THE DYNAMICS OF YOUNG FATHERHOOD

Understanding the Parenting Journeys and Support Needs of Young Fathers

Bren Neale and Anna Tarrant

First published in Great Britain in 2024 by

Policy Press, an imprint of
Bristol University Press
University of Bristol
1–9 Old Park Hill
Bristol
BS2 8BB
UK
t: +44 (0)117 374 6645
e: bup-info@bristol.ac.uk

Details of international sales and distribution partners are available at
policy.bristoluniversitypress.co.uk

© Bristol University Press 2024

British Library Cataloguing in Publication Data
A catalogue record for this book is available from the British Library

ISBN 978-1-4473-5161-0 hardcover
ISBN 978-1-4473-5171-9 paperback
ISBN 978-1-4473-5173-3 ePub
ISBN 978-1-4473-5172-6 ePdf

The right of Bren Neale and Anna Tarrant to be identified as authors of this work has been asserted by them in accordance with the Copyright, Designs and Patents Act 1988.

All rights reserved: no part of this publication may be reproduced, stored in a retrieval system, or transmitted in any form or by any means, electronic, mechanical, photocopying, recording, or otherwise without the prior permission of Bristol University Press.

Every reasonable effort has been made to obtain permission to reproduce copyrighted material. If, however, anyone knows of an oversight, please contact the publisher.

The statements and opinions contained within this publication are solely those of the authors and not of the University of Bristol or Bristol University Press. The University of Bristol and Bristol University Press disclaim responsibility for any injury to persons or property resulting from any material published in this publication.

Bristol University Press and Policy Press work to counter discrimination on
grounds of gender, race, disability, age and sexuality.

Cover design: Nicky Borowiec
Front cover image: Adobe Stock/Aliaksei Lasevich

To the 34 young fathers who generously shared their life stories with us, and to John May and Kate Bulman for their groundbreaking work with young fathers.

Contents

List of figures		vi
List of abbreviations		vii
About the authors		viii
Acknowledgements		ix
Introduction		1
PART I	**Young fatherhood: contemporary knowledge and debate**	**9**
1	The lives of young fathers	11
2	Policy responses and public discourses: the neglect of young fathers	31
3	Researching young fatherhood through time	52
PART II	**Living young fatherhood: changing identities, relationships and practices**	**71**
4	Becoming a young father: transitions, identities, choices, constraints	73
5	Co-parenting: the gendered dynamics of young relationships	97
6	Reconfiguring families: intergenerational care and support?	117
7	Young breadwinners? Education, employment and training trajectories	137
8	Finding a place to parent: young fathers' housing needs and pathways With Linzi Ladlow	157
PART III	**Supporting young fathers: lived experiences and policy challenges**	**177**
9	Professional support for young fathers: support, surveillance, sidelining?	179
10	Enhancing the social engagement of young fathers through qualitative longitudinal impact research	197
11	Rethinking young fatherhood: citizenship and compassionate social policy	216
Appendix: Pen portraits of the participants		236
Notes		254
References		255
Index		288

List of figures

2.1	Ten key factors for effective local strategies	37
4.1	Ben's future life map, aged 20, wave 2	87
4.2	Jason's future life map, aged 22, wave 1	88
5.1	Typology of parenting relationships at close of fieldwork	101
8.1	Typology of living arrangements/ontological security for young fathers	162

List of abbreviations

APPG	All-Party Parliamentary Group
CAFCASS	Children and Family Court Advisory and Support Service
CV	curriculum vitae
EET	education, employment and training
ESRC	Economic and Social Research Council
FYF	Following Young Fathers
FYFF	Following Young Fathers Further
GDC	Grimsby Dads Collective
GCSE	General Certificate of Secondary Education
HGV	heavy goods vehicle
IT	information technology
MP	Member of Parliament
MPLC	Men, Poverty and Lifetimes of Care
NEET	not in education, employment or training
NHS	National Health Service
NSPCC	National Society for the Prevention of Cruelty to Children
NVQ	national vocational qualification
PHE	Public Health England
PRS	private rented sector
QL	qualitative longitudinal
RSE	Relationship and Sex Education (from March 2017)
RYD	Responding to Young Dads in a Different Way
SRE	Sex and Relationship Education (to March 2017)
TPIAG	Teenage Pregnancy Independent Advisory Group
TPS	Teenage Pregnancy Strategy
TPU	Teenage Pregnancy Unit
UKRI	UK Research & Innovation
YDC	Young Dads Collective

About the authors

Bren Neale is Emeritus Professor of Life course and Family Research (University of Leeds, School of Sociology and Social Policy, UK) and a fellow of the Academy of Social Sciences. Bren specialises in research on the dynamics of family life and intergenerational relationships and has published widely in this field.

Bren is a leading expert in qualitative longitudinal (QL) research methodology. From 2007 to 2012 she directed the Economic and Social Research Council-funded Timescapes Initiative (www.timescapes.leeds.ac.uk), as part of which she advanced QL methods and archiving across academia, and in government and non-governmental organisation settings. She continues to provide support and training in this methodology for new and established researchers across the disciplines.

Anna Tarrant is Professor of Sociology at the University of Lincoln, where she is also the Director of the Centre for Innovation in Fatherhood and Family Research. She has been funded to the tune of £1.7 million by the UKRI Future Leaders Fellowship scheme to lead Following Young Fathers Further (https://followingyoungfathersfurther.org/), a seven-year qualitative longitudinal and participatory study about the lives and support needs of young fathers. Her research specialisms include men and masculinities; family diversity and dynamics; and methods of qualitative secondary analysis and co-creation.

Anna has built a corpus of publications in these areas including monographs and edited collections. Notable recent contributions include *Men and Welfare* (2023, Routledge, with Linzi Ladlow and Laura Way), *Fathering and Poverty* (2021, Policy Press), *Men, Families and Poverty: Tracing the Intergenerational Trajectories of Place-Based Hardship* (2023, Palgrave Macmillan) and *Qualitative Secondary Analysis* (2020, Sage) with Kahryn Hughes.

Acknowledgements

The research programme upon which this book is based has been a long time in the making and involved the collective efforts of a great many people over the years. Funding for the original study was provided by the Economic and Social Research Council, under the Timescapes Initiative (www.timescapes archive.leeds.ac.uk) and subsequently under the dedicated Following Young Fathers (FYF) study (grant no. ES/J022993/1), with additional support from the University of Leeds, for which we are very grateful. We'd like to extend our special thanks to the original team of researchers who conducted the Following Young Fathers study and contributed to the corpus of early publications: Carmen Lau Clayton, Laura Davies, Linzi Ladlow and Ruth Patrick. Carmen's input to the fieldwork with the young men was vital to the success of this project, while Linzi's contributions to the housing dimensions of this study have been invaluable. Thanks also to Esmée Hannah for helping to prepare the first phase data for archiving.

The practice partners whom we were fortunate to work with over many years (and who continue to support Anna's work) not only enhanced the development of this research; without them the project would not have got off the ground. Our biggest thanks go to John May and Kate Bulman, but we'd also like to extend our thanks to our collaborators from the FYF strategy group, including Jessica Cundy, Mark Osborn, David Lammy and teams from Barnardo's, St Michael's Fellowship, Leeds City Council, The Young Dads' Collective, and Coram Family and Childcare. It has also been a great pleasure to work with Alison Hadley, who sharpened our thinking about policy developments for teenage pregnancy and parenthood; and our network of academic colleagues and advisors, including Mark Kiselica, Jean-Paul Deslauriers, Harry Ferguson and Tina Miller, whose insights on young fathers in different contexts and settings of change have greatly enriched our own thinking. Being part of a network of family law researchers proved most helpful when we were considering our findings on this topic: grateful thanks to Richard Collier, Emma Hitchings and Rosemary Hunter for useful discussions and suggestions, although, in the event, this was not a theme that we were able to pursue. We are also grateful to Jay Allan and the publishing team at Policy Press, who waited so patiently for the manuscript to appear and were encouraging and supportive throughout its development.

Our biggest debt, of course, is to the 34 young men who took part in this study and shared their life journeys with us, in some cases over many years. Their rich accounts form the core of this book, and they have immeasurably enriched our findings, and indeed our own lives, as we have lived with the ebbs and flows of their journeys over time. Some of these young men are continuing to work with Anna and Linzi for the Following Young Fathers Further study, for which we extend our further thanks.

On a final note, Bren would like to extend her personal thanks (and many apologies) to her family members, not least to her children, Jess and Danny, for their technical wizardry and enthusiasm, and to her husband Alan, whose patience, love and steadfast support over many years made it all possible. Finally, Bren would like to pay a special tribute to Anna for being such a wonderful colleague over the past decade; without her commitment, enthusiasm, drive and support this book would never have been written. Anna extends her personal thanks to Professor Kahryn Hughes, whose early mentorship was foundational to the decision to conduct a secondary analysis of the Following Young Fathers dataset. To my own children, Lorelei and Wilf and husband Jamie, whose unwavering love, understanding and support is unparalleled. And finally, to Bren; not only for 'passing on the torch' and for your continued intellectual generosity over the years; but also for paving the way for future researchers through the establishment of the Timescapes Archive. In creating that resource, your leadership has shaped diverse methodological fields and debates and has facilitated the preservation of the rich history of family life in contemporary Britain. This may well be your last book and I am extremely honoured to have written it with you.

Introduction

This book is the first major research monograph to be published in the UK on the dynamics of young fatherhood. The evidence presented here is drawn from an Economic and Social Research Council-funded programme of qualitative longitudinal research (principally, the Following Young Fathers (FYF) study, 2010–15), which was carried out in a Northern industrial city in the UK. The study followed a sample of young fathers through the early years of parenthood, generating new insights into their lived experiences over time and their support needs. A collection of articles and briefing papers from this research was published as the FYF study came to an end. Our objective here is to draw these findings together into a composite whole and update the longitudinal picture for selected young men. These findings are placed within the context of a growing body of contemporary research evidence on young parenthood, and against a backdrop of shifting welfare policies and professional practice. The overall aim of this book is to create a state-of-the-art picture of contemporary young fatherhood in the UK. We begin by introducing some of the key themes and methodologies that underpinned the FYF study, and present an overview of the structure of the book and the contents of the chapters.

Patterns of early parenthood

The entry of young people into early parenthood has long been regarded as an issue for social policy and for professional practice in the UK and internationally (Brown, 2016; Hadley and Ingham, 2018; PHE/LGA, 2018). Since 2000, the under-18 conception rate in the UK has more than halved, to the lowest level since 1969 (PHE/LGA, 2019). However, young conceptions continue to be concentrated in the most socially deprived areas of the country, and the rates remain relatively high in comparison with other Western European countries (Hadley and Ingham, 2018; ONS, 2023). The majority of young pregnancies are unplanned, and about half result in the birth of a child. The vast majority of babies born to young mothers (those under the age of 20) are fathered by young men up to the age of 25, a third of whom are estimated to be in their teens (PHE/LGA, 2019). Considerable research evidence exists on the experiences of young mothers, with a range of interventions designed to meet their needs. However, until recently, young fathers (defined as those who enter parenthood up to the age of 25) were neglected in both research and policy. While a great deal of evidence about these young men has been amassed in recent years, it has remained scattered and inaccessible to policy and practice audiences, resulting in a paucity of knowledge about their lives.

In much of the research evidence in the UK and elsewhere, young parenthood is seen within a *social problems framework*, characterised by low-income, single-parent families headed by mothers, and with a presumed high incidence of absent fathers. Evidence from large-scale studies shows a clear correlation between early parenthood and indices of social deprivation, although how this correlation should be understood, and how far young people themselves should be blamed for this state of affairs, are contested issues (Duncan et al, 2010). A growing body of qualitative research evidence has also emerged that is set within what we have called a *social engagement framework*. Painting a more nuanced picture of the practices, values and support needs of young fathers, this evidence finds that young men commonly embrace their roles as fathers and are highly committed to their children (see, for example, Robinson, 1988; Kiselica, 2011; Tuffin et al, 2018; Weber, 2018; Tarrant, 2021). However, what their contributions and commitments mean in practice, and how far they can be sustained over time remain open questions.

Despite the emergence of a social engagement framework for understanding these young men, in the public imagination a social problems framework has proved to be remarkably resilient. Young fathers are commonly labelled as 'feckless'; they are assumed to be absent or uninterested in 'being there', or worse, are regarded as a potential risk to their children (Robinson, 1988; Johanssen and Hammarén, 2014; Weed et al, 2015; Tuffin et al, 2018). Here, the focus on social problems shades into a *deficit model* of young parenthood, which identifies young fathers as the root cause of the problems. More benignly, perhaps, practitioners commonly regard young fathers as 'hard to reach', a pejorative view that places the responsibility for engaging with services firmly with the young men themselves. Historically, these perceptions have fed into and shaped policy and practice responses to young fathers, resulting in the marginalisation of young fathers within mainstream policy responses and service provision.

Young parents: new adults?

At this point it is worth considering why the idea of young fatherhood (and young parenthood more generally) has evoked a sense of moral panic and condemnation in the popular imagination. We draw here on an earlier analysis presented in Neale (2016). Of the many challenges facing young parents, perhaps the foundational issue relates to their youthful and dependent status. In transitioning to parenthood at a young age, and most often outside marriage or cohabitation, teen and young parents openly disrupt cultural expectations about an appropriate time to have a child (Weber, 2012).

At the same time, transitions into adulthood in contemporary Britain are acknowledged to be increasingly fluid, varied and difficult to navigate

(Furlong and Cartmel, 2007). As a life course category, youth has expanded in ways that blurs the boundaries between childhood and independent adult life. In the 1950s, as post-war employment opportunities flourished, key life course trajectories relating to age, employment, family and household were bound together for young people, reflecting new, normatively prescribed pathways into adulthood. An orderly progression could be expected involving leaving school or college, securing work, entering a stable relationship, setting up an independent marital home and starting a new family. Timespans for these set transitions were also prescribed, with progress expected to occur over a decade or so, starting at the point of leaving full-time education.

However, for many young people these prescribed pathways have been largely disrupted (McDowell, 2014). In 1975, over 60 per cent of young people in the UK moved straight from school to work at the age of 16. But by the mid-1990s the rate had dropped to less than 20 per cent (Coles, 2000). The collapse of the youth labour market in the 1980s led to a steep rise in youth unemployment, an expansion of youth training schemes and, by the 1990s, an expansion of post-16 education and routes into further and higher education. By the year 2000, nearly 80 per cent of young people were extending their education beyond the traditional school-leaving age (Coles, 2000). The trend has been reflected and reinforced through successive legislation: since 2015, young people have been required to stay in education or training until the age of 18, and a far greater proportion go on to further or higher education. These demographic trends mean that disadvantaged young people are more likely than others to experience insecure working lives, with 'transitions characterised by flux and rapid movement around different economic statuses ('unemployed', 'in training', 'in education', 'employed')' (MacDonald, 2013: 2).

The extended trajectory from compulsory education into employment has been accompanied by rising housing costs and parallel delays and variations in transitions from dependent to independent living. This has created a growing pattern of nomadic young people living in temporary forms of accommodation well into early adulthood. Accompanying these material changes there have been widespread transformations in normative family practices: a substantial loosening of marital ties and a slow but discernible uncoupling of parenting from partnering or cohabitation as the basis for family life. These changes, in turn, have created shifts in the gendering of parenthood; we are witnessing the rise of 'new' fathers, whose parenting may no longer be mediated entirely by mothers and who are striving to forge more direct ways of engaging with their children (Smart and Neale, 1999).

These far-reaching changes in life course trajectories have substantially unravelled the post-war, normatively prescribed transition to adulthood. The key trajectories relating to age, employment, home, family and parenthood are no longer necessarily synchronised or intertwined: they may or may not unfold in chronological order, in a linear direction or at a uniform pace; indeed, some elements of the transition may be extended while others have accelerated (Bynner, 2007): '[F]ar more common are complex and contradictory patterns in which the achievement of independence in one sphere of life may well involve compromises in others' (Allen and Crow, 2001: 36). As Bynner (2007: 378) observes, there is a need to 'move from blanket categorisations of individuals in terms of stages bound by chronological age towards a broader conception based on a range of trajectories'.

Young parents occupy a unique place within these processes. In 1981, around 50 per cent of teenage conceptions occurred within marriage, but the delayed trajectories and changing mores of family formation mean that only a small minority of conceptions now take place as part of a planned entry into parenthood within a stable relationship (Furstenberg, 2003). Moreover, values surrounding youthful transitions into parenthood vary across social groups. A close layering of the generations, whereby the children of young parents become young parents themselves, is a more commonly accepted feature of family life in low-income communities (Emmel and Hughes, 2014; Brown, 2016). Viewed historically, it is not so much that young people are having children at an earlier age; it is more the case that we are witnessing delays in transitions to 'full' adult status, which now occur later in the life course. Young parents may therefore be seen as pioneers of a 'new' adulthood (Wyn, 2014) that is no longer tied to a prescribed and wholesale transition to a 'finished' and fully independent adult state, where all the pieces of the jigsaw fall neatly into place. Indeed, in a political climate of austerity, welfare reform and wholesale changes in labour markets (Bochel and Powell, 2016; Vizard and Hills, 2021), a secure and orderly transition into such a state may be beyond the reach of many disadvantaged young people.

In this shifting historical picture, young people from lower-income families are more likely to enter parenthood without skills, employment, resources, stable relationships or independent homes. In effect, they represent the ultimate confounding of the post-war normative pathway to adulthood. It is this confounding of normative ideals, coupled with evidence for a strong correlation between early conception and social deprivation, that has profoundly influenced public and policy perceptions of young parents and, in some government and media circles, created such opprobrium towards them (Swann et al, 2003; Ingham, 2005; Arai, 2009).

The dynamics of young fatherhood

The FYF study was designed to consolidate knowledge of young fathers in research and policy settings and address the lack of engagement of these young men with professional support services. The study sought to uncover new insights about the 'hidden' lives of these young men: to explore how far their lived experiences chime with policy and practice responses, and to understand the challenges faced by practitioners in supporting them. Perhaps the most notable aspect of the study design is its qualitative longitudinal (QL) methodology (detailed in Chapter 3). Relatively few studies have been able to shed light on the changing experiences of young fathers over time, or to tease out the causes and consequences of change in their parenting journeys. Relatively little is known, for example, of young men who drop out or fail to engage in their children's lives. The recruitment of such young men in a 'snapshot' (single visit) study is likely to be a challenge. However, in a longitudinal study, such experiences may emerge as a study unfolds, affording opportunities to trace how these processes unravel and their longer-term effects. The study also sought to recruit a highly varied sample of young fathers, beyond the stereotypically disadvantaged young men that are the focus of most studies of young parenthood. The inclusion of young men who were both well and poorly resourced, partnered and non-partnered, resident and non-resident, has yielded valuable insights into the commonalities and differences in their experiences, and it has sharpened our thinking about the place of relational and socio-economic factors in the practices and sustainability of young fatherhood. The findings from this study are reported in Part II of this book. In what follows, we set out details of the organisation of the book and the contents of the chapters.

Organisation of the book

Part I of this book (Young fatherhood: contemporary knowledge and debate) reviews how young fatherhood is constituted in pre-existing research, in policy settings and in the public imagination. Chapter 1 presents a detailed review of the wider body of research and demographic evidence on young fathers, both in and beyond the UK. It establishes the social problems framework that shapes much of this evidence and goes on to consider the power of a counter-narrative that recognises the social engagement of young fathers. Finally, the chapter reveals gaps in the evidence base that the FYF study seeks to address. Chapter 2 traces UK policy and popular responses to young fathers since the 1990s. The main focus is on New Labour's ten-year Teenage Pregnancy Strategy, and more recent responses under the Coalition and Conservative governments. We show how negative portrayals of young fathers have fed into policy responses to these young men. In the final part of the chapter, we consider how far the principle of evidence-based policy has been adhered to in shaping policies and professional practice that impact on young fathers.

Chapter 3 introduces the linked projects that make up the FYF programme and the methodologies that have shaped these studies. Particular attention is given to the qualitative longitudinal design of the programme and its value in discerning the complexities of causal processes over time. We also give space to our modes of data generation and analysis and, in outlining the purposive sampling strategies that were devised for this study, we address the vexed question of how representative this sample is.

Part II of the book (Living young fatherhood: changing identities, relationships and practices), presents the broad empirical evidence from the FYF study. The chapters are organised thematically to develop a nuanced, dynamic picture of the many factors that shape the lives of these young men. They also reflect a conceptual development from the micro-sphere of interpersonal relationships and family practices (Chapters 4, 5 and 6), to the macro-sphere of structural opportunities and constraints, with a particular focus on employment and housing provision (Chapters 7 and 8).

In each of these chapters, the empirical evidence is placed in a wider policy and/or historical context, relating, for example, to Relationship and Sex Education (RSE), social welfare, employment, housing and parenting support. The range of challenges that young fathers are likely to face are woven through these chapters: their lack of reproductive agency and preparation for parenthood; their changing identities as they strive to be good dads and co-parents; the heartache of constrained or diminishing contact with their children where co-parenting relationships break down; the vagaries of intergenerational support; the sheer hard work of finding employment and the triple burden of learning, earning and caring; and for disadvantaged young men, the nomadic nature of their lifestyles, and experiences of homelessness. The additional challenges that are experienced by young offender fathers and those with anger management problems are also represented here, and we touch upon the mental health issues that arise for many young fathers as they attempt to establish and sustain a role as a parent.

In Part III of the book (Supporting young fathers: lived experiences and policy challenges), we explore young fathers' perspectives on their support needs, and their experiences in engaging with statutory and voluntary sector support services (Chapter 9). Across these chapters, we highlight the fragmented nature of current provision, consider how far existing provision is 'in tune' with the lived realities of young fatherhood and what the implications are for the development of effective policy and professional practice. In Chapter 10, we describe the Responding to Young Dads in a Different Way (RYD) project, a QL practitioner-led impact project that aimed to translate the findings of the FYF study into father-inclusive practice developments. In this project, practitioners supported and trained selected young fathers as 'experts by experience' to develop advocacy, mentoring and training roles that gave them both a voice and an audience.

Chapter 11 draws the findings of this study together and highlights the complex constellation of factors that influenced the parenting journeys of the participants. We go on to consider how the findings from the FYF study sit within the wider body of evidence reviewed in Chapter 1, showing where they accord with the broader picture, and where they advance our knowledge and understanding. We conclude the book by exploring the implications of our findings for the social citizenship of young fathers and the development of compassionate social policy (Gregory, 2015; Vizard and Hills, 2021). This seeks to develop policies based on a culture of support rather than blame, particularly for vulnerable young people. Returning to the dynamic threads woven into this book, we consider the value of policies that take a future orientation (including, where needed, an ethos of redemption) towards young fathers, and that recognise and seek to nurture the potential of these young men to engage positively with their children, and their families, for the benefit of all.

PART I

Young fatherhood: contemporary knowledge and debate

1
The lives of young fathers

Introduction

This chapter presents a detailed review of demographic and social research evidence on the lives and support needs of young fathers, drawing on an existing body of research literature beyond the findings of the Following Young Fathers (FYF) study. Our main focus is on published evidence from the UK, but selected international studies, particularly from the US and Canada, are also included. We highlight insights from some early studies, conducted in the 1980s (reviewed by Miller, 1997), whose findings are just as pertinent today as they were over 30 years ago. Our main sources are dedicated studies on young fatherhood. We also draw on key reviews of the literature, alongside studies with a broader young parenthood or fatherhood focus, which incorporate some limited insights on young fathers (for example, Edin and Nelson, 2013). As the discussion unfolds, we draw out the nature of this evidence, whether it is produced through qualitative/quantitative research and/or 'snapshot' or longitudinal methodologies, and we consider how robust this evidence is in generating measured findings.

Our discussion is shaped around two key orientations found in the literature: a *social problems framework*, which can shift seamlessly into a *social deficit* understanding of young fathers; and a *social engagement framework*, which reveals the efforts of young men to engage with and care for their children. While both frameworks have value and are complementary, they produce very different insights into the lives of young fathers. We finish the chapter by considering the methodological implications of the picture developed here, and we highlight gaps in the evidence base to which the FYF study responds.

Historicising young fatherhood research: the nature of the existing evidence

Academic interest in young fatherhood, particularly in the US and the UK, can be traced back to the 1980s and 1990s (Lane and Clay, 2000; Lau Clayton, 2016; Kiselica, forthcoming). At this time, scholars conducting research on teenage pregnancy and parenthood in the US began to acknowledge that young fatherhood was a topic of 'empirical neglect' (Klinman et al, 1985; Robinson, 1988; Glikman, 2004). In the process, young fathers had become anonymous and invisible (Lane and Clay, 2000, see also Parikh, 2009). Early studies were found to be overly impressionistic, lacking in sufficient data, and they grouped fathers of all ages together. These methodological limitations had produced skewed findings that perpetuated negative views of young fathers (Parikh, 2009).

In addressing these issues, research in the 1990s and 2000s began to develop a more nuanced picture of the antecedents for adolescent fatherhood, producing important findings about the hardships experienced by this population and the harmful stereotypes perpetuated about them (Achatz and MacAllum, 1994; Florsheim and Moore, 2020). The policy and public health implications of the evidence, and considerations about the most effective ways to support young fathers also grew into important areas of interest (Klinman et al, 1985; Brown, 1990; Kost, 1997; Romo et al, 2004). An especially early evaluation of a US support programme for young fathers (Klinman et al, 1985), made significant strides towards increasing recognition of the support needs of young fathers, and encouraging services to extend their provision beyond young mothers. Through their evaluation of service provision, these authors were able to identify young fathers as a diverse rather than homogenous population, particularly with regard to their ethnic and cultural background. Most were poor, under- or uneducated and often unemployed, but all were deeply committed to their co-parent and child.

Methodological challenges

Despite these early contributions, the body of research evidence on young fathers has some ongoing limitations. Much of the evidence is drawn from opportunity samples of a handful of young men, resulting in small pockets of data that are scattered across a wide range of studies. This has limited their utility and impact, at least in relation to the considerable weight of evidence on young mothers. It has also increased the challenge of piecing together an adequate picture of these young men's lives. Reviews of the literature tend to be selective in their coverage (for a recent example, see Rantho and Matlakala, 2021), thereby perpetuating a partial view of the evidence base. International reviews that generate comparative insights are also sparse (although see SmithBattle et al, 2019a; Kiselica, forthcoming), as are historical reviews that rediscover past insights.

Even so, these reviews have produced some valuable insights into the nature of young fatherhood, and the shaping of the evidence base. For example, in their overview of evaluations of pregnancy prevention and parenting support for young men, from 1996 to 2008, Trivedi et al (2009) identified only 3 quantitative and 15 qualitative studies about young fathers, of which 9 were UK based (see also reviews in Swann et al, 2003; Bunting and McAuley, 2004; Parikh, 2009, Trivedi et al, 2007; Tuffin et al, 2010).

Many of these studies focus on young mothers and include only a handful of young fathers, who are 'tacked on' by virtue of their status as the mothers' partners (for example, Quinton et al, 2002; Gibbin, 2003; Higginbottom et al, 2006; Formby et al, 2010; Alexander et al, 2010). This has led Parikh (2009) to conclude that much teenage parenthood research might be more accurately identified as young motherhood research. Overall, relatively few studies have recruited young fathers directly or focused exclusively on their needs and experiences.

An over-reliance on recruiting young fathers via the mothers has led to a neglect of the substantial proportions of young men who are single, and may therefore face different, and arguably greater, challenges in establishing and sustaining a paternal role and identity (Wiggins et al, 2005; Trivedi et al, 2009; Lohan et al, 2010). The effect of this imbalance is that young fathers who parent at a distance have either been rendered invisible or knowledge about them has been gleaned predominantly from mothers (for example, Mollborn, 2017). This means that they are often regarded as part of the phenomenon of teenage motherhood (Hendricks and Montgomery, 1983; Tuffin et al, 2010), obscuring the particularities of their experiences as parents in their own right.

Other factors may also contribute to this rather skewed picture, including a lack of externally funded and well-resourced studies that could explore a more purposively chosen range of experiences, and the existence of a raft of studies that are unpublished and/or hard to identify (for example, doctoral dissertations (Osborn, 2007; Rouch, 2009; Graham, 2013), and 'grey' literature such as reports produced for local service providers (Birbeck, 2004; Ayoola et al, 2010; Mensah, 2017; Clayton and Fletcher, 2023)). Recruiting young fathers for a dedicated study can also be a challenge: researchers report a range of difficulties in gaining access to young men, not least the objections of young mothers to their involvement, and a shying away of young men amid concerns over negative attitudes towards them, or fears about the illegality of underage sex (Reeves, 2006).

A more recent qualitative meta-synthesis of research about teen fathering confirms that little has changed methodologically, despite an increase in empirical research with young fathers since 2005 (SmithBattle et al, 2019a). This review identifies 29 international studies about teen fathers, aged 20 and under, in countries with advanced economies. It suggests that less than half of these studies had recruited teen fathers exclusively (n = 15). It is worth noting, however, that coverage in this review is not comprehensive; the focus on teenage fathers excludes a range of studies that use a broader age definition of young fathers, including earlier findings from the FYF study.

In terms of the methodologies employed to generate the available evidence, there is a strong strand of research that is quantitative in nature. Drawing on large-scale survey and cohort data, these studies shed some light on the socio-demographic profiles of young fathers, including the antecedents and consequences of young parenthood for boys and men (see, for example, Kiernan, 1995, 2005; Quinton et al, 2002; Berrington et al, 2005; Pirog et al, 2018). In parallel to these studies, a body of qualitative evidence has developed that focuses on the lived experiences of young fathers. Taken together, these studies present a more rounded picture of young fatherhood. But there are still some gaps in the evidence base. With a small number of exceptions (see Chapter 3) the evidence has been generated from 'snapshot' studies of young fathers, conducted at one point in time. As we show in Chapter 3, longitudinal studies are rare, and since most of these are drawn from large-scale surveys and cohort studies, there remains a paucity of qualitative longitudinal evidence on the dynamics of these young lives, and on subjective understandings of the causes and consequences of change.

Methodological challenges notwithstanding, it is to the knowledge generated from these existing literatures that we now turn, beginning with socio-demographic profiles of young fathers.

Socio-demographic profiling

Young fathers are commonly defined as young men who enter parenthood up to the age of 25. A quarter of these are estimated to be in their teens when they first become a father. A substantial majority of these young men are thought to be in the same, or slightly older, age bracket as the mothers of their children (Speak, 2006; Pirog et al, 2018). This evidence provides a corrective to popular notions that vulnerable young women are coerced by older, predatory fathers. More generally, demographic data on young fathers are sparse because of the way that birth statistics are generated (Speak, 2006). There has been no routine collection of information by frontline staff that finds its way into surveys, the census or local authority databases. The data that would enable young fathers to be identified, recognised, counted and built into national statistics or statutory policy responses are therefore negligible. However, this situation may be changing with the take-up of specially designed auditing tools for local authority use (Trivedi et al, 2009; Lammy, 2015; Osborn, 2015) and further calls to produce more baseline data, both locally and nationally (Goldman and Burgess, 2017).

Internationally, teenage pregnancy rates are measured on the basis of data about young mothers. Global trend data produced in 2021 indicate that an estimated 14 per cent of young women gave birth before age 18 (UNICEF, 2021). Overall, adolescent pregnancy rates are decreasing around the world although there are variations in different regions. Low-income countries, in particular, continue to report higher rates (Baxter et al, 2021). Where there has been a sharp decline in Southern Asia, slower declines are observable in Latin American, Caribbean and sub-Saharan Africa regions (Baxter et al, 2021).

More generally, longitudinal trends in teenage pregnancy rates globally demonstrate a commitment to reduction and prevention. In the UK, where rates have steadily fallen in the wake of the ten-year Teenage Pregnancy Strategy (discussed in Chapter 2), teenage or adolescent pregnancy rates in disadvantaged neighbourhoods remain stubbornly high (Hadley and Ingham, 2018). These area variations indicate that child poverty and unemployment are two key indicators for under-18 conception and birth rates (Hadley and Ingham, 2018). Overall, the latest international comparisons rank the UK 22nd out of 28 European countries in terms of its record on tackling young pregnancies (RCPCH, 2021).

There is continued uncertainty about the exact number of young fathers globally and in different regions of the world, although there are notable attempts among researchers to estimate these figures. Across comparable Western democracies, estimates suggest that roughly 5–10 per cent of all births are likely to be fathered by young men (for example, Ayton and Hansen, 2016 for Australia; Kiselica, forthcoming, on the US), a figure that roughly aligns with teenage pregnancy rates among young mothers. In the US, rates of young men becoming fathers are thought to be rising (Pirog et al, 2018). In the UK, up to a quarter of young men aged 25 and under who are fathers are thought to be in their teenage years, although as noted, fathers often fall under the radar of national surveys and census data (Fatherhood Institute, 2011; Goldman and Burgess, 2017). Moreover, some men themselves may not know that they have fathered a child. The linked under-reporting of teenage paternity is also an enduring issue (Pirog et al, 2018), particularly in countries where conceptions outside marriage are a source of moral concern.

In the UK, the national proportion of young men who become young parents is also difficult to gauge. British Household Panel data from the early 1990s suggest that about one third of fathers conceived a child when they were still under the age of 25, and that 3 per cent of fathers were still in their teens (Burghes et al, 1997; Speak, 2006). However, these proportions are likely to have receded over the intervening years, in line with a more than 70 per cent reduction in birth rates for young parents since 1997 (see Chapter 2). In 2017, the average age of fathering a child in the UK was reported to have risen to 33.4 years (ONS, 2022). These trends indicate a growing gulf between the average age of first-time fatherhood and the age of young fathers.

It is well established that the majority of young conceptions are unplanned (Alexander et al, 2010; Kiselica, forthcoming), but there is limited evidence to suggest that fathers may be positively ambivalent, and quickly able to adjust to the idea of fathering a child (Alexander et al, 2010; Deslauriers, 2011).

A pregnancy may occur within a non-partnered or tentative relationship, or in a committed relationship between the parents (Speak et al, 1997; Mollborn and Jacobs, 2015). Incidences of teenage pregnancy may also be more prevalent among certain minority ethnic groups, with Caribbean, Pakistani and Bangladeshi women more likely to become teenage mothers than White women and a relatively common incidence of early fatherhood among African Caribbean and Latino young men (Berthoud, cited in Lau Clayton, 2016; Wei et al, 2002; Paschal, 2006; Paschal et al, 2011).

While the exact prevalence of young fatherhood is difficult to determine, the demographic picture presented here demonstrates that young fathers are far from a homogenous population.

The social problems framework

As well as highlighting diversity, numerous intersecting factors have been observed that are associated with the prevalence of young fatherhood. These reflect a social problems framework that, we suggest, has tended to dominate existing research and analyses. In identifying cases of early pregnancies, cohort studies have contributed important evidence about the risk factors associated with teenage parenthood and explanations for the factors that lead to young fatherhood and its prevalence. In their analytic interrogation of antecedents and consequences, these literatures tend to paint a rather woeful picture of the biographies of young fathers, both prior to the arrival of a child and in the aftermath.

In an analysis of data from two UK longitudinal cohort surveys (Avon Longitudinal Study of Parents and Children (ALSPAC) and the 1970 British Birth Cohort Study (BCS70)), for example, Berrington et al (2005) found that men who had become fathers at the age of 22 years and under were more likely than others of their age to be living in social housing, to be unemployed and in receipt of social security, to have lower educational qualifications and lower earning power. They were also more likely to be separated from the mother of their child and re-partnered.

More generally, large-scale evidence on the lives of young fathers establishes a strong correlation between young fatherhood (and young motherhood) and a range of social ills. As it has developed, the qualitative evidence-base about young fathers, has largely followed suit, with a tendency to give priority to the life experiences and contexts of vulnerable young fathers (Glikman, 2004; Tuffin et al, 2010; Johansson and Hammarén, 2014). Such a focus indicates a presumed causal link between young fatherhood and social problems, obscuring from view a diversity of experiences among young fathers and how and why these may change and evolve over time. Mirroring research with teenage mothers (for example, Cook and Cameron, 2017), teenage fatherhood continues to be associated with poor social and health outcomes for mother and child, even after adjusting for pre-existing social, economic and health concerns.

Scholars have also reported an established risk profile for the heightened chance of adolescent fatherhood (Enderstein and Boonzaier, 2015), comprising a multitude of biographical factors and hardships that characterise the early lives of these young men (Berger and Langton, 2011; Lewin et al, 2015; Enderstein and Boonzaier, 2015; Pirog et al, 2018; SmithBattle et al, 2019a; Kiselica, forthcoming). Early analyses of data from the National Child Development Study, and the British Household Panel Study in the 1990s, for example, demonstrated links between the low educational achievement of boys at different points in their childhoods, and an increased likelihood that they would become young fathers (Kiernan, 1995; Burghes et al, 1997).

Several studies confirm that young fathers' childhoods are often marked by family insecurity and isolation, rejection, loss, stress and mental ill health. These are associated with other shared features of the childhoods of these young men, especially when compared to older fathers. These include growing up in small, fragmented family networks, frequent house moves, periods spent in care or in prison, and experiences of neglect or abuse (Glikman, 2004; Berger and Langton, 2011; Lewin et al, 2015; Enderstein and Boonzaier, 2015; Pirog et al, 2018; SmithBattle et al 2019a; Kiselica, forthcoming). Other identified factors include being a child born to young parents, a history of exposure to domestic violence and/or street and neighbourhood violence, and parental separation and divorce (Lemay et al, 2010). This leads much research to conclude that young fathers either lack their own male role models through father absence or bring their own histories of trauma and stress into parenting (Dukes and Palm, 2019).

The longer-term trajectories of young fathers are often assumed to be shaped by their earlier disadvantages and complex childhood histories. With limited material or financial resources to contribute to parenting, for example, disadvantaged young fathers often navigate a combination of socio-economic and relational constraints that impact upon their parenting efforts (Kiernan, 1995; Pirog-Good, 1995; Johnson, 2001; Swann et al, 2003; Bunting and McAuley, 2004; Tyrer et al, 2005; Reeves, 2006; Trivedi et al, 2009; Ladlow and Neale, 2016; Donald et al, 2022; Kiselica, forthcoming). Compared to older fathers, evidence suggests that young fathers are more likely to be unemployed, on low incomes, engaged in risky behaviours, in custody or on remand, living in disadvantaged families or away from their birth parents (Kiernan, 1995; Wei et al, 2002; Berrington et al, 2005; Berger and Langton, 2011; Lewin et al, 2015; Enderstein and Boonzaier, 2015; Pirog et al, 2018; SmithBattle et al, 2019a; Kiselica, forthcoming).

In international contexts, being unemployed with insufficient income has been observed as a core problem for young fathers, who often need to rely on their own families or the families of their co-parent for necessities such as food and housing (Chirawatkul et al, 2011; Uengwongsapat et al, 2017). In the UK, a high proportion of young fathers experience financial insecurity associated with disrupted education and employment trajectories and the increasing precarity created by reduced welfare entitlements (Donald et al, 2022; see also Chapter 2). Each of these factors is assumed to erode the possibilities for father engagement, locking young fathers out of a relationship with their child, which, as we will show, is the more socially accepted trajectory (Donald et al, 2022).

The influence of street culture as a neighbourhood risk factor, combined with housing instability, may also limit opportunities for young fathers to participate frequently and actively in their children's lives (Achatz and MacAllum, 1994; Dukes and Palm, 2019). Berger and Langton (2011) conclude that disadvantaged young fathers are less likely to be involved fathers than older men because they are both socio-economically disadvantaged and unmarried. In sum, a combination of disadvantages including poverty, neglect, violence and criminality are often considered to blame for young men's failure to father (Weber, 2020).

The social deficit framework

While the link between social disadvantage and young fatherhood has remained relatively stable over time, the extent to which these social ills are seen as a cause or consequence of young fatherhood remains a contested issue (Pirog et al, 2018). It is undoubtedly important to establish the factors that can lead to young fatherhood and the implications of social disadvantage for longer-term outcomes. However, interpretations of this evidence may slip into and reinforce a deficit view of young fathers (Johannson and Hammarén, 2014).

A sizeable body of evidence about young fathers, particularly in the field of psychology, is framed in terms of the risk factors associated with young parenthood (for example, Miller-Johnson et al, 2004). The vacuum in the research evidence on the lived experiences of young fathers has contributed to the impression that they are either invisible or absent (Coleman and Dennison, 1998: 311). The earliest studies of young fathers assumed they were psychologically unstable and able to offer nothing of value to support young mothers (reported in Glikman, 2004). The knowledge that most young fathers are socially disadvantaged has increased the tendency among some researchers to perpetuate negative stereotypes of them as uncaring, indifferent or 'risky' (critiqued, in particular, by Miller, 1997; Parikh, 2005; Tuffin et al, 2010; Johansson and Hammerén, 2014; Tarrant, 2021). Wei et al (2002), for example, frame their research with a key question: how many of the offspring born to teenage fathers are produced by repeat serious delinquents? They report a close link between delinquency and the early onset of sexual activity, with rates of conception and fatherhood twice as high among repeat serious delinquents. Perhaps even more problematically, Khatun and colleagues (2017) ask, 'Do children born to teenage parents have lower adult intelligence?' The findings reported by Wei et al (2002) are relatively measured (suggesting the need for better interventions to tackle the link between delinquency and early conceptions). Nevertheless, the language of such reporting is laden with a social deficit perspective.

Researchers may also uncritically buy into the public stigma that tarnishes the reputations of young fathers (see Chapter 2 for a detailed discussion). In the process, their writings may reinforce and encourage such views (Speak, 2006). For example, an early study of teenage mothers reports that young fathers run away from their responsibilities: 'the last stages of teenage pregnancies echo to the sounds of slamming doors as the fathers make their dash for anonymity and freedom' (Hudson and Ineichen, 1991: 66). As a further example, in her analysis of data from the US National Longitudinal Survey of Labor Market Experiences, Pirog-Good suggests that the poverty and lack of agency that marks the lives of young fathers goes hand in hand with 'irresponsible behaviour concerning one's children' (Pirog-Good, 1995: 373; for further critiques of this study, see Chapter 6).

However, there is a growing awareness that seeing young fatherhood through a social problems lens is too narrow: a range of perspectives is needed (Paschal et al, 2011: 63). Encouragingly, a strand of historical and more recent literatures has developed a much more nuanced picture of young fathers and their engagement in the lives of their children. Building on the foundation that young fathers are more involved than first assumed (see Glikman, 2004 for a review), there is ample evidence of young fathers' intentions to be there for their children, regardless of the challenges and circumstances through which they experience fatherhood. Such insights have also been enabled through alternative theoretical frameworks for understanding young fathers, as we will go on to show.

The social engagement framework

A social engagement framework offers a strong counter-narrative to the 'problem's findings outlined earlier. It has emerged, in the main, through qualitative studies that focus on the lived experiences of young fathers. One of the first major studies to adopt this view sought to challenge the deficit framework for understanding young fathers and replace it with a compassionate approach that would support their parenting efforts (Robinson, 1988). The evidence generated through what we have called a social engagement lens offers a very different picture from the social problems framework, not least because it gives more weight to young fathers' own accounts. It is consistently reported that young fathers, whether single or partnered, resident or non-resident, care about and want to be engaged in their children's lives, and that they aspire to being treated as clients of services that will support their parenting efforts. The accounts of the young men are often framed in terms of 'being there' for their children, or 'doing the best they can' (Osborn, 2007; Edin and Nelson, 2013; Shirani, 2015). A commonly reported rationale is a wish to do better than their own fathers (Bunting and McAuley, 2004; Tuffin et al, 2010; Kiselica, 2011; Paschal et al, 2011; Edin and Nelson, 2013).

Engaged young fathers

This alternative way of framing the lives of young fathers is part of a broader pattern of engaged fatherhood, which began to emerge in Britain in the latter decades of the 20th century. It was stimulated by ideals of gender equality, the rise in working motherhood, and the growing incidence of divorce and separation, which required fathers to find new ways to relate to their children (Smart and Neale, 1999). This emerging ideology has been described in increasingly nuanced language as the emergence of 'new' men, shared or co-parenting, or engaged, involved or intimate fathering (Clark, 1991; Dermott, 2008; Featherstone, 2009; Miller, 2011). How far this ethos is accepted among contemporary parents, and is being used to shape their family practices, has been the subject of sustained academic interest and debate, as we show below (see, for example, Clark, 1991; Dermott and Miller, 2015; Mollborn, 2017; Tarrant, 2021; Grau Grau et al, 2022).

Evidence that young men recognise and value the notion of engaged fatherhood is not new. A purposive study of 26 expectant young fathers carried out in the early 1980s, for example, found that an overwhelming majority of the young men possessed strong feelings of obligation to both mother and child (Barret and Robinson, 1982; see also SmithBattle et al, 2019a). Moreover, widespread patterns of parental aspiration and commitment are evident among young fathers across the UK, Europe, the US and further afield (for example, Rouch, 2005; Andreasson et al, 2023; Donald et al, 2022). South African evidence, for example, shows how early fatherhood provides an opportunity for young men to privilege care, respect and active involvement in their children's lives, thereby shifting dominant constructions of men and masculinities (Enderstein and Boonzaier, 2015; Elkington, 2017; for similar evidence in a Thai context, see Srion, 2014; Uengwongsapat et al, 2017).

There is also mounting evidence to suggest that, regardless of age, where men are engaged as parents, this can be beneficial for them, the mothers and their children (Robinson, 1988; Speak et al, 1997; Rolph, 1999; Kiselica, 2011; Wilson and Prior, 2011; Norman and Davies, 2023; see also Welsh et al, 2004). The correlation between engaged fathering and positive outcomes for children has been demonstrated along a range of measures, including children's mental health, antisocial behaviour and academic motivation (Flouri, 2005; Duncan, 2007, Paranjothy et al, 2009; Mollborn and Jacobs, 2015; Mollborn, 2017; Norman and Davies, 2023). In the UK the new ethos has been reflected in and reinforced through legislative changes (notably, the Children Act 1989 and the Children and Families Act 2014).

Researchers report that young men commonly see fatherhood as an accomplishment, a source of pride and responsibility and a potential source of giving and receiving love (Arai, 2009; Ayoola et al, 2010; Elkington, 2017; SmithBattle et al, 2019a). Wider benefits for the citizenship of young men have also been reported when they invest in their identities as fathers. Researchers note, for example, that an early entry into fatherhood can be an important impetus to secure education, training and employment (Duncan, 2007), while for previously incarcerated young men, fatherhood represents an important turning point that may trigger a rejection of riskier behaviour and aspirations to follow more productive paths in life (Meek, 2007; Shannon and Abrams, 2007; Landers et al, 2015; Neale and Ladlow, 2015a; Ladlow and Neale, 2016). Such commitments reflect the re-establishment of life goals (Sriyasak et al, 2016) and a greater commitment to family life in otherwise disrupted life trajectories (Torres de Lacerda et al, 2014; Rua, 2015; Ayton and Hansen, 2016; Elkington, 2017).

In short, young fatherhood may therefore be acknowledged as an opportunity for young men, rather than a catastrophe (Duncan, 2007). This body of evidence also suggests that young fathers matter: they deserve to be supported in their efforts as parents, and included as clients of services (Neale and Davies, 2015b; Neale, 2016). Across this body of research, these central themes are filtered through a consistent understanding of the heterogeneity of young fathers' lives across contexts and global settings, warning against the tendency to essentialise their experiences (Klinman et al, 1985; Speak et al, 1997; Neale and Davies, 2015a; Lau Clayton, 2016). To give one example, in a study of 30 young fathers set in Worcester, UK, commissioned by a local Sure Start service, 70 per cent of the sample was employed, including 5 per cent who were at university (Birbeck, 2004, cited in Speak, 2006). The circumstances of this sample of young men offers a very different picture from that generated through research that focuses on disadvantaged young men and that sees them through the lens of a 'social problems' framework. Overall, across a disparate body of research, attention is now being paid to the varied circumstances and experiences of young fathers, in different cultural and ethnic contexts, in urban and rural settings (Clayton et al, 2022) and across different contexts of time and place (Tarrant and Neale, 2017b; Diverse Dads Collective, 2021; Tarrant, 2021).

Absent young fathers?

This mixed evidence on the lives of young fathers raises an important question: across the population of young fathers, how prevalent are those who deny or disregard their paternity and, from the outset, run away from their responsibilities? This is the foundation for the deficit view of young fathers, yet to what extent is it supported through the available research evidence? Our review of the literature suggests that most of the evidence for the existence of these absent young men comes from young mothers (see, for example, Hudson and Ineichen, 1991; Speak et al, 1997), whose accounts are bolstered by public discourses that denigrate their absence (see Chapter 2). Direct evidence from absent young men themselves is harder to find; by definition, they fall outside the mould of engaged young fathers. For their study of young single fathers, for example, Speak et al (1997: 10) recruited 40 young men who were actively engaged with their children, but a further 28 declined to take part on the grounds that they had had little or no involvement with their child since the birth.

However, two US studies, conducted prior to the births of the young men's children, offer interesting insights into the motives and rationales of nine absent, single, disadvantaged young men, most of whom were from African American backgrounds (Leite, 2007; Paschal et al, 2011). The presenting issue seemed to be a simple denial of paternity in a context where these 'autonomous' young men held dear to their teenage lives, had no desire to become a parent, expressed doubts about the mother's fidelity, and felt trapped by what they saw as the mother's duplicity over using contraception (Paschal et al, 2011).

However, these considerations mask an underlying range of social factors that, taken together, led to the withdrawal of these young men. The key issue was the lack of social recognition, encouragement and support, primarily from the mothers (but also from grandparents, professional workers, and/or peer group), that could foster their fatherhood identities, at a time (pre-birth) when these identities felt unreal to them. Without encouragement to engage with the process, and compounded by the stigma associated with their position, they felt excluded from the pregnancy and had no means of countering their deep anxieties about their abilities to provide for and nurture a child (Leite, 2007; Paschal et al, 2011; see also Wilkes et al, 2012 and Ncayiyane and Nel, 2023; we return to these important themes in Chapters 3 and 4).

The prevalence of such experiences across the wider population of young fathers is difficult to gauge, given that we do not know with any certainty how many young men become fathers, who they are and where they can be found (Deslauriers and Kiselica, 2022). However, the social engagement framework outlined earlier points to strong and consistent evidence, across time and space, for the existence of young men who wish to be there for their children. Statistical evidence supports this picture: in 2008 in the UK, 77 per cent of births to women aged 20 years and younger were jointly registered by young mothers and fathers, while only 23 per cent of births were registered solely by the mothers (ONS, reported in Graham, 2013). Moreover, sole registrations of births by mothers have been falling steadily since 2008 (Statista, 2023), indicating a possible rise in the proportion of young men who jointly register the birth of their child.

This is not to deny the existence of young men who, from the outset, may decline a role as a father. But it does suggest that these absent young men are likely to form a relatively small minority within the general population of young fathers. This reworking of the evidence provides a challenge to popular understandings of the overriding prevalence of young men who simply run away from their parenting responsibilities.

Contextual influences on the engagement of young fathers: socio-economic, geopolitical and relational factors

The social engagement framework outlined earlier provides an important counter-narrative and corrective to the orthodox social problems literature on young fathers (especially where it drifts into a deficit framework of understanding). But it does not replace it. Both frameworks are needed and have value. Taken together, they provide a more rounded and nuanced understanding of the complicated lives of young fathers. The rather rosy picture that emerges from the social engagement evidence is tempered by the realities of the many factors that may hinder young fathers in fulfilling their aspirations to be there for their children.

A common analytic dimension of both frameworks that must be held in tension are the socio-economic contexts through which young fathers are supported or challenged as parents. For many young fathers, entry into and transitions through fatherhood are undeniably achieved on 'shaky ground', a metaphor employed by SmithBattle et al (2019a) to describe the challenging social and contextual conditions through which teen paternity occurs and is navigated. As Deslaurier and Kiselica (2022) show, an ecosystemic framework can be of great value in piecing together the wide constellation of factors that might converge to influence a young father's journey from the time of the pregnancy through to the first year of a child's life.

Personal, socio-economic and geopolitical factors

As we have seen, the socio-economic standing of young fathers is a key issue that shapes their journeys into parenthood. In the context of enduring values surrounding a provider role, the challenges are all the greater for young men with few resources to contribute. Alongside this, a host of other factors can make a difference. For example, the transition into early fatherhood is often associated with concerns about finances, completing education and finding ways to be there for the mother and child, which may result in considerable levels of personal stress (Robinson and Barret, 1987; see the review in Miller, 1997).

An early US study of 95 adolescent fathers (Fry and Trifiletti, 1983) identifies a range of stress factors, including fears of emotional rejection from significant others, the weight of responsibility as a parent, blame for the pregnancy, and personal anxieties and feelings of guilt, all of which may impact on the capacity of young fathers to take up a caring role. Accounts of pregnancy from young fathers are permeated with discussions of challenging childhoods and prospects for 'bleak futures'; they commonly report feeling ill-prepared and daunted by their uncharted journeys and new responsibilities, a finding that is also reported in more recent international research (for example, Chili and Maharaj, 2015; Madiba and Nsiki, 2017; Matlakala et al, 2018; Astuti et al, 2021; Mukuna, 2020). Young fathers in impoverished communities in South Africa, for example, are more likely to deny paternity because of the stigma associated with young parenthood and teenage pregnancy (Ncayiyane and Nel, 2023). Qualitative researchers have found that fear of stigma may be expressed through fears of ridicule from the maternal family and anxieties over limited financial resource in a context where breadwinning is considered a key component of fatherhood (Swartz and Bhana, 2009; Ncayiyane and Nel, 2023).

These findings accord with those of Miller (1997) who was reviewing research evidence on these themes from the US in the 1980s. When impoverished young men become fathers, they are likely to feel burdened by their multiple roles and changed priorities, and preoccupied by feelings of inadequacy and dissatisfaction with the barriers that hinder their engagement as fathers (Chili and Maharaj, 2015, see also Uengwongsapat et al, 2017 in a Thai context). Such findings sit alongside the evidence that young fatherhood can introduce purpose and meaning in the lives of young men and offer redemption and a turning point in otherwise disrupted trajectories.

In the growing international literature, wider geopolitical and geographical factors have also been found to influence young fathers' reported readiness to participate as engaged fathers. In countries like South Africa, the separation of fathers from their children has been linked to the need for men to secure employment in more distant places, especially where they reside in rural areas (Chili and Maharaj, 2015). Poverty and the HIV/AIDS pandemic have also been identified as contributing factors (Ncayiyane and Nel, 2023). Distinctive cultural norms such as *inhlawulo* (the payment of damages for impregnating a woman before marriage) and *lobola* (an obligatory payment of a 'bride price'), can also contribute to the separation of some young men from their children (Ncayiyane and Nel, 2023). These international comparisons of the lives of young fathers indicate that the idiosyncrasies of historically embedded welfare, cultural and political systems may strongly influence how these young men perceive their roles as fathers, and their capacity to sustain this role over time.

Co-parenting relationships

As the evidence suggests, one of the key factors that that can make a difference to the parenting journeys of young fathers is the nature of their relationships with the mothers of their children, and how these relationships unfold over time. In terms of their quality and construction, co-parenting relationships are varied and fluid. It is worth teasing out here the changing nature of these relationships, both historically, in terms of wider patterns of social change, and biographically, in terms of changes in individual lives. The specific issues that arise for young parents are considered here within a broader discussion about patterns of co-parenting for all fathers, regardless of age.

Our starting point is the observation that reproductive agency tends to reside largely with mothers (although the maternal family and, to a lesser extent, male partners may also have some influence, Mann et al, 2015). This is part of a strongly ingrained and widely held assumption that mothers are the primary carers of their children, a presumed essentialist and indissoluble tie between mothers and their children to which fathers or father substitutes can be serially and conditionally attached. Mothers are perceived to have the power to decide how a child will be raised and by whom. A decade ago, as we write, estimates in the UK indicated that around 97 per cent of primary caring parents were mothers (ONS, 2013); little seems to have changed since (ONS, 2021). This suggests the continuing strength of the mother/child dyad as the basis for organising the care of a child, while alternative framings around gender equality and engaged fatherhood have been relatively slow to emerge.

For example, notions of a *package deal* for fathers became institutionalised in 20th-century American society (Furstenberg and Cherlin, 1991; Townsend, 2002; Tach et al, 2010). According to this model, fatherhood cannot operate independently of the mother's involvement; it flows through and is contingent upon the relationship that binds the mother to the child. Mother and child operate together as a 'package' which shapes the father's involvement. This pattern was observed to be most common among low-income families (Edin and Nelson, 2013).

The ways in which fathers are connected to mothers and their children has shifted over time. Marriage was traditionally seen as the institutional backbone of family life, creating a supposedly indissoluble tie between a couple and binding them closely to their children. Widespread values in which sexual relationships were tied to marital status created a major fault line in society between legitimate children and those who were deemed illegitimate for being born 'out of wedlock'. The idea of marriage as a social good has remained in evidence; in some international contexts, for example, young fathers regard marriage as a key protective factor for their involvement, because it is an assumed indicator of a stronger, more stable relationship (for example, Edin and Nelson, 2013; Florsheim and Moore, 2020 for the US; Enderstein and Boonzaier, 2015 for South Africa). However, with the rise in unmarried partnerships and parenthood, cohabitation and, more recently, civil partnerships, marriage has lost much of its institutional force, although it remains as a residual and symbolic force that continues to shape people's aspirations for a stable and settled family life.

As shown in the Introduction, with the rise in divorce and separation, a slow uncoupling of parenthood from marriage and cohabitation has occurred. The more peripheral role allotted to fathers is reinforced in these circumstances; they are increasingly parenting *at a distance*, across households and outside partnered relationships, rather than parenting *at close hand* within a shared household. In the last decades of the 20th century this was a growing trend (DWP, 2010; ONS, 2013; Poole et al, 2016). Estimates suggest that, for much of the 20th century, and regardless of the routes into single or non-residential fatherhood, between 40 and 70 per cent of non-resident fathers of all ages lost contact with their children over time, particularly where they were living in disadvantaged circumstances (Simpson et al, 1995; Bradshaw et al, 1999; Dermott, 2016). This pattern has been observed across Europe and the US (Elke Graf and Wojnicka, 2023).

Driven by the idea of a 'clean break', mothers and their children would commonly seek a new family unit with a surrogate father, while fathers would commonly start a new family, or join a pre-existing unit of single mother and her children (Bradshaw et al, 1999; Smart and Neale, 1999). Moreover, where either parent re-partners, this may 'crowd out' the fathers' obligations to their original children (Tach et al, 2010). Tach et al (2010) speculate that it is easier for fathers to use their scarce resources to fulfil the demands of a new family, rather than retaining a commitment to their original children (see also Edin and Nelson, 2013). Other evidence, however, suggests that it is the change in the mother's circumstances (rather than the father's) that provides most of the momentum for a change in paternal contact arrangements. In effect, fathers tend to be 'pushed out' rather than 'drop out' (Corlyon and McGuire, 1999: 85; see also Tach et al, 2010)

Regardless of these intricacies, recent shifts in historical patterns of partnering and parenting show that fathering at a distance is a growing practice that is becoming more sustainable over time. Poole et al (2014) for example, report a rise in the incidence of sustained contact between non-resident fathers and their children, with only 10 per cent losing all contact over time (in most cases, among those living in impoverished circumstances (Poole et al, 2014; also, Simpson et al, 1995; Bradshaw et al, 1999)).

How far these relationship dynamics characterise the practices of *young* fathers and mothers is a key question. The general patterns and trends we have outlined would seem to be accentuated for this age group. For example, evidence from both the UK and US suggests a relatively high incidence of relationship breakdown between young parents. This is particularly the case during the pregnancy or in the first year of a child's life (Tabberer et al, 2000; Lloyd, 2010). It is also more likely to occur for disadvantaged young men, in a context where poverty and high levels of stress are linked to parental conflict (Donald et al, 2022). For young fathers it is commonplace to be fathering at a distance, without the advantages of an income, a shared home (and in some cases without any kind of stable home base), or a closely aligned couple relationship upon which to build a cooperative parenting project.

Based on a nationally representative sample of fathers interviewed for the *Understanding Society Study*, Poole and colleagues (2014) found that 34 per cent of young fathers aged 16–24, are non-resident, compared with 14 per cent of fathers aged 45 and over. They are also more likely than older fathers to have been in casual or fleeting relationships with the mothers at the time of conception, and, therefore, to have entered parenthood as single and/or non-resident fathers (Kiernan, 2005; Poole et al, 2014). It seems that, for many young parents, it is not so much that couple ties have been broken, for they were never strongly forged in the first place. As Gilligan and colleagues (2012) note, in these fragile circumstances, young mothers alone are seen to have a legitimate claim to their children, and the right to determine the nature and extent of a young father's involvement.

These patterns raise further questions concerning the extent to which parenting at a distance is sustainable over time for this age group. Where relationships between young parents are fragile, researchers commonly report that paternal contact decreases or becomes intermittent over time (Bunting and McAuley, 2004; Lewin et al, 2015). Longitudinal evidence on this theme is rather limited, reliant largely on mothers' accounts, and also dated (relating to earlier generational cohorts, see the reviews in Bunting and McAuley, 2004, and Mollborn and Jacobs, 2015). But it is worth providing a brief overview here of evidence from the US and UK.

In their study of 89 African American young mothers, Toledo-Dreves et al (1995) report a comparatively high incidence of stable relationships between the parents, with 66 per cent maintaining their family relationships at the two-year follow-up. Kiernan (1995) also found that the majority of young single parents were in relatively stable, long-term co-parenting relationships that supported their parenting efforts. Analyses of national data from the US 'Fragile Families' study demonstrate that at the time of the birth of the child, 82 per cent of young unmarried fathers were still romantically involved with their female partners, 50 per cent of whom were cohabitating and 32 per cent visiting. Only 10 per cent of mothers reported a loss of contact with the father (Carlson and McLanahan, 2010).

Data from the UK reveal a similar picture. In a longitudinal study of 74 young couples, Quinton et al (2002) found that by the time the child was nine months old, 63 per cent of the young men were still engaged, while 37 per cent had largely dropped out. A qualitative retrospective study of 40 young single fathers in the UK (Speak et al, 1997), report comparable rates of engagement, with well over 50 per cent of the sample having amicable relationships with the mothers. In 50 per cent of these cases, the fathers had weekly contact with their child, while 60 per cent had sustained some ongoing contact with their child and co-parent for more than three years.

However, longitudinal research conducted over more extensive periods of time indicates that these relationships are more likely to deteriorate over the longer term. Larson et al (1996), for example, observe that, among their sample of 241 teenage mothers, 60 per cent of fathers were involved with their children in the immediate aftermath of the birth, but at the follow-up, some three and a half years later, only 25 per cent were still involved and child contact was increasingly intermittent. Similar findings are reported by Furstenberg et al (1987a,b), who conducted a 17-year follow-up of a sample of 400 African American teenage mothers. While nearly half the fathers had resided with their children for some time after the birth, only 17 per cent were co-resident at the long-term follow-up, while a further 16 per cent had weekly contact with their children. Comparable rates are reported in a UK context (Bunting and McAuley, 2004). Most of the 13 young fathers recruited by Wiggins et al (2005), for example, were in a relationship with the mothers at the time of the pregnancy, but none of these relationships were sustained, resulting in tenuous contact between the fathers and their children over time.

Overall, this evidence indicates that young fathers are likely to face challenges in sustaining long-term partnerships with the mothers of their children, although they still aspire to be there for their children, and will seek to do so through co-parenting relationships that operate at a distance. It also seems clear that the ingrained 20th-century pattern of mothers taking a primary caring role for their children has been slow to change. Young parents themselves tend to give conflicting reasons for this: young women tend to lament the father's lack of interest, while young men lament the mother's resistance to their involvement (Rhein et al, 1997). Despite, or perhaps because of a growing awareness of the principle of father engagement, neither parent is willing to take the blame when it does not materialise.

Overall, the evidence presented here suggests that whether separated fathers can sustain a role as an engaged parent depends on how far they are able to negotiate and sustain a working relationship with the mothers of their children (Furstenberg and Cherlin, 1991, Smart and Neale, 1999; Bronte-Tinkew and Horowitz, 2010; Poole et al, 2014). Regardless of marital or residential status, it is the strength of co-parenting relationships that determines the engagement of a father with his child. These relational factors would seem to be just as salient in determining father/child contact as a father's socio-economic status and resources (Tach et al, 2010; Elkington, 2017; Pirog et al, 2018). To date, however, there is limited evidence on these more distant patterns of co-parenting, the extent to which they are sustainable over time, and the factors that are likely to make a difference (Mollborn and Jacobs, 2015).

Concluding discussion

Our overview of this rich body of empirical research reveals that studies on young fatherhood are many and varied when seen in historical and international context. Young fathers are heterogeneous and may face a wide range of challenges in establishing and sustaining a role as an engaged parent. Nevertheless, across this body of evidence, key findings and enduring themes relating to the commitments of young fathers to their children are remarkably similar. Two key orientations are evident in this literature: a social problems framework (that may shade into a social deficit understanding of young fathers), and a social engagement framework that establishes their commitment to be there for their children. These are complementary modes of understanding that, taken together, create more rounded insights into the issues that young fathers face. In exploring the range of factors that may impact on young fathers' parenting journeys, we have drawn particular attention to their socio-economic circumstances and the nature of their relationships with the mothers of their children.

We have also reviewed the nature and robustness of the existing research evidence and have found it wanting in some respects. The oft-repeated mantra that there is a paucity of evidence on young fatherhood is beginning to wear a little thin in the face of a burgeoning body of international literature. It is not clear why some researchers perpetuate this view (see, for example, Donald et al, 2022, and a recent review of existing evidence in Rantho and Matlakala, 2021). But there may be unfortunate effects. Researchers may fail to do justice to the existing body of evidence. And there is a continual recourse to relatively minute, opportunistic and exploratory samples of young fathers that do not adequately capture the range and variety of their experiences and circumstances.

We have noted too that the body of research evidence on young fathers is relatively scattered across numerous studies and, at the time of writing, had not been systematically integrated to create a more rounded and comprehensive picture. Finally, some notable gaps exist in this body of evidence, not least a paucity of dynamic evidence that traces the lives of young fathers qualitatively through time. The piecing together of presumed trajectories based on 'snapshot' research produces a less nuanced understanding of the shifting dynamics of these young lives and the causes and consequences of change. The FYF study was designed to overcome these limitations and shed new light on the rich constellation of factors that shape young fathers' parenting journeys over time. Our aim has been to complement and further advance an impressive body of evidence that has already yielded many important insights into the lives of young fathers.

2

Policy responses and public discourses: the neglect of young fathers

Introduction

In this chapter we turn our attention to the national policy context within which the Following Young Fathers (FYF) study took place, drawing on a range of academic and policy related commentaries, including our own earlier contributions (Neale and Davies, 2015a, 2015b; Neale, 2016; Tarrant and Neale, 2017a, 2017b; Neale, 2021b). Our main focus is on UK policies relating to teenage conceptions and young parenthood since the 1990s. These form part of a broader complex of family and youth policies that are detailed elsewhere (Churchill, 2016; Edwards and Gillies, 2016; Davies, 2019).

Starting with policy developments during the last years of the Conservative administration in the 1990s, we move on to the bold strategies introduced in the late 1990s under New Labour, with particular attention to the ten-year Teenage Pregnancy Strategy (TPS). More recent developments, under the Coalition and Conservative administrations from 2010 onwards, are also explored. Through this evolving policy landscape, we also trace the impact of successive government responses on the socio-economic fortunes of disadvantaged families and young people. Specific policy initiatives relating to Relationship and Sex Education (RSE), health and social welfare, parenting support, and provisions for youth employment, benefits and housing, are touched upon here, but given more detailed attention in our empirical chapters.

We then turn our attention to young fathers, discerning how they are perceived in these policy processes. Three interrelated issues emerge: first, the dominance of the social problems framework as a lens through which to respond to these young men; second, the stigma that they face by virtue of their early entry into parenthood (the persistence of a social deficit framework of understanding); and third, their general neglect in a policy process that is focused, by and large, on young mothers. We conclude with reflections on the reasons for this state of affairs. Drawing together insights from Chapters 1 and 2, we consider how far the principle of evidence-based policy has driven policy responses in relation to young parents, and to what extent the existing research evidence has been skewed to fit dominant constructions of young fathers.

Teenage pregnancy and parenthood: policy developments

In recent decades, UK policy concerns about young pregnancy and parenthood have been sharpened in response to changing patterns of family practices. In the late 1960s and early 1970s, a significant growth was observed in teenage conception rates in Europe and the US (in the UK, the rate peaked in 1971, at 50.6 live births per 1,000 women aged under 20; Arai, 2009). This change occurred within the context of broader historical shifts in patterns of partnering and parenting (detailed in the Introduction). As numerous commentators observe, the rate then fell quite sharply, in line with the introduction of free NHS contraception services in 1974 (Alison Hadley, pers. comm.). By 1981, rates had fallen to 28.1 live births per 1,000 young women and remained relatively stable over the next two decades. However, the rates were an ongoing concern in the UK because they remained high in comparison with other European states. They also varied across localities, with the highest levels found in disadvantaged communities across the UK (Wellings and Kane, 1999; Furstenberg, 2003; Arai, 2009; Duncan et al, 2010; Hadley and Ingham, 2018).

A correlation between young parenthood and indices of social deprivation has long been noted by policy makers. It became commonplace to observe that these young lives are marked by a range of inequalities, including poverty, poor educational skills and qualifications, unemployment, dependency on state benefits and housing, crime, 'troubled' family backgrounds, and poor physical and mental health outcomes, including postnatal depression, lower rates of breastfeeding and higher infant mortality rates (SEU, 1999). As shown in Chapter 1, research evidence on the characteristics of young fathers, and the risk factors associated with them, have bolstered this view, although the assumption that all young parents face all of these social ills is speculative. Exactly how and to what extent young parents are implicated in these social problems, and whether young parenthood is understood as a cause or consequence of the problems (or both), are long-standing and contentious issues (Kiernan, 2002; Duncan, 2007; Arai, 2009; Duncan et al, 2010). Nevertheless, these research findings fed into growing concerns about early conception rates and young parenthood in late 20th-century policy circles.

In tracing policy concerns and developments over time, it is possible to discern four underlying concerns that, at various times, have helped to shape the responses of successive governments: *moral concerns* about teen sexual practices; *social concerns* about the exclusion and poverty of young parents; *financial concerns* about the costs of supporting young parents; and *public health* concerns about the fragile health profiles of young mothers and babies (Daguerre, 2006). Our discussion begins in the 1990s, when Conservative policy was driven by a moralistic concern to reduce teenage pregnancy rates. A policy target designed to reduce these rates was built into the five-year Health of the Nation initiative (1992–97), although its effects were limited (Arai, 2009). Dedicated contraception services for young people were expanded, but little attention was given to those aged 16 and 17, who accounted for 80 per cent of the high conception rates. Moreover, the initiative was narrowly focused on health provisions and failed to consider partnership working across different agencies (Hadley and Ingham, 2018).

In 1999 the New Labour government instituted the ten-year TPS (SEU, 1999), a national framework coordinated by a dedicated Teenage Pregnancy Unit (TPU). Detailed appraisals of the TPS are available elsewhere (see, for example, TPIAG, 2010; Hadley and Ingham, 2018), but an outline of developments is given here. The main focus of the strategy was to reduce teenage conception rates, whether they resulted in a birth or abortion, and with a particular focus on young women under the age of 18. The strategy also aimed to provide socio-economic, housing and parenting support for young parents (Hadley and Ingham, 2018). Under this policy, concerns about young pregnancy were reframed in the less moralistic language of social exclusion. The then prime minister, Tony Blair, castigated the previous administration for attacking teenage mothers, while ignoring 'the damage [pregnancy] does to the education, employment and life chances of young women and girls' (cited in Arai, 2009: 59).

The TPS was anchored in the principle of multi-agency joined-up working. It was rolled out nationally at all tiers of government, via local and regional teenage pregnancy coordinators. The TPU produced regular evidence reviews, progress reports and non-statutory guidance to help local authorities work towards their targets, including reaching out to boys and young men (TPU, 2000). Measures were designed to improve Sex and Relationship Education (SRE, replaced by Relationship and Sex Education in March 2017) provision; give better access to contraception and sexual health advice through a variety of frontline health services; and to change public perceptions through a national communications campaign targeted at young people and their parents. Underpinning this preventative strategy was a financial concern to save costs; teenage pregnancy was estimated to cost £63 million a year to the NHS alone, a drain on the public purse that could be avoided with more effective and timely interventions (DfES, 2006a; TPIAG, 2010).

The second plank of the TPS strategy aimed to better support vulnerable young parents, and to address the inequalities that they faced. The objective over the decade was to increase (to 60 per cent) the take-up of education, employment and training (EET) opportunities among teenage mothers. This was seen as the most meaningful form of citizenship for young parents and the main route out of poverty and protection from social exclusion. The strategy also encompassed support for the housing needs of young parents, with £12 million allocated for housing and childcare support over the first three years (SEU, 1999). At mid-term, plans were announced to evaluate a pilot housing scheme, developed across seven local authorities. In 2009 extra support was announced for all those aged 16 and 17 who were in supported housing (DCSF and DoH, 2010: 37, 54; see Chapter 8 for a more detailed account).

It is worth noting here that the TPS formed part of a coordinated range of initiatives designed to support the health and well-being of families and young people, including drug, alcohol and child safeguarding policies and the National Healthy Schools programme. For example, support for disadvantaged families, including vulnerable young parents, was built into the Sure Start Plus programme, a flagship initiative that developed in parallel with the TPS. Between 2004 and 2007, the programme was established in 35 of the most disadvantaged localities of England. Based on fledgling ideas about the value of early intervention (described later), the aim was to support low-income families with children under the age of five. The overall programme was later expanded to a network of 3,500 Sure Start Children's Centres. These were established in a wider range of communities, beyond those identified as deprived, and with budgets devolved to local governments.

Returning to the TPS, while the specific targets of the strategy were not reached, positive impacts were achieved over the decade. Mid-term reviews (DfES, 2006a, 2006b) helped to drive forward implementation strategies, including inter-agency collaborations and mechanisms to set targets and monitor progress. The focus at this point was to iron out continuing high rates of conception in the most deprived localities and give examples of good practice from innovative services. There were also renewed efforts to challenge the defeatist mindsets of many frontline staff (discussed further in Chapter 9). Services were actively encouraged to reach out to young people and make a difference to their lives (Hadley and Ingham, 2018). Drawing on recommendations from the Teenage Pregnancy Independent Advisory Group (TPIAG, 2002), the government began, for the first time, to incorporate the needs of young fathers into its statutory guidance for local authorities ([DCSF/DoH], 2007).

By 2010, teenage conception rates in the UK were falling steadily and they continued to fall in the aftermath, although variations across localities remain, and conceptions resulting in the birth of a child continue to be concentrated in the most disadvantaged communities (PHE and LGA, 2018, 2019). Whether the falling rates can be attributed solely to the TPS or would have occurred in any case is a matter for debate (Baxter et al, 2021). However, with its range of accessible, welcoming and targeted support services, alongside a new-found commitment from frontline staff, the strategy contributed to a gradual sea change in reproductive values among young people, with an increased preference to delay parenthood through the use of contraception and abortion.

Attempts under the TPS to improve the life chances of young parents also bore some fruit, with more than a 30 per cent increase achieved in EET rates for young mothers over the decade. Given the young age of the mothers, much of the success related to engagement or re-engagement in education and training as a route into eventual employment, rather than securing employment per se (see also the critiques in Duncan et al, 2010: 42). Overall, the TPS offered new ways to tackle the issues of teenage conception and support for young parents; its achievements were made through a unique national framework around which wider policy and practice responses could cohere (Hadley, 2014; Neale, 2016; Wellings et al, 2016; Hadley and Ingham, 2018).

In 2010, shortly before the end of New Labour's term of office, plans emerged for the continuation of the strategies developed under the TPS. Initiatives were to be integrated into the work of local and regional governments through a range of universal and targeted services: maternity and Sex and Relationships Education (SRE) provision; youth-friendly contraception and sexual health services; Children's Centres (the successors to the Sure Start programme); education and housing support services; and the Connexions service, which offered a range of socio-economic and relational advice to young people aged 13 to 19 (DCSF and DoH, 2010). TPS strategies were also to be built into structured family interventions programmes, notably the Family Nurse Partnership scheme, which was set up in 2007 to offer a two-year package of support to young mothers through home visits from a specially trained nurse (Ferguson and Gates, 2013; Ferguson, 2016; see Chapter 9 for further details).

Policy developments under the Coalition and Conservative governments

From 2010, these broad strategies were accepted by the Conservative–Liberal Democrat Coalition government (Hadley, 2014; Hadley and Ingham, 2018). But there were some notable shifts in emphasis and implementation. Responsibilities for TPS initiatives were now devolved to local government without national support or coordination. In the process, support for young parents became much less visible. Reducing the under-18 conception rate was once more framed as a public health issue, with monitoring (but no clear targets) set up through a new framework for national health (DoH, 2012, 2013; Hadley and Evans, 2013; Hadley, 2014).

Central government commitment to these strategies was clearly beginning to wane: 'national funding for the strategy, including the media campaign, stopped, visible government leadership ceased, and the structures for strategy implementation began to be dismantled' (Hadley and Ingham, 2018: 68). From 2011, the teenage pregnancy coordinators were gradually decommissioned, and the TPU was closed in the following year. As a result, policy responses on teenage pregnancy became fractured and diluted across diverse agencies, running the risk of patchy and uncoordinated service provision, and an over-reliance on isolated 'local champions', operating outside, or on the fringes, of statutory provision.

The Coalition offer in terms of family intervention was more targeted and conditional. Further investments were made in early intervention services (for example, the Family Nurse Partnership scheme), which were targeted at families with very young children, since this was seen as the best way to prevent an escalation of problems over time, and thereby to save on the public purse. The bigger ambition was to break what was seen as a cycle of disadvantage in 'troubled' families (Allen, 2011; Eisenstadt, 2011; discussed further in Chapter 6). This shift in investments, however, resulted in a loss of the Connexions service and other dedicated services and community facilities for teenagers (Churchill, 2016).

Despite the erosion of central government support, valiant attempts were made by frontline staff to maintain the momentum of the TPS, aided by continuities in the appointment of key advisors. In 2013, an independent Teenage Pregnancy Knowledge Exchange, based at the University of Bedfordshire, was set up to provide an ongoing source of central expertise to guide the work of local authorities and non-statutory service providers (Hadley and Ingham, 2018). Hadley, former lead for implementing the TPS, directed this new unit and, from 2013, was appointed as policy advisor on teenage pregnancy for Public Health England (PHE). This new executive agency of the Department of Health was given operational autonomy in its task of improving the nation's health and reducing health inequalities.

During the first term of the Conservative administration (2015–19), at the behest of a number of local authorities, PHE produced two policy frameworks on young pregnancy and parenthood (PHE/LGA, 2018, 2019). Despite advances under the TPS, it was recognised that more needed to be done in tackling inequalities within and across varied localities of the UK. The initial priority was to reinvigorate the work of supporting young parents, which was beginning to slip down the policy agenda. In effect, the documents resurrected and further developed the twin planks of New Labour's TPS. While officially the TPS had come to an end, operationally the strategy was revitalised.

The need for joined-up services was re-envisioned through a 'whole system' approach, based on the appointment of lead professionals for young parents in each organisation or locality, and the establishment of structured care pathways that linked these agencies together (PHE/LGA, 2019). From the early days of the PHE, Hadley had repackaged these ideas in a new and

Policy responses and public discourses

Figure 2.1: Ten key factors for effective local strategies

- Relationships and sex education in schools and colleges
- Youth friendly contraceptive and SH services, and condom schemes
- Strong use of data for commissioning and monitoring of progress
- Support for pregnant teenagers and young parents – including prevention of subsequent pregnancies
- Strategic leadership and accountability
- Targeted prevention for young people at risk
- Consistent messages and service publicity to young people, parents and practitioners
- Support for parents to discuss relationships and sexual health
- Advice and access to contraception in non-health education and youth settings
- Training on relationships and sexual health for health and non-health professionals

Source: Alison Hadley (PHELGA, 2018)

eye-catching format (see Figure 2.1), which was now imported into the new PHE frameworks.

The 2019 framework (PHE/LGA, 2019, originally published in 2016) focused on support for young parents. While the needs of young mothers were prioritised, the framework took a lead from the DCSF/DoH (2007) guidance, and actively considered the needs of young fathers, against a backdrop of emerging research evidence about their lives (including some early findings from the Following Young Fathers study). The key actions needed to support young parents, including the development of local monitoring tools, were specified across a wide range of specialist and statutory services, from GP practices to safeguarding agencies.

How far the PHE frameworks were endorsed by the Conservative administration is difficult to gauge. They were made available on the main government website. But by 2019 it was clear that the political will to invest in these policies had eroded further, in line with falling rates of under-18 conception rates in the UK, and with other pressing issues weighing on the government. In the process, the ongoing support needs of young parents (which were never a priority for the Coalition and Conservative governments) slipped further from view (Jamie and Brown, forthcoming). From 2015, public health funding was increasingly eroded, and directors of public health marginalised (Griffiths et al, 2021). In 2021 PHE was abolished, its agendas diluted, and its budgets redirected to the Department of Health and Social Care and the newly established UK Health Security Agency (Griffiths et al, 2021). The attempts to open up the TPS at national level were effectively closed down again. Moreover, the issues that arose under the Coalition government relating to service fragmentation and welfare retrenchment intensified during this time. These constraints on support for young parents look set to continue under the current Conservative administration.

In this shifting climate, how far the PHE frameworks have been implemented, and what impact they may have had on local service provision is equally unclear. These processes would have stalled in any case during the COVID-19 pandemic, while coordinating a plethora of services, with variable delivery across localities, remains a challenge. Inequalities in pregnancy rates across localities in the UK are still prevalent, while the under-18 birth rate remains higher in the UK than in many comparable Western European countries (RCPCH, 2021). Policy documents warn against complacency.

Even so, the contemporary picture in England is positive when seen in historical perspective. Teenage pregnancy rates have continued to fall (despite a small increase at the start of the pandemic), with statistics for 2021 showing a 72 per cent decrease since 1998 (Hadley, 2023; RCPCH, 2021). Through the Local Government Association, the PHE frameworks have revitalised national benchmarks for professional practice and helped to sustain local efforts to provide pregnancy and parenting support for young people (Hadley, pers. comm.). In effect, the TPS has continued in new guises, with longer-term impact at grassroots level. The original policy, with its strong central leadership, active communications strategies and substantial budget (£280 million over a decade) has contributed to a sea change in the climate of local support for young parents that, despite the waning of central government interest, continues to build under its own momentum.

Poverty and changing family fortunes: UK policy responses

Alongside the policy developments already traced, broader policy responses were shaping and reshaping the socio-economic fortunes of young people and their families, with associated impacts on the correlation between young parenthood and social disadvantage. During the 1970s, when teenage conceptions were peaking, relative child poverty rates in the UK were also rising, with an increase from 15 per cent to 29 per cent of families living on incomes below the national average (Churchill, 2016). Over the whole course of the Conservative government (1979–97), and despite falling rates of unemployment, the number of children living in poverty tripled, with a quarter of the population (one in three children), living below the mean level of income by the time New Labour came to power (Piachaud and Sutherland, 2001).

These poverty rates, just like teenage conception rates, were the highest for any European country (Piachaud and Sutherland, 2001). During this period, stark social inequalities were increasingly apparent among UK families in terms of life expectancy, income levels, standards of living, and physical and mental health. The Conservative response to the rise in poverty and inequality was lukewarm. At this time, there was no acknowledgement of the problems that families were facing or, indeed, any attempt to define poverty, let alone address it (Piachaud and Sutherland, 2001).

This changed radically under New Labour. At the core of Blair's new government was a 20-year mission to eradicate child poverty, which was broadly defined to include lack of income, access to good-quality health, education and housing, and the quality of the local environment (Piachaud and Sutherland, 2001). In the wake of the Thatcher years, a broad neoliberal consensus had emerged that stressed the importance of work rather than 'welfare' and the value of individual responsibility and self-reliance, rather than social rights. While New Labour accepted elements of this approach, the government maintained a central, state-led set of strategies, combined with a strong will to tackle child poverty and inequalities (McKay and Rowlingson, 2016). Importantly, too, in his foreword to the 1999 Social Exclusion Unit Report (SEU, 1999), Blair acknowledged the failures of government to tackle the issues of poverty and the lack of opportunities that had dogged the lives of many young parents:

> Some of these teenagers, and some of their children, live happy and fulfilled lives. But far too many do not. Teenage mothers are less likely to finish their education, less likely to find a good job, and more likely to end up both as single parents and bringing up their children in poverty … Our failure to tackle this problem has cost the teenagers, their children, and the country dear. (SEU, 1999: 4)

A raft of measures was put in place across different areas of provision, with the aim of halving child poverty by 2010 (Walker, 1999; Piachaud and Sutherland, 2001). The main objectives were to improve income levels for disadvantaged families through the tax and benefits system, and promote and facilitate opportunities for paid work, which (despite the steady downgrading of employment conditions and benefits) was seen as the main route out of poverty. The strategies for supporting young parents were part and parcel of these broader policy agendas. Moreover, both had a good measure of success. It is worth noting here that most of the young men in the Following Young Fathers (FYF) study were growing from childhood to adolescence during these years.

From 2010, under the Coalition government, the neoliberal ideologies we have referred to were more fully articulated and embraced, with a particular focus on individual responsibility and the drive to reduce the 'nanny' state through welfare retrenchment and the gradual privatisation of public services. Responses to poverty during the second decade of the new century were as muted as the responses to the problems faced by young parents. The government introduced a range of benefit caps, conditions and sanctions for people of working age (including those with children) that marked a major change from the past (McKay and Rowlingson, 2016; Dwyer et al, 2022).

Tax credits and housing benefits were withdrawn from young people aged 18–21 (including young people with children), which increased their socio-economic vulnerability and forced them into a prolonged reliance on their parents (Churchill, 2016; Edwards and Gillies, 2016). The retrenchment of support for young people, parents and families affected many areas of community provision. For example, one in three Children's Centres was axed under the Coalition administration, while real-term spending on this provision in 2015/16 was 47 per cent less than in 2010/11 (Bate and Foster, 2017). During this period, when the FYF study was under way, the social disadvantages faced by young parents undoubtedly become more pronounced.

In this increasingly rigid, conditional and pared down welfare regime, child poverty rates began to rise once more. In the wake of New Labour, denying the existence of poverty was no longer an option. But the Coalition government sidestepped the issue by redefining what poverty was, and how it might be tackled. With the focus firmly on individual responsibility, poverty was now reframed as 'a lack of opportunities, aspirations and skills', and the root causes of childhood disadvantage were said to be 'educational failure, worklessness, family breakdown, severe debt, and poor health, including alcohol and drug addiction' (HM Government, cited in Churchill, 2016: 276). Poverty, then, was recast as an individual behavioural issue (with a marked downplaying of structural issues related to poor labour-market conditions, the reduced safety net of social security, and degraded neighbourhoods).

From 2015, after five years of austerity in the UK, and a Conservative government no longer fettered by Coalition partners, welfare retrenchment was intensified. This led to a widening of deep-rooted structural inequalities across multiple dimensions of life (Vizard and Hill, 2021). Rates of relative poverty, which had risen sharply from 2013/14 onwards, rose to 4.2 million in 2018/19. Some 43 per cent of larger households (with three or more children) were living in relative poverty by this time. It is worth stressing once more that these rates do not map onto employment trends. As labour markets became more precarious and less regulated, more in-work poverty appeared. Nearly 2 million full-time employees were living in relative poverty by 2017/18. At the same time, while the number of young people who were engaged in EET had risen steadily since the days of New Labour, progress had stalled by 2017, and further decreases were projected. Employment rates were now lowest among those aged 18–24 (see Chapter 7). On a range of other measures, including life expectancy, the roll-out of new apprenticeships for young adults (down by a third from 2015 to 2019), and the health and mortality of young children in disadvantaged households, family fortunes were facing a notable downturn, with a widening gap now evident in socio-economic inequalities (Vizard and Hills, 2021).

In order to tackle these formidable deficiencies, a range of urgent measures have been proposed (Vizard and Hills, 2021): the need for sustainable funding models to tackle underinvestment; mechanisms and resources for strengthening accountability at local level; holistic, multi-agency strategies and interventions to join up different policy areas (as showcased in the TPS); prioritising the needs of those most in need; and, finally, a new values-based approach to social policy, based on embedding dignity, respect and recognition into the fabric of public services. The last is a vital challenge that we revisit in Chapter 11.

To return to our main theme, in a context where policy is dynamic and ever-changing, we have traced two sets of policy developments, relating (1) to teenage pregnancy and parenthood and (2) to issues of poverty and social inequality. These policies run in parallel, and for disadvantaged young parents they are interrelated; the fortunes of young parents are continuously shaped through the varied and undulating responses of successive governments. There is a great deal that governments can do to lift young people and their families out of poverty, to encourage and facilitate their self-sufficiency and to minimise the social ills that they face. Whatever its successes and failures, this was the thrust of New Labour's approach. Whether future governments in the UK will find the will to resurrect these commitments remains to be seen.

Perceptions of young fathers

The broad policy developments traced here raise important questions about how young fathers are perceived in these processes, and to what extent they are included. Our discussion spans three interrelated observations: first, the dominance of the social problems framework as a lens through which to respond to young fathers; second, an ingrained tendency in policy and public discourses to denigrate and stigmatise these young men (and young parents more generally); and finally, the overall neglect of young fathers in a policy process that focuses on the needs of teenage mothers. We explore each of these issues in turn.

The social problems framework

The first observation concerns the correlation between young parenthood and indices of social deprivation. Young pregnancy and parenthood were described as somewhat 'invented' social and public health problems when they first arose in the US in the 1970s (Arney and Bergen, 1984). After all, social 'problems' are rarely based on objective conditions. They are social constructions: images of specific groups of people, for good or ill, that are legitimised and entrenched through collective definitions and the momentum of public and professional opinion. The policy process 'is the dynamic element through which governments anchor, legitimise or change social constructions' (Schneider and Ingram, cited in Collins and Mead, 2021: 493).

Under New Labour, the social ills associated with young parenthood were framed in terms of inequality and social exclusion. Although the precise relationship between early parenthood and social exclusion is not clearly spelt out, in New Labour rhetoric early parenthood is presumed to carry significant risks for the majority of young parents and their children, with impacts for society more broadly. The development of the TPS was driven by a particular understanding of these issues: a general assumption that having a child at a young age disrupts the life course and creates downward paths for young parents and their children (DCSF and DoH, 2010). The focus on social responsibilities in New Labour thinking meant that the problems were perceived to be rooted in young people's ignorance and low expectations. But, in practice, the 'low expectations' argument, which points towards tackling social disadvantage, carried less weight (Duncan et al, 2010). In other words, teenage conceptions were cast as individual problems that required remedying through changes to young people's attitudes and behaviour (DCSF/DoH, 2010). Overall, early parenthood was not seen as a legitimate choice (Arai, 2009).

These negative correlations were reinforced through evidence that was oriented to a social problems framework (see Chapter 1). However, as we have seen, this evidence offers a partial account of the lives of young parents (Weed et al, 2015). Prior to 2007, a social engagement framework of understanding was notably absent from the policy script. In a parallel development, despite New Labour's recognition of the structural issues facing disadvantaged young parents and their families, doubts were raised about whether Blair's poverty strategies were robust enough to improve people's lives (Piachaud and Sutherland, 2001; Kidger, 2004; Arai, 2009; Duncan et al, 2010).

The social deficit framework

These negative portrayals of young parenthood were feeding into moralistic public discourses that stigmatise young parents and condemn their behaviour (Robinson, 1988; Duncan et al, 2010; Ellis-Sloan, 2013; Johansson and Hammarén, 2014; Neale, 2016; Weber, 2020). Stigma has been defined as 'spoiled' identities, and the felt and experienced discrimination and disapproval which results from being castigated as a public burden (Titmuss, in Deacon 2002: 18). It is commonly articulated through the creation of 'in and out' groups (for example, 'strivers', in contrast to 'scroungers' or 'shirkers') along with the process of 'othering', which defines who is deserving of support, and who is to blame for their own misfortunes (Gregory, 2015). Young parents and their families are common targets, alongside those who are unemployed, living on state benefits, homeless, seeking asylum, or from 'troubled' families or ethnic minority groups. In this climate, assumptions, misconceptions and stereotypes about young parents take on a mythic quality (Weed et al, 2015); they have little grounding in empirical reality, for they sidestep young parents' own experiences and aspirations.

While young mothers continue to face stigma (SmithBattle, 2013; Conn et al, 2018) attacks on young parents' behaviour are commonly directed at young fathers (Johansson and Hammarén, 2014; Weed et al, 2015; Sheeran et al, 2021). They are blamed for the pregnancies and assumed to be absent, uncaring and uninterested in taking up their parenting responsibilities. As a result, they are labelled feckless (worthless) or, worse, as a potential liability and risk to their children (Robinson, 1988; Luker, 1996; Paschal, 2006; Speak, 2006; Kiselica, 2011; Weber, 2012, 2020; Johansson and Hammarén, 2014; Tuffin et al, 2018). Robinson (1988) for example, reports that young fathers are commonly depicted as 'Don Juans', 'Super Studs' and 'Phantom Fathers', who move from one damaging sexual conquest to the next, leaving a trail of abandoned mothers and children in their wake.

These social constructions straddle the dual identities of young fathers. As teenagers, they carry the characteristics of dependants, who are immature and irresponsible. But they also carry the stigma of deviance (Collins and Mead, 2021), characterised by risky, illegal and unpredictable behaviour (Robinson, 1988; Wenham, 2013; Kiselica, forthcoming). As shown in Chapter 1, researchers themselves are not immune to such stereotypes, which feed into perceptions of the irresponsible absent young father.

These derogatory views find expression in the simple binary distinctions that are commonly drawn between 'good' (hard-working, fully engaged) fathers, and 'bad' (absent, feckless, scrounging, troubled) fathers; and between vulnerable young mothers and the 'runaway' young men who deny paternity and abandon them (Edin and Nelson, 2013; Gregory, 2015; Weber, 2020). Stigma is reinforced where one set of stereotypes is overlaid with others.

A decade ago, 'bad' fathers were increasingly vilified in public discourses: 'It's high time "runaway" dads were stigmatised, and the full force of shame was heaped upon them' (David Cameron, Prime Minister, quoted by Hennessy, 2011, in the Telegraph). While young fathers may be painted in a variety of ways in these discourses, they are generally cast as a social problem, with the root of the problem presumed to lie with them (Sherriff, 2007; Arai, 2009; Johansson and Hammarén, 2014). Overall, this elaboration and hardening of the social problems framework has created an 'alarmist paradigm' (SmithBattle, 2013) and a culture of blame among policy makers that has infected the public imagination. It is worth observing, however, that these stigmatising discourses are not universally found: they are a particular feature of targeted welfare states, such as the UK and US, that view young parents not with empathy, but as a cost to the taxpayer (Nativel with Daguerre, 2006; we return to this theme in Chapter 11). In what follows, we illustrate how a deficit view of young parents may find expression in public discourses.

The deficit framework exemplified

During the 1990s, public hostility to teenage pregnancy was at its peak, with press reports suggesting it represented the collapse of family life in the UK. As Daguerre (2006: 74) notes, the problem was commonly portrayed in terms of illegitimate access to scarce social housing. In 1992, the Social Security secretary, Peter Lilley, declared at a Conservative Party conference: 'I have a little list of young ladies who got pregnant just to jump the housing list', while in 1998, Margaret Thatcher suggested an alternative solution: young mothers and babies should be shipped off to convents where some good family values could be instilled (reported in Daguerre, 2006: 74). During New Labour's terms of office, these traditional moralistic discourses on young parenthood continued to find a voice through media reports and speeches delivered by Conservative opposition MPs. These sought to place young parents in a presumed 'underclass': from large, poor, 'broken' and troubled families, who live on welfare at the expense of hard-working taxpayers, and engage in antisocial behaviour, crime and drug addiction. Former leader of the Conservative Party, Iain Duncan Smith was particularly vociferous in linking teenage parenthood with moral and cultural breakdown, placing the children, parents and extended families beyond the pale of 'civilised' society. He also criticised 'ineffective remedial policies, whether they take the form of more prisons, drug rehabilitation, or supporting longer and more costly lifetimes on benefits' (*The Sunday Times*, 15 February 2009, cited in Duncan et al, 2010: 2–3).

Under the Coalition government, an increasingly moralising and divisive narrative sought to distinguish responsible, deserving citizens from those who are irresponsible and undeserving. Conservative rhetoric, that decries the 'broken society' and 'family breakdown', and equates the rise of single-parent families with a descent into poverty, 'welfare' dependency and diminished citizenship, intensified during this period (Patrick, 2017). The following speech from a Conservative MP is a prime example:

> 'I think it's absolutely outrageous that so many young men in our society feel they can go out, get women pregnant, allow them to have children, make them bring them up by themselves, often on benefits, and then just disappear. It is utterly shocking, and I hope ... the ministers will get hold of some of these feckless fathers, drag them off, make them work, put them in chains if necessary.' (David Davies MP, 12 November 2013, House of Commons; reported in Cornock, 2013)

Such inflammatory discourses reinforce wider prejudices, and also serve to deflect attention away from the underlying structural issues (poverty, low pay, reduced benefits, poor education and housing, degraded neighbourhoods) that disadvantaged young parents may face, along with the responsibilities of governments to address these issues (Churchill, 2016; Edwards and Gillies, 2016; see also Chapter 1).

As a further example, the TPS strategy of supporting young parents is commonly justified on the grounds that it is an integral part of a long-term preventative strategy (Hadley and Ingham, 2018: 146). But in the right-wing press, an opinion piece (published in both the Telegraph and the Daily Mail) ridiculed the strategy as antithetical to the main aim of discouraging early entry into parenthood. Providing support for young fathers was seen to endorse and encourage their deviant behaviour. The headline banner reads, 'Teenage fatherhood and underage sex glamorised in Government guidance' (Telegraph, 2009; also, Doughty, 2009). The 'guidance' in question is a booklet of sympathetic photographs of young fathers with their babies (Clark, 2002), accompanied by a supportive commentary from Cathy Hamlyn, former head of the TPU. The booklet and accompanying posters were distributed to all maternity units in England to help to make these services more welcoming to young fathers and to increase their engagement with the impending birth (Hadley, pers. comm.). The article heaped scorn on the TPU for supporting young fathers instead of condemning them:

> The [New Labour] Government says teenagers should be equipped with skills, knowledge and attitudes to prepare them to bring up babies ... and told about 'the pleasures of early fatherhood'. ... However, the Tories warned that the guidelines, from the Government's Teenage Pregnancy Unit, glamourises teenage parenthood and condones irresponsible sex. The publication includes pictures of boys with babies, and was described by Cathy Hamlyn, then head of the TPU, as 'a

timely resource'. Miss Hamlyn said, 'popular attitudes to teen fathers have been shaped by the examples which the media have chosen to feature'. The initiative challenged prejudice and showed that teenage boys could be 'proud and able' parents. ... Patricia Morgan, a researcher [for the Institute for Economic Affairs] said, 'fatherhood before the age of 18 should be a matter for the police. The parents of the teenagers involved should be charged with neglect ... This is child abuse. After 16, fathers who want to bring their children up should be given one piece of advice: get a job'. (Doughty, 2009)

While opposing views are included in this article (and later articles in the *Daily Mail* give space to young men's own accounts), the deficit view of young fathers that emerges here is hard to ignore. Moreover, it is a view that continually surfaces in an increasingly neoliberal culture that tends to shun, sideline or neglect those who are in need. As commentators note (Paschal et al, 2011; SmithBattle, 2013), these attacks on 'deadbeat' dads and 'feckless' young men are likely to create a further burden for young fathers that adds to the social problems that they commonly face (we return to this theme in Chapter 4).

The neglect of young fathers

The social problems framework and the denigration of young men that stems from this framework lead to a third observation about the place of young fathers in these policy processes: they have been marginalised and neglected (Quinton et al, 2002; Pollock et al, 2005; Shields and Pierce, 2006; Sherriff, 2007; Hadley and Ingham, 2018). This is despite strong evidence to suggest that where young fathers are engaged, this can offer significant benefits for children and families, particularly in the early years (Flouri, 2005; Sherriff, 2007; Sardaki et al, cited in Cundy, 2016; Wilson and Prior, 2011). Commentators frequently observe that 'parenthood' in the TPS and in subsequent policy directives really means motherhood; young fathers are largely invisible in the equation.

This situation has not been helped by the lack of reliable data on young fathers, around which policy targets could be built, and effectiveness monitored and appraised. But it also reflects a more general lack of knowledge and understanding of the lives of these young men. For example, many young fathers are financially disadvantaged, without the resources to pay maintenance or provide materially for a child (Cundy, 2016). Yet in the early days of the TPS, New Labour's policy focus was on the responsibilities of young fathers for financial provision, rather than on any direct nurturing role:

Young men are half of the problem and the solution. ... Young men ... need to be targeted with information about the consequences of sex and fatherhood, including their financial responsibility to support their children. Fathers of children born to teenage mothers will therefore be pursued by the Child Support Agency to reinforce the message that for this group, regardless of age, they are financially responsible for their children. (SEU, 1999: 97)

This preoccupation with the financial responsibilities of young fathers left little room to consider the aspirations of young men to be there for their children, or their own needs for support as young people with parental responsibilities (Quinton et al, 2002). As we saw earlier, the social engagement of young fathers was recognised in the early days of the TPU, but largely through the commissioning of a booklet on young fathers for maternity units, and through the recommendations of the TPIAG (2002). Even then, these initiatives ran the risk of ridicule in the media.

It was not until 2007 that the engagement of young fathers was incorporated into statutory guidance (DCSF/DoH, 2007), with an acknowledgement of their neglect across statutory services. The tone of this guidance marks a significant departure from earlier directives:

We need … to develop a culture in which the starting point is that young fathers' involvement in the pregnancy and birth is beneficial for the mother and child, and that services should be designed so that they are inclusive of young fathers, rather than starting with the presumption that young fatherhood is a problem. … Currently, work with young fathers is patchy and there is limited commissioning of discrete [services] to support them. Its funding is insecure, and it is often not sustained. (DCSF/DoH, 2007: 60)

However, despite these recommendations, there were, and continue to be, no mechanisms or national frameworks in place to turn principles into practice, and virtually no national or local datasets to benchmark or monitor improvements in outcomes. Moreover, when guidance on the further roll-out of the TPS was published in 2010 (DCSF/DoH, 2010), young fathers were accorded little attention. As New Labour's ten-year strategy drew to a close it became clear that while significant support had been operationalised for teenage mothers and their children, there was very little information or evidence on outcomes for young fathers (Trivedi et al, 2009).

This general neglect of young fathers has continued under the Coalition and Conservative governments. Using gender-neutral language (parents, families, carers) their family policy directives barely mention fathers of any age, let alone young fathers (see, for example, announcements for revamping Children's Centres (DfE, 2013) and family hubs (DHSC and DfE, 2022)). However, pockets of important developments have sidestepped the government's stance. The PHE framework on young parents (PHE/LGA, 2019 [2016]), was innovative in flagging up young fathers in the title of this document and, offering a framework for meeting their needs based on earlier guidance under the TPS (DCSF/DoH, 2007).

Pockets of specialist provision for young fathers have also been developing in piecemeal fashion since the early 2000s (Sherriff, 2007; Hanna, 2018; Hadley and Ingham, 2018; for a more detailed account, see Chapter 9). In the voluntary sector, many of these services have stepped in to provide support at a time when public sector cutbacks have intensified (Hanna, 2018). Such provision is also under development in child protection, social work and custodial settings, with the rationale that it is much better to engage with, and effectively assess and manage the risks that a small minority of young fathers might pose than to simply sideline them (Neale and Ladlow, 2015a; Bulman and Neale, 2017; Robinson et al, 2023; Brandon et al, 2017; Tarrant, 2021). Whatever their direct impact, the PHE frameworks have helped to raise awareness of the value of young-father-inclusive practices across a range of mainstream statutory agencies.

Despite these important grassroots developments, the marginalisation of young fathers has become entrenched in a culture that continues to see them as a problem and, in some quarters, continues to denigrate them or treats them with mistrust. Since the turn of the century, statutory provision for parents has continued to reflect the motherhood orientation of (maternal) health services (RCPCH, 2021), and targeted schemes such as the Family Nurse Partnership. Young men may be included in these services as the partners of young mothers, or as co-parents. While marginalised young men may see this intervention as intrusive and disengage from it, others find it valuable, especially where they are given quality time with professionals to build trust, skills and confidence (Ferguson and Gates, 2013; Ferguson, 2016). Either way, such provision is discretional and dependent on the gate-opening capacity of the young mothers. In effect, young fathers are 'tacked on' to these services, rather than treated as clients in their own right. Moreover, their engagement is rarely monitored or evaluated (McAllister et al, 2012). This is part of a larger problem: young fathers don't seem to count because they are simply not counted (Osborn, 2015; Neale and Davies, 2015a). But the underlying issue here is one of gender inequality, which is thrown into sharp relief in comparison to Nordic countries, where a culture of equality for mothers and fathers prevails (Lammy, 2015; Andreasson et al, 2023).

The neglect of young fathers in statutory service provision represents a major barrier to their social engagement. In health services that focus on the maternal, or in social work with its surveillance remit, a policy vacuum has developed that creates a culture of discretion for professionals in their dealings with these young men. This perpetuates their invisibility, and the tendency for them to remain unrecognised and underserved. This neglect has its own language and rationale. Young fathers are commonly described as 'hard to reach', disengaged, or potentially 'risky' (Osborn, 2015). This is stigmatising language, which places responsibility for a perceived lack of engagement with the young men themselves (Neale, 2016). Placing young fathers on the margins means that they are not accorded and cannot command the basic conditions of social citizenship for young people: recognition, respect and participation (Neale and Flowerdew, 2007).

This, in turn, impacts on the behaviour of young fathers themselves. Despite consistent research evidence that they want to engage with mainstream services (Speak et al, 1997; Quinton et al, 2002; Pollock et al, 2005), they tend to shy away from contact with professionals and remain passive and invisible (Shields and Pierce, 2006; Speak, 2006; Deslauriers et al, 2012; Fatherhood Institute, 2013a; 2013b). Researchers report that young fathers often have limited or no contact with midwives and health visitors, and have negative experiences of these services, feeling that they are mother-focused and not appropriate for their needs (Bunting and McAuley, 2004, Fatherhood Institute, 2013b; Paschal et al, 2011; Osborn, 2015; Cundy, 2016; Bateson et al, 2017). These patterns sustain a vicious circle of non-engagement and mistrust between practitioners and young fathers. By and large, the challenges identified under the TPS have remained in place: there is an ongoing need to change the culture of professional practice so that young fathers are no longer discounted as 'hard to reach', 'disinterested' or 'risky', but sought out and welcomed as clients with a valuable contribution to make.

Concluding discussion

Tracing the development of the TPS and related policies since the late 1990s has revealed some valiant efforts to tackle the complex issues of teenage conception, and to offer varied forms of support for young parents, particularly those experiencing social disadvantage. It has also revealed some limitations in the underlying assumptions that drive these policies, which have attracted a raft of criticisms. Commentators have questioned the presentation of young parenthood as an inherently problematic state, and teenage parents as victims of ignorance, misinformation and low expectations (Carabine, 2007; Duncan, 2007; Arai, 2009; Duncan et al, 2010; Wenham, 2013; Owens, 2022).

How far official understandings of young pregnancy and parenthood map onto young people's own perspectives are key issues, suggesting a mismatch between policy processes and young people's lived experiences (Higginbottom et al, 2006; Neale, 2016). The parameters imposed on disadvantaged parents would seem to reflect a socially conservative sensibility and set of normative concerns about (in)appropriate parenting that may not match the realities of young people's lives (Owens, 2022). Commenting on the TPS and its relationship to whole family policies, Morris and Featherstone observe that: '[T]he last decade represents a lost opportunity to construct family policies which engage with the complexity and diversity of the lived experiences of families and contemporary family practices. Policies have not been rooted in dialogue with vulnerable and marginalised families about their needs and the challenges they experience' (Morris and Featherstone, 2010: 563).

Moreover, while quantitative research evidence confirms a correlation between young parenthood and socio-economic disadvantage, along with an increased likelihood of disrupted trajectories for young parents and their children, these findings do not adequately explain the nature and causes of these disadvantages (Graham and McDermott, 2005). How government and popular responses feed into these processes is clearly important and deserving of greater scrutiny. Overall, there was strong support for the TPS from professionals and the voluntary sector as a long-awaited initiative to equip young people with the knowledge and skills to make informed reproductive choices. Even so, some serious questions have been raised about the ideologies that have driven recent policies for teenage pregnancy and parenthood, and to what extent they are appropriate and ethically justified (Hadley and Ingham, 2018).

More specifically, these limitations in policy and practice responses tend to be magnified for young fathers. Three interrelated issues are of particular significance: the over-reliance on a social problems framework, which has cast young fathers in a negative light; the related tendency to blame these young men for a range of social ills, and to stigmatise them as 'feckless' and untrustworthy; and the ingrained habit of marginalising and neglecting young fathers in policy and in professional practice. There is still a great deal to do to break down the stigma and neglect that has dogged provision for young fathers, particularly in mainstream services. It seems that these issues for young fathers are part of a wider, gendered pattern that treats all fathers in much the same way, particularly where they are separated from the mothers. At the end of the Coalition government, a parliamentary enquiry into parenting and social mobility noted that:

> The present parenting support offer across the UK is fragmented, with little leadership from national government. With family policy spread across ... departments, a lack of joined up government is a key barrier to any successful parenting support. ... Any parenting support scheme must not be overly prescriptive and cannot be seen by parents as a punishment if it is to be successful. ... Fathers are an important source in early years child development ... but are underused and often side lined when family services are developed. (APPGPF/APPGSM, 2015: 5)

As we have seen, however, despite these observations and recommendations, little has changed since 2015. If anything, these issues have become more pronounced, particularly for disadvantaged young fathers. In the current climate, the potential for young fathers to make a positive difference to their children's lives, and to improve their own life chances, is only slowly being realised (Maxwell et al, 2012). We will return to these important issues in the empirical chapters of this book and in our concluding chapter.

Finally, these limitations in current policy responses and the lack of knowledge and insight into the lives of young fathers arise, at least in part, because of a growing chasm between policy making and empirical research evidence. The principle of evidence-based policy (endorsed in the late 1990s under New Labour) was perhaps unrealistic given that there will always be other factors that shape policy responses. Evidence-informed policy is perhaps a more realistic goal (Bochel and Daly, 2021). Nevertheless, with some recent exceptions, the research evidence on the social engagement of young fathers has been slow to feed into national policy responses.

In this research vacuum, a deficit understanding of young fathers has become more firmly entrenched in the popular imagination. Changing public perceptions is not an easy matter (Collins and Mead, 2021). Like all social constructions, images of feckless young fathers are pervasive. Nevertheless, change is possible, and may occur through the arrival of new evidence, particularly from young fathers themselves when they are given a voice and an audience (see Chapter 10). Media reports can also be catalysts for change. While alternative accounts may jostle alongside each other, gradual shifts in perceptions may occur over time (see, for example, the sympathetic portrayals of young fathers in a BBC documentary, *Lads to Dads* (Black, 2009); in the *Observer* (Y. Roberts, 2013); and in the *Mail Online* (Hilpern, 2009), published four months after the inflammatory *Daily Mail* article (Doughty, 2009) that was cited earlier.

In light of the commentary provided in this chapter, the task for the FYF study was clear. Beyond the production of new dynamic evidence on the lives of young fathers, the objective was to consolidate a growing body of research evidence, and to engage in partnership working with professional agencies, including participatory work with young fathers themselves. These strategies were designed to shape more effective responses to young fathers in policy and practice settings, and to contribute to a sea change in public perceptions of these young men, enabling them to be seen in a different and more compassionate way. It is to the methodology and findings of this study that we now turn. In the concluding chapter of this book, we return to the policy issues raised here and reconsider them in the light of our empirical findings.

3

Researching young fatherhood through time

Introduction

Following our review of the research and policy contexts in which the Following Young Fathers (FYF) study was conducted, we turn here to the study itself and its methodological drivers. The programme comprised a core study and three follow-on projects that form the basis for our empirical reporting:

- Following Young Fathers (FYF) (Economic and Social Research Council, Neale and Lau Clayton; two-phase study, 2010–12; 2013–15, involving a total of 34 young fathers);
- Responding to Young Dads in a Different Way (RYD) Impact Initiative (University of Leeds, Tarrant and Neale, 2016–17, involving the post-custodial settlement journeys of a further 5 young fathers);
- Men, Poverty and Lifetimes of Care (MPLC), involving a secondary analysis of data from the FYF study (Leverhulme, Tarrant, 2014–18); and
- Following Young Fathers Further (FYFF), involving an extensive follow-up of ten young fathers from the FYF study (UKRI Future Leaders Fellowship, Tarrant, 2020–27).

These projects are described in this chapter. We have also drawn selectively on evidence from two linked projects. Published interview data have been incorporated, where appropriate, from a small-scale project (New Pathways for Young Fathers, Clayton, et al, 2021) that reinterviewed a subsample of the young men from the original FYF study. For Chapter 8 we have also drawn on evidence from a linked doctoral study, Housing Young Parents (Economic and Social Research council [ESRC], academic-led studentship, conducted by Linzi Ladlow, 2014–17; Ladlow, 2021), which explores the housing journeys and needs of young fathers and mothers.

In reviewing the methodologies that shaped the FYF programme, we begin with a brief discussion of qualitative longitudinal (hereafter, QL) research, and its distinctive features. We go on to explore the design and conduct of the FYF study, including sampling strategies, data generation and analysis, and the co-production of knowledge with service providers. Ethical considerations are also touched upon here; detailed discussions of longitudinal ethics that draw extensively on insights from the FYF study are presented elsewhere, along with considerations of the rigour and integrity of QL enquiry (Neale, 2013, 2021a).

The final sections of the chapter focus on the three projects that build on the core FYF study. We start with the impact initiative (RYD) that followed on from the completion of the FYF study. This initiative extended the collaborative ethos of the original study, finding innovative ways to co-produce knowledge across the research/policy/practice interface (Tarrant and Neale, 2017a). We then provide an outline of the MPLC study, which involved a secondary analysis of FYF data, and conclude with a brief discussion of the Following Young Fathers Further (FYFF) study (Tarrant, 2020–27), an ongoing longitudinal research programme that has conducted a more extensive follow-up of selected young men from the original FYF study.

Qualitative longitudinal research

While qualitative longitudinal (QL) research has a long pedigree, stretching back to the early days of the 20th century, since the early 2000s a critical mass of methodological scholarship has developed among QL researchers (Neale, 2021a). The five-year Timescapes Initiative (ESRC, Neale, 2007–12, https://timescapes-archive.leeds.ac.uk/), under which the first phase of the FYF study was funded, was a critical landmark in this development. In its wake, a widespread international interest in and uptake of QL research has occurred across a broad range of disciplines. QL enquiry is now recognised as an established approach to social enquiry that offers new and exciting ways to know and understand the social world.

A detailed exploration of this methodology is available elsewhere (Neale, 2021a), but it is worth teasing out some key features here. First, as a mode of longitudinal enquiry, QL research follows the same individuals or groups in real time, as their lives unfold. While revisiting a panel of participants may occur extensively, over decades, giving valuable longitudinal reach to a study, most QL research begins by following lives intensively over the relatively short term. This has been described as 'walking alongside' participants (Neale, 2021a). The aim is to look forward, prospectively, and backward, retrospectively, to give a detailed, processual understanding of change in the making.

Second, as a mode of qualitative research, rooted in the interpretivist tradition, QL research engages with and seeks to mirror real-world processes. If longitudinal enquiry turns a 'snapshot' of the social world into a 'movie', this is the 'up-close-and-personal' movie, with enhanced depth and explanatory power. Ethnography, life-journey interviewing and participatory methods, including narrative and visual tools, are commonly combined to gain insight into the inner logic of people's lives and their lived experiences of continuity and change. It is an approach that recognises the dynamics of human agency and subjectivity and takes these seriously. Subjective understandings are a crucial dimension of social explanation, just as important for our verifications of the social world as any objectively defined fact or process (Midgley, in Neale, 2021a). This approach feeds into and enables a participatory ethos of working with study populations; the research is not conducted *on* specific groups but *in collaboration with* them.

Third, this methodology is driven by a complex, fluid ontology. A century of rich temporal theorising and the recent rise of social complexity theory have established that lives do not necessarily unfold in chronological order, through discrete stages, in one linear direction or at a uniform pace. Processes of continuity and change are just as likely to be unpredictable and non-linear (cyclical, spiralling, a-synchronic, cumulative, oscillating, erratic, random). Discerning a simple, sequential, moving picture that charts what happens next can be a useful starting point for investigation. But beyond this, lives are shaped through multiple contingent events, actions and interactions, flowing at different speeds, in all directions, through different horizons of time (past to future, short term to longer term), and at different scales of the social fabric (personal to social, micro to macro). Investigating this fluidity yields a more complex and nuanced understanding of how lives unfold, one that reflects the flux of the social world.

This fluidity is not simply a temporal framework within which change occurs; it shapes the nature of change, exerting considerable causal power and influence. This has implications for our understanding of the causes and consequences of change. Causal processes are necessarily complex, requiring an understanding of their multiple, fluid and relational elements (Neale, 2021b). Engaging with the flux of the real world entails a focus on the *nature* of the journey, not just the *destination*; the *process*, not just the *outcome*; and the *how* of change, not just the *what* or the *why* of change (Neale, 2022).

Finally, QL research not only documents the fluidity of real-world processes; the methodology itself, from sampling to data generation and analysis, is fluid: it becomes part of the moving picture. As a craft that balances creativity with precision, and flexibility with continuity, QL enquiry is responsive, interactive and adaptable. Each wave of fieldwork informs the next in a cumulative process of knowledge building. This approach enables a dynamic interweaving of case, thematic and processual analysis and insights. This three-dimensional logic shapes the whole research process, yielding a powerful combination of case depth, thematic breadth and temporal reach.

Law (2004: 7) observes, 'we begin to imagine what research methods might be if they were adapted to a world that included and knew itself as tide, flux and general unpredictability'. QL research could not be better suited to this enterprise. It derives its explanatory power and methodological rigour from its unique capacity to mirror the flux of the world: to reflect real-world processes, up close, in real time, and through a temporal momentum that is sensitive and responsive to change. In the process our vision of the social world is transformed from monochrome to vivid technicolour (Ridge, 2015).

The Following Young Fathers (FYF) study

Following Young Fathers was designed as a prospective QL study that would explore the dynamics of young fatherhood over time. This represents a departure from most existing research on young fathers. As shown in Chapter 1, there is a paucity of evidence that takes a dynamic perspective on young fatherhood. A small number of QL studies in the US and Canada have generated valuable insights (see, for example, Glikman, 2004; Shannon and Abrams, 2007; Negura and Deslauriers, 2010; Deslauriers, 2011; Deslauriers and Kiselica, 2022). However, in the UK no comparable QL studies have been dedicated to young fathers, although small pockets of dynamic evidence have emerged from studies of fathers in general (Miller, 2011; Shirani, 2015), and from a study of eight young couples who were followed through the first year of their parenting (Graham, 2013).

The picture is hardly better in respect of large-scale longitudinal survey and cohort studies. These shed light on the wholesale movement of populations into or out of a particular state, usually over extensive populations and periods of time. Where such studies focus on birth cohorts or on child or youth development, or where disadvantaged populations are oversampled, there is a greater likelihood of generating data on young fathers (Pirog-Good, 1996; see, for example, Kiernan, 1995, 2005; Quinton et al, 2002; Berrington et al, 2005). However, the published evidence from these studies relates to older cohorts, born in the second half of the last century, thereby creating a lag in our knowledge of contemporary patterns of young fatherhood. More generally, most national-level longitudinal studies are not designed to target specific populations (let alone shed light on people's lived experiences); young fathers are likely to fall under the radar of such studies.

It is only through real-time, up-close, intensive enquiry that the complex ebb and flow of life course transitions can be discerned, along with insights into how these processes are negotiated, lived and experienced. We were able to chart the changing fortunes of the young men, and capture something of the volatility or stability of their lives over relatively short periods of time. This volatility is evident in their housing and living arrangements (with some moving frequently between temporary abodes); their relationships; and their education and employment trajectories. Had the young men been interviewed just once, it would not have been possible to build up an understanding of this volatility or of its impact on their capacity to be a parent. Nor would it have been possible to investigate how professional support was perceived and utilised or what kind of impact it had on the young men over time. By adopting QL methodology, the FYF study therefore filled a significant gap in the longitudinal evidence on young fathers.

The broad aim of the study was to trace the changing lives, experiences, relationships and the support needs of young fathers; to draw out their lived experiences of the transition into parenthood, and the causes and consequences of a major and generally unplanned transition in their lives; and to explore the complex biographical and historical/structural processes that shape their practices and identities. The research was located within a growing body of studies that have used a *social engagement framework* to explore the lives of these young men, but which also recognised the particular challenges that these young men face (see Chapter 1). The following dynamic research questions guided the study:

1. How is young fatherhood constituted, practised and understood over time in varied socio-economic, relational and familial contexts?
2. How and why do young men enter into early parenthood and how is young fatherhood 'worked out' over time? How do their individual life histories and circumstances impact on their subsequent experiences and practices?
3. What opportunities and constraints are associated with an early entry into fatherhood and how do these impact on the capacity of young men to establish and sustain a role and identity as a parent?
4. What impact do policy interventions and other kinds of support have on the lives of young fathers? How is professional support for young fathers perceived by young men, service providers and practitioners?
5. How effective is current policy and practice in meeting the needs of young fathers and what might lead to more effective strategies and provision?

Study design

The design of the FYF study is fully documented elsewhere (Neale et al, 2015), but some key features are drawn out here. The study was based at the University of Leeds and carried out in two phases over a five-year period, beginning in 2010. The initial 'baseline' phase (2010–12) formed part of the Young Lives and Times study, one of seven empirical projects on family change funded under the ESRC Timescapes Initiative. Designed and directed by Bren, it was carried out with the support of Carmen Lau Clayton. The follow-on phase of the study (funded by ESRC, 2013–15) was co-directed by Bren and Carmen, with support from Laura Davies and Linzi Ladlow. The follow-on funding gave the study an independent identity, a boosted sample, a larger team and an extended longitudinal reach, enabling it to grow from its relatively modest beginnings.

Sampling strategies and recruitment

Sampling in a QL study is not a static, one-off event; it is a fluid and dynamic process. The FYF baseline sample consisted of 12 young fathers, aged between 15 and 22. They were residing in a West Yorkshire city, including localities with some of the highest rates of teenage pregnancy in the country. Ten of the young men were interviewed three times, and the remaining two on two occasions, starting, where possible, when they were expectant fathers and following their transitions into early parenthood. Where participants had already undergone this transition, we sought retrospective accounts of the process and tracked their ongoing journeys as they occurred. The tempo of this phase of the study was intensive. In some cases, the young men were interviewed two or three times over the space of a year.

This was an opportunity sample: in all but one case the young men were recruited via a specialist educational mentoring service, provided for school-age young fathers (detailed later). During the second phase of the study, the original 12 young men were tracked less intensively: two further waves of interviews were conducted, yielding up to five waves of data for these participants over a two- to four-year period. The sample was also boosted to include a new cohort of 19 young fathers, giving a total of 31 young men in the longitudinal sample. Of these, 15 young men were interviewed on two occasions between 2013 and 2015, giving a total of 27 young men who were followed over time for the FYF study. The remaining four dropped out after the first wave. However, we generated useful 'snapshot' accounts of their journeys into parenthood and their aspirations for the future, and two of these young men were eventually followed up over the longer term for the Following Young Fathers Further study. An additional three young men were recruited for one-off interviews, in two cases to capture their experiences as young offender fathers (Neale and Ladlow, 2015a; Ladlow and Neale, 2016). Overall, we generated data from 34 young men over the two phases of the study and across five waves of fieldwork (see the pen portraits in the appendix). Our reporting here is based largely on the accounts of the 31 young men who were recruited to take part in the longitudinal study.

The limited method of recruitment for the baseline study had skewed the sample towards lower-income, disadvantaged young fathers of school age. For the follow-on phase, a purposive sampling strategy was devised that required a wider range of recruitment routes. Our objective was to recruit a subsample of well-resourced young men, including those who were at university, to create a more balanced range of socio-economic circumstances across the sample. This gave us sub samples of 10 well resourced young men, 11 who were less well resourced and 10 who were poorly resourced over the course of the study. Our aim was to discern how the relative socio-economic fortunes of the participants were implicated in their parenting journeys. Similar profiles were achieved in an unpublished study of 30 young fathers, carried out for Worcester Sure Start in the UK (Birbeck, 2004, cited in Speak, 2006; see Chapter 1 for details), and in an opportunity sample of 26 young men from an American rustbelt town, generated for a doctoral study (Weber, 2012, 2018, 2020). But such sampling is rare. Including a purposive range of socio-economic circumstances across a sample of young fathers was innovative when this follow-up study was designed in 2012, and it has since been identified as a vital axis of comparison that is ripe for further development (SmithBattle et al, 2019a). In dividing our sample into higher or lower income categories we sought to convey the relative nature of these categories and their fluidity over time. Income levels were derived from the young men's accounts, rather than directly elicited, and were based in large part on the resources available to the young men via their families of origin. The levels varied greatly within each group, as well as across them, creating a broad spectrum of income levels across the sample as a whole. These resources were not static or stable, but liable to shift over time in line with the changing fortunes of the young men and their families. On the whole, however, there was relatively little movement between the two groups over time.

We also boosted the proportion of young men who were in their late teens and early 20s to create a broader age range across the sample; wider evidence suggests that age matters, with younger teenagers more likely to be single and disadvantaged, and less likely to sustain their parenting than their older counterparts (Quinton et al, 2002; SmithBattle et al, 2019a). Finally, we incorporated a broader range of experiences of professional support, including participants who were reliant on generic service provision alone (Neale et al, 2015). Across the two phases of the study, 27 young men were recruited via professional referrals (including 17 via our specialist practice partner), 5 via higher-education settings, and 2 through chance encounters or personal contacts.

A key methodological question arises at this point: how far is this sample representative of the wider population of young fathers in the UK? Given that demographic knowledge of young fathers is sketchy (see Chapter 1) it would be difficult to give a precise answer to this question. The notion that a sample can be representative of a wider population has been critiqued as an elusive and rather idealistic goal, even among large-scale quantitative researchers (see, for example, Rothman et al, cited in Neale, 2021a). Qualitative researchers, who work with smaller and more targeted populations, use a different sampling logic, one that obviates the need to measure similarities and differences across strictly comparable cases. Purposive sampling aims to generate evidence from an appropriate *range of complementary cases* that straddle the circumstances and experiences of a study population. The inclusion of a particular experience is the critical factor, not the number of times it is represented. This creates an alternative and arguably more grounded understanding of what it means to be representative.

The young men in this study were anchored in one particular urban conurbation, with a shared backdrop of local policies and support services. But within these parameters, the sample reflected a wide range of experiences and circumstances. Alongside the attention to the age range of the sample, a spectrum of socio-economic circumstances, and their access to a mixed economy of support, the young men were living in varied family, relational and housing circumstances, including those who were married, single or partnered at the birth of their child, and who were residing at close hand or at a distance from their families of origin and/or from their children (detailed sample characteristics are reported in later chapters). The sample was predominantly white and of British origin (those from minority ethnic communities are identified in the appendix). It also includes young offender fathers, those with experience of the care system, and those with mental health issues. Through serendipity, this fluid sampling strategy reflects the heterogeneous nature of young fatherhood and allows for the discovery of unanticipated connections between different circumstances that a more rigid sampling frame might obscure (Neale, 2021a: 116).

A further pertinent question arises here: is the sample skewed towards young fathers who are committed to their children, thereby under-representing those who absent themselves from their children's lives? Could our findings on young men's aspirations to engage with their children be a mere by-product of our sampling strategy? In addressing this question, two broad observations are worth making.

First, as shown in Chapter 1, direct evidence drawn from the accounts of 'absent' young men is very hard to find. Researchers commonly report that when young men drop out of a study, or fail to engage in the first place, the reasons stem from problems in their parenting relationships and/or their estrangement from their children (Speak et al, 1997; Wilkes et al, 2012). This was certainly the case in this study. Given the stigma that surrounds their position, these absent young men are all the more invisible and uncounted, and more likely to fall outside the orbit of studies such as FYF.

At the same time, and despite the paucity of direct accounts from absent young men, wider evidence from a range of sources (including men themselves) shows that fathers of any age may drift in and out of their children's lives or may disappear altogether over time (Bradshaw et al, 1999). The FYF study was able to explore the experiences of ten young men with fragile parenting trajectories. Over the course of the study, three of these young men had intermittent contact with their children, a further three had negligible contact, while the remaining four lost contact with their children over time (including one young man who had been barred from establishing contact in the first place; see Chapters 4 and 5).

The fluidity of QL sampling was a real boon here: we were able to tap into the ever-changing circumstances of the participants and gain insights into the causal factors that could lead to their engagement or disengagement from their children over time. The longitudinal design of FYF, then, was a crucial factor in our ability to draw out these important convergences and divergences in the young men's parenting journeys as they unfolded. Whatever the prevalence of absent young men within the general population of young fathers (discussed in Chapter 1), the purposive sample generated for this study was an appropriate reflection of these experiences.

Sample maintenance

In general, QL researchers report relatively low rates of sample attrition over time; the focus on sustaining meaningful research relationships with participants undoubtedly helps (Neale, 2013, 2021a). However, maintaining a sample can be more challenging where participants are disadvantaged or leading chaotic or nomadic lives (see, for example, Williamson et al, cited in Neale, 2021a). This was certainly the case here. It involved a great deal of effort and perseverance from Carmen, who took the lead on the fieldwork with the young men. Over the course of the study, three young men from our baseline sample who had moved, changed their phone numbers or were in custody could not be contacted for a particular wave. However, Carmen was able to retrace these young men and draw them back into the study for the next wave of fieldwork, working with our practice partner and/or through family contacts.

Attrition rates for our baseline sample were relatively low. Our practice partner gave invaluable help, including, on some occasions, finding the young men in their localities and bringing them for interview at the university. However, attrition was somewhat higher for the second phase sample. We lost four of the 19 young men between the first and second waves of interviews. The reasons for this varied, but difficulties relating to their relationships and their roles as parents were reported in these cases. These participants had been recruited via a range of generic services and agencies (including the Connexions employment service and training colleges), to which they were loosely attached, and who quickly lost track of them. The young men did not have sustained relationships with these practitioners that the research team could build upon. This highlights the vital role played by practice partners in facilitating and sustaining contact with this population over time (see also Emmel et al, 2007). It also reinforces the insight that maintaining a QL sample relies on sustaining high-quality relationships with participants (Neale, 2013, 2021a), particularly when working with marginalised groups who face stigma in their daily lives.

Generating data

Our initial encounters with the young men were through focus groups, which brought the panel members together in small groups. These were useful icebreakers, introducing the participants to the study and the research team, documenting group reflections on the broad themes of the research, and generating a sense of rapport and group identity among the participants (Neale et al, 2015). Thereafter, individual young men were tracked intensively over time using in-depth, life-journey interviews (Neale, 2021a). Both prospective and retrospective techniques were employed. Weaving back and forth through time, revisiting both past and future at each research encounter, created a rich biographical picture of these young lives, giving insights into how past experiences impact on current circumstances and future aspirations, and uncovering changing perceptions as well as changing practices (Neale, 2021a).

The study used interview rather than ethnographic methods for generating data; the decision to interview the young men in neutral settings or at the university rather than in their home settings gave limited direct insight into their lives in their own localities (see Neale et al, 2015 for further discussion on this point). However, this was a pragmatic choice, judged to be suitable for a 'nomadic' group of participants, many of whom lacked a stable home base (see Chapter 8).

The strategy of balancing continuity with flexibility was built into each wave of fieldwork. Core continuity questions about the young men's parenting journeys enabled us to build 'though lines' in the data that aided case analysis. As the same time, the flexibility of our topic guides enabled new themes to be introduced as their significance emerged, and to revisit existing themes with individual participants to clarify or expand on past narratives. We were able to build specific modules of questions into each wave of fieldwork and revisit issues that impacted on the parenting journeys of selected young men, for example, aspirations for further or higher education and training; nomadic lifestyles and situations of homelessness; experiences of constrained contact; and accounts of offending and custodial sentences.

The interviews were supplemented with a range of participatory visual mapping methods, including life maps, relationship maps and self-portraits, along with vignettes designed to tease out values on sexuality and early conception (Hanna and Lau Clayton, 2012; Neale, 2021a). These are good tools to think with, enabling the articulation of sensitive or difficult disclosures that can be hard to glean through interviews alone. The life maps were particularly useful in enabling participants to visualise their unfolding trajectories. In each case, these participatory tools were used to draw out accompanying narratives, which form the basis for our reporting here.

The quality of the data generated for this study is a testament to Carmen's skill and empathy as a fieldworker. Over time, the young men disclosed a great deal about the challenges in their lives, including illiteracy, anger management problems, domestic violence, illegal activities and a host of relationship problems. Such disclosures often took time to emerge and were most usually made when the young men felt that they could talk about these as past experiences, that were now well behind them (what we have referred to in our writings as 'redemption' scripts, Ladlow and Neale, 2016). Feedback from the young men revealed satisfaction with the interview process:

> 'It's not enjoyable [talking to you] 'cos I've been talking about sore subjects. … It's always about problems, every time, but it will be good to know that it is potentially helping someone else. … I don't really talk to anybody, but I know I've just sat and spoke for the last three hours. … I've spoken to you about loads of stuff which I wouldn't normally speak to people [about]. So, it's probably helped me actually, 'cos it gets it off my chest.'
> (Jason, aged 25, lower income, single, intermittent contact, wave 4)

The young men commonly spoke of these encounters as therapeutic, enabling them to explore difficulties in a 'safe space'. These are commonly reported side effects of the sustained research encounters of QL enquiry (Neale, 2021a).

Analysis

Longitudinal case analysis was of central importance in this study. A suite of longitudinal cases was constructed by drawing out and piecing together case data from across the waves of fieldwork. The focus was on the particularities of individual trajectories, their upward, downward or undulating pathways, and their stability or volatility through time. Once the longitudinal cases were in place, they were brought together to explore how these trajectories converged or diverged across the sample, and to discern the complex range of factors that could produce these different pathways. This was the prime form of analysis adopted for the FYF study. We also utilised thematic framework grids that enabled a three dimensional mapping of key themes against individual cases and across the time span of the study (described in Neale, 2021a).

In terms of our reporting, we nested our longitudinal case studies within a thematic analytical framework that runs across different scales of the social fabric: from the micro-sphere of interpersonal relationships to the macro-sphere of institutional opportunities and constraints. This has been described as an 'ecological' approach to social enquiry (Bronfenbrenner, cited in Neale, 2021a), which has been utilised recently to good effect in young fatherhood research (Deslauriers and Kiselica, 2022). In this way, we were able to discern the degree of 'fit' between lived experiences and wider policy processes (Neale, 2016).

Policy and practice engagement: building collaborative research

The FYF study was also distinctive in the variety and scope of its policy engagement. It was founded on a collaborative and participatory research ethos designed to co-produce knowledge and impact with policy and practice partners (Neale and Davies, 2015b; Neale, 2021b). Approaches to working collaboratively with practitioners have developed significantly over recent decades. In the 1970s, the focus was on knowledge transfer, seen as a one-way process in which researchers disseminate their findings to practice organisations. By the 1990s, this was being superseded by the idea of knowledge exchange, a two-way process involving the translation and mobilisation of research knowledge for practice groups, but still premised on the idea that research and professional practice operate in separate and distinct domains.

By the first decade of the 21st century, these ideas had moved on again, with the development of the concept of knowledge co-production (Best and Holmes, 2010). This is an integrated approach in which practitioners and/or policy makers are more centrally engaged with researchers in the design and execution of a study, with the potential to develop practitioner-led research and research-led practice (Neale and Morton, 2012; Neale, 2016, 2022). The approach is premised on the idea that knowledge can be co-produced by bringing different stakeholders together to create something new that one group alone could not have produced. It also fosters a culture of improvement in policy and professional practice, based on an understanding that provision needs to be refined over time through an evolving approach to service development and delivery (Neale, 2021c). Part of the rationale for these historical developments was a growing expectation from funders that researchers should create some societal impact with their studies. Intensive QL research designs offer clear advantages here, for they enable impact to evolve as an integral part of the research process (Neale, 2021a, 2021b).

An early engagement with practitioner groups became the catalyst for the development of the FYF study. In late 2009, Bren attended a meeting of the Regional Coordinators for Teenage Pregnancy and Parenthood in what was then the Yorkshire and Humber Regional tier of UK government. The practitioners listened politely as Bren pitched her ideas for a tracking study of teenage mothers, a proposed 'bolt-on' sample to an existing study on young people that was being conducted under the Timescapes programme. However, they observed that existing evidence on young mothers was quite substantial, while very little was known of young fathers. As they astutely observed, since these young men were viewed as 'hard to reach', this tended to make them invisible to practitioners and researchers alike. Concerned that they had no means of engaging with these young men, let alone support their parenting efforts, they suggested that a new evidence base on young fathers would be of great value to policy and professional practice. It was the disclosure of this major gap in professional knowledge that led to the design of the FYF study; it was a practitioner-inspired initiative.

Following this meeting, Bren was referred to John May, a local authority educational practitioner who had set up a specialist mentoring service for school-age fathers and fathers-to-be in a Yorkshire city. This practitioner became a valued and long-standing partner in the study, playing a pivotal role in recruiting young fathers to the study and sustaining their involvement over time. He often brought the young men to interview, encouraged their involvement and fostered trust with the research team (Neale et al, 2015). He also mediated between the research team and a wider network of practitioners tasked with supporting young parents.

Sustaining productive links with practitioners in a QL study can be a challenge. Grassroots practitioners are busy people, who may not have the time or inclination to commit to a research project. Researchers may invest time in nurturing these relationships, only to find that they come to a sudden end as organisations lose their funding, or as practitioners lose interest or move on. We were fortunate here. Our key practice partners were highly committed and compassionate 'local champions' for young fathers, who were keen to enrich and advance their professional practice, and to benefit their clients. Despite changes in their working lives, they played a sustained and active role in the FYF programme, including more recent engagement with the Following Young Fathers Further study.

For the second phase of FYF funding, these forms of professional engagement were developed further. Through our involvement in an advisory group for the Strategic Family Partnership Initiative on young fatherhood, with whom we shared some of our early data and findings (Barnardo's, 2012; also, Cundy, 2016) we had established links with practitioners from a range of statutory and voluntary agencies who were supporting young fathers. The Barnardo's group was now reconvened as a policy strategy group and sounding board for the FYF study, with membership drawn from 14 organisations, straddling frontline service providers and campaigning groups. Through our twice-yearly meetings, the group contributed to the development of the research and the dissemination of findings, feeding in ideas, enhancing our knowledge of policy and practice issues, and generally anchoring the study in the policy and practice landscape. Bringing the group together for regular discussions was also helpful for the member organisations; they were able to forge stronger networks, share insights and good practice, and debate key challenges and strategies for change.

In addition, we developed closer links with key organisations (a local housing charity, an employment and training service, a youth offending agency, a local Children's Centre) who could offer specialist input to the study. For example, a Sex and Relationships Education (SRE) provider contributed to the development of a suite of questions for young fathers on their experiences of this provision (see Chapter 4). We developed a productive and enduring collaboration with Kate Bulman, a staff nurse working in a secure training centre for young male offenders. Her pioneering work with young offender fathers helped to shape our findings on their support needs and led to a critique of the 'risk' framework that dominates professional thinking in this field (Neale and Ladlow, 2015a; Neale and Davies, 2015b; Ladlow and Neale, 2016; Bulman and Neale, 2017; see also Chapter 9).

Over time, varied policy and practice groups invited our input into their meetings and networks: our researchers contributed to father-inclusive training programmes organised by the local Teenage Pregnancy and Parenthood Team, gave presentations on emerging research findings to grassroot organisations in the city where the fieldwork took place and regularly attended meetings of the Teenage Pregnancy Forum in the local authority. The team also engaged with national policy makers and strategic think tanks, including membership of the expert advisory panel for the Early Intervention Foundation. We engaged in a consultation meeting with colleagues from the Department for Work and Pensions, who were interested in the factors that shape young fathers' material contributions to their children's lives, and we contributed to meetings at the House of Commons of the All-Party Parliamentary Group on Fatherhood (chaired by David Lammy, MP), and its offshoot, an all-party parliamentary subgroup on young fatherhood.

Under phase two of FYF, we also recruited a range of practitioners as research participants, who were interviewed about their experiences of working with young fathers (Davies and Neale, 2015; Davies, 2016). Semi-structured one-off interviews and focus groups were conducted with 20 practitioners, ranging from frontline workers to managers and commissioners of services. They were drawn from 15 organisations that represented a broad spectrum of family support and related services in health and social care, employment and housing advice, and in support for young offenders. Fieldwork for this part of the study was carried out by Laura Davies between May 2013 and October 2014, with some additional support from Linzi Ladlow (Davies, 2016).

To complement this cross-sectional approach, we developed longitudinal case studies with two organisations: the specialist mentoring service provided through the local education authority, and a phase one Children's Centre serving an inner-city area of the locality (Davies and Neale, 2015). For the latter, we utilised a stakeholder approach to our fieldwork. Key staff members, including the centre manager and assistant manager and family outreach workers were interviewed and took part in a focus group discussion. Interviews were also conducted with two young fathers who used the Centre for both childcare and other family support services. This strand of the study generated insights into where young fathers 'fit' into a generic family support service, how the service responded to them over time, and what this meant for the broader operation and development of children's centres.

Finally, the breadth and variety of our policy and practice engagement was reflected in our collaborative forms of dissemination. Towards the conclusion of the initial phase of the study, a presentation on young fatherhood was jointly delivered with our key practice partner at an international Timescapes conference in London (Lau Clayton and May, 2011). During the second phase of the study, we developed an innovative writing project called Seeing Young Fathers in a Different Way, with contributions reflecting a range of perspectives, from policy makers, think tanks, and voluntary and statutory sector organisations, to young fathers themselves. The contributions were published as a themed section in a leading family research journal (Neale and Davies, 2015a). Finally, we held a UK practitioner conference, attended by over 80 practitioners. This was jointly organised with selected practice partners. A tentative list of Ten Top Tips, developed for discussion in the final break-out sessions, was turned into a more proactive Must Do list of 15 recommendations, reflecting a new-found enthusiasm and commitment among the delegates.

The engagement of young fathers

In our writing and our FYF conference, we were able to mobilise our participatory principles by actively engaging young fathers in the co-production and dissemination of the study findings. Selected young men, all *experts by experience*, were able to document their own lives, speak for themselves and represent young fathers in general. However, we stopped short of training young men as co-researchers and peer interviewers (see Braye and McDonnell, 2013 for a discussion on the potential and pitfalls of this approach). Relatively few of our sample would have been interested in or willing to engage in these processes, but some were keen to move beyond the relatively safe – and anonymised – space of an interview to engage in the public realms of publishing, presenting, training and advocacy. They were supported in this by their professional mentors (see Colfer et al, 2015, who point to the sustained professional training and support that young fathers need to develop such roles).

Two young men contributed to our collaborative writing project (Colfer et al, 2015; Johnson, 2015). Subsequently, three young men (Daniel from our study, and Anthony and Reuben from the Young Dad's Council) actively contributed to the FYF conference, speaking on behalf of young fathers, sharing their direct experiences with delegates, engaging in break-out discussion groups and giving a plenary feedback session at the end of the day. Through these processes we gave both a voice and an audience to the young men, mobilising our commitment to the principles of 'shared authority' with our key participants and enhancing their social citizenship (Neale and Flowerdew, 2007; Neale, 2013, 2021a). The young men were able to speak for themselves and be heard by a professional, captive and clearly captivated audience. The very presence of the young men, their measured voices, and their willingness to share their personal accounts with practice communities were critical factors in our ability to convey the central messages of this study to a practice audience. Their voices in this context were at least as powerful as our own, enabling these young men to be seen, heard and responded to in a different way.

Responding to Young Dads in a Different Way (RYD)

In the final part of this methodological account, we provide an outline of three projects that have followed on from and enhanced the work of the core FYF study. We start with RYD (Responding to Young Dads in a Different Way), an impact initiative that followed on from the completion of the FYF study. Funded by the University of Leeds Social Sciences Institute (2016–17), it was directed by Anna with support from Bren, and carried out in collaboration with three teams of service providers. They received funding to develop and pilot new forms of provision for young fathers, building on the findings of the FYF study (Bulman and Neale, 2017; Tarrant and Neale, 2017a, 2017b; Way et al, 2022; Tarrant, 2023). Across three case studies, the project explored the possibilities and outcomes of implementing more creative and sustained forms of self-help, peer support, advocacy and mentoring for young fathers, as well as creating and providing enhanced training and education for professionals that was led by young fathers themselves.

This initiative is explored in some depth in Chapter 10. But it is worth pointing out here that this participatory action research project further developed our collaborative mode of engagement with practitioners and with young fathers, including engagement with a further five young men whose journeys were traced through the resettlement process following a period in custody. The initiative was also foundational to the design of the Following Young Fathers Further study, described later in this chapter. RYD embodied the idea of father-inclusive practice and represented a high-yield form of participatory action research, which was practice-informed and translated into research-based practice (Neale, 2021b). This required a dynamic, flexible and interactive approach, a cumulative process that unfolded through iteration between research and practical action, as well as successive cycles of reflecting, planning, acting, observing and back to reflecting (Neale, 2021b). In RYD, we provided the impetus for practice developments and then walked alongside to document how these unfolded and their evolving impact on the stakeholders. At the close of the year, the findings were co-disseminated by the young fathers and our professional partners at a practitioner training event (Tarrant and Neale, 2017a). This raised awareness of new ways to work at the interface of research and professional practice, and the creative strategies needed to proactively work with and support young fathers.

Secondary data analysis: the Men, Poverty and Lifetimes of Care (MPLC) study

A secondary analysis of FYF data was carried out by Anna under the aegis of the Men, Poverty and Lifetimes of Care study (MPLC, Leverhulme Trust, October 2014–July 2018). Using the principles of qualitative secondary analysis, ten disadvantaged young fathers from the FYF study were included in a dataset that had been reconstituted for the MPLC study. The substantive aim was to develop a sociological account of the lived experiences of men's caring and parenting practices and intergenerational identities in low-income settings and circumstances. Alongside a literature review, Anna carried out a fresh analysis of existing data on these themes, drawn from two Timescapes datasets: FYF and Intergenerational Exchange. Findings on these themes have fed into our discussion of intergenerational relationships in Chapter 6.

The MPLC study built on a collaborative ethos of data sharing and reuse that was instituted under the Timescapes programme and has since developed further (see, for example, the suite of publications by Irwin and Winterton cited in Neale, 2021a; also Tarrant, 2017; Tarrant and Hughes, 2019; Hughes and Tarrant, 2020; Weller et al, forthcoming). Such studies have the capacity to generate new forms of qualitative generalisations by bringing together a mosaic of empirical evidence drawn from different studies, contexts and settings of change (Neale, 2021a). For MPLC, innovative approaches to qualitative secondary analysis were developed, including the use of continuous, collaborative and configurative analytical techniques (Tarrant and Hughes, 2019; Hughes et al, 2021).

One of the innovative features of MPLC was the capacity to work concurrently and collaboratively with the FYF team. While legacy datasets are commonly revisited a decade or more after their initial generation, a concurrent sharing of data between 'primary' and 'secondary' researchers is relatively unusual. In this case, the secondary analysis of data was carried out hard on the heels of their original production. The status of MPLC as an affiliated project to FYF enabled a series of data-sharing and analysis workshops that helped to sharpen insights across the two studies (Tarrant, 2017; Tarrant and Hughes, 2019; Hughes et al, 2021; Tarrant, 2021; Hughes and Tarrant, 2023). Overall, MPLC was the first study of its kind to utilise qualitative secondary analysis to extend the temporal reach and explanatory power of an original study, and to feed into new project designs in a developing field of enquiry (Tarrant, 2017; Hughes and Tarrant, 2023).

Following Young Fathers Further (FYFF): creating historical reach

The final study to be considered here is of central importance in extending and enhancing the original FYF programme. Following Young Fathers Further

(FYFF, UKRI Future Leaders Fellowship, Tarrant, 2020–27), grew out of the suite of projects outlined earlier. This ambitious QL study aims to extend knowledge of the parenting journeys and support needs of young fathers, building on the foundational knowledge and insights generated in the FYF study and the RYD initiative. It employs QL and participatory methods to advance and extend the existing evidence base. The study also adds a valuable comparative dimension to the growing body of young fatherhood research, enabling insights into how young fathers are understood and responded to across different cultures and welfare regimes in the UK and Sweden (Tarrant et al, 2022; Andreasson et al, 2023). Of relevance for our purpose here, FYFF includes an extensive follow-up of ten young fathers from the original FYF sample. Six of these participants have been interviewed on three further occasions (and a further three on two occasions), yielding longitudinal data on their lives that runs over a decade of change. We have drawn selectively on these data to extend our longitudinal reporting on these young men. Initial publications from this study are beginning to appear (see, for example, Tarrant et al, 2020a, 2020c; Tarrant et al, 2021; Way et al, 2022; Tarrant, 2023).

Concluding discussion

In this chapter we have seen how a QL research framework can offer flexibility, continuity and creativity in study design and development. This was fully reflected in the FYF programme; the research evolved through several phases of funding, and was bolstered through several follow-on studies that, in combination, have enriched our insights, extended the longitudinal reach of the original research, and enhanced its impact.

The QL methodology made it possible to document the changing lives, experiences, relationships and support need of young fathers as they underwent a major transition in their lives, and to do so in 'real' time through a processual, qualitative lens. The study yielded rich biographical data on the young men, discerning how past experiences impact on current lives and future aspirations. As we will show in Part II of this book, the life journeys of the young men did not unfold in planned, prescribed or predictable ways, or at a uniform pace: rather they were fluid and contingent.

Researching over time also provided the flexibility to follow up themes that had emerged in earlier interviews. For example, the importance of grandparental support became apparent in the first wave of interviews for the baseline study and became a particular focus in the second wave of interviews with these young men. Undertaking a series of interviews over time also aids the process of building relationships of trust with participants as a study progresses. For example, we found that the young men were more likely to reveal sensitive information over time, as trust grew, and that we could revisit past events beyond the heat of the moment and with the benefit of hindsight. Such benefits have also carried over into the Following Young Fathers Further study.

A longitudinal design also opened up opportunities for creative means of collaboration with policy and practice partners and with young fathers themselves. Flexible forms of engagement were necessary, given the plethora of practice and campaign organisations that are concerned with young fatherhood. This wide-ranging exploration sharpened insights into 'what works' in policy terms, enabling a more nuanced and grounded understanding of 'how things work', through the stream of time (Neale, 2021b).

Given the qualitative framing of this study, we have prioritised depth (as opposed to breadth) of exploration, and intensive (as opposed to extensive) explorations of change over the relatively short term. As acknowledged in our earlier documentation (Neale et al, 2015), the prospective, longitudinal window afforded by the original study was relatively modest, in most cases tracking the parenting journeys of each young father over two to four years. The development of the Following Young Fathers Further study has enabled us to combine intensive and extensive explorations over time, and reinforced the insight that these trajectories are very much in the making. Over the longer term and with hindsight it becomes possible to discern more clearly the overall shape of a life trajectory and the host of factors that may lead to new directions or reinforce existing ones. At the same time, the more intensive tracking that characterises the core FYF study has afforded a unique opportunity to discern the ebb and flow of these young lives, and the fluid twists and turns in their biographies. Having completed our overview of the FYF programme, and its methodological drivers, we now turn to Part II of this book, where we introduce our empirical findings.

PART II

Living young fatherhood: changing identities, relationships and practices

This part of the book introduces the empirical evidence from the Following Young Fathers study, exploring the young men's transitions into parenthood, and their lived experiences during the pregnancy and following the birth of their children. The chapters reflect a conceptual development from the micro-sphere of interpersonal relationships and family practices to the macro-sphere of structural opportunities and constraints. As the chapters unfold, we build up layers of meaning about the complex constellation of factors that shape young fathers' experiences and practices.

Chapter 4 explores the changing identities of the young men as they try to prepare for parenthood and establish a relationship with their children. We map out their diverging trajectories to gauge their success or otherwise in engaging with their children over time and what it means to 'be there' for a child. How their transitions into parenthood are triggered – how and to what extent they exercise their reproductive agency – is a key theme of this chapter, with implications for the development of Relationship and Sex Education (RSE) provision.

The subsequent chapters explore the raft of relational, environmental and socio-economic opportunities and constraints that shape these transitions. Chapter 5 focuses on the relationship between the young parents, set in the context of shifting ideologies about the gendering of parenthood. The importance of intergenerational relationships, and how they are implicated in the young men's journeys, is detailed in Chapter 6. Finally, the part played by wider environmental and socio-economic factors (education, employment and housing) is explored in Chapters 7 and 8. In Chapter 7 we explore how the ideology of engaged fatherhood meshes with the enduring 'breadwinner' model of fatherhood (Neale and Davies, 2016), and illuminate the diverging socio-economic fortunes of the young men. In Chapter 8, we document the trajectories of young fathers who yo-yo between different households. Seeking to secure a home for themselves and their families involves 'walking a tightrope' in a housing system that is in crisis.

Taken together, the chapters reveal how transitions into early parenthood are shaped through a complex blend of personal and relational factors, along with familial, environmental and socio-economic opportunities and constraints. The specific issues that arise for young offender fathers, those living in impoverished circumstances or with backgrounds in care, and those with mental health issues are threaded through these chapters (and are given more detailed attention elsewhere: Neale and Ladlow, 2015b; Ladlow and Neale, 2016; Lau Clayton, 2017).

The evidence presented in these chapters is based primarily on the accounts of the 31 young fathers who were recruited at two points in the main longitudinal study (see Chapter 3). At the time of first conception, the participants ranged in age from 14 to 24. Over half of the sample (18 young men) were school-age fathers, having conceived their first child between the ages of 13 and 16, with most (15) clustered in the age range 15–16. The remaining 13 young men conceived their first child between the ages of 17 and 24, with a fairly even spread across this age range. When we first met these young men, five were expectant fathers, affording an opportunity to follow the young men prospectively, though the transition itself. A further 22 had recently become fathers; in 17 of these cases the children were small infants at the start of the study, while the rest were two to three years old. In these cases, experiences of the transition to fatherhood were relatively recent at first interview, enabling us to capture the young men's reflections at an early stage, and to discern changes in circumstances as they occurred. The remaining four fathers had primary-school-age children at the time of first interview; here we relied on their retrospective accounts of their journeys into parenthood.

It is also worth noting that of the 21 young men from lower-income families, 17 were low-skilled and living in relatively precarious financial and material circumstances. Ten of these young men disclosed various family hardships as part of their childhoods, and in their own lives since (and these may have been under reported among the remainder). Problems included drug or alcohol addictions; physical abuse and domestic violence; custodial sentences; mental health and anger management problems; unstable housing; periods in social care; and tenuous or volatile relationships within and beyond their families. Although the nature, extent and severity of these problems varied across the sample, the widely reported correlations between young parenthood and social deprivation were particularly evident among these ten low-skilled, lower-income young men (see also Quinton et al, 2002; Swann et al, 2003; Lemay et al, 2010).

4

Becoming a young father: transitions, identities, choices, constraints

Introduction

'[B]ecause you're young, you don't tend to get the respect. I mean, I remember a nurse coming in and saying to us, "oh, have you got a social worker coming in or something?" I turned round to her. I just said, "I don't know why they'd be coming to see me! ... I'm not some scumbag that's just having kids willy-nilly, here, there and everywhere. I'm not from the estates round here." ... In the heat of the moment, it just came out.' (Tommy, aged 24, higher income, married, wave 1)[1]

As we saw in Chapter 2, the most pernicious public perception of young fathers is that they are 'feckless', in other words, that they impregnate young women 'here, there and everywhere' while running away from the responsibilities of parenthood. Young men are fully aware of these negative portrayals of themselves, as our opening quotation reveals, and commonly seek, through a process of 'othering', to distance themselves from these pejorative views. Even so, the stereotype of the young 'scumbag' referred to by Tommy can impact on their personal relationships and professional engagements and colour the way they think and feel about themselves and their social standing.

In this chapter we map out the young men's transitions into parenthood, and their success or otherwise in keeping in touch with their children. We address three themes. First, we explore how this transition is triggered: to what extent and in what ways the young men exercise their sexual and reproductive agency. Against a backdrop of public assumptions that young men enter parenthood irresponsibly, we explore their views and experiences of contraception, abortion and the decision to keep a child, and the gendered character of reproductive-decision making. Second, we chart the processes through which young fathers inculcate an identity as a committed father, and the challenges they face in doing so. We map out the diverging fortunes of these young men: those who establish and sustain a parenting role and identity over time, and those who experience fragile trajectories, including those who lose contact with a child over time. We also consider the different ways in which young men can 'be there' for a child. The many factors that shape these varied trajectories are given detailed attention in subsequent chapters.

Third, we consider the experiences of young men who fathered more than one child during the lifetime of this study, in some cases with more than one mother. In the process we gain insights into those who, at first glance, appear to closely fit the 'feckless' image of young fathers that Tommy describes and denounces in our opening quotation. Finally, we place our findings in the context of broader debates about Relationship and Sex Education (RSE). We consider the policy context that pertained during the lifetime of the FYF study, and we gauge the impact of recent changes in RSE legislation and practice.

Sexual practices

The participants were developing their sexual identities and fertility practices within a particular framework of government policies. As we saw in Chapter 2, the prevention and reduction of teenage pregnancy was a central driving force for New Labour's Teenage Pregnancy Strategy (TPS), a key plank of which was the provision of Sex and Relationships Education (SRE, until replaced by RSE in March 2017) in government-maintained schools. The aim was to reduce unprotected and unwanted sex, promote healthy sexual practices and encourage respectful, non-exploitative relationships. It was also designed to prepare young people for their future responsibilities as parents (Epstein et al, 2003; Lindberg and Maddow-Zimmet, 2012; SEF, 2015).

Despite these laudable aims, at this time there was no statutory requirement to deliver SRE in schools and provision that was suitable for young men was very limited (Limmer, 2010). Despite some strenuous efforts, attempts to put a legislative framework in place under the TPS had been unsuccessful, largely because of a moral backlash against initiatives that were seen to condone or encourage early sexual practices (Daguerre, 2006; Hadley and Ingham, 2018). Other than the need to provide information about HIV, AIDS and sexually transmitted infections, schools had discretion in deciding what to deliver and how. Inevitably, provision was patchy. In 2013, the need for improvements was identified in over a third of UK schools (Ofsted, 2013), while estimates suggest that one in four students received no provision at all (Brook, 2011). Overly perfunctory, irregular and untimely sessions, a lack of partnership working with parents, and limited training for SRE educators were identified as major barriers (SEF, 2015; Alldred et al, 2016).

The views of our participants on SRE provision in schools reinforce this rather woeful picture. Several young men learned about contraception at school, but their key reference points were friends, pornography and, to a lesser extent, family members:

'They (teachers) didn't show us anything. It was just, like, a mess-around lesson. ... It's just [through]... me mum [laughs]. ... she's just fun.' (Adam, aged 16, lower income, partnered, wave 1)

'I just picked it up, like, when I were round with me mates ... and from porn ... they always used to have porn on their phones. It's just how everyone is [laughs].' (Karl, aged 16, lower income, single, wave 3)

'It seemed one of those gradual things ... especially round high school friends. It's just through talking obviously, hearsay. There were no sorta "the bees and the birds" chat with, with my father and stuff like that ... obviously round that age you are embarrassed about anything. ... They had sex education lessons [in the early years of high school] ... Obviously, [SRE] is quite juvenile at that point. ... its more of a, I dunno, like with boys, it's sort of a bravado subject. It's a chance to show off, or brag, or some people shy away from it. But obviously ... it's very formal lessons there.' (Dominic, aged 18, higher income, single, wave 3)

SRE tended to focus on factual information about preventing pregnancies at the expense of developing literacy in managing respectful and fulfilling relationships and exercising sexual and reproductive agency (Youth Parliament, 2007; House of Commons Education Committee, 2015; SEF, 2015, 2016; Brown and McQueen 2018). There was no support for young people who were expecting a child, or had become a parent:

Did you have like any sex education at school or any of that?

'After she fell on! It wor a bit late to be honest! ... And me teacher went "you don't even need to be here do you?" ... and he sent me home.' (Darren, aged 21, lower income, partnered, wave 3)

Wider evidence points to the existence of a knowledge/practice gap, where SRE messages are not well absorbed or acted upon (Elley, 2013). Young men tend to express dissatisfaction with SRE provision, to respond less well or to disengage from its messages (Forrest, 2007). Perhaps not surprisingly, promoting abstinence has been found to be particularly ineffective (Swann et al, 2003; Trivedi et al, 2007).

Planned conceptions?

Reflecting wider evidence that most teenage pregnancies are unplanned (Wellings et al, 2013), 27 of the sample of 31 young men conceived their child without advance planning, and most often in casual, fleeting or fledgling relationships with the child's mother. In these cases, the accounts reflected the tempo of young lives lived 'in the moment', with a discernible lack of intentionality or future planning. It was common for sex to be perceived primarily as a recreational activity that may or may not involve any commitment. Issues of safe sex and contraception were a lower priority, particularly for the less well-resourced participants. Edin and Nelson (2013: 63) suggest it is a 'don't ask, don't tell' approach to birth control. For these young men, sexual practices were linked to the persistence of traditional masculine ideologies of sexual prowess, competition, gender dominance, risk taking and antipathy to contraception. There was also a marked lack of interest in engaging with or discussing these issues with adults, or becoming more informed, either at home or at school:

So are you just happy to be using the pill?

'Yeah I am at t' minute 'cos obviously I trust [girlfriend] and I don't think she's, she'd forget to take it.' (Simon, aged 16, higher income, single, in a new relationship, wave 3)

'I think she were on the pill – I can't remember. ... Yeah, I knew [where to get condoms] but I just didn't bother. ... I just wanted to go out all the time. I didn't want to waste my day going all the way to the sexual health clinic.' (Jimmy, aged 16, lower income, single, wave 3)

'I don't know any lads that use condoms. ... I wouldn't have a sexless relationship. If it were sexless, we wouldn't be together ... She told me she were on the pill. ... So it were a big shock. She said she forgot to take it.' (Jason, aged 22, lower income, single, wave 4)

'It should be both, really [taking responsibility for contraception]. But I think people leave it to their partners half the time. I mean, she was actually meant to be on the pill. ... I think she just stopped taking it, to be honest, but obviously you forget. ... I've got to have sex. And it's usually on the first date. ... I really can't do johnnies [condoms]. I don't like them.' (Callum, aged 19, lower income, single, wave 3)

'I think she [partner] were on the injection but I weren't sure. I didn't ask her, we didn't use condoms.' (Adam, aged 16, lower income, partnered, wave 3)

'We used a condom ... But I don't think we knew or realised it had split.' (Dominic, aged 18, higher income, single, wave 3)

'I was about 14. I didn't really think. ... I had no common sense. I didn't think you could get pregnant the first time.' (Darren, aged 21, lower-income, partnered, wave 3)

Wider evidence confirms the picture that emerges here: on the whole, young men are not generally well informed or prepared. They are less preoccupied with pregnancy prevention and there is a strong tendency to leave responsibility for contraception to their partners (SmithBattle et al, 2019a). Rather than engage in life planning, the young men tended to live 'in the moment', with shorter-term horizons and goals.

Reactions to the pregnancy

Three lower-income young men (Adam, Jax, Darren) welcomed the pregnancy as a way to cement their relationships with the mothers. Two higher-income young men (Tommy and Martin), both in their 20s and in longer-term relationships, responded by marrying their partners (although Tommy's marriage came to an end during the study). These findings support wider evidence (drawn mainly from studies of partnered young fathers) that young men may be 'positively ambivalent' and able to adjust quickly to the idea of a pregnancy (Alexander et al, 2010; Deslauriers, 2011; Graham, 2013).

However, for the 27 young men who had not planned to enter parenthood, the overriding response was shock, disbelief and emotional turmoil, particularly where relationships were casual or had come to an end. In some of these accounts a fatalistic approach to the impending pregnancy is evident, with events seen as outside the young men's control:

> 'I knew that the condom had broken. … [but] I just didn't see it coming at all. … I just felt blind shock. And then a gradual panic set in. … I just kind of freaked out a bit … cut myself off from the world … for a couple of weeks, just while I tried to deal with it. … I was terrified to be honest.' (Ben, aged 20, higher income, single, wave 1)

> 'Accidents happen. … We didn't have us own place, no job, no income or anything. Really rock bottom.' (Peter, aged 17, higher income, single, wave 2)

> 'I was upset … nervous, shaking … because I just thought, within myself, I felt a bit young, and still a bit, well, not wild [laughs] … I felt that would be the end of my fun basically.' (Orlando, aged 24, lower income, single, wave 1)

The stress and anxiety expressed by these young men reflected their perceived lack of agency over the pregnancy, their lack of commitment to the mothers, fears over what would happen next, and deep worries that they were not ready and would not cope with the responsibilities of parenthood. These are widespread and consistent responses (Barret and Robinson, 1982; Miller,

1997; Higginbottom et al, 2006; Tyrer et al, 2005; Trivedi et al, 2009; Lohan et al, 2010).

With the benefit of hindsight, a substantial majority felt that, given the choice, they would have delayed entry into parenthood:

Had you thought about having children?

'Well, only in the general sense that, you know, the vague kind of plans of, you know, graduate, get a job, get married, have kids. ... It's not, it wasn't anything serious. It was just the general standard life plan, kind of thing. ... The problem is I am still growing up, I am discovering who I am and what I want to do. If I was 25, 26, I'd know who I am a bit, and would have a more established life.' (Ben, aged 20, higher income, single, wave 2)

'I wouldn't change [daughter] for the world, but maybe I wish I would have waited until I had a job ... and a little bit more money. ... But things happen, don't they?' (Andrew, aged 16, lower income, partnered, wave 5)

'It weren't planned ... I would never have had kids when I did, never. It's a ridiculous idea. It weren't to the right woman, it weren't at the right time in my life. ... I were 20 years old ... getting a girl pregnant that I weren't even in a full-time relationship with. ... 'Cos I've always wanted kids ... in a stable life ... work, having a nice home, doing healthy things ... didn't even have a garden for him to play in. ... You have to step up, don't you, but I ... don't even have a job, don't even have much life experience ... I regret that. Like I say, it weren't planned. ... I wouldn't advise being a young father ... because I weren't ready to be a dad.' (Jason, aged 25, lower-income, single, entered parenthood at the age of 22, wave 4)

Whether for good or ill, these transitions into early parenthood represented a major and mostly unanticipated rupture in these young lives, which was compounded by the stigma that surrounds young fatherhood.

Keeping a child? Reproductive decision-making

As with contraception, decisions about keeping a child were acknowledged to reside, ultimately, with the mother, even among those young men who raised the possibility of an abortion:

'It's up to the girl, obviously, they're bringing it [up]. But, be good to have opinion [from] lads as well, 'cos at sixteen, you've still got all your life to live ain't you. ... If I'd have known straight away, I'd be – definitely told her to have an abortion.' (Simon, aged 16, higher income, single, wave 3)

'I were a bit annoyed 'cos, obviously I didn't want a kid then. 'Cos, obviously, I'm still only young. ... She just texted me and said, "I'm keeping it". ... Her mum started saying "oh you need to think about it because if you get rid of it, it's just like killing somebody". So she just decided to keep it.' (Jimmy, aged 16, lower income, single, wave 3)

'I even spoke about abortions before they were born ... it still sickens me to think that I even mentioned that.' (Jason, aged 25, lower income, single, wave 4)

'We managed to keep it a secret for five months. ... by then it were too late to get rid of it. ... Abortions – I don't believe in all that. So, at end of the day you have to cope.' (Darren, aged 22, lower income, partnered, wave 4)

The idea of abortion was raised in seven cases, mostly by well-resourced young men, but quickly abandoned. An anti-abortionist ethos, founded on moral sensibilities about heartlessly taking a life, was particularly evident among the less well-resourced young men, a finding mirrored in other studies (Holmberg and Wahlberg, 2000):

'Her mother ... managed to persuade my ex to not have an abortion. ... it was down to her dad and mum, saying "we're having him". And obviously, I just felt, "this isn't your right, it's down to ... me and her". I've let it go now. Whatever has happened has happened. I said, you know, "whatever you want, it's your body".' (Dominic, aged 18, higher income, single, wave 3)

'I was 18 years old at the time. It wasn't how I saw my life going. So, I decided to suggest ... as it were, the easy [nervous laugh] the easy solution, but it didn't mesh. ... And then ... I suggested adoption. And, again, she said, "well no I want to, want to keep it". So ... it was kind of a difficult situation because both of us wanted very different things. ... it's like she'd already planned everything. ... And ... it ended up being on me whether I wanted to be involved or not. So, I, obviously, I chose to be involved. ... But she made it perfectly clear that if I chose one thing and then later changed my mind, she wouldn't be happy.' (Ben, aged 20, higher income, single, wave 1)

Ben's account reveals the emotional turmoil that these young men face: a moral ambivalence about abortion tempered by a desperation to resume a carefree teenage life. The young men's agency was often restricted to decisions about whether to be involved in the child's life, although one 16-year-old father was not given this choice during the pregnancy (see Simon's account, later, which reveals the circumstances that led him to make a different choice from Ben).

Adjusting to the pregnancy?

How these young men engaged with a pregnancy and sought to adjust to it over time varied across the sample. The shaky ground identified by SmithBattle and colleagues (2019a) is perhaps particularly noticeable during this fragile time. Impending fatherhood is a state that may seem unreal and marked with anxieties about future responsibilities (Quinton, et al, 2002; Pollock et al, 2005). Young fatherhood emerges here as a socially constructed state that is only legitimised and made tangible through recognition and support within the young man's social network, notably from the child's mother, and by extension, grandparents and professional workers (Leite, 2007; Paschal et al, 2011; Wilkes et al, 2012). In accord with wider evidence, we found that the configuration of these relationships during the pregnancy was a vital factor in the shaping of the young men's fledgling identities as parents.

In most of these cases, and in line with wider evidence, the young men adopted narratives of emerging adult responsibility as a marker of their transition into parenthood:

> 'It's just that challenge of growing up, manning up, knowing you've got a child on the way.' (Senwe, aged 16, higher income, single, wave 4)

> 'My mum, she was disappointed in me ... it's the fact I am so young, but if I take responsibility for what I've done then that'll be ok.' (Trevor, aged 15, lower income, single, wave 1)

> 'I only started getting some common sense when our lass fell on. ... I needed to stop acting like an idiot. ... Most blokes, as soon as they find their girlfriend's pregnant, they are gone, but I didn't see it that way. ... I just saw it as a better start ... a better way to change my life.' (Darren, aged 23, lower income, partnered, wave 4)

> 'It's like, sugar, it's happened, I need to grow up major now. So, like, you try to do the best you can to be able to support your baby and girlfriend, or whatever. It kind of hits you, "Oh God, I've gotta do this,

I've gotta do that". ... I'm gonna have to help out by cutting out my social life a bit more.' (Adam, aged 16, lower income, partnered, wave 2)

Adam began to save his pocket money to help prepare for the new baby. Saving up, and/or looking for work or other sources of income were common preoccupations among these young men (see Chapter 7). And, with varying degrees of success, they began the process of curtailing their youthful practices of smoking, drinking, soft drugs, nights out with their mates, and physically dangerous pastimes (Reeves, 2006; Neale and Lau Clayton, 2011). In these ways, the young men sought to inculcate a new identity as a responsible adult and engaged parent. These narratives of 'growing up', 'stepping up' or 'manning up' are commonly reported in studies of young fatherhood (Reeves, 2006; Tuffin et al, 2010; Weber, 2020). A participant in Weber's study (2020: 54), for example, observes that: 'boys can make children, but only men can care for them'.

In demonstrating their commitment to engaged fatherhood, young fathers commonly used the language of 'being there' (Speak, 2006; Osborn, 2007; Edin and Nelson, 2013) This can be interpreted in a number of ways but is commonly understood as a physical presence in a child's life based on the provision of love and emotional support, spending quality time, and helping out with caregiving activities (Paschal et al, 2011). More broadly, it is a relational orientation and a set of moral sensibilities.

Before the birth, where relationships with the mothers allowed, the young men began to 'be there' by taking an interest in the pregnancy and attending hospital scans and antenatal classes. This made the impending pregnancy much more real for them:

'I just go round there and make sure she's alright. And we do talk, daily ... like every two hours, I'm texting her. ... Well, she's carrying a precious load ... so that kind of connects us, although we're not together. ... So she's bonded to me and my family.' (Iman, aged 16, higher income, single, wave 1)

'I've been to the scans and antenatal classes, all the doctors' appointments that she's had ... I didn't want her to feel like, just 'cos we're single, like, I can't come and help her.' (Orlando, aged 24, lower income, single, wave 2)

'[The hospital staff] involved both of us. ... There was a lot of laughing and joking. ... The staff and the scans ... they was all fantastic. ... They explained what the pregnancy's going to be like and giving birth. ... It was really good.' (Kevin, aged 24, lower income, single, aged 18 and partnered during the pregnancy, wave 1)

'When my girlfriend saw the midwife I could hear my baby's heartbeat, or at night-time I'm listening to her belly ... how she's moving. ... and I can feel that she's kicking. ... It was just, wow, "that's my child in there" ... I just couldn't wait to meet her.' (Marcel, aged 24, lower income, partnered, wave 1)

There are two important observations to be made about these narratives. First, whatever the aspirations of these young men, an abrupt transformation from young lad to responsible dad cannot be achieved overnight; it may take considerable time. In this sample, it was more likely to occur in piecemeal fashion over some years, as young men zig zagged between their identities as carefree lads with their own social lives, and their fledgling identities as grown-ups with new relational and socio-economic responsibilities. Negotiating the fast track to adulthood, then, created substantial challenges for these young men and was not always achievable in the short term (Edin and Nelson, 2013; Weber, 2020).

A second observation concerns the role of stigma in the drive to 'step up' and 'be there'. Making a commitment to an impending child becomes imperative in a context where the only alternative is to be branded as a 'scumbag' (as Tommy so graphically describes it). 'Being there' is the only way these young men can distance themselves from such labels (see Darren, earlier) and salvage their moral reputations. These narratives help well-resourced young men, like Tommy and Ben, to preserve their existing moral standing, while disadvantaged young men like Darren, use them to elevate their moral standing above their 'scumbag' peers (Weber, 2020).

The stigma attached to young fatherhood, then, cannot easily be taken out of the picture. It creates a moral benchmark against which young men judge the responses and behaviour of themselves and others. This stigma, moreover, is by no means a temporary state; it may linger with pernicious effects for years (Formby et al, 2010). This is illustrated in Ben's follow-up account, generated ten years after his entry into parenthood. He reveals a tendency, as a part-time parent living at a considerable distance from his daughter, to compartmentalise his life and hide his status as a parent:

What would you say is the most challenging thing about being a dad?

'I think I might have mentioned this in the original research, but it's ... still the same sense of judgement I get from other people when they find out I have a [ten-year-old] child. ... Young fatherhood is very frowned upon. ... It's like, "oh you look really young and you've had a kid?" It's like, "I fucking know. I was there". ... It's not their business. The biggest struggle is dealing with other people's prejudices. ... Maybe I'm just being paranoid ... but that line of questioning still happens ... which has made it hard just to kind of talk about. ... I am trying to be more forthcoming about it these days, because ... a few years ago, I had quite a bad mental health blip and I realised that part of it was because I wasn't really accepting and embracing my role as a parent ... So I've been working on myself more, to be more honest, to not hide it ... and trying to think, 'well, if people are gonna judge me, fuck 'em', you know.' (Ben, aged 28, higher income, single, part-time father, FYFF study, wave 1)

Ben's account points to the deep and enduring shame associated with having a child 'out of time', which may be accentuated for well-resourced young men who feel that their lives should have progressed along another track entirely (Formby et al, 2010).

Birth as a turning point

The birth itself, attended by 26 of the young men in this study, was regarded as a culminating event in a significant transition. It was described as an emotional moment, a turning point, where the enormity of bringing a new and fragile life into the world was finally brought home to them:

'Well, if I'm honest, before he was born I was a bit negative ... I didn't want to be a dad 'cos for starters I'm unemployed. ... And living in a council flat in a block of smackhead flats in [deprived area of the city] wasn't ideal. ... So I can't give him the best possible life. But it's quite crazy. Once he were born and I seen him, like, it changes everything. ... Nothing else matters. Everything you do is for him. ... It's impossible to describe, I think. It's just overwhelming. You are responsible for something that can't be independent and needs help. ... You have to be there for him, don't you – sacrifice things to make [his] life better. Like I used to ... smoke weed. But I just stopped. ... I've got a crap dad, so obviously I want to be total opposite and be a good example to him. I would never consider putting [son] in an ounce of life I've had – that's not a normal upbringing.' (Jason, aged 22, lower income, single, wave 2)

'It were just like the biggest joy I've ever had in my life. ... it hits you like a ton of bricks when, when they're born, and you realise that it's not about *you* anymore.' (Callum, aged 19, lower income, single, wave 2)

'I were crying and I've never cried like that before. The first time he cried, the first time he took a bath, had a bottle, I was there to witness all that, which is important for being a father ... not just for the kids but for his mum. I was there for her as well.' (Kevin, aged 24, lower income, single, partnered during the transition to parenthood, wave 1)

'[During the pregnancy] it felt ... very distant. It wasn't really happening. And then when you're actually holding [the baby] it was just very ... very emotional. And it kind of hit me then ... completely overwhelming. It just changed everything. ... and I was "right, I can, I'll be able to do this, I'll find some way to do it".' (Ben, aged 20, higher income, single, wave 1)

'I just thought, if this is going to come about, this is something that I am going to take on and I am going to be responsible because I don't understand how, when a child comes along, you can't have that love for him. As much as you don't expect it, it just hits you.' (Dominic, aged 18, higher income, single, wave 1)

These accounts reflect the rise of a new emotional literacy among young fathers that aligns with cultural imperatives and ideologies of engaged fatherhood (Dermott and Miller, 2015; Neale and Patrick, 2016). Their efforts to 'be there' as responsible adults were instrumental in the process of generating new paternal identities for these young men (see also Kiernan, 2005; Edin and Nelson, 2013). They also became workable strategies for managing and deflecting the stigma attached to their position (Nayak and Kehily, 2013; Conn et al, 2018). Whatever the circumstances at the point of conception and during the 'unreal' time of the pregnancy, by the time of the birth these children were far from unwanted.

Engaged fatherhood?

After the birth, a substantial majority of the young men in this study strove to develop their practices as engaged fathers. For both partnered and single young men there were notable examples of stable working relationships between the parents and wider families that developed as a solid foundation for a joint parenting project, often across two households. But at the other extreme there were examples of relational, socio-economic, familial, emotional and behavioural problems that led to tenuous contact or its cessation over time. It is important to note that the journeys of these young men were far from linear or straightforward; in many cases they were fluid, undulating, volatile and unstable. The complexities of these journeys are explored in subsequent chapters, but here we draw a distinction between two broad groups of young men: those who managed to sustain a relationship with their children over the course of the study, and those whose relationships with their children remained fragile or ceased altogether.

Sustained father–child relationships

In the years following the birth, 21 of the 31 young men established ongoing and relatively stable relationships with their children. They expressed a distinct desire to be emotionally engaged and active carers. In some cases (see Jason, earlier) they were motivated by the wish to be more available to their children than their own fathers had been to them (Bunting and McAuley, 2004; Shannon and Abrams, 2007; Tuffin et al, 2010). This commitment was evident regardless of their relationship or co-residence status with the mother. Echoing findings from other studies (Ayoola et al, 2010), parenting for these young men became a rationale for seeking a new and more fulfilling direction in life:

'It's challenging, its exciting, it's interesting. It makes you proud. It makes you tired. It keeps you busy. It makes you a family – it makes you feel like you are a family.' (Martin, aged 25, higher income, married, wave 2)

'I want to be the person who [my son] can turn to. And who, obviously, who is always gonna be there for him. ... You know, when I've got him, and when he does something, when's he's growing up, you know, it's the happiest emotion 'cos you just wanna give him a kiss and a cuddle. He's my little man. ... He's so – you feel really proud.' (Dominic, aged 18, higher income, single, wave 1)

'People say it ruins your life, but it doesn't. It makes you a better person.' (Orlando, aged 24, lower income, single, wave 1)

'Back then, I used to get into trouble, I was selling drugs and stuff. ... I could have got sent to jail. But ... after having my kids it opened up a better side to me ... I were getting into training schemes, football, college and stuff like that.' (Tarrell, aged 21, lower income, single, wave 1)

'My attitude to life is a lot better. Yeah, I've become a lot calmer. ... A couple of years ago the slightest thing would really, really get me angry. ... Now it just flies straight over my head. It's 'cos you've got the responsibility of looking after another human being.' (Joe, aged 18, lower income, partnered, wave 2)

'I was only 18, so it was ... a shock, like I said, it forced me to grow up, to take responsibility. ... [A good dad is] one that listens, always there, no matter what. And teach you things ... bedtime stories and just spending time, that important time. I think it's important to provide – not just financially, but in all the other areas. ... It's not just about buying them ... this and that. It's – it runs a lot deeper than that. It's having that bond. ... My son ... wants to be like me ... get my hairstyle, support the same football team. ... It's wonderful to see 'cos I never had that ... I grew up with [my dad] in and out of my life. ... My advice [to other young dads] is just keep positive. Having kids is going to be the most exciting and terrifying moment of your life. ... They're always gonna be your babies and just, just love them. ... Enjoy every minute of it.' (Kevin, aged 24, lower income, single, wave 1)

Contemporary understandings of engaged fatherhood emphasise emotional connectedness as the key marker of good parenting (Dermott, 2008; Weber, 2020). As these accounts show, these young fathers were striving to be *emotionally engaged* fathers, a connection that goes beyond a traditional provider role. Moreover, for young men who are not (yet) in a position to define themselves in terms of a provider role, an emotional engagement has even greater resonance (Tyrer et al, 2005; Neale and Patrick, 2016). The young men saw their new role and status as beneficial for themselves, as well as for the child and mother. The arrival of a new generation, then, may have a transformative effect, providing a fundamental source of meaning and identity, and creating new pathways and aspirations to enhance young men's life chances (Edin and Nelson, 2013: 211).

By the end of the study, 19 of these 21 young men were seeing their children at least once a week, and often much more frequently. Over time, one of the fathers became the primary carer for his child where the mother was incapacitated. Ten of these fathers developed an element of shared care with the primary caring mothers across two households, with their child regularly visiting or staying overnight during the week or at weekends. Meanwhile, those who were co-resident (eight cases by the close of fieldwork) were sharing their daily lives with their children.

It is worth noting that the idea of socially engaged fatherhood masks extensive variations in what it means to 'be there' and how it is practised. For example, comparing the accounts of two higher-income young men (Dominic and Ben) who were both parenting at a distance, reveals very different levels of commitment to their children and ways of interacting with them. While Dominic lived near his son, played a regular and flexible role in his care over the years (as already shown), and strove to see more of him where possible, Ben had become very much a part-time 'fun' dad:

'I'm maybe not as involved as I could [be]. ... I could do more. ... I'm told by my parents that I'm a good dad. ... I don't think I've ever felt competent as a father. ... I hang out with [my daughter] ...

because I feel like we're cultivating as much a friendship as a parental relationship. ... I don't live with her full-time or anything like that and she's not – she's a force in my life, but she's not the dominant force in my life.' (Ben, aged 28, daughter aged 10, higher income, single, FYFF, wave 1)

Ben's orientation to parenthood is reflected in the life map that he constructed for his future (see Figure 4.1). His daughter does not appear on this map, although he later added her in response to prompts from the researcher.

Figure 4.1: Ben's future life map, aged 20, wave 2

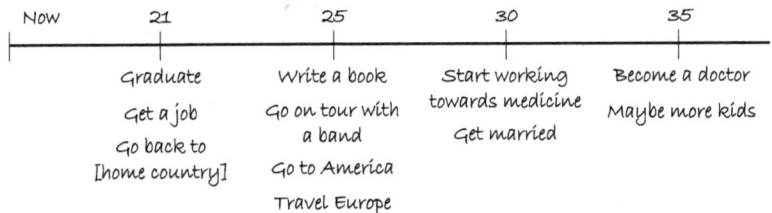

As we show in Chapter 5, a primarily emotional and fun way of 'being there' for a child was not only characteristic of non-resident parents; it was also evident among young men who were living with their children. In some cases, 'being there' occurred almost by default, by virtue of a young man's residence in the same household, rather than any staunch commitment to a more 'hands-on' parental role.

Fragile father–child relationships

The remaining ten young men in the sample reported a range of difficulties in establishing and sustaining a role as a parent, with experiences of constrained or intermittent contact with their children during the pregnancy and/or in the early years following the birth. Their parenting was indeed built on shaky ground (SmithBattle et al, 2019a). In seven of these cases the young men were leading highly impoverished lives, marked by various forms of social deprivation and in some cases, prolonged mental health issues. As Adam explained at a follow-up interview: "My brain doesn't stop. I have anxiety and depression, like, I've got severe anxiety problems, so my brain does not stop worrying about everything" (Adam, aged 26, low income, partnered, New Pathways Study, Clayton et al, 2021).

With few resources of an emotional, relational or material nature to bring to the task, these young men were working with idealised notions of engaged fatherhood that were difficult to put into practice, especially for the teenagers in the study (Early et al, 2019). We identified three interrelated barriers that constrained the engagement of these young men, bound up with youthful offending, child protection issues and the curtailing of contact by gatekeeping mothers. We introduce each of these scenarios here.

Youthful offending

Spending time in the criminal justice system, with its focus on surveillance and a culture of risk, engenders spoiled identities that can run counter to the identities of these young men as good fathers (Buston et al, 2012; Neale and Ladlow, 2015a; Ladlow and Neale, 2016). The stigma surrounding the deviance of young fatherhood looms large here, compounding the view that young fathers are a risk to their children rather than a resource for them (Neale and Ladlow, 2015a; Ladlow and Neale, 2016). More pragmatically, doing time in prison prevents young men from spending quality time with their children and building trusting relationships with them. The issues are as much emotional as practical. Young fathers may find it emotionally difficult to see their children under the unnatural conditions of supervised contact, leading them to withdraw even further (Shannon and Abrams, 2007; Neale and Ladlow, 2015a; Ladlow and Neale, 2016; see also Chapter 9).

Jason provides a good example of these issues. As already shown, he was transformed by the birth of his son, and saw the potential for new opportunities in his life. These are reflected in his future life map which, in contrast to Ben's, is built entirely around the arrival of his son (Figure 4.2).

As a new father, Jason professed that he had put his criminal career behind him and would do all he could to stop losing his temper and getting into violent fights: "I'm glad I went to jail … because it's just changed me. … What I've done in the past, before [son] were born, I can't alter that. But now I've got my son, I definitely wouldn't [get into a fight]. It's not worth it" (Jason, aged 22, lower income, single). In practice, however, such behavioural changes tend to occur in fits and starts. Jason describes a slippery

Figure 4.2: Jason's future life map, aged 22, wave 1

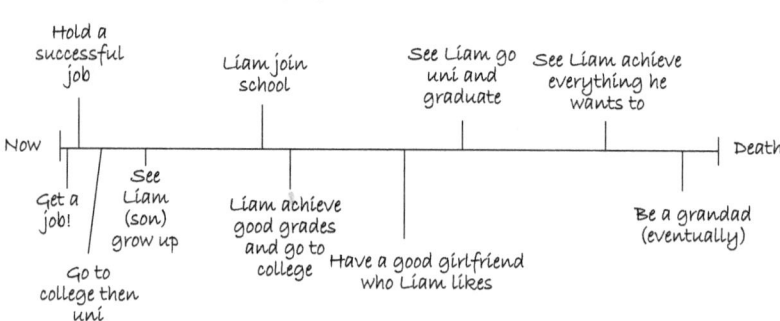

protracted journey towards an ideal self, a state of fragile desistance that may not happen overnight (Neale and Ladlow, 2015b; Ladlow and Neale, 2016). This is perhaps not surprising given his background (he suffered from anger management and mental health problems, after spending years in care following the death of his mother from a drug overdose). When his son was a year old, Jason was given a second custodial sentence for violent assault following a 'heat of the moment' brawl in a pub:

> 'It were horrible not seeing my son ... knowing that I were missing the most important part of his life, where he's learning how to walk and talk. I just felt I'd let him down big time. I've let his mother down, 'cos she's had to cope on her own for fifteen months. And I weren't supporting him financially. He'd come on visits and I'd pick him up and he'd want me to put him back down ... and run to her. It'd hurt me. It's hard, it breaks my heart. ... And I'd say, "I don't want to see him for a bit" and Carla would be like, "Why? You need to see him more often, not less". ... If you got to see [your child] like, in a playroom, with a camera in there ... playing toys together and having a laugh ... that'd be good, 'cos you're not bonding sat on a seat, with a table and a drink and a packet of crisps. ... he gets bored and restless ... How are you bonding? I did that for fifteen months. When I got out, we didn't have a bond. That's the price I paid for being an idiot. I weren't someone important to him.' (Jason, aged 24, lower income, single, wave 3)

Related issues of constrained contact that were imposed by child protection agencies arose for Callum, Andrew and Adam, who were regarded as a potential risk for their children, and for Karl, whose child was taken into care (see his account in Chapter 9).

Curtailed contact

In five of these ten cases, mothers sought to curtail contact between the young men and their children. These experiences created a rupture in the young men's parenting journeys; they were effectively barred from 'being there' and expressed a sense of powerlessness in finding a connection to their child, or in simply being recognised as a parent. In some cases, the cessation of contact was tied to a deep estrangement between the parents (and by extension, the families), most usually triggered when a couple relationship ended, or one or both re-partnered, or the mothers moved away, creating a geographical barrier to contact (see further accounts in Chapter 5). In other cases, it was triggered by concerns over erratic behaviour, or mental health and anger management problems for the young men, arising from their earlier life experiences. Where these issues occur concurrently, they could create significant barriers to an engagement as a father.

By the close of the research, three young men with fragile parenting trajectories had intermittent contact with their children, a further three had negligible contact, while in the remaining four cases, contact had ceased altogether. We recount here the experiences of two young men, Jimmy and Simon, who lost contact with their children in different circumstances.

For Jimmy, the loss of contact was not of his choosing, but arose through a complex mix of volatile relationships with the maternal family, anger management problems, concerns over safeguarding issues, and barred contact:

> 'Her mum [maternal grandmother] won't let me go up to her house no more. … And, like, I want to see [my son]. … It'd have to go through courts wouldn't it? [But] I don't wanna do that 'cos then it'll just cause bigger arguments. … I've got nowhere to go, nowhere to live. And I'm like sponging off people's mums and that. And then obviously I can't go and see [my child's mum], she can't bring [my son] down to see me. So … it's just harder on me.' (Jimmy, aged 16, lower income, single, wave 3)

Jimmy had been followed initially, through three waves of interviews spread over the course of a year. By the time he was 17 (wave 4), Jimmy had started court proceedings to reinstate contact with his son. By the close of the fieldwork in 2015, he had not seen his son for 18 months, although he hoped to rekindle supervised contact in future. When asked about his relationship with his son, he reflected:

> 'I haven't got one. I couldn't describe it. … I don't know if he actually does remember me. … At first it were, like, upsetting and that, but now I'm just getting used to it, 'cos I know I'm not going to see him for a while, so just come to terms with it. … I just won't think about it, just do something else. … I don't really feel nothing anymore. … Sometimes I even forget that I haven't seen him, 'cos it's that normal to me now. I feel like disappointed in myself, like … that I don't feel upset. … It don't come into my mind hardly any more. Very rarely. … it would be good to see him, just for ten minutes. Mind you, I … I'd rather wait till it was consistent, instead of seeing him for ten minutes and then not seeing him again for months … [just] get through each day and just wait till I see him eventually.' (Jimmy, aged 19, lower income, single, wave 5)

Contact had also ceased for 16-year-old Simon. Having learned of the pregnancy two weeks before the birth, there had been no opportunity for him to build a paternal identity beforehand. This was in the context of a serious rift with the maternal family and their seeming reluctance to involve him in the child's life. The pattern established during the pregnancy continued in the aftermath. Simon was offered one supervised visit to see his son at the maternal house, although his mother visited the baby on several occasions. Requests to bring the child to his family home were rebuffed. At his first interview, he was undecided about his future involvement:

> 'I wanted to see him … just to try and see if I felt any better … but it just didn't feel right … [The family] are always watching you. … I just felt like I shouldn't be there. … Just hard to take. … I'd be able to step up to it if I'm fully committed … I think … like I should be [committed], 'cos it's my kid and I should be there. Well, her mum just said, "go think about it, and talk to your mum". … But I don't know if I [want] to be involved. … They're only willing to let my mum see him like an hour a fortnight. I'm leaning more to not being involved … With all the past as well and getting threats [from her family] … It's just not a family to be with. … And with the girl I'm with now … it's like a second family and proper close.' (Simon, aged 16, higher income, re-partnered, wave 2)

In deliberating about his future, Simon considered the quality of his new relationship and the stress experienced by his family. But the main issue was the estrangement from the maternal family, which left him without a foundation to build a meaningful relationship with his child. Given the circumstances in which his paternity had been revealed, his status as a parent remained unreal to him:

> 'I do think about the future, and I'd be happy to have a future, obviously, as a dad. But just not with [son]. It's not real. I don't feel – it don't feel any different. He might want to see me when he's a bit older. … [We] just seemed to drift away. … my mum stopped going and … nothing being spoken about, … [that] calmed me down and I weren't as stressed out. And I ain't thinking about it as much. And I think my mum's just thought, "let's just get on with our lives". And that's what I have done.' (Simon, aged 16, higher income, re-partnered, wave 2)

By the end of the study what marked Jimmy and Simon out from the rest of the sample was their emotional disengagement from their children, and their acceptance that, currently at least, they did not have a role in their children's lives. These changes in perception and emotional distancing were, in themselves, critical transitions in their fatherhood journeys.

There are some parallels here with the broader experiences of non-resident fathers who face losing contact with their children after a separation or divorce. Although this pattern is receding, it has been well documented, particularly for lower-income fathers (see Chapter 1). There are heavy health and financial costs involved in pursuing child contact through the courts, which have to be weighed against the benefits of abandoning the struggle and simply letting go (Bradshaw et al, 1999). The lack of continuity of contact, and the powerlessness associated with this circumstance can create a heavy emotional burden (Bradshaw et al, 1999: 121). For vulnerable young men, these burdens may become too much to bear (Mazza, 2002; Quinton et al, 2002). At the same time the loss of a potentially fulfilling role as a parent may compound their sense of failure and marginalisation, with longer-term implications for their mental health and well-being (Caldwell and Antonucci, 1997; Lowenthal and Lowenthal, 1997; Mazza, 2002; Parikh, 2005).

Multiple pregnancies? Multiple children?

The young men in the study were generally more aware of the value of contraception once they had become fathers, and more likely to use it to avoid a second pregnancy. As Jax explains:

> 'I want more kids, definitely. ... I want a son. ... Me and Janie have already decided. Not yet, obviously! ... I go to the doctors with Janie every few months to get that injection thing. ... obviously, like, we're too young to have another kid now. I mean, one kid ... it's easy, but if you had ... another baby in the equation, it'd blow the whole thing to smithereens. And I think another kid right now would absolutely ruin our relationship. ... it would make us argue proper. And then it would make us split up and then Janie would be stuck with two kids. ... I wouldn't want to do that to her.' (Jax, aged 18, lower income, partnered/co-resident, wave 1)

However, during the course of this study, six of the 31 young fathers conceived a second child. The pregnancies arose under a variety of circumstances. In two cases the fathers were in relatively stable relationships with the mothers, but contraception remained sporadic. Darren had planned a second pregnancy with his partner, but, despite an avowed pro-life stance (see earlier account), a third pregnancy was terminated, since the couple were not ready for three children.

A termination was also the chosen path for Adam and his partner, whose circumstances were far from settled. A child protection plan was in place for their first child, which involved Adam in supervised contact once a week. This would have been extended had a further pregnancy gone ahead. The couple were still in their teens and had no sources of income, and few educational or training skills. Moreover, Adam was living in a hostel for homeless, single men, where he was not allowed to bring a child (Neale and Ladlow, 2015b):

'It was about a month into her [pregnancy] ... I sort of put the question ... "I don't think we should". So she feels like I pressured her into that. ... I said, "that's fine, you can blame me for it". ... So I do feel responsible. ... But I don't think we would have managed and with what's gone on since then, I don't think it would have been the best thing. Bringing up another kid in that sort of environment, no. And I don't, personally, I don't think I was ready for another one.' (Adam, aged 18, lower income, partnered, wave 4)

The agency exercised by these two young men is significant, given our earlier findings about the powerless of young men in reproductive-decision making. In both these cases, the more established partnerships between the parents, and shared sense of family meant that decisions could be negotiated directly between the couple themselves. Earlier sensibilities over the morality of abortion now gave way to practical considerations and a greater appreciation of the relentless nature of parental responsibilities.

In four of the five cases where a second pregnancy went ahead, relationships between the young parents were highly volatile and the fathers were excluded from decision making. For Jason, a second conception occurred 'in the moment' when he was attempting to rekindle good relationships with the mother and re-establish contact with his first child:

'We'd not seen each other for, like, five weeks. ... she ended up coming to mine and got pregnant. ... I don't think it's nice to have wanted two kids to be aborted. I think it's quite wrong. It just happened. And you always think that it's never gonna happen, don't you. I never thought in my life that she would have got pregnant then. ... I should – you should take precautions. But the fact of the matter is that she did get pregnant. So, it weren't ideal. ... If she'd be using precautions, then you wouldn't need abortions would you. ... And then [weeks later] she messaged me. ... I said, "that's not mine, I haven't seen you for six weeks". ... She said, "I've not been with anyone. I wouldn't even consider having a baby to another man. I'm not having kids to two different men". I were just in a shell for about three days, didn't know what to do.' (Jason, aged 24, lower income, single, wave 3)

The remaining three young men had further children with different mothers. For Karl, who felt anguished and powerless when his child was taken into care (see Chapter 9), this was a fresh start and a second chance to forge a family (see also Edin and Nelson, 2013: 92). A similar motivation may have been in place for Callum. Like Jason, he found that contact with his twins was curtailed when he tried to withdraw from a relationship with the mother. A protracted court case ensued, which required supervised contact for

Callum. In the meantime, he sought out a new relationship, which resulted in the birth of two further children over the study period:

> 'We literally just had our daughter [third child]. And then, within God knows how long, she were pregnant again. And, genuinely, I didn't actually think you could get pregnant so quick after. I thought that it'd be, like, kind of messed up down there, if you know what I mean. ... After [fourth child] it's just I haven't been feeling the same. I haven't been thinking about things. I haven't been feeling things. It's like I'm not here. I have no emotion and that. It's weird. I don't think properly anymore. It's more like just depression side of things. Thinking things, and just how my head is. I don't know why, it's since [fourth daughter] has been here. I think that's just like tip of iceberg: *four* kids!' (Callum, aged 19, lower income, single, wave 2)

As a final example, Tarrell had fathered twins at the age of 14, some years before the start of the study. But when these family ties were disrupted by a long spell in custody, he sought out new relationships and a fresh start. By the end of the study, he had fathered five children with three different mothers, the last one following a casual encounter.

One of the significant features of these multiple pregnancies, particularly where they occur across households and with different mothers, is the pressure that they place on the young men's ability to be there for their children. These young men were committed fathers. Yet they struggled to maintain contact with all their children, let alone put the principles of engaged fatherhood into practice. Their parenting efforts were simply spread too thin. Moreover, they could face tensions from mothers who were not happy with 'sharing' a father and his limited resources (Donald et al, 2022). For Callum, fathering four children during his teenage years had deleterious effects on his mental health. Logistically, it was not possible for him to give an equal commitment to all his children, or to maintain the emotional attachment that (as shown earlier) he had strongly felt upon the arrival of his first child. The presence of multiple children, particularly across different households and mothers, forms yet another significant barrier for young fathers in being able to put the principles of engaged fatherhood into practice.

The four cases where there were serial partnerships and multiple pregnancies share two striking features. First, these young men were unable to exercise any agency over their subsequent fertility and/or had no choice over the continuation of the pregnancies. For young men like Jason and Callum, the prospect of another unplanned child was devastating. The patterns set for their initial entry into parenthood, with their sense of fatalism, and their lack of knowledge, planning and agency, were simply repeated. Yet

Callum had been recruited into this study via a specialist learning mentor, who had not only provided him with tailored support and contraceptive advice but had actively engaged him in the delivery of an SRE peer-support programme (detailed in Chapter 9). This reinforces our earlier observation that young men may have difficulties in absorbing sexual and reproductive health messages and using them to shape their own practices.

Second, it is significant that these young men were some of the most marginalised in our sample, having experienced particularly difficult journeys through childhood and into adolescence. We have suggested elsewhere (Neale, 2021a) that where lives are impoverished, time horizons shrink as people become preoccupied with day-to-day survival. Living in the moment in this way engenders risky practices, for it reduces one's capacity to care for or learn from the past, or to plan for the future.

Concluding discussion

Our findings in this chapter demonstrate the significant emotional impact of the transition into early fatherhood, with implications for young men's identities and their mental and emotional health and well-being. Young fathers care about and attach importance to 'being there' and investing in a loving, personal relationship with their children. This is irrespective of their age, the nature of their relationship with the mother, or their socio-economic background. It is also irrespective of whether the pregnancy is unplanned, unexpected or the cause for initial ambivalence. Tracing the journeys of the young men reveals the subtle and cumulative processes through which new paternal identities are forged, and we have begun to map out the factors that may consolidate or disrupt these processes over time.

For some young men the entry into parenthood can be an opportunity to form new attachments, to create family (Tyrer et al, 2005) and to reinvent themselves as responsible adults. The adherence of these young men to an ethos of emotionally engaged fatherhood is a significant finding here; over the course of the study, contact between father and child had dwindled or ceased in just seven of 31 cases. A substantial majority not only held to the ideology of engaged fatherhood but were actively striving to put it into practice. Arguably, their strong awareness of the 'scumbag' image of young fathers who absent themselves from their children's lives may have reinforced their efforts to engage with their children, although what 'being there' means and how it is practised is highly varied.

We have also seen that the young men entered parenthood in ways that were not planned or well informed, creating an unwelcome and deeply unsettling rupture in their lives. The highly gendered nature of this process left little room for them to exercise their reproductive agency. In some cases, the pattern repeated itself in subsequent, sometimes multiple conceptions for these young men, in ways that could create yet further barriers to their effective engagement with their children.

Our findings about the limited reproductive knowledge and skills of the young men have implications for the provision of Relationship and Sex Education (RSE). As shown earlier, provision at the time of the FYF study was inadequate and lacked statutory force. This picture has improved over the years. SRE has been rebranded to give priority to the relational elements of provision. Legislation passed in the Children and Social Work Act 2017 mandated compulsory Relationship and Sex Education in secondary schools and Relationships Education in primary schools (SEF, 2018; DfE, 2020). New guidance and a road map for implementation were published in early 2019, with expectations that schools would set this up by late 2019.

However, a recent survey has found that major gaps continue to exist between the laudable aims of the legislation and its implementation (SEF, 2022). Despite widespread recognition of the crucial role of such provision in supporting the relational and sexual health of young people, delivery remains inconsistent, underfunded, and of poor quality, and with no pathway to specialist teaching. There are also few opportunities for young people to ask questions or input into discussion. The survey found that boys remain less likely than girls to have a trusted adult with whom they can confide about RSE issues. And, despite the name change, the relational components remain a low priority. There are urgent calls to rectify this situation to avoid letting down another generation of young people (SEF, 2022).

In terms of delivery, there is an obvious need for provision that is timely, provided early enough to make a difference to young people, and that is sustained and delivered flexibly at keys points in a young person's journey, rather than scheduled as a one-off event. The use of informal settings, and delivery by trained staff, specialists and peer groups (young parents and their babies) are likely to make such provision real, accessible and meaningful for participants.

In terms of content, researchers have long called for a less didactic, 'top down' and instrumental approach (lecturing young people on the do's and don'ts of their sexual behaviour), in favour of a more participatory, facilitative approach, based on discussion and debate about sexual attitudes and values, and the nurturing of healthy sexual practices (Allen, 2007, 2008; Lohan et al, 2010, 2017). There have been calls, too, for a greater focus on preparing young people for conception, pregnancy and parenthood, rather than focusing solely on how to avoid becoming a parent in the first place. Overall, a better balance is needed between the 'sex' and 'relationship' elements of RSE provision, to create a more nuanced understanding of how relational factors shape fertility decisions and journeys into parenthood. It is to these important relational issues that we now turn.

5

Co-parenting: the gendered dynamics of young relationships

Introduction

In this chapter we explore how young fathers work out their relationships with the mothers of their children over time. The discussion builds on the evidence presented in Chapter 4 and draws on and updates our earlier writings (Neale and Lau Clayton, 2015; Neale and Patrick, 2016; Tarrant and Neale, 2017a, b). As we saw in the Introduction and in Chapter 1, ideologies around the gendering of parenthood are continually shifting through time. These shifts have been linked to the waning of the nuclear family as the dominant form of family life and the rise of a more diverse range of family forms and practices. However, there remains a strongly ingrained and widely held assumption that mothers are (and should continue to be) the primary carers of their children. In the fragile circumstances of early parenthood, young mothers alone are seen to have a legitimate claim to their children and the right to determine the nature and extent of a young father's involvement (Gilligan et al, 2012).

Gendered relationships, then, are clearly important in shaping the parenting journeys of young fathers; they emerged as central themes in this research, just as they have in a range of similar studies (see Chapter 1; also, Rhein et al, 1997, Speak et al, 1997, Quinton et al, 2002; Florsheim et al, 2003; Bunting and McAuley, 2004; Mollborn and Jacobs, 2015; SmithBattle et al, 2019a). The value of co-parenting – the collaborative process by which two parents care for their child – has been much debated. Yet dynamic understandings of how this pattern evolves biographically is less well developed, while evidence on young fathers' co-parenting practices and experiences is equally sparse (see the review in Chapter 1; Mollborn and Jacobs, 2015; Neale and Patrick, 2016). From this starting point, our aim was to contribute new dynamic knowledge on co-parenting from the perspectives of young fathers, and to gauge how far they were able to forge workable arrangements with the mothers as the basis for maintaining a relationship with their children (Mollborn and Jacobs, 2015).

The discussion begins with a brief summary of sociological insights on gendered patterns of parenthood (detailed in Chapter 1). Turning to our empirical evidence, we map out the nature of co-parenting relationships across the sample of young men, and document shifts in these relationships over time. We also develop a typology that shows how varied parental relationships map onto varied child-contact arrangements. This reveals three broad configurations of co-parenting relationships that were operating across the sample at any one time.

We complement this mapping exercise with accounts from young fathers that reflect their lived experiences of co-parenting. We distinguish here between the experiences of young men who were parenting at close hand (through a co-resident partnership with the mother) or at a distance (through a non-partnered relationship operating across households). Woven into the discussion are considerations of the nature and quality of these gendered relationships. We explore further some of the barriers that may prevent young men from being there for their children, including issues of oppressive or violent behaviour, and curtailed contact, which in some cases led the young men to seek mediation or legal redress through the family courts.[1] In our conclusion, we return to the inherent tensions between the established ethos of the mother/child dyad and the emerging ethos of engaged fatherhood, and we draw out some policy implications from our findings.

Gendered patterns of parenthood

As shown in Chapter 1, gendered patterns of parenthood in the UK and further afield are underpinned by the strength of an enduring mother/child dyad. Statistical evidence backs up this picture: the vast majority of primary caring parents are mothers, an overriding pattern that places fathers in a more peripheral position in relation to their children (HM Government, 2019). These gendered patterns are not inevitable; as shown in Chapter 1, some Scandinavian states embrace gender equality as the basis for parenting relationships. But to varying degrees these patterns are widespread across international contexts. Mirroring the experiences of contemporary fathers more generally, early parenthood for young fathers is usually mediated through the mothers (and reinforced through the influence of the maternal family). This pattern is perceived as a natural extension of the maternal choices that, as we saw in Chapter 4, led these young men into parenthood in the first place.

As primary caring parents, mothers hold the main responsibility for the care of children, and the power of decision making about how their needs should be met, and who should be involved. Trinder (2008) identifies a range of maternal gatekeeping strategies that may be either passively or proactively used to encourage, discourage or otherwise shape the involvement of fathers. Gate-opening serves to enhance the engagement of fathers, while gate-closing inhibits or prevents such engagement (see also Edin and Nelson, 2013). In Trinder's (2008) study, each strategy and its mode of delivery was shaped by maternal perceptions of a fathers' competence to meet the needs of a child, and the quality of the co-parenting relationship. These strategies were employed by the parents in the Following Young Fathers study and were also utilised by the grandparents (see Chapter 6). They were particularly apparent where relationships between the parents were volatile, or where parents were operating in separate spheres, that is, where they were not partnered or cohabiting.

Mapping co-parenting relationships

At the start of this study, 17 of the 31 young men in the longitudinal sample were in a relationship with the mother, albeit some of these relationships were newly formed or relatively tenuous. In 11 of these cases, the young men had moved in with their partners, including two higher-income young men who had married their partners. The remaining 14 young men were single, having entered parenthood and lone parenthood simultaneously.

By the close of fieldwork, some four years later, 12 of the 17 partnered young men had retained their partnership status; and of these, eight were co-residing with their partner and child. One was married, while a further four saw this as a viable goal for the future (Lau Clayton, 2015). However, five relationships had come to an end, including one of the marriages. Overall, 19 young men were separated from the mothers and attempting to sustain their parenting at a distance. The reasons given by the fathers for separating included disputes and tensions over childcare responsibilities and resources, a growing distance and lack of trust and empathy between the couple, and poor relationships with the maternal family. The duration of these young men's intimate relationships ranged considerably, from two weeks to four years (Lau Clayton, 2015).

The participants described a diverse range of relationships with the mothers of their children, which were fluid and fluctuating over the course of the study. The longitudinal design of this study reveals that neat categories of partnered and single do not always fit the fluid circumstances of these young men: some were loosely partnered and either in unstable relationships or serially partnered with new young women/mothers. Neat categories of living together or apart are also inadequate to describe the flux of living arrangements that occurred for these young parents: frequent changes of abode were evident, with a great deal of to-ing and fro-ing across the grandparental households, interspersed with a variety of other living arrangements (from sofa-surfing with friends to periods in hostel accommodation, see Chapter 8).

Whatever their aspirations to take on the mantle of settled adult lives, these shifting relationships and living conditions reflect the more fleeting and experimental patterns of intimacy that commonly characterise the lives of young people (Tillman et al, 2019). This meant that seemingly established relationships could swiftly unravel, while highly tentative or volatile relationships could suddenly improve. Given the flimsy foundations for parenting experienced by most of these young men, it is perhaps not surprising that there was a sense of precarity and conditionality in the way their relationships unfolded over time.

In these fluid circumstances, the nature and quality of relationships between the young parents presented significant challenges for many of these young men. As shown in Chapter 4, for both partnered and single young men there were notable examples of stable working relationships between the parents, often across two households, which provided the basis for a sustained role as a father. But, at the other end of the spectrum, there were examples of multiple problems that led to constrained, unstable or fragile contact or its cessation over time (Neale and Patrick, 2016).

The typology presented in Figure 5.1 maps variations in the young men's engagement with their children against variations in their relationships with the mothers, enabling a more nuanced understanding of how these two sets of relationships intersect. Our reporting here takes a snapshot of the young men's lives at the close of fieldwork. The grid can be 'read' in varied ways. First, the spectrum of child contact arrangements is represented along the horizontal axis. Two thirds of the sample (21 of 31 young men, located on the left-hand side of the grid) were seeing their children at regular and usually frequent intervals by the close of fieldwork. Second, the spectrum of co-parenting relationships is represented along the vertical axis. 60 per cent of the sample (18 of 31 young men, located in the bottom half of the grid) were experiencing fragile or volatile relationships with the primary caring mothers at this point. In some cases, these relationships were described as highly volatile or non-existent. Tensions between the gendered ideologies of parenting (engaged fatherhood and the mother/child dyad) were particularly evident for these young fathers.

A third way of 'reading' this grid focuses on the different quadrants into which the young men have been placed. This reveals three constellations of co-parenting relationships that pertained at the close of our fieldwork. These groupings are summarised briefly here.

Sustained relationships/sustained contact

The first group of 13 fathers (located in the top left-hand quadrant of the grid) were enjoying sustained contact with their children by the close of fieldwork, in circumstances where they had developed a relatively stable co-parenting relationship with the child's mother. In eight of these cases the young men were partnered, seven of whom were cohabiting. In five of these seven cases, the young men had lived with their partners and children

Figure 5.1: Typology of parenting relationships at close of fieldwork

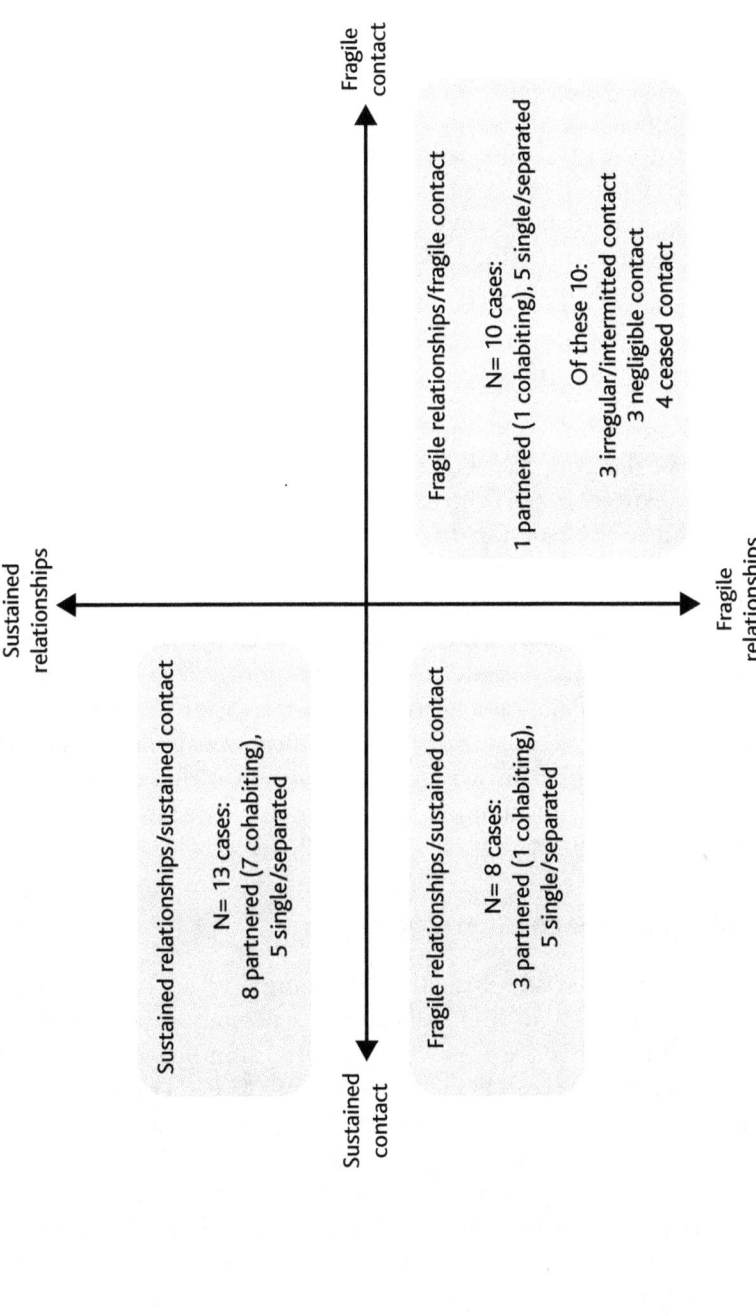

Source: Based on Neale and Patrick, 2016

throughout the course of the study. A further five young men in this group were single; they had sustained a co-parenting relationship despite having separated from the mother during the study, or having never formed a stable relationship with her.

Fragile relationships/sustained contact

The second group of eight fathers (located in the bottom left-hand quadrant of the grid) also had sustained contact with their children, but in circumstances where relationships between the parents were fragile or fluctuating over time. In three of these cases, the parents were partnered (and in one case, cohabiting), while the remaining five young men in this group were single or separated from the mother.

Fragile relationships/fragile contact

The final group of ten young fathers (located in the bottom right-hand quadrant of the grid) had fragile or no contact with their children by the close of fieldwork, in a context where relationships between the parents were highly unstable or non-existent. In nine of these cases, the young men were single or separated from the mothers. By the close of fieldwork, three of these young men had intermittent contact with their children, a further three had negligible contact, while in the remaining four cases, contact had ceased. For this group, the challenges commonly faced by young fathers were magnified. Practical and material barriers were extensive and more severe in their effects. Seven of these ten fathers were leading impoverished lives, marked by varied forms of social deprivation, including periods in care, disengagement from education, training or employment, a lack of a stable home base, mental health problems and offending behaviour.

The dynamics of co-parenting

This mapping exercise reveals that sustaining a relationship with a child does not necessarily go hand in hand with stable relationships between the parents. Moreover, there is no evident correlation between child contact and partnership status or living arrangements. Whether young men were parenting at close hand or at a distance they were striving to work with the mothers to sustain a relationship with their children.

As already noted, this typology presents a snapshot of the young fathers' positions at the close of fieldwork. While we have placed the young men in particular quadrants of the grid, relatively few stayed in one place over time. Ben, for example, began his parenting journey in the Fragile Relationships/Sustained Contact group, reflecting the early tensions that existed in his relationships with the mother, and his own uncertainties about his role as a father. Over time he moved into the Sustained Relationships/Sustained Contact group as relationships improved. Other young men, Iman and Tommy for example, moved in the opposite direction as relationships deteriorated, while Andrew and Adam frequently moved back and forth between these groupings over time as their relationships fluctuated. Similarly, Dominic, who was parenting at a distance, moved from long periods of relative stability to sudden deteriorations when contact with his child was temporarily curtailed. Finally, for young fathers like Jason and Callum, the journey was all downhill; their relationships and contact with their children deteriorated to such an extent that by the end of the study that they had fallen into the Fragile Relationships/Fragile Contact group. This fluidity in the young men's relationships can run counter to the stability needed for parenting, creating extra challenges for young parents.

In order to complement and flesh out the picture produced by this mapping exercise we draw on the accounts of selected young men to illustrate their lived experiences of co-parenting. Following the axis from sustained to fragile relationships, the accounts that follow illustrate the varied and nuanced ways in which these relationships unfold over time. The rather neat categories we have outlined tend to mask the many complexities of these co-parental relationships, and the differences that may arise for those parenting at close hand or at a distance. We also explore in greater depth the barriers to engaged fatherhood that were introduced in Chapter 4: those relating to curtailed contact through a rupture in the parents' relationships, or those associated with offending or child protection issues. As our discussion will show, these barriers are often bound up with a loss of trust and respect between the young parents, issues that are foundational in shaping how young co-parenting relationships unfold and the extent to which they are sustainable over time.

Sustaining relationships at close hand

The young men who were attempting to develop and sustain their co-parenting roles and relationships tended to use the language of 'being there' and 'helping out' to describe their contributions, reflecting a conventionally gendered form of parenthood that is based on complementary roles (Weber 2020: 42). There was a general recognition of the need to support the mothers, as the primary caring parents. Helping out with childcare was part and parcel of what was required. The young men were generally inexperienced in the basics of looking after a baby (feeding, bathing and so on) and they placed little emphasis on related domestic duties (housework, cooking, shopping, laundry; Miller, 2011). Yet many learned the basics of childcare to support the mother and child, sometimes with the help of professionals: "Sterilising milk, changing bums. That sort of basic stuff

I learned from the Family Nurse Partnership … I would have been a lot less prepared. I wouldn't even know how to change a bum" (Adam, aged 16, lower income, partnered). However, supporting the mother involved much more than this. The arrangements worked most effectively where a child's well-being and upbringing became a common and collaborative goal between the parents:

> 'I feel this real sense of responsibility that I have to be successful at something, to make life as easy as possible for my partner and son. It is quite a burden in fairness … Like you've got this weight on your shoulder to do that, so yeah … Generally I think I do an okay job. Like I don't want to say for eighteen I'm a good dad because I don't think that age comes into it. You're defined by what you are, right!' (Zane, aged 18, higher income, partnered, wave 1)

> 'You build a really good respect for each other … Before you were just girlfriend and boyfriend, kind of separate, but now you're conjoined, you're going for a common goal.' (Zane, aged 20, higher income, partnered, wave 2)

Whatever the nature of practical help for the mother, the ability to offer emotional support and build relationships of care and respect for her were seen as key components of effective co-parenting. In some cases, 'being there' meant an emotional and leisure-based engagement with mother and child, which sat alongside a broader commitment to gain employment and provide materially for a young family (see Chapter 7).

As we saw in Chapter 4, the younger men commonly zig zagged between their efforts to take on the mantle of adult responsibilities, and a drift back into their laddish behaviour with their mates. This was the case for Adam, whose relationship with his partner was volatile throughout the study and who resided intermittently with her. Adam saw the need to 'grow up fast' to support his partner and child, but recognised the challenges of putting this into practice:

> 'It's like, sugar, it's happened, I need to grow up major now. So, like, you try to do the best you can to be able to support your baby and your girlfriend … with your relationship. It kind of hits you, "Oh God, I've gotta do this, I've gotta do that".' (Adam aged 15, lower income, partnered, wave 1)

> 'I just couldn't cope. … [I felt] "I need to grow up, I need to do this, I need to do that" and I couldn't do it. It was all at once and it were too much for me. … Last night I went out for a little bit … and then … [partner] was feeding him, changed his nappy and all that. And

then when I got back, she had a little bit of a go at me 'cos she wanted me to be there and help her out and all that. So ... I'm gonna have to help [partner] out by cutting out my social life a bit more. And ... well when he's a bit older if I ... want to do something with my mates I'm not gonna be able to ... 'cos I'd have to do it with [the child]. So, I think, just basically, just cut social life out.' (Adam, aged 16, lower income, partnered, wave 2)

'I went to bed, fell asleep for about two, three hours, then [partner] got back, woke me up straight away. I was like "oh couldn't you have just done him [changed the nappy]" ... We just argue constantly.' (Adam, aged 16, lower income, partnered, wave 3)

'There are no arguments. It's just getting on with each other ... I think it's because I've started pulling my socks up now and being a proper dad and trying to support my partner better. ... Being in a relationship makes things harder. It's just all the stress from everything, and not seeing your mates that much as well.' (Adam, aged 19, lower income, partnered, wave 5)

As shown in Chapter 4, without a magic fast track to adulthood, the transition to responsible parenthood could occur in fits and starts over many years, with ongoing tensions simmering between the parents.

In some of these cases, 'being there' occurred simply by virtue of the young man's presence in a shared household, rather than any staunch commitment to a more 'hands-on' paternal engagement. This was the case for Jax (who by the close of fieldwork remained in the Sustained Relationships/Sustained Contact group). Jax had a history of offending (criminal damage and burglary, including a time when he "smashed up" his mother's house). These events were shaped by significant relational problems in his earlier life. He was regularly "battered" by his mother, whom he rarely saw, disengaged early from school, avoided any form of officialdom (including health visitors and parenting classes) and described anger management problems and an argumentative personality. His partner, Janie (aged 16 during the pregnancy) "stood by him" and "waited for him" during two spells in custody. Jax was on remand for the second time when he learned of the pregnancy. But he was released onto an Intense Supervision Surveillance Programme after six months and was able to be there for the birth of his daughter.

He was one of the few young men in the study who welcomed the pregnancy, seeing it as a way of "making a go of it" with the mother and bettering himself. He moved into his partner's flat shortly after the child was born and was still living there a year later. He described his circumstances during his first interview, when his daughter was three months old:

'I were a totally different guy then ... all I wanted were to just go out and do loads of drugs and just party. ... and then ... I did change. ... I stopped offending, obviously. I stopped drinking altogether. ... If it weren't for my daughter, I'd probably be in jail now ... slip back into my old ways. One of the biggest challenges ... were staying away from my mates, 'cos, obviously, I got into a lot of trouble with them. ... I had to do that for myself and for my daughter ... stop ... being a fucking idiot, basically, do you know what I mean? See, there's a time to grow up, isn't there. ...

When I got Janie pregnant ... I just decided to sort my life out a bit. ... I told her to keep [the baby] straight away ... and we decided we'd try to make a go of it. ... It made our relationship a lot stronger. ... I've never gone a day, like, without seeing [the baby]. ... The longest time Janie's spent away from that kid is about an hour and a half, since she were born. She does everything for her, literally. She's a proper good mum. ... I wind her up sometimes. ... It's a bit horrible ... I say, "she [daughter] loves me more [than you]" ... and all this lot. But I'm only winding her up. ... I don't like to look after [the baby] by myself, just in case, I don't know, 'cos if something happened, I'd just panic. ... I do help to look after her ... get up in the night, but I prefer for someone to be there as well. ... To be a good dad, all you need is just to be there for your kid, just love it, give it attention ... provide and protect, do the man things. ... Everyone goes on that it's really hard ... It's not hard at all ... I love it. It's got its bad times when you're tired ... But you've just got to have patience, 'cos ... all babies do is drink their bottle and then go back to sleep. ... Even if me and Janie split up, I'd still want to be in the baby's life ... but I think while me and Janie are together and we're all living there as a family, I think it's nice. Well, I've got it easy, an alright life, just chilling. ... If you've got a good relationship with the mother ... then you'll have a better relationship with your child.' (Jax, aged 18, partnered, lower income, co-resident, wave 1)

At his second interview nearly a year later, Jax recounted that he had become "proper lazy" and was going out with his mates whenever he wanted. He reported that the mother found this difficult because she was providing more extensive care for a lively and demanding one-year-old. In comparison with the rather rosy picture of family life painted in Jax's first interview, there was now a growing sense of divergence in these young lives, with Jax less engaged with his daughter than he was before. He also revealed that his status as a partner and co-resident parent was conditional upon the strictures laid down by his supervision programme, which were being reinforced by the mother:

'I don't like it when my daughter cries ... she doesn't cry, she proper screams the house down, it's like, fuck! ... I don't like it 'cos I just think like I've done something proper bad to her, something wrong. ... I'm scared to look after her by myself. ... We say it's our kid, but it's just hers really. ... Janie says to me the other day ... if I get with another girl, like if we split up, she ... would not want me to see [the baby]. But if I want to see my daughter I will. ... I'm on the birth certificate, so we've got the same rights. She couldn't stop me anyway, 'cos she's like a fucking five-foot girl ... she isn't going to tell me what I can't [do]! ... She's joking anyway. ... She's not the type of person to make the baby a bargaining chip. ... I can't see her doing that ... unless I did something proper bad – like if she found out ... I were talking to one of my old mates, she'd go mental. ... If I were back on drugs ... she wouldn't let me see the baby. But obviously I'd accept that 'cos I'd think, "it's your own fault, you're a dickhead". That's why I've stopped doing all that stuff.' (Jax, aged 19, partnered, lower income, co-resident, wave 2)

Jax's account suggests that he had few resources to respond directly to the needs of his child and that he relied very heavily on the mother. He was also well aware of his contingent position as a parent. Being there at close hand with his daughter was conditional upon his ability to sustain a good relationship with Janie and keep away from a life of drink, drugs and offending.

Sustaining quality relationships at close hand?

Further complexities arise at this point. Existing evidence on co-parenting suggests that it is the quality of relationships in families, rather than the mechanics of 'contact' that makes a crucial difference to family members (Smart and Neale, 1999; Neale and Flowerdew, 2007). However, parenting at close hand does not necessarily guarantee supportive, high-quality relationships between the young parents or indeed between parent and child. Our findings here are drawn from the accounts of three young men who gradually disclosed relationship problems to the researchers, including controlling and abusive behaviour between the parents. Darren, one of the older fathers in the study, had long been in a joint household with his partner and their first child, who was now of school age. Throughout the study, Darren fell into the Sustained Relationships/Sustained Contact group, ostensibly showing a great deal of stability in his family life. However, during the latter stages of the study, social care teams had been contacted by the child's school over allegations of Darren's physical abuse of the child. A home visit also resulted in serious concerns about the squalor of the family home. By the close of fieldwork, both parents had been referred for compulsory parenting classes.

Similar circumstances were in place for two teenage parents, Adam and Andrew, both of whom fell into the Fragile Relationships/Sustained Contact group for most of the study. Relationships with the mothers were volatile and sometime violent throughout the study period, with the fathers moving in and out of the mothers' homes. In both cases social services intervention involved child protection plans, placements on parenting and domestic violence programmes and periods of supervised contact for the fathers:

> 'It's a lot lot better [now]. Me and Jade went through a stage of … of … of domestic violence in past. … and it was in front of [daughter] – it isn't a nice thing to see, obviously. And that's all stopped … I mean, we have us ups and downs. … Both of us went through a court hearing about it. And we got put on a parenting course and … completed it now. … Not only do we have to stop arguing just for [daughter] but for me and Jade as well.' (Andrew, aged 19, lower income, partnered, wave 4)

Like Jax and Darren, these young men had socially disadvantaged backgrounds: poor family relationships, mental health and anger management problems ("smashing up" doors) and few resources or relational skills to fashion supportive, trusting adult relationships. These young fathers expressed love for their children and pride in their parenting commitments. They were able to maintain close relationships with their children by virtue of their close ties to the mothers and their residence (intermittently) in a shared household. However, where co-parenting relationships were volatile, these close-at-hand relationships could mask ongoing oppression and domestic violence in these young families.

Sustaining relationships at a distance

We have seen that parenting at close hand does not necessarily guarantee mutually respectful, high-quality relationships between the young parents or indeed between parent and child. Equally, it should not be assumed that parenting at a distance (where parents are not partnered and living separately) entails poor quality or unsustainable co-parenting. As shown in Chapter 1, parenting at a distance is a common practice among young fathers. It involves developing a relationship with a child without the advantage of a stable home or a closely aligned couple relationship as the basis for a joint parenting project.

In these circumstances, co-parenting takes on a different meaning. For the young fathers in this study, it meant fostering enduring friendships with the mothers as the basis for securing an ongoing relationship with a child:

> 'As long as you've got that strong friendship, or strong bond together, and that togetherness, you don't need to be in a relationship.' (Senwe, aged 17, higher income, single, wave 4)

'I think separating is just a thing that people use as an excuse. We are separated and we do get along and we do what we need to do. ... I probably do more than people who actually live with their kids in the house. ... it's like the best bond you can have [with your child].' (Orlando, aged 24, lower income, single, wave 1)

With shaky foundations for their parenting, single young men often had to work harder than partnered fathers to build trust and respect for their co-parent. They described a number of strategies to make it work, including being open and honest, listening and compromising on decision making, showing respect for the mother, providing financial support or goods in kind where possible, and being flexible with visiting or childcare arrangements. In effect, these forms of co-parenting relied on the young men 'being there' emotionally and materially for the mothers, as well as for their children.

Building trust and respect does not occur overnight; it often requires patience on the part of the young men, a capacity to bide their time. Ben, for example, split up with the mother during her pregnancy, leaving tensions between them. For the first year, he was only able to visit his child at the maternal home (see Chapter 6) but he was eventually able to take his child out on his own and care for her at his parents' home. A key factor in this change was the improved relationship with the mother: "We get on really well. ... She is one of my closest friends, actually, and we can talk about pretty much anything" (Ben, aged 21, higher income, wave 2). The fact that Ben was studying for a degree, with good socio-economic prospects, and enjoyed well-resourced and stable relationships with his own parents, may well have helped. His credentials for his future as a father were impeccable.

Over time, other young men who were fathering at a distance managed to develop an element of shared care with the primary caring mothers across two households, with their child regularly visiting or staying with them overnight during the week or at weekends. This meant that they had to develop a much more direct and hands-on role in caring for their child than those young men who were co-resident; their parenting was less directly mediated by the mothers.

Jock, for example, had moved into his parents' well-resourced house with the mother and his son after the birth, but tensions in the household soon led the young couple to separate and for the mother to take the child back to her own family. By the close of fieldwork, Jock was seeing his child every night at the maternal grandparents' home, and his son came to stay with him for one night per week. He described the relationship with the mother as:

'On and off. ... Very casual at the moment, yeah, getting along absolutely fine but she wants to make another go of it. ... So I says, "look, you know, I can't see us being together at the moment, but

I really want us to, you know, get along, I still want us to, at the very least, be friends. I don't want my son growing up with a mum and dad that hate each other". I just want to make it as amicable and friendly as we can, even if we aren't together.' (Jock, aged 20 higher income, single, wave 1)

By wave 2, a year later, Jock was veering back towards a relationship with the mother (see Chapter 8). Sustaining a supportive relationship with her during these early years gave Jock a chance to consolidate his relationship with his child. A follow-up interview, conducted six years later under the Following Young Fathers Further (FYFF) study, showed that over time he had established a stable relationship with the mother and child, and had also moved on in his own life and found a new partner.

Fragile relationships at a distance

For other young men who were parenting at a distance, securing a co-parenting relationship was very difficult. In each case the problems were bound up with the fragility of trust and respect between the parents. Eight of the young men in this study found that their contact with their child was curtailed by gate-closing mothers. The circumstances in which this occurred varied. Dominic, who fell into the Fragile Relationships/Sustained Contact group throughout this study, had looked after his baby son on a weekly basis at his parent's home. But when his son was a year old, this arrangement came to an end when he decided to end his relationship with the mother. At the age of 18 he sought help from the family courts to reinstate contact. This resulted in a mediated agreement that enabled Dominic to have his child to stay every other weekend. He was helped in this in no small measure by his stable home environment (with his parents), his office employment, which gave him good credentials as a provider, the high quality of his care for his child, and his perseverance in attempting to negotiate with the mother:

> 'I feel the strain of not having an off switch. ... Either I'm too wrapped up in my child, and I'm just constantly stressed 'cos I'm worrying about stuff. I don't want my former partner messing me about, I need to get to work, I need to earn money. Then, there's the balance of "oh, I'll go see my mates" ... Sometimes I just want to literally go off the rails, and to forget all the worries and stress that's come from having a child. ...
>
> I found out, ultimately, that I wasn't going to be happy in that relationship, [but] it became quite hard to maintain a separate parent relationship. ... She's tried to make life as hard as possible for me with our son. ... Since he's been born, I've always wanted to be there ... to take

on the responsibilities ... I've always been supportive of us both being there. ... But it's turned into a fight, which I didn't want. She's sort of forced the issue purely out of spite. And emotionally it's been draining. ... I don't involve myself now in her life. ... I've no interest in it, 'cos of what she's done.' (Dominic, aged 18, single, higher income, wave 1)

Having to fight for the right to see his child impacted on Dominic's willingness to co-parent amicably. In the aftermath of the legal proceedings, he stuck rigidly to the mediated agreement, rather than working flexibly with the mother. His narratives, gathered over the years, reflect a gradual settling in the relationship with the mother:

'We're civil now. We can have conversations. I think she's grown up and we've become more of a team. I think she sees me more as a form of support as opposed to being someone against her. ... [But] I haven't felt like I've had that sustained period where I've enjoyed being a father because of the issues that's come with it.' (Dominic, aged 20, single, wave 4)

Despite reaching some equilibrium with his co-parenting there was little sense that Dominic could ever forge a friendship with the mother. Follow-up interviews, generated six years later for the FYFF study, reveals that while he continued to share the care of his son, there had been a further cessation of contact linked to a dispute over maintenance payments. Overall, there were emotional costs for Dominic in managing such a volatile relationship over many years.

Several other young men in the study had their contact with their children curtailed when relationships between the parents came to an end, when either parent was seeking a new partner, or where the mothers moved away, creating a geographical barrier to contact. Where trust and respect between the parents had broken down, it was much harder to rekindle a co-parenting relationship. These young men reported feeling sidelined or excluded by the mothers and/or the maternal family (see Chapter 6), and by practitioners, who would commonly take their lead from the mothers (Neale and Davies, 2015b):

'I feel like I've been replaced. ... It's hard. I used to see [daughter] every day. And then I've gone from seeing her on the weekend, to not seeing her at all. She [the mother] has bullied me out really.' (Richard, aged 18, lower income, single)

'She were just ... well, making me last as long as I can without seeing [the twins]. She'd do owt to stop me. And, well, it's about, going on three years I've been to court now. I get to see them once a week now, on a Saturday. ... I feel, fair enough, she wants a new boyfriend ... and live a life with him. I ain't really bothered about that. But I'm bothered about her not wanting me to see the kids. It should be fair to let me have 'em, well, not when I want, but at least part of the day, and then things would be fine.' (Callum, aged 21, lower income, single, supervised contact, wave 4)

These young men expressed anguish at not being able to see their children and in being given so little recognition as parents. The contingent state of their parenthood could also be reinforced where a mother re-partnered. Wider evidence (see Chapter 1) suggests that relationships between young men and the mothers of their children may become more distant over time. This does not necessarily lead to loss of contact with a child. However, this outcome is more likely where relationships of trust and respect between the parents (and by extension with the parents' families) cannot be sustained (as was the case for Jimmy and Simon, reported in Chapter 4).

A curtailing of contact may be triggered not only by parental separation or re-partnering; it may also be driven by a mother's concerns over the capacity of young men to be good parents, particularly where there is domestic violence, dependency on drugs or alcohol, and/or fears of physical or emotional harm to a child (see also Caldwell and Antonucci, 1997; Smart and Neale, 1999; Reeves et al, 2009). These concerns may be reinforced by the widespread 'deficit' labelling of these young men.

Teasing out these different scenarios is not always easy; they may occur in combination. Jason, who had fallen into the Fragile Relationships/Fragile Contact group by the close of fieldwork, provides a useful illustration of these complex issues. This young man had multiple problems in his earlier life, including time spent in prison. He was parenting at a distance over most of the study period, in a context of ongoing tensions with Carla, the mother of his child:

'I'm sick of [her] changing the times ... [During a telephone argument over contact] I heard her mum in the background ... "tell him he's immature and he needs to grow up". So I said to her, "tell your mum, immature is not wanting to see your son, and not caring. Mature is wanting to see your son and asking why the times have been changed".' (Jason, aged 22, lower income, single, wave 1)

Jason also recounted some of the "silly arguments and fall outs" that he had with Carla, which he reflected on further in his second interview:

'I went home after I spoke to you, and I just thought about how I'd spoken and how it must have looked. ... It sounded crazy. So, I ... said [to her], how we've been acting childish, and all that … and that we just need to get along for [son's] sake. … I said, "we've got a son and it's all about him". And we weren't arguing … and now she's just like a different girl. We go and meet each other, drop [son] off. Yesterday, we went for a walk round park, we make arrangements and stick to them. It seems a lot better, and we wouldn't have been able to do that before. … I knew what were happening were wrong. It's like we're mates now, good mates.' (Jason, aged 22, lower income, single, wave 2)

This cultivation of a friendship was greatly valued by Jason. As shown in Chapter 4, Carla had remained supportive during Jason's second prison sentence and had facilitated his contact with his son. But subsequently she turned from gate-opener to gate-closer. By wave 3, when Jason was building his bond with his son, he reported that Carla curtailed contact whenever she learned of his attempts to move into another relationship. By the end of the study (by which time the couple had a second child; see Chapter 4) contact was curtailed once again. The problems had escalated when Carla sent Jason an inflammatory text about his son's feelings towards him, to which he responded with a loss of temper and threatening behaviour. With a previous record of violent offences, he was given a restraining order that reinforced the blocked contact.

Jason's anguish at this turn of events was evident in our last interview with him, when he seemed to be at breaking point:

'I'd love to be able to get on with her. … Obviously she's my kids' mum. … I still respect and care about her, but I kind of hate her as well. … I would love to be a family, love to wake up with them in the morning, but … If you aren't [suited] then you can't just make it work for the kids. …

She uses our son as a weapon when we don't get on. It's the only way she can hurt me. … I don't even know where the kids are. … She's got all the power … I've got no power whatsoever. I don't have a leg to stand on. … I … kept on her case. I contacted solicitors. They've stopped legal aid now but at the time they'd not. So I thought, "this is my last chance". I've rung her. I said, … "I want to see [child]. I really don't want to take you to court. Can we not just have this one last chance?" …

I were constantly begging, "please let me see them". … And then it'd be, like, "I've got £50, can I come and see them?" Those were the times when she were letting me. … Once I rang her and I were crying. I said, "you don't know what you are doing to me. It's breaking me".

> ... I don't want them growing up, seeing tension between us. That's the last thing I want. ...
>
> I've just felt like giving up, and just not trying. But then I think I owe it to my son ... just for him to know that I care. ... I know I'm not the best dad in the world, and I don't even work. But I'd still always care about them, and I'd never let them down. ... I'm going through double the heartache. ... Sometimes I just think about, like, going to nursery and taking my son ... but I know it'd cause more problems than its worth. ... It just hurts bad.' (Jason, aged 25, lower income, single, wave 4)

Fathering at a distance is not simply a geographical state. It is a relational and experiential state that in such challenging and volatile circumstances may produce severe anguish for young fathers.

Concluding discussion

In this chapter we have highlighted the significance of relational factors in shaping young men's parenting journeys. Their capacity to develop an effective relationship with their co-parent is a pivotal issue that determines how and to what extent they can 'be there' for their children (Edin and Nelson, 2013). In effect, being an engaged father is not simply about being there for a child; it depends on being there, at least to some degree, for the mother. Our evidence suggests that co-parenting relationships are more likely to be effective where they are founded on mutual trust and respect between the parents. The quality and conduct of these relationships are vital factors, but they are often overlooked in discussions about the involvement of young fathers in their children's lives. As we have seen, 17 of the young fathers in this study were attempting to parent at a distance by the close of fieldwork, and the majority were grappling with relatively fragile or volatile relationships, reflecting the shaky ground upon which many of these relationships were forged in the first place. In these circumstances, sustaining a co-parenting relationship can be a particular challenge.

Turning to the broader context of gendered ideologies of parenthood, our findings point to the continued strength of the mother/child dyad as the basis for organising the care of a child: a presumed essentialist tie between mothers and their children to which fathers or father substitutes can be serially and conditionally attached. However, this well-established ethos is increasingly in tension with the newer ethos of engaged fatherhood. The tensions are present to some degree for all parents, but they may become polarised for young parents, especially where young men are parenting at a distance (across households) and without a closely aligned relationship with the mothers, or where there are concerns over their behaviour and mental health. Fatherhood for these young men was conditional, requiring them to prove their credentials as parents who could support both mother and child. Clearly the idea of engaged fatherhood as an unquestionable good or an inherent right, regardless of the circumstances and the *quality* of parent–child and mother–father relationships, does not stand up to scrutiny. In the tenuous circumstances in which young men become parents, engaged fatherhood is likely to remain a contingent state.

We have seen that achieving an effective co-parenting arrangement relies on good relational skills. It requires cooperation, tact, mutual respect and trust, flexibility, the ability to negotiate and compromise, emotional maturity and a joint focus on the needs of the child. It requires much more than simply 'being there'. Such relational skills need a certain level of confidence, and they have to be inculcated over time and put into practice by both young parents. The young men in this study had had variable opportunities to acquire, test out or hone such skills. Those who were at the younger end of our age range and less well-resourced struggled to put these skills into practice. For those involved in offending, anger management, or abusive behaviour and domestic violence, the problems were all the greater. We have seen, too, the anguish felt by young men who hold dear to the ethos of engaged fatherhood but lack the capacity to turn it into practice. While effective co-parenting relationships can help to bridge the gap between the competing ideologies of engaged fatherhood and the mother/child dyad, across our sample these ideologies continued to exist in uneasy tension with each other (Dermott and Miller, 2015).

At the same time, we have seen that many of these young fathers were developing distinctive moral scripts around good fatherhood. Alongside their commitment to 'stepping up', and 'being there' for their children, they were promoting ideals of friendship, respect and teamwork with the mother, particularly when they were co-parenting at a distance. In this way, they were asserting the viability of non-partnered parenthood that operates across separate households. And they were challenging the idea that 'being there' for a mother and child necessarily means being in an intimate and exclusive relationship with the mother. As their accounts show, they commonly denigrated what they saw as the dubious maternal practice of using a child as a weapon in disputes over money, lifestyles or a father's exclusive commitment to the mother.

These moral scripts were not operating simply at an ideological level; they were feeding into and unsettling young parenting practices and negotiating processes. In effect the young men were actively seeking to move on from a deficit view of young fatherhood (Jaffee et al, 2001; Weber, 2020). Despite the inherent tensions, this suggests that the ethos of engaged fatherhood may slowly gain ground for these young parents and, in future, could take a more established place alongside the primary caring role of mothers.

More broadly, our evidence suggests that, in terms of gendered ideologies and expectations, the contemporary context in which men become fathers is more fluid than in previous times, offering new possibilities for younger generations of men (Miller, 2011; Tarrant, 2021; Andreasson et al, 2023). There is evidence to suggest a gradual generational and cultural shift towards engaged fatherhood, alongside increasing recognition of the value of co-parenting (Brannen and Nilsen, 2006; Dermott and Miller, 2015), especially in post-separation contexts (Elke Graf and Wojnicka, 2023). The evidence presented here for the engagement of many young fathers in the lives of their children is part of this growing trend and represents the incremental steps through which wider transformations may eventually occur.

Finally, ideological assumptions about the gendering of parenthood not only underpin family practices: they also form the backdrop to decision making in policy and professional practice (see Chapter 2), and in the resolution of parental disputes in family law (MoJ, 2020). A greater awareness in policy and professional practices of the gendered dynamics of early parenthood, the competing ideologies at play, and issues of the quality and integrity of co-parenting relationships, seen from the perspectives of both parents, would help to inform policy responses and provide a platform for more tailored interventions.

Our findings on the quality of co-parenting relationships also have implications for the provision of parenting support programmes. We have seen that where professional concerns are raised about the quality of parental and parent/child relationships, parents are likely to be referred to compulsory parenting or domestic violence programmes. However, preventative parenting programmes, delivered as part of early intervention strategies, are much less evident, including professional provision that focuses on co-parenting (Mollborn and Jacobs, 2015). As shown in Chapter 4, there is currently very little provision of a generic nature for the development of relational and parenthood skills, and even less that is tailored to the particular needs of young fathers. The evidence presented here reinforces just how important such provision is, and why its delivery, through a variety of specialist and generic routes, including relationship counselling, maternity and post-natal services, and Relationship and Sex Education in schools and other community settings, is an urgent matter. This would give young people the opportunity to develop the vital relational skills that they need to develop as future partners and parents.

The relational and gendered dimensions of early parenthood highlighted in this chapter also extend to and are reflected in wider family relationships across the generations. Having touched upon these issues in Chapters 4 and 5, we now turn to an exploration of these important intergenerational themes.

6

Reconfiguring families: intergenerational care and support?

Introduction

In this chapter the relational themes introduced in Chapter 5 are broadened to consider the wider constellation of family relationships that impact on the trajectories of young fathers. Drawing on earlier findings (Neale and Lau Clayton, 2014), a secondary analysis of the Following Young Fathers (FYF) dataset (see Chapter 3), and longitudinal data generated under the Following Young Fathers Further (FYFF) study, we examine the shifting nature of intergenerational relationships in these young men's families. Existing knowledge comes largely from the accounts of grandparents; there is very little evidence on how these relationships are perceived and experienced by young parents, especially by young fathers (Tan et al, 2010; Neale and Lau Clayton, 2014).

Drawing on the young men's perspectives, we chart how the grandparent generation reacted to news of the pregnancy; their engagement and influence in decision making; the kinds of support – practical, financial and emotional – provided for the young men; and how gendered patterns of care (or neglect) and support (or interference) may evolve or dissipate over time. We place our evidence in the context of broader debates about family relationships and we consider the implications for family policy and professional practice, in a context where grandparent care is increasingly assumed and relied upon by state agencies.

Grandparenting and intergenerational family relationships in contemporary society

Research into intergenerational chains of family members, who are held together 'vertically' by their genealogical ties, has increased in recent years, offering insights into the interconnecting lives, influences, legacies and internal dynamics of those who are linked through the bonds of kinship (Neale, 2021a). Family trajectories are interlocking, with the fortunes of each generation (changes in relationships, employment, health, housing and parental status) impacting on the lives of both older and younger family members. More broadly, intergenerational relationships of care or neglect, closeness or distance, are formed and transformed in different socio-cultural and historical contexts

(Brannen and Nilsen, 2006; Neale, 2021a). As we will show, these patterns are also fluid and evolve within individual families over time.

An important tranche of this research has focused on the role of grandparents in contemporary societies and their informal family practices (Arber and Timonen, 2012). As societies have aged, growing numbers of grandparents are engaging in childcare, adding to the complexity of family structures and relationships (Arber and Timonen, 2012). In these contexts, grandparent practices have diversified, reflecting a spectrum from occasional caring to legal guardianship (Tarrant et al, 2017). Grandparenting is also a gendered experience (Arber and Timonen, 2012; Tarrant, 2014; Mann et al, 2015). Traditionally, it has been seen as synonymous with the care provided by grandmothers (Mann et al, 2012). Yet more recent evidence demonstrates how grandmothers and grandfathers practise their roles in different ways. In later life, grandfathers may be more directly involved than they were as fathers (Tarrant, 2012, 2014; Buchanan and Rotkirch, 2016).

For young parents and their children, both sets of grandparents are likely to play a significant role. Paternal grandparents provide important practical and economic help and housing for young fathers and enable ongoing contact between them and their children (Shepherd et al, 2011; Neale and Lau Clayton, 2014; Tarrant, 2021). Maternal grandmothers continue to be the most consistent providers of support to young mothers, with up to 60 per cent of teen mothers living with or heavily relying on their own mothers. While grandfathers have received limited sociological attention, they may act as significant role models or reference points for young men's own actions, as well as giving other forms of practical and economic help (Tarrant, 2012, 2014; Mann et al, 2016).

In some disadvantaged communities, older women may provide informal kinship care (as the main carers or substitute parents) to successive cohorts of young children, sometimes over decades. They can strengthen fragile parent–child relationships and enable young parents to find and sustain employment (Ben-Galim and Silim, 2013). This has been described as a rescue-and-repair model of grandparenting, far removed from the leisure-pleasure model that is based on family gatherings, top-up childcare and babysitting (Hughes and Emmel, 2011; Hughes and Tarrant, 2023). It has particular salience in a context where young people enter parenthood when they are still dependent themselves. The extent and impact of grandparental involvement is likely to be all the greater for young fathers who are in their teens and still at school.

Beyond the family, this blurring of care across the generations may go largely unnoticed and unrecognised. Yet it is likely to be relatively common, especially where there is a close layering of the generations: that is, where grandparents entered parenthood early in their lives, and are relatively young (commonly aged 35–55) when their children become parents (Emmel and Hughes, 2014). This early entry into grandparenthood and compression of the generations is a relatively common feature of family life in disadvantaged communities, generating distinctive patterns of intergenerational parenting (Emmel and Hughes, 2014; Neale and Lau Clayton, 2014).

It is worth observing here that these intertwined patterns of intergenerational care are perceived in some policy and professional discourses as the defining feature of a 'cycle of deprivation' that is perpetuated down the generations. This notion, coined by Keith Joseph, Conservative secretary of state for social services in the early 1970s, holds that poverty and disadvantage are the product of psycho-social factors – family lifestyles and cultures that fall outside respectable norms of middle-class behaviour, creating a presumed underclass marked by moral decline and disorder. The root cause of this cycle is seen as a failure of parenting (Welshman, 2008). The notion of a 'a long-standing culture of early pregnancy' (DfES, 2006b: 37) that cannot easily be dismantled, continues to find a voice. For example, it has fed into a fatalistic and neglectful view among health professionals that 'you'll never stop young people round here getting pregnant' (reported and critiqued in McNulty, 2010: 111).

This is part of the wider social deficit framework of understanding that stigmatises young parents, along with their families of origin (see Chapters 1, 2 and 4). While researchers generally eschew notions of entrenched cycles of deprivation, the idea is occasionally resurrected by young fatherhood researchers (see, for example, Pirog et al, 2018 and Donald et al, 2022). Pirog et al (2018: 318–19), observe that, 'pre-existing deficits ... in childhood and early adolescence are predictive of becoming a teenage father, and having become a teenage father is predictive of subsequent disadvantage'. In such accounts, young fatherhood becomes the lynchpin through which socio-economic disadvantage is perpetuated down the generations.

As we saw in Chapter 2, numerous critiques of such thinking point instead to persistent structural inequalities that shape and reshape low-income families over time (Macdonald et al, 2020). Creative forms of intergenerational care and support are the necessary responses to successive cycles of structural inequalities. In policy circles, grandparents are commonly viewed as a key resource, a form of social capital for young parents that is too often taken for granted (Griggs, 2010). However, the nature of grandparent support, and the extent to which it is sustainable and relied upon over time, is much less clear. The notion that relations of care and support inevitably flow down the generations may or may not be the case – with implications for the provision of professional services for young parents. Moreover, reliance on the older generation can result in a 'missing generation in the middle', with a double care burden for the grandparents, particularly where they step in to keep families together and avoid their grandchildren being fostered. In these circumstances, kinship care can impact negatively on the grandparents' health, income and future lives. Concerns have been raised about the stress felt by younger grandparents who juggle work and leisure lives with caring responsibilities, especially where they face higher levels of disadvantage and poverty (Tarrant et al, 2017; Hunt, 2018; Hughes and Tarrant, 2023). This clearly becomes a multigenerational family matter rather than a challenge for young parents alone.

The intergenerational characteristics of the sample

As reported earlier, 21 of the 31 young fathers were from lower-income families, and the remainder from higher-income families. Paternal grandparents were employed mainly in semi-skilled or low-skilled occupations, while in six families, grandparents were long-term unemployed and receiving out-of-work benefits. Wider evidence has shown that most young fathers have strong, locally based kin ties and enduring relationships with their families (Quinton et al, 2002; Ross et al, 2010). This was the case for the vast majority of these young men: only two had tenuous links with their birth families, having spent part of their childhoods in the care system. Paternal grandmothers played a significant role in the lives of these young men and invested heavily in supporting their sons and grandchildren. Relationships with paternal grandfathers were more variable. Only four young men were living with their birth fathers at the time of first interview, while eight young men reported poor or neglectful relationships with them.

By the end of the fieldwork 15 young fathers were living with their parents, while a further three were living with their partner and child in the home of the maternal grandparents. The remaining 13 young men were living independently in the same localities. These patterns evolved in highly varied ways over the course of the study, with considerable movements in and out of parental homes and across households (Neale and Ladlow, 2015b; see Chapter 8).

Family circumstances and relationships for the older generation also varied across the sample. The young men reported that eight paternal grandparents were in stable relationships, while in the remaining cases, grandparents were separated or widowed – although the majority had re-partnered and had more children. Based on the young fathers' reports, at least a third of the paternal grandparents were under the average age of grandparenthood, that is, in their late 30s to mid-40s, as opposed to their 50s. In at least ten cases, a close layering of the generations was evident: entry into early parenthood (under the age of 25) was a feature of the lives of the grandparent as well as the parent generation and also evident among the siblings of the young parents.

Reactions to news of a pregnancy

In a context where young parenthood is highly stigmatised and associated with negative outcomes for young people, it is not surprising that most grandparents expressed dismay or disappointment when a pregnancy was disclosed. Since most of the pregnancies were unplanned and conceived in otherwise fragile relationships with the mothers, they were also unexpected. Concerns over how grandparents would react to the news of a pregnancy were major preoccupations of these young men, especially where they were still in their mid-teens. Only five grandparents were reported to be happy with the news. As other researchers have found (Shepherd et al, 2011; Brown, 2016) they were particularly shocked or disappointed where the parents-to-be were of school age or were planning to enter, or had entered, further or higher education. This was the case even where they had been young parents themselves.

Manuel's mother, for example, gave birth to Manuel in her mid teens, and become a grandmother at the age of 33. Unusually for this sample, Manuel used this to justify his own entry into parenthood at the age of 17:

> 'My dad just went, 'oh, wasn't there, like, any protection? And I said to him ... 'you didn't use protection, so why are you moaning at me now? And he was like, 'yeah, yeah'. ... My mum didn't say nothing, 'cos she had me when she was ... just 16 ... so I just thought, if she can afford it, then I can afford it as well'. (Manuel, aged 18, lower income, partnered, wave 1)

Negative reactions were regarded as natural and a display of care and concern by some young men, while others found themselves subjected to anger and condemnation:

> '[It was a] shock for them. 'Cos at my age, at my point in life, circumstance wise, education wise, that wasn't the right time for, for me to come with the news that, like a baby was on the way. But I think that's a natural reaction if they care about someone.' (Dominic, aged 20, conceived a child at the age of 16, wave 3)

> 'Oh, my mum went crazy and she was like "if you can't look after him, I'll take him on as my own, but he'll still be calling you both mum and dad" and all this. ... Her mum and dad wanted me dead, literally! ... My stepdad was like, "yeah, you've screwed up your life".' (Darren, aged 22, lower income, partnered, wave 3)

Paternal grandfathers, some of whom were stepfathers, tended to focus on the impact of a new baby on the financial and employment futures of the young men. They reinforced the need for the young men to find work as a means of fast-tracking into adulthood. As shown in Chapters 4 and 7, it was a message that young men themselves readily took on board. Richard's account of his father's response illustrates this theme:

So you said your dad was mad at first. Do you know why he was mad initially?

'I don't know. He just … he were. I could just tell. … [he said] "Gonna have to buck your ideas up now aren't you?"'

What did he mean by that then?

'Stop being naughty at school and stuff. Get a job. All he says to me "get a job".' (Richard, aged 16, lower income, partnered, not cohabiting, wave 1)

Maternal grandfathers also tended to blame the young men for the pregnancies, and would sometimes respond with anger, thereby reinforcing the stigma of the young men's position (see Dominic and Alex, later). However, the precise influence of grandfathers on young fathers-to-be is complex. As we saw in Chapter 4, young fathers' aspirations to be there for their children were often couched in terms of a desire to do things differently from their own fathers, who had not been there for them. Yet in other cases they looked up to the father figures in their lives and saw them as role models:

'Me stepdad knows loads o' different trades, he started off as a mechanic. So as I were growing up I learned mechanics with him and that. And I were doing up motorbikes and all that lot. So I wanted to do that. And then I went and did work experience in a garage. … He's always brought me up doing the trade stuff and all that lot. Like he's a right grafter and that and he decorates house proper nice and all that lot. And he's, he's learned me all these skills and that. And it's really helped in me life, so yeah.' (Callum, aged 19, lower income, repartnered, wave 2)

Whether the young men were seeking to emulate their fathers (or father figures) or to distance themselves from them, the actions of the older generation became a benchmark against which to establish their own priorities and aspirations.

In contrast to the grandfathers, maternal grandmother reactions were more generally bound up with the pros and cons of terminating a pregnancy, reflecting their greater role in decision making and care of a new baby. Despite uniform expressions of disapproval and concern, they exerted a great deal of influence over these decisions (see Chapter 4). Seven young men who discussed a termination with the young mothers-to-be, for example, were upset to find the decisions reversed, and their wishes and feelings dismissed. In some cases, the moral and religious scruples of the maternal grandmothers were major considerations:

'Her mother is very religious and Catholic. She managed to persuade my ex-girlfriend to not have an abortion.' (Dominic, aged 18, higher income, single, wave 3)

'Her mum didn't want her to [have an abortion]. My ex-girlfriend probably thought, "my mum knows best". You're going to listen to your mum, aren't you?' (Callum, aged 19, lower income, single, wave 1)

'Her mum started saying "oh you need to think about it because if you get rid of it, it's just like killing somebody". So, she just decided to keep it. And now her mum and her nanna have a go, saying "oh you shouldn't have had him if you can't look after him". But they were the ones that said all that to her. And they seem to forget that.' (Jimmy, aged 16, lower income, partnered, wave 3)

It is worth drawing out two observations from these accounts. First, the reactions to the pregnancy by the grandparents indicate the momentous change that entry into young parenthood entails for both generations. Like the parents, grandparents also undergo a period of adjustment to resolve their ambivalence over the pregnancy. As we will show, this is in large part linked to the degree of perceived and actual commitment that they will need to make to support their child and new grandchild. Where grandparents have responsibilities for teenage or school-age young parents, who may need substantial amounts of support themselves, the commitments of the older generation are all the greater.

Second, the responses of grandparents are shaped in relation to gendered and generational patterns of care and support. As Chapters 4 and 5 show, mothers are seen as the primary decision makers regarding the continuation of a pregnancy. Our evidence here shows that, by extension, it is the maternal grandparents – particularly grandmothers – who exercise agency in these decisions, creating a marked contrast with the agency of the young men and their families. A clear pattern emerges whereby decision making and hands-on responsibility flow vertically down the generations, particularly in the maternal household, rather than flowing horizontally between the young parents themselves (Neale and Lau Clayton, 2014). These transitions, then, are critical moments in which gendered ideologies and assumptions are transmitted down the generations, from parent to child. In the process, the primacy of the mother/child dyad and the inequalities that it generates between mothers and fathers are reinforced, leaving the young men in a more peripheral position in relation to their children. As we show, once these early patterns of influence and control are established during the pregnancy, they can set the pattern for the subsequent care of a child.

Birth as a turning point

Regardless of the presence or otherwise of the young men, 11 maternal grandmothers were chosen as the birthing partners of their daughters, while a paternal grandmother who had been housing her son and his partner, had also planned to be there (but arrived too late):

> 'She decided that she wanted her mum to be her birthing partner rather than me.' (Ben, aged 20, higher income, single, wave 1)

> 'Her mother was there as well.' (Cade, aged 21, lower income, partnered, wave 1)

> 'Her mum tried to be there for the birth. But I weren't having none of it if you know what I mean. And yeah so, her mum always came to the appointments, but she never actually went into the room for the scans and stuff. It were always just me and her for the scans if you know what I mean. I think that's actually brought us closer together ... and made bonds stronger between us both ... So having her mum there is sort of like, yeah, ruins the scene ... and makes it, makes me uncomfortable.' (Darren, aged 23, lower income, partnered, wave 4)

Darren's retrospective account nicely reflects the tensions that may arise between the vertical flow of support and influence down the generations, and the horizontal flow between the parents themselves. In such cases, co-parenting as a joint parental project (see Chapter 5) may be recast as a co-parental relationship that runs across successive generations of mothers, daughters and babies, creating a clear division between the responsibilities and influence of the maternal and paternal households.

Grandparental support

By the time of the birth, most grandparents were reported to be reconciled to the arrival of a new baby and had made a commitment to support their child and grandchild. Wider evidence suggests that grandparents are generally positive about their grandchildren, and often go on to form deep attachments to them, even where the pregnancy was initially seen as problematic (Kirkman et al, 2001; Sadler and Clemmens, 2004; Brown, 2016). As Ross et al (2010) argue, the arrival of a grandchild can bring families together, creating stronger ties or repairing broken ones across the generations. In line with traditional gendered roles, maternal grandmothers are most often directly involved in the provision of emotional and practical support during the pregnancy and birth, and in the early years of a child's life.

In 23 of these cases, both sets of grandparents were described as significant providers of practical, emotional and financial support. In the majority of these cases their support was sustained and in five cases it increased over time. Grandmothers, particularly in the maternal home, were the main source of support, striving to ensure basic standards of care for the baby, and encouraging the young parents to develop their parenting skills. Paternal grandmothers also provided practical help, and were the most consistent source of emotional support for the young men, that is, talking things through, listening and offering advice (Tan et al, 2010). They were usually better confidantes than the young men's peers, who would not necessarily understand the issues at stake.

But grandfathers, both paternal and maternal, also played a role in supporting the parenting efforts of the young men and offering guidance on strategies for engaging with their co-parent:

'I've walked in on [partner's dad] holding him, just singing him to sleep. And I'm like "oh that's proper cute". And I'm thinking 'I think I should do that'. I did it last night, it didn't work for me! It's usually her dad that comes out [at night]. And just stands there or sits there downstairs rocking him like this, seeing to him till he goes to sleep.' (Adam, aged 16, lower income, partnered, wave 2)

'My dad gives like a neutral point of view. Like he'd say to me, he'd emphasise [my daughter's] point of view. Like he once said to me, "when [daughter's] eighteen, do you think she'll want to be seeing you and [co-parent] still like this?" [arguing]. And it just, that one sentence just made me think a lot really.' (Trevor, aged 16, lower income, separated, wave 2)

The provision of a home for many of the young fathers was perhaps the most tangible dimension of grandparental help, although this could also cause difficulties in terms of overcrowding and stretched financial resources within the household (Neale and Ladlow, 2015b; see Chapter 8). For the youngest fathers in the study, and those who were single, such support was critically important. Several of the young fathers who remained in a relationship with the mother also lived with parents, who supported them to remain together and jointly care for their child (see Chapter 8). Adam and his partner moved in with his mum shortly after the baby first arrived: "[The mother] wanted to live wi' me. I was living at my mum's. So, she moved in wi' ma mum ... [My mum] will just do everything that a parent does basically, but she's grandma" (Adam, aged 16, lower income, partnered, wave 2).

In terms of financial support, this too tended to flow down the generations. For the young fathers this might mean the receipt of funds or material goods from the paternal grandparents, which could then be passed on to the mother as part of a reciprocal exchange between the parents. Similarly, the young fathers benefited indirectly from help and support offered to mother and baby by the maternal grandparents. Even minimal help from the grandparents was greatly appreciated. "She always took us places we needed to go. ... She did do quite a lot for us money-wise as well" (Callum, aged 19, lower income, partnered, wave 2). However, some frustration was felt at having to rely on the grandparents, especially when their resources were also limited: "I'm the one who's meant to support the baby. Obviously without my mother's financial support or anything, I don't know where I would have got the money from. I'd have been really stuck" (Senwe, aged 16, higher income, separated, wave 2).

Overall, the support of grandparents was not simply a useful supplement to the care provided by the young parents: in many cases it was a crucial foundation for the care of the next generation (Neale and Lau Clayton, 2014).

Grandparental power and influence

The power and influence of grandparents in this study was reflected in their gatekeeping activities. The varied forms of gatekeeping outlined in Chapter 5 are not confined to young mothers; they are strategies that grandparents may employ in varied circumstances to support or inhibit a young father's engagement with his child. For example, gate-opening could occur where grandmothers played a mediating role between the young parents, particularly where their relationships had broken down. This was the case for Tommy, whose marriage had ended in bitter circumstances during the study: "[Me and the mother] have no contact. ... I've done everything through [the maternal] grandmother. She's amicable and understands both sides" (Tommy, aged 24, higher income, separated, wave 2).

Iman had developed a close friendship with the mother of his twins during the pregnancy (see Chapter 4). But this had quickly unravelled in the aftermath of the birth, when the young man became aware of his peripheral role and felt that he was under surveillance at the maternal family home. However, Iman's mother acted as gate-opener and mediator with the maternal family:

> 'I am going into someone else's territory, and I didn't feel like I could be myself around my [twins]. ... There isn't a relationship [with the mum]. I don't think about her, I don't speak to her. ... [She] was causing me a lot of stress. ... All the arrangements are through my mother. She's my saviour.' (Iman, aged 17, higher income, single, wave 2)

By the close of fieldwork Iman was seeing his children once a month but, on the advice of his mother, was working hard to develop his credentials as a breadwinning parent (see Chapter 7). The circumstances of these young fathers who were estranged from the mothers were far from ideal, and there was a sense that these were makeshift arrangements, often held together by the grandparent generation, which would need to be resolved with the mothers over the longer term.

Changing patterns of support, interference and neglect

Over time we were able to discern how grandparental involvement unfolded, revealing complex and changing patterns of support, influence, interference and, in some cases, oppression and neglect. Wider evidence suggests that grandparents tend to tread a delicate line between 'being there' in a supportive role for their children and grandchildren, and not interfering (Mason et al, 2007; Ross et al, 2010). However, as these studies show, finding the right balance between these states can be a challenge. Blurred boundaries around parental and grandparental care are perhaps inevitable in a context where teenage or school-age young fathers are themselves dependants: they are responsible for their infant children, and yet remain the responsibility of their parents (Neale and Lau Clayton, 2014). Moreover, where young parents are living with grandparents, this can create a lack of clarity around lines of responsibility across the generations.

The young men in this study defined support in terms of offering advice when asked, rather than 'taking over':

> 'I have to ask for [advice] … I have to say [to my mum], "oh I don't get this, can you help?" And she'll help, she won't like take over and do it. She's just like, "oh you do that, do this". And stuff like that. Then that's really good 'cos that's like teaching you. That's teaching us to be parents instead of, instead of like taking over and just doing it.' (Senwe, aged 17, higher income, separated, wave 3)

> 'Well, she's there for whenever I need to talk. I can talk about owt. And she's not one of them that'll be in your face and say "look what's up, what's up" and all that lot. She won't nag me. She'll just say "oh if you wanna talk, talk", and she, she's just, she's been really good to me. She's really supportive.' (Callum, aged 19, lower income, partnered, wave 2)

However, it was common in this study for young fathers to report interference and surveillance from maternal grandparents, a passive form of gatekeeping that could deskill them, undermine their confidence and unsettle their parenting efforts. Even where relationships were relatively supportive, this could be the case. Maternal grandmothers often appeared to 'know best' and would take over or supervise in a way that the young men described as 'annoying' or 'upsetting':

'Generally, the maternal grandmother is trying to hold on to being a mum still. She acts like we still need approval or guidance for everything. ... She doesn't treat us properly like adults yet.' (Martin, aged 23, higher income, married, wave 2)

'It gives me little niggles sometimes because my parents are always there with me.' (Ben, aged 20, higher income, single, wave 2)

'I'd just like her to sit back and be a grandmother instead of a mother. Normally I would argue with people if they've tried to be so controlling ... but it's not in my son's best interest. I just had to bite my tongue.' (Jason, aged 22, lower income, single, wave 1)

Being a young and inexperienced father in the maternal household was a particular trial for these young men, which could generate deeply ambivalent feelings about their new role. Ben's experience mirrors that of Iman (see earlier) and Simon (recounted in Chapter 4):

'Having, you know, quite a hostile relationship with [the mother] there was also a hostile relationship with her family as well, though they were much better at hiding it [laughs]. ... So, I would always have to spend time at her house with [my daughter], and then all of her family and stuff. So it was, it was very uncomfortable because ... there was always a really tense atmosphere. ... If I was changing a nappy or anything everyone would be watching me. ... It was something I'd never done before, and I'd never had practice doing. It felt like I couldn't do what, what I felt would be natural to do. ... It almost felt like it was someone else's baby ... I could just feel eyes on the back of my neck [laughs]. So yeah, it did feel like I was kind of, it was someone else's child that I was being reviewed on my performance with.' (Ben, aged 20, higher income, single, wave 1)

Unlike Simon, Ben persevered with these difficult arrangements and was eventually able to see his child on his own. What made a difference was his capacity to build a relationship of trust and friendship with the mother (see Chapter 5).

In seven cases in this study tensions and conflicts between the generations and across the two households were particularly severe. Several young men in their mid-teens reported that grandparenting had tipped over into overt control of the pregnancy and child, policing of the young parents' behaviour or interference in the young people's relationship. As Jimmy recounts in Chapter 4, there were instances of overt gate-closing, where young fathers were barred from the maternal homes, forbidden to see the mothers and effectively denied an opportunity to see their children. This was also the experience of Dominic, who found himself navigating the contradictory responses of his own parents and those of the maternal grandparents. In each of his five interviews, Dominic reflected on the moral and practical support offered by his parents, despite their initial shock and disappointment. He contrasts this with the long-standing difficulties that he faced with the maternal grandparents. The moral outrage expressed by the maternal grandfather carried the threat of violence and led to an enforced separation between the young parents:

> '[The mother] hadn't spoken to me at all. It was down to her dad and mum saying, "we're having him". And obviously I just felt "this isn't your right – this isn't your right as a person to decide whether or not me and [the mother] should have this child". Her parents, her parents stopped me seeing [the mother]. You know, said to her, "you're not seeing him again". So, but obviously we didn't, didn't speak to one another for a while ... My parents ... said "whatever you decide we'll stick to it, but, you know, you can go places, you know ... you're a bright lad, we want the best for you".' (Dominic, aged 18, single, wave 1)

As shown in Chapter 5, by the time of the birth, Dominic had managed to rekindle his relationship with the mother and was able to establish a co-parental relationship across households.

In a variation on this theme, Adam and his partner switched households after their baby first arrived, following a violent argument with the maternal grandfather about the pregnancy:

> 'I fell out with the [maternal grandparents] 'cos I don't like people getting in my face and blocking me off and that. And her dad did that to me. And I just flipped out at him. And he didn't like it. ... Fair do's, it's their house and everything. I was respecting their rules, but they didn't like me there. ... I was sick of them telling me what to do. They're not my parents. And I lost it. ... So, I decided not to go back there again. And then because I didn't go there, [my girlfriend] didn't go there. And she wanted to live wi' me. I was living at my mum's. So, she moved in wi' my mum.' (Adam, aged 16, lower income, partnered, wave 1/2)

As Adam shows, such actions were most likely to occur in the context of highly volatile intergenerational relationships, and where young fathers were in their mid-teens and still dependent on the older generation. But they suggest too that maternal grandparents may adhere to and seek to reinforce the ideology of the mother/child dyad (see Chapter 5). They may also act upon the stigma associated with early fatherhood by treating the young men as feckless, irresponsible and/or a risk to mother and/or baby. In cases such as these, grandparent involvement can be experienced by young parents as a curse rather than a gift (SmithBattle, 1996; Neale and Lau Clayton, 2014).

Oppressive relationships

Interestingly, if grandparents could be critical of young fathers, the reverse was also the case. In six cases young men expressed concerns about the behaviour and motives of the older generation, reporting that the maternal families were dysfunctional, or leading lifestyles (typically involving drug or alcohol abuse and associated violence) that were not conducive to 'good' grandparental behaviour. Sometimes these criticisms arose in the context of cultural and socio-economic differences between the two families:

> 'I think there are a lot of negative influences in [the mother's] family. ... My parents have never got on with her parents. ... At the moment I'm getting on with her parents but ... they are dysfunctional ... because both parents have got past history problems in terms of mental health ... which is quite hard for 'em to be rational. So, you know, it's always been quite, walking on eggshells with the family as a whole.' (Dominic, aged 18, higher income, wave 1)

Oppressive relationships across the generations were most evident among the most poorly resourced families There were several instances of grandparents misusing their position as custodians of a grandchild's welfare benefits: "Like, my son's child benefits and all that, she [maternal grandmother] claims them because my girlfriend's too young. And when my girlfriend asks ... she won't give her it, she spends it on herself. So we can never ... go buy him anything" (Jimmy, aged 16, lower income, partnered, wave 3).

There were also instances of abuse between the young fathers and their fathers that had left scars in their relationships. Darren's father had initially provided some financial support for Darren and the new baby, although he struggled to sustain this support since he had a young child of his own who was the same age as his new grandchild. But he had also spent time in prison for assaulting Darren: "Literally, last time he were drinking he battered me and I got him sent to prison" (Darren, aged 22, lower income, partnered, wave 3).

Andrew's experiences provide a striking illustration of the volatility of complex intergenerational relationships that involve drug dependency and domestic violence (see also Chapter 5). His account reveals that his parents separated when he was six years old, and that, because of an ongoing addiction to Class A drugs, his father had subsequently spent four years in prison. On leaving prison, his father had re-partnered. Andrew and his new de facto stepsister were both in their early teens; they entered a relationship and were soon expecting a child. At the same time, Andrew's father and de facto stepmother were also expecting a child, creating a complex blurring of the generations in this family, and an intertwining of the maternal and paternal families.

Just as Jimmy had found, the flow of intergenerational support in this family was very much two-way, with the grandparents receiving the child benefit payments for Andrew's new baby. This increased the dependency of the young couple and constrained their ability to provide directly for their child. Moreover, the financial arrangement depended on the young mother residing in the grandparent household, while Andrew was forced to reside at various times in a local hostel or move in with his mother.

These financial tensions were bound up with the drug dependency of the grandparents, an issue that led to ongoing social services involvement with this family and concerns about the care of the new infants. Andrew was equally concerned about these issues: "When you're on drugs, you're not interested about anybody but yourself and the drugs" (Andrew, aged 16, lower income, partnered, wave 3). By the third interview, Andrew had informed social services anonymously of the grandparents' drug use, and his father had returned to prison. By the fourth interview, Andrew's disclosure had caused rifts with his father and with his young partner (whose loyalties were divided between Andrew and her mother). Eventually, the grandparents separated, and their small child was taken into care.

During this turbulent period, Andrew was rendered vulnerable by his intermittent residence in a hostel that was also inhabited by drug users; it was not an environment into which he could safely bring a child. Combined with little to no family support and instances of domestic violence between the couple (see Chapter 5) this placed a great deal of strain on their relationship. However, they were reconciled and co-residing with their child in their own flat by the fifth wave of interviews.

The two accounts given here represent extreme instances of how oppressive relationships may flow down the generations and confound assumptions surrounding intergenerational care and support. These were not isolated instances but reported elsewhere among the most poorly resourced young men in this study. The cases reflect further complex issues that may also arise in these poorly resourced households. We have seen (in Chapter 4) that young men who have more than one child in quick succession, particularly with different partners or across households, may struggle to be there for their children because their efforts are simply spread too thin. This same problem arises where the generations are so closely layered that young parents and grandparents are simultaneously striving to raise small children. In these circumstances, grandparents are doubly overstretched. They may have few resources of an emotional, relational, practical or financial nature to give to their teenage children and young grandchildren. Moreover, the issues are compounded where associated child protection, domestic violence and/or addiction difficulties arise in these families.

Neglectful relationships and tensions over parental rights

We have seen that inappropriate or oppressive grandparent involvement could be experienced as a curse by young fathers. The opposite scenario, where grandparental support was withdrawn, could also be experienced in this way (Bunting and McAuley, 2004; Mollborn and Jacobs, 2015). A withdrawal of support could be triggered by conflicts over household chores, infant care, and the differing priorities of the generations, with both generations perceiving a lack of responsibility in the other (Sadler and Clemmens, 2004; Neale and Lau Clayton, 2014). It could also be triggered by the changing circumstances of the grandparents and challenges in their own lives. At various times a substantial minority of young men reported a cessation of support from either a maternal or paternal grandparent, particularly where relationships were fragile and volatile:

> 'You could ring her, and she's like, "well, I'm busy now, you'll have to ring back tomorrow". I'm like, "well I don't need you tomorrow, I need you now" … She wanted to move [house] … and start afresh, which I can understand, but obviously, still see your grandkids. But she doesn't want it like that … she goes, "oh my life doesn't involve children now".' (Darren, aged 21, lower income, partnered, wave 2)

> 'It's hard, just with the two of us.' (Adam, aged 17, lower income, partnered, wave 3)

In Adam's case, social services had been involved with the family for most of his life, with issues of domestic violence arising in the family while Adam was a child. His mother had been largely supportive of Adam and his young partner during the pregnancy and early days after the birth and had informally taken over the care of her grandchild when things became difficult for the parents. She then withdrew her support and instead sought parental responsibility for her grandchild as an official kinship carer. She was supported in this by Adam's social worker. This created serious rifts in this family, placing Adam's mother and the young couple in legal conflict as they both sought to secure rights to the child. Over time, Adam's staunch commitment to his son and partner bore some fruit. By the time he was interviewed for the Following Young Fathers Further study (conducted some five years later, in 2020 and 2021) he and his partner had married and were living in the private rental sector with their nine-year-old son. However, parental relationships remained volatile.

As a final example of the limits of grandparental involvement, Callum recounts how his mother's otherwise staunch support was withdrawn followed a period of difficulties for the young man. After attending court to secure access to his twins (discussed in Chapter 5), he began to drink and to sell drugs. The strain on his mother led him to move out of the house and into a hostel:

> 'When I stopped seeing the kids for so long when I was still going through court and it were just taking proper ages, I went off rails a bit and I were going out drinking all the time and getting in fights and in trouble with police and all that lot. And after a while my mum just got sick of it. ... One night I came home pissed ... at, like, three in't morning and all that lot, and she were proper pissed off. ... When she came down the next day she were crying and ... she just said "look Callum I've had enough, I want you out, I can't deal with it anymore". And since then, it's been up and down. ... [B]ut ... after about three months ... of being in the hostel we started seeing each other again. ... And then she were really supportive. ... She were getting me things for the flat and all that lot. And yeah, she were just there for me all the time, yeah.' (Callum, aged 19, lower income, partnered, wave 2)

The value of consistent and dependable support to young fathers by grandparents cannot be overestimated. It was more likely to be provided in relatively well-resourced and harmonious households; where relationships across the generations are volatile, support can be unpredictable and intermittent. These complex and undulating patterns of dependency and interdependency had variable implications and outcomes for the young men. Support from parents could not always be relied upon over the long term, adding to the sense of insecurity in the lives of these young men.

Concluding discussion

Broadening the relational themes introduced in Chapter 5, this chapter has explored the important influence of grandparents on the practices of young fatherhood, the varied ways in which intergenerational relationships operate and evolve over time, and the impact that they have on the capacity of young fathers to care for their children. As shown in Chapters 4 and 5, the arrival of a new child presents a raft of emotional and practical challenges for young men. Regardless of whether they are partnered or single, living with parents or living independently, they are likely to have few material and financial resources to contribute, and commonly lack skills and experience in childcare and in managing relationships. This is in addition to their own care needs, as young people who are still dependent on their families (Swann et al, 2003).

In these circumstances, grandparents can be a vital source of sustained and reliable support for young fathers, helping in the provision of housing and practical, financial and emotional support, including the direct care of a child. Our evidence suggests that support that flows down the generations, from grandparents to young parents and their children, is not a mere supplement to the care provided by the young parents; the younger the young parent, the more vital such support becomes as a foundation for the care of the next generation.

These patterns of intergenerational support are also clearly gendered. Our evidence suggests that grandfathers and stepfathers can play an active role in supporting their adolescent children and grandchildren. They are most likely to promote and reinforce traditional gendered ideologies around the financial constitution of good fatherhood (discussed further in Chapter 7). But it is grandmothers, especially on the maternal side of the family, who are likely to play the most active role in supporting young parents with their new grandchildren (Neale and Lau Clayton, 2014, 2015). They may be extensively engaged in decisions to keep the child and may take on a co-parental role, or, in some cases, secure a role as a statutory kinship carer.

We have seen that these forms of engagement can result in patterns of power, responsibility and decision making that flow 'vertically' down the generations, particularly in the maternal household, where mother and child are most likely to live. Where young parents are in their teens, inexperienced, unprepared and poorly resourced, it is not uncommon for the ideology of the mother/child dyad to be extended to a triad of mother, child and grandmother (Neale and Patrick, 2016). This can create additional difficulties for the young men in establishing relations of care and responsibility that flow 'horizontally' between the young parents themselves. It is a pattern that also establishes clear divisions between the responsibilities and influences of the maternal and paternal households.

Overall, however, our evidence shows that grandparent engagement is highly variable in its extent, quality and sustainability. It may have mixed effects on the fatherhood identities of the young men, and may be unsustainable, particularly in families with complex needs. Even where grandparental support is of good quality and highly valued, finding the right balance between support, interference and neglect is notoriously difficult, particularly in a context where young parents are themselves dependent and remain the responsibility of the grandparent generation. This may result in blurred lines of responsibility that become a burden for both the young parents and the older generation (Neale and Lau Clayton, 2014).

Overall, good-quality grandparental care is far from given. We have highlighted here cases where relationships are highly volatile, or where grandparents themselves have complex needs or are stretched too thin in terms of their own caring responsibilities, particularly where a close layering of the generations may mean that they are producing children at the same time as their teenage children. In these cases, grandparental involvement may be experienced by young fathers as interference, oppression or neglect. In some cases, it may have damaging longer-term consequences for the younger generations. There is no simple correlation between the involvement of grandparents and positive outcomes for their children and grandchildren – the picture is complex and requires a more nuanced understanding of the constellation of factors at play across the generations, across households and over time.

The young men's accounts reflect the overriding significance of intergenerational support for young parents. But at the same time, they exemplify what can happen when grandparents lack the material, financial and emotional resources to offer positive support to their children and grandchildren. Grandparent involvement has rarely been the focus of attention in policy and professional circles, and its variable nature, including the possibility of its detrimental and unstable effects over time, has been too little understood (Hughes and Emmel, 2011; Emmel and Hughes, 2014). In the main, grandparents have been marginalised in legislation and in social policy, while their contributions have been taken largely for granted (Grandparents Plus, 2010).

This reliance on family support has been sharpened in recent years. In a context of growing austerity and the retrenchment of welfare support and front-line services for young people and children (see Chapter 2), the financial and parenting support of grandparents has become ever more crucial. Combined with the UK housing crisis and the shortage of affordable housing for young people (see Chapter 8), there is evidence that grandparents are increasingly relied upon by state agencies to fill in the gaps in professional support. This is illustrated, for example, in the increase in kinship care orders, whereby grandparents take on statutory responsibilities for their grandchildren where their children are incapacitated or there are safeguarding issues (Grandparents Plus, 2017; Tarrant, 2018; Tarrant, 2021). Whatever the good intentions of grandparents, tensions and conflicts across the generations are likely to continue and, for a whole host of reasons, the ability of the older generation to provide sustained support over time may be compromised. Recent evidence on the experiences of children and young people who live with their grandparents and other family members suggests that such care does not necessarily provide full protection for vulnerable children, many of whom remain disadvantaged in terms of their general development and mental health (Grandparents Plus, 2017). In poorly resourced families in particular, kin care may not be an adequate substitute for the range of benefits that could be provided through statutory forms of family support.

In policy and practice circles a more nuanced approach that takes into account the fluid and contingent nature of inter-generational relationships and, in some cases, its deleterious effects on young parents, would be helpful. Using a partnership model of service provision would enable the inclusion of grandparents within family centred services, to the benefit of family members across the generations. There would be scope, for example, to offer bespoke support that would operate flexibly and in line with the shifting dynamics of kin care in families. Tailoring support for families where the generations are closely layered would also be helpful, and lead to a better balance of care across the generations and between the young parents themselves. And it may ease the pressure on poorly resourced young fathers whose options for independent living and/or for financial security are extremely limited. It is to these pressing issues that we now turn.

7

Young breadwinners? Education, employment and training trajectories

Introduction

> 'I think it's important to work ... to be a father figure for [my son]. ... I don't want my son to be on the dole. I want him to be able to provide for his family when he eventually has one. God forbid it'll be when I did, but hopefully like come 20, 25 years from now he'll have a family. And he'll be able to support them with a job. And he'll be able to look after them. I mean I don't want to be on the dole all my life doing nothing for no one. I want to be able to help people ... the way I can do that is by getting a job.' (Adam, aged 26, Following Young Fathers Further, lower income, partnered, wave 1)

In this chapter our focus shifts to the wider institutional opportunities and constraints that impact on young fathers. Drawing on and updating earlier findings (Neale and Davies, 2016), we explore the economic resources available to these young men and how they seek to make ends meet. We begin by considering the aspirations of young men to provide materially and financially for their children (the 'breadwinner' ideology). We go on to chart their varied pathways through education, employment and training (EET) and we show how these pathways are shaped through a complex constellation of life circumstances. The discussion is shaped around the distinctions between the EET trajectories of young men who were skilled, semi-skilled or low-skilled at the start of our study, and their attempts to maintain or improve their skills levels and employment prospects over time. We also show the varied ways in which young fathers attempt to balance learning, earning and caring, and the very real burden that this can produce, often over considerable periods of time.

Extending our discussion in Chapter 2, we set our findings in the context of contemporary debates about the socio-economic fortunes of disadvantaged young people, and their marginalisation within policy processes. Over the course of the Following Young Fathers study (FYF, 2010–15), welfare policies in the UK become increasingly punitive under the Coalition government, with adverse effects particularly evident for young parents. Finally, we reappraise a normative framework that assumes that early parenthood 'causes' social deprivation, and a welfare framework that regards the needs and aspirations of young people as a low priority (France, 2008).

'Breadwinner' ideologies

Providing financial and material support for children has traditionally been seen as the defining feature of fatherhood, while primary caring responsibilities are assumed to reside with mothers (Roy, 2004). Earning and caring have always been shared by parents to varying degrees, creating a more fluid picture than these traditional models imply, and giving rise to newer ideologies based on a 'cash and care' model of parenting (Speak, 2006; Miller, 2011). Nevertheless, the default ideological framework remains a gendered one (Weber, 2018).

While paternal care is mediated through mothers, who are gatekeepers to their children, paid work and family provisioning continue to be bound up with ideas of adult masculine identity, status and reputation, particularly within working-class households (S. Roberts, 2013). The cultural stereotype of the male breadwinner tends to be reinforced in the UK through a variety of policy and legislative frameworks that take an 'economic' view of fathering. Not providing for their family is a key characteristic of the absent, 'bad father', who is at the heart of a social deficit understanding of young fatherhood (see Chapter 2; Miller, 2011; Neale, 2016; Weber, 2018; Tarrant, 2021). Whatever factors may lead to a blurring of parental roles over time, fathers are more likely to start from an imperative to earn (with some discretion over when, where and how they care), while mothers start from an imperative to care (with some discretion over when, where and how they earn; Neale and Smart, 2002).

Evidence from young fathers suggests a similar balancing of these gendered constructs. As reported earlier, despite the relational constraints that they face, young fathers wish to 'be there' for their children and not simply as 'weekend dads'. Nevertheless, they regard breadwinning as a taken-for-granted part of their emerging adult status and identity (Glikman, 2004; Duncan et al, 2010; Negura and Deslauriers, 2010; Shirani, 2015; Weber, 2018).

However, despite these values and aspirations, they are likely to face significant constraints in providing financial or material support for their children, born of a range of social and structural barriers to both caring and earning (Speak, 2006; see Pirog-Good, 1996 and related evidence reviewed in Chapter 1). This is particularly so where they lack formal educational skills and qualifications to propel them into training or employment. Their youthful and dependent status compounds these problems. Young fathers of post-school age may have fragile EET trajectories that are still very much in the making, while school-age fathers, who enter parenthood before the age of 17, are simply too young to earn a living or access welfare benefits in their own right.

The policy context: EET opportunities and constraints

At the time of the FYF study, the challenges faced by young fathers were compounded by a climate of limited educational opportunities, inadequate training provision, insecure youth labour markets and reduced welfare entitlements. As shown in Chapter 2, these issues became more pronounced over the course of the study as welfare reforms brought in under the Coalition government began to take effect.

Despite strong evidence for the value of post-secondary education for young people, provision for longer-term learning or training pathways for disadvantaged young people were limited. Under New Labour's Teenage Pregnancy Strategy, 'Care to Learn' grants were introduced in 2004. These were designed to help pay for childcare while parents under the age of 19 studied in school, school sixth forms or sixth-form colleges. Local education authorities were also required to ensure that young parents were able to reintegrate into education promptly after the birth of their child. However, these grants were only available to the main carer of the child (the mothers), with no recognition of shared care arrangements for parents who live apart. Young fathers living apart from their children were not eligible for educational support payments.

Job training and employment opportunities were equally limited for disadvantaged young people. By the end of the study in 2015, 22.2 per cent of young people in the UK aged 16–24 were gauged to be NEET (not in education, employment or training), a comparably higher figure than for other Western countries, including the US (Lawton, 2013: 6; Mirza-Davies and Brown, 2016). NEET trajectories are particularly prevalent among highly disadvantaged young people, including those who have spent periods of time in social care (Mortune, 2021).

More broadly, at the time of the FYF study, nearly 2 million young people in the UK were estimated to have incomes considerably below the poverty threshold (below 50 per cent of median income). This represents over 30 per cent of young people, including those who were churning in and out of work. The adverse effects of these early experiences on young people's health, well-being and life chances are by no means short-lived. Follow-up studies of disadvantaged youth, conducted over decades, reveal that, for many young people, these effects may extend over the long term and result in entrenched poverty and precarity (Laub and Sampson, 2003; MacLeod, 2009; Mawn et al, 2018; Williamson, 2021).

Since 2015, there has been little improvement in this picture. Despite an overall rise in employment rates, youth unemployment has remained a significant problem. Rates are higher for this group than any other age group, and with a greater proportion of young people at risk of long-term unemployment (NPI, 2015; APPGYE, nd). Economic downturns (wrought through recession, austerity measures, rising housing costs and, more recently, the COVID-19 pandemic) have been found to have disproportionately adverse effects on young people (Churchill, 2016; Davies, 2019; Tarrant et al, 2020a, 2022; Youth Employment UK, nd; Garthwaite et al, 2022; MacDonald et al, 2022).

The dominant perception is that unemployment and disadvantage are individual problems, caused by a deficit in skills and motivation among young people. If they are not work-ready, they are likely to labelled as 'shirkers' rather than 'strivers', 'sinkers' rather than 'swimmers' (Jones, 2002). These dualisms do a disservice to young people, obscuring the complexities of EET transitions and polarising debates about welfare entitlements. In the process, 'stronger' explanations for social disadvantage and exclusion, that they are the product of neoliberal, capitalist economies that rely on a flexible and casual labour force, are submerged and not addressed (Veit Wilson, cited in MacDonald, 2011; Ward, 2015; Ward et al, 2017; Macdonald et al, 2020).

Moreover, as shown in Chapter 2, being employed no longer solves the issues of poverty and disadvantage. Dynamic research that moves beyond static understandings of young people as either in or out of work (EET or NEET), has uncovered the fluidity and volatility of employment trajectories over time. The evidence shows that poverty has increased most rapidly among those who churn in and out of temporary work and benefits receipts (MacDonald, 2011; Shildrick et al, 2012). This churning is not merely a feature of early employment experiences, which later settle into something more secure; it is becoming a long-term pattern, stretching into later life, creating insecurity for young people as a way of life. As MacDonald (2011) observes, it is *under*employment that is the deeper and more pervasive problem. For semi-skilled or low-skilled workers, work itself has become 'poor': it is sufficiently precarious that it can no longer be relied upon to offer a good enough wage in the here and now, or security for the future.

The effects of these structural changes on disadvantaged young people have been well documented. They face the prospect of precarious EET trajectories; 'patchwork' careers in which they churn between training, unemployment and insecure zero-hours jobs that are low paid, low status and without any of the contractual safeguards that come with settled employment. They work on shop or factory floors, on construction sites, in bars and fast-food outlets, taking casual jobs as cleaners, drivers, security guards or labourers, or in home delivery services.

In policy debates about how best to support young people in these volatile labour markets, young parents remain an under-represented and seldom heard group (Tarrant, 2021). Yet their employment needs, as parents with a child to support, are all the more pressing. They also face extra challenges in accessing the labour market, including the lack of flexible and affordable childcare provision, and little acknowledgement for the time constraints and extra commitments that parenthood brings (see also Swann et al, 2003; Lemay et al, 2010). The particularly woeful picture for young men from disadvantaged backgrounds has also been highlighted, with adverse effects on their transitions to adulthood observed across a range of international welfare regimes (Nayak, 2006; McDowell, 2014; Ward et al, 2017; Walker and Roberts, 2018; see also Tarrant, 2021).

Compounding these problems, the UK has also seen a shift towards increasing welfare conditionality and a drift away from the insurance principles of the post-war welfare settlement (Dwyer et al, 2023). The fortunes of young people are shaped not only by market immobility and precarity, but by a diminishing safety net of security through the benefits system (Simmons et al, 2014). Towards the end of the Coalition government, the chancellor defended plans to remove benefits from young people on the grounds that the imperative was to ensure they were either 'earning or learning'. The first budget of the new Conservative administration (July 2015) reduced entitlements to housing benefits for young people and announced a living wage available only to those over the age of 25. Two schemes to help young people into work and training, the Future Jobs Fund and Educational Maintenance Allowance, were axed during the first years of the Coalition government. A replacement scheme, the Youth Contract, was found to be too narrowly focused and ineffective in its design, delivery and impact (Newton, 2014). Successive government schemes, for example, the more recent Kickstart scheme, reflect similar issues.

Young people on Jobseeker's Allowance (a basic working-age employment benefit in the UK) are encouraged to take up any form of work, regardless of how insecure or poorly paid it is, and, with the threat of sanctions if they do not comply, the process may deskill and impoverish them further (France, 2008; Rao, 2021; Dwyer et al, 2023). They may be assigned to training schemes in an instrumental fashion that pays scant attention to matching skills and interests with available opportunities, resulting in high drop-out rates. They may be subjected to routinised and largely ineffective strategies to find work, for example, cascading their CVs to all employers in an area, regardless of the supply of jobs or the degree of fit with young people's training needs and capacities (MacDonald and Marsh, 2005).

Despite the efforts of a scattered and uncoordinated range of youth employment initiatives, there is a continuing and unresolved mismatch between job opportunities and the training and career needs of young, disadvantaged people (APPGYE, nd). Along with the tightening of welfare conditionality in the UK, this mismatch has further entrenched the inequalities gap across the generations.

Policies that reduce wages and benefits for young people are driven by an assumption that young people's needs are less than those of other age groups (France, 2008). Underpinning this assumption is another: that as dependants, young people can and should rely on the support of their families, rather than the state. Yet, as we have seen in Chapter 6, such support cannot be relied upon, particularly where families are living in precarious circumstances.

The EET trajectories of young fathers

It was against this backdrop that we set out to understand the values and experiences of young fathers in navigating their (N)EET trajectories. In light of the widely reported correlation between young parenthood and social deprivation, including lack of EET skills and experience (see Chapters 1 and 2), we sought to explore the many factors that were making a difference to the fortunes of these young men. We wished to understand the effects that early entry into parenthood might have on their life chances, and whether it could be said, in any sense, to 'cause' social deprivation.

As noted earlier, FYF (2010–15) followed the lives of 31 young fathers from varied socio-economic backgrounds. Of these, 10 young men were from higher-income families, while the remaining 21 were from lower-income families. Overall, the sample fell into three skills categories at any one time. By the close of fieldwork, six of the well-resourced young men were following skilled trajectories, involving higher education. Eight young men, four from higher-income families and four from lower-income families, were following semi-skilled trajectories. The remaining 17 were low-skilled and living in relatively precarious financial and material circumstances that, as noted in Chapter 2, were becoming more pronounced under the Coalition government. While the nature and extent of these disadvantages varied across this group, the widely reported correlation between young parenthood and social deprivation was evident for many of these low-skilled, lower-income young men (see also Quinton et al, 2002; Swann et al, 2003; Lemay et al, 2010).

The diverse circumstances of the young men in this sample enabled us to explore variations in their EET skills, qualifications and experiences over time, and the causal processes involved. Our reporting relates to the positions of the young men at the close of our fieldwork and the journeys undertaken to arrive at these positions. These EET states are inherently provisional and porous; some individuals were striving to move up a level or prevent slippage down to the level below. Nevertheless, it is possible to discern clear differences in the way these pathways took shape and how they were unfolding. In what follows, we chart these upward and downward transitions over time and the ensuing trajectories-in-the-making. In the more detailed cases, we illustrate how these socio-economic pathways intersect with the young men's unfolding lives as parents and the relational aspects of their fathering journeys.

Aspirations and values surrounding paid work

In line with existing evidence, the young fathers in our study uniformly held to the values of both 'earning' and 'caring' as core attributes of fatherhood. This is reflected, for example, in Adam's opening quotation for this chapter, an account that also illustrates how breadwinning ideologies consciously flow down the generations from fathers to sons. While the young men clearly attach importance to 'being there' in a loving, personal relationship with a child, the provision of material and financial support for their children was a 'given' (Edin and Nelson, 2013). Indeed, these roles were intertwined: being a provider was inextricably bound up with being 'close' to a child:

> 'I was only eighteen, so it was ... a shock, like I said, it forced me to grow up, to take responsibility ... to go and look for work ... [A good dad is] one that listens, always there, no matter what. ... It's not just about buying them clothes, buying them this and that. ... [Their mum] is ... unemployed. ... Obviously, things like new jumpers for school ... we'll go out and get them. Yeah, I think me working full-time ... it can be the difference for her. ... I think it's important to provide – not just financially, but in all the other areas.' (Kevin, aged 24, semi-skilled, employed, separated, wave 1)

As we saw in Chapter 4, and as other researchers have found (Chapter 1), the arrival of a child can be a catalyst to take responsibility and better oneself. The young men often spoke starkly about the imperative to fulfil their provider role:

> 'I want any job that's possible, 'cos if I didn't have money, that'd mean I'm a bad dad 'cos I'm not making a living or anything.' (Jackson, aged 16, low-skilled, unemployed, partnered, wave 2)

> '[I'm on] benefits money – you haven't earned it, so I haven't provided ... getting up in morning and grafting all day, and then coming home ... that's providing. I'd much rather be in a job, earning.' (Jax, aged 18, low-skilled, unemployed, partnered, wave 2,)

> 'I wouldn't change [daughter] for the world, but maybe I wish I would have waited until I had a job ... and a little bit more money ... You need a job just to pay your bills ... But things happen, don't they?' (Andrew, aged 16, low-skilled, unemployed, partnered, wave 1)

Whatever their age and skills at the point of entry into parenthood, very few young fathers in this study felt they had had sufficient time to consolidate their EET aspirations. However, for the low-skilled young men, all of whom were living on low incomes, employment and financial security were remote goals. School-age fathers lacked funds for basics such as milk, nappies and bus fares to visit their children. They relied heavily on their parents in the short term, saving pocket money and other handouts for essentials. Ironically, and despite a drive to 'grow up' and be responsible as parents, the imperative to provide for their children could engender criminal activity among these young men (Shannon and Abrams, 2007; Paschal et al, 2011; Neale and Ladlow, 2015a; and for further evidence on 'survival' crime, see Ladlow and Neale, 2016):

> 'It was hard at first, 'cos that's when you have to buy everything – a cot and clothes and all that lot. And when I were at school, I were selling cigarettes ... and more [laughs wryly] and that's how I made me money to pay for everything. ... I've got basically no money. I'm trying to do good in me life and all that and everything's piling on top. It's a lot of pressure on me. It does your head in. ... It's just been a constant struggle, relationship-wise as well. I [can't] take the kids out, nice places. ... You want the best for your kids. You want 'em in nice clothes. ... I'm struggling to put decent food on the table. ... Yeah, [finance] does play a lot in it. Definitely, 'cos if you ain't got money, I mean you can love your child and that, can't you ... nowt can beat that love. ... But I mean ... when it comes to feeding and stuff like that, if you can't do that, then you're fucked aren't you, basically.' (Callum, aged 19, low-skilled, unemployed, separated, waves 2 and 3)

> 'I've just been smoking weed really badly, and that's obviously not helping me, going through a lot of things, depression and all that lot. So, yeah, I've been going a bit downhill.' (Callum aged 21, unemployed, separated, wave 4)

As we can see from Callum's account, the cumulative weight of multiple problems, relational and socio-economic, can create mental health problems for young men over time. More specifically, the challenge of being out of work and losing hope of finding work can create a disjuncture between young fathers' values and aspirations around breadwinning, and what they can achieve in practice. In what follows we examine the different skills levels of these young men and how these shape their EET trajectories over time.

'Skilled' trajectories

Six of the young men in our study, all from higher-income families, were at university or on track to secure a university place; they had developed academic identities during their secondary schooling. Three had entered parenthood in their early 20s (in two cases as a welcome transition that led to marriage to the primary caring mothers). A further two were in their late teens, and one was still at school. While the EET trajectories of the older fathers were relatively well defined and stable, the journeys of the younger men were more circuitous. Two of them were combining their studies with part-time work, as well as some direct care of their children.

Jock modified his aspirations to go onto a higher degree because he faced a triple burden of earning, learning and caring that became relentless when his relationship with the mother came to an end. Ben, in contrast, continued to pursue his education. He was 18 and in his first year of university when his child was conceived within a transitory relationship. He considered giving up his degree to find a job, since his course involved a one-year placement abroad. But with support from his parents, and the acquiescence of the primary caring mother, he focused on securing his degree, continued to live in student accommodation, and fitted his caring responsibilities around his studies. In common with all the young men, his child provided an additional motivation to pursue his career:

> 'It's just completely altered my trajectory as it were – it's like a responsibility that's always there. ... I'm really pleased I went [abroad] actually, yeah. Rather than dropping out of uni and in a substandard job. It felt like ... you know, the most logical course of action to take. And the one that was kind of most in line with the plan I'd had. ... and then hopefully get a decent job. ... I find it quite a difficult situation because on the one hand I don't have the money to provide, but on the other hand I really do want to be able to provide. ... But it's worth a short period of ... struggling through it for potentially quite a comfortable existence after university. ... And it would be, ultimately it would be better for [my daughter]. ... In my hometown the twenty-year-olds are unemployed and going out and getting drunk. I'm not like that, I'm working towards something better. ... I can still be a good dad and also do what I want.' (Ben, aged 19/20, skilled, full-time university student, waves 1 and 2)

As other researchers have found (Shirani, 2015; Weber, 2018), this strategy of investing in education to secure long-term employment benefits was an attractive option for these skilled or potentially skilled young men, which became viable because of the resources that they could draw upon in their families of origin.

When, at the age of 29, Ben was reinterviewed for the Following Young Fathers Further (FYFF) study, his need to balance his fatherhood commitments with his personal fulfilment had recently been revived. In the wake of his first degree he had taken up IT work, since it fitted better with his role as a part-time, non-resident parent. Finding this work less than fulfilling over time, he had recently left his job to embark on a higher degree in language teaching and, with much less income, had moved from his own flat (with a room for his daughter) to a temporary residence in a shared house.

At the time of the interview, he was seeing his daughter every other weekend at the home of his parents. While Ben described this as a backward step in terms of his role as a father, he was giving priority to his needs for personal development. He was able to do this because of his well-resourced family support, and his good relationship with his child and co-parent. For young skilled fathers like Ben, balancing aspirations for personal fulfilment with responsibilities as a parent are not necessarily one-off choices; they are complex, longer-term considerations, with opportunities to reconfigure the delicate balance between earning, learning and caring over time.

As a further example, Dominic's entry into parenthood at the age of 16 triggered a disruption to the longer-term, skilled trajectory that he had been forging through his earlier school years. He managed good grades for his GCSEs, which gave him entry to a sixth-form college, but to support his child he combined studying with part-time, semi-skilled office work. During college Dominic separated from the mother (see Chapter 5) and contact with his child was curtailed. His earning power then became a critical factor in his efforts to reinstate contact. Like Jock and Ben, he was engaged in a triple burden of earning, learning and direct care of his child, which he was trying to sustain with strong support from his parents. However, these events took their toll, and he dropped out from his A-level course. At the time of his first interview, Dominic had moved to full-time office work; he was on a stable, semi-skilled trajectory that did not match his educational profile and aspirations:

> 'I'm not best pleased I'm in this job ... 'cos it's really mind-numbing. ... So it's not for me. ... I'm purely there just to, just to take money out, 'cos of financial constraints. ... I have to get some sort of income when it comes to a child. ... Regardless of ... what I feel I can do, it is just a case of keeping my job. ... Before this happened, you know, I'd, I'd had aspirations of what I wanted to do. ... But I feel quite trapped at the moment. I'm quite aimless. What's the point in having any ambition if you just, you know ... Everything's a struggle.' (Dominic, aged 18, semi-skilled, employed, separated, wave 2)

Four years later, Dominic's life was back on track: he was studying part-time for a degree and with plans for a professional teaching career. He was supported in this by his learning mentor, and his parents, who helped him find a regular pattern for combining part-time, degree-level study through a remote-learning provider, a part-time job, an unpaid internship, and direct care of his child:

> 'Going down to part-time from full-time is a massive shift in your lifestyle. … In some ways, it's lucky how it's turned out where I've had three years' work experience. … [I knew] I wasn't going to uni just for the sake of going. … I've got a direction: it gives me motivation. … I work evenings, so I have the full days to commit to uni. … As I say it's very tiring 'cos I'm up at eight … and then it's a case of I'm working till ten at night. … It's all building towards, hopefully, a career path in future. … I'm genuinely a lot more happy.' (Dominic, aged 21, skilled, part-time student/part-time employed, separated, wave 4)

By the time Dominic was 30 years old, his trajectory had shifted again. His follow-up interview for the FYFF study revealed the challenges that he faced in trying to sustain the triple burden of earning, learning and caring over many years on a part-time, remote-learning degree. Despite the support of his parents, the delicate balance of this process was undermined by the difficulties in his relationship with his son's mother and her family. As shown in Chapter 5, Dominic's contact with his son was curtailed as the mother sought an increase in his maintenance payments.

When he was offered a full-time, well-paid senior management role at his office, Dominic decided to consolidate his existing career, and maximise his financial security. This gave him a strong negotiating position with the mother and her family, and greatly helped to secure his relationship with his son at times of tensions across the two households (see Chapter 5; Tarrant, 2017; Tarrant et al, 2020a). While Dominic remained keen to complete his degree for his own personal fulfilment, he was resigned to deferring the process to a later date.

The engagement of these young men in higher-education opportunities challenges popular assumptions that young parenthood inevitably leads to educational failure or limits employment prospects (see also Ellis-Sloan, 2022). At the same time, these cases illustrate the complex challenges and choices that these relatively skilled young men faced as parents, and the impact on their life plans.

'Semi-skilled' trajectories

Eight fathers were in this group at the close of our fieldwork (four from higher-income families, and four from lower-income families). One had entered parenthood in his early 20s, two in their late teens and the remaining five were of school age. Relationships with the mothers varied, but these young fathers had maintained a regular commitment to their children over time. Iman, who had been in a fleeting relationship with his co-parent, had an academic identity and background. Much like the skilled young men, his aim was to secure a longer-term strategic pathway through sixth-form college and university, which would take him into the skilled category over time:

> 'It's given me that drive and determination ... Although I did have my aspirations ... But it's made me ... you know, it's made it concrete – the only way I can do that is by studying hard – or winning the lottery overnight [laughs] ... I've explained the bigger picture – you know, I said to [the mum], "I could just get a job now, you know ... stop my studying and just, you know, any money I give it to the kids. But then what is that benefiting the kids? That's just money for now. That money goes. It's not putting nothing in place for them kids".' (Iman, aged 16, semi-skilled, full-time student, single, wave 1)

This strategy offered other advantages for Iman. By wave 2, after the birth of his twins, he had become estranged from the maternal household and was struggling with being a hands-on parent. As he explained, in these circumstances, developing a breadwinner identity through a continued engagement in his education was a contribution that he felt he could more easily make:

> 'My mum spoke to me, she goes, "why stress about something when you've got no control over it? ... The best impact you can have on [the children] is by getting good grades, and making sure you can secure their future in a good way." So I just see it like that now. ... it's like the best I can do.' (Iman, aged 17, full-time student, single, wave 2)

But other young men, with few family resources to fall back upon, made different decisions. Kevin, for example, prioritised paid work over his construction college course, with the aim of directly supporting his child and the mother (they were partners for seven years). With great regret, he left college at the age of 18 and held several temporary jobs before securing a full-time stock control job at a warehouse. At the time of this interview, he was studying for a national vocational qualification (NVQ) in warehousing. NVQs can be combined with work or schooling, and were ideal for Kevin, enabling him to continue earning and opening up opportunities to apply for promotion or a higher-paid position in future:

> 'To come out of college, no real grades from school, not even completed a year of college, I was worried ... who would employ me?

'... I had four cleaning jobs and I just worked and worked and worked and provided. It was hard, yeah [laughs] ... looking back maybe I could have stayed at college and got a few years under me.' (Kevin, aged 24, semi-skilled, full-time employee, separated, wave 1)

Like Kevin, most of the semi-skilled group felt they had no choice but to prioritise work and its earning power over the acquisition of further qualifications (Shirani, 2015). They were following shorter-term EET strategies, attempting to accrue skills and qualifications through a piecemeal mix of study, training and low-paid, insecure employment, often with more than one part-time job at a time. A key aim for these young men was to secure better work: a pay rise or promotion, extended or better hours, improved conditions or a more permanent contract. It was striking that, for this group of young men, finding a job was simply not enough; they were striving to find a *secure* job, to move from underemployment to full employment. This was a difficult and protracted process, necessitating relentless searching and changes in direction.

Training opportunities

If finding the right kind of work was a challenge, so too was securing appropriate training and apprenticeships. Senwe had attended a decorating course on day release from school, followed by a full-time college placement for an NVQ. Unable to meet the standards to progress to the second year, he faced a demoralising period of unemployment and low-skilled, low-paid short-term work in a fast-food outlet, which he was able to sustain with additional support from his mother. Motivated by his daughter, mother and Connexions worker, he eventually secured a two-year apprenticeship in bricklaying through the Construction Industry Training Board. This 'snakes and ladders' process, on the borders of semi- and low-skilled status, took three years:

'It's just that challenge of growing up, manning up, knowing that you've got a kid coming on the way ... I was really upset and down, 'cos most of my friends have gone to uni or college and stuff, doing something with their life ... and I didn't want to let my mum down as well – just stay at home ... and do nothing.' (Senwe, aged 16, semi-skilled, partnered, wave 1)

'I applied for three apprenticeships and went to an interview. Yeah, I got it! ... Really happy ... every day I just try my hardest and work hard so after two years I'll get the job. Not to just finish with nothing and just go back down on the dole. Now it's less stressful 'cos I'm earning instead of relying on my mum ... So it's made me a better person to provide for my daughter, and just knowing that I'm working for her. And I feel proud of myself for doing that.' (Senwe, aged 19, semi-skilled, apprentice, separated, wave 5)

The perseverance of these young men in improving their lot in life was striking; their accounts revealed the sheer hard work needed to secure, sustain and consolidate a breadwinner role in a context where they could not take their EET trajectories for granted. Like Senwe, Richard, Simon and Orlando all moved from low- to semi-skilled positions over time. Through protracted and circuitous routes, including debilitating periods on the dole, they found full-time jobs: in garage and warehouse work and in a sorting office. They saw these as staging posts on the way to the kind of work that they would eventually like to do, and, with good family support, they were sustaining their motivation.

Most of the young men in this group were strongly committed to securing semi-skilled occupations. In many cases, they fitted the traditional working-class model that is centred around the idea of male breadwinning for their families (Weber, 2018). At the same time, these EET trajectories bear all the hallmarks of a casual and 'patchwork' labour market, necessitating shorter-term aspirations and choices, and more uncertain futures.

'Low-skilled' trajectories

Seventeen young men, all from lower-income families, fell into the 'low-skilled' category at the close of the study. As shown earlier (Introduction to Part II) ten of these young men were grappling with multiple disadvantages in their family lives that impacted on their EET trajectories. Nine were school-age fathers, but in each case their engagement with school was tenuous. Some had been excluded or had poor levels of attendance that had impacted on their self-confidence and achievements.

The young men who had conceived a child later in their teens or early 20s were faring no better. They had accrued negligible qualifications, skills or experience upon which to build an EET trajectory. Their opportunities to compete for work in the labour market were slim, and their journeys through school and post-school training were chequered, with higher drop-out rates for both. The precarious EET trajectories of these young men bore all the hallmarks of their insecure lives. Jed explains here why he dropped out of his college course:

'Just too much, can't, I have the baby and that. And if I have college, I won't have much time with the baby. And I really don't want that.'

Right, yeah. So what, what about with working though? Would that not take time away from baby as well or …?

'Yeah, but it'd, hopefully I'd be able to provide for her. When I was at college you don't really get owt do you. You have to, well you get a free bus pass. That's about it [laughs]. ... I've already got two' GCSEs in construction so ... I don't really need to go back [laughs].' (Jed, age 17, low skilled, partnered, wave 2)

The financial circumstances of these low skilled young men were often precarious. They were dependent on out-of-work benefits and, crucially, they had negligible financial support from their families. Since these young men had accrued very few skills since leaving school, their low-skill status was becoming an entrenched part of their credentials and identity. Their aspirations to work as an integral part of their fatherhood role were no less strong than those of the other young men in the study, but the gap between aspirations and achievements was more pronounced, both in terms of embarking on a particular path and sustaining it over time:

'So I've worked ... a couple of times but it's just because it's always been temporary. So around these times ... they always lay me off. So, it's – I'm always looking again and looking again, until I find something again and I just start right over again. But it's just, it's just really hard to find something permanent this time because I didn't, I didn't finish my studies well and I didn't do no apprenticeship courses. So it's really got a bit hard for me to go to the, to, to the level of job that I, I was really supposed to, I really wanted to go to.' (Marcel, aged 24, low-skilled, unemployed, partnered, wave 1)

The strategy of investing in training and qualifications as a more secure route into employment was well known among these young men and seen as an attractive option. Jakie, for example, hoped to gain skills and a qualification in plastering:

'If I do get a full-time job ... it's never 100 per cent guaranteed that I'm always going to have it ... six months down the line. ... [If] the company has fall backs and has to let people go, I just feel I'm going to be in the same boat again. So, I'd rather go and get a certificate saying I can do something, and I've got more chance of getting a job.' (Jakie, aged 23, low-skilled, unemployed, partnered, wave 1)

However, as we have seen, tailored routes into training were not easy to secure or sustain.

Overall, this group did not progress up the skills ladder during the study, while some of the young men continued on a downward trajectory. Andrew, for example, one of the youngest fathers in the study, revealed the multiple factors that can lead to a downward path, including a lack of support from his family, which led to his disengagement from primary school:

> 'I had to go [to school] on us own. And that's how come I ended up … acting an idiot. … 'cos I thought, obviously, I, I aren't having any help so I'll just do … as I please now. And I – look where I've ended now. But obviously, I mean I still could … change it. But it's just, it's like hard isn't it, really.' (Andrew, aged 16, low-skilled, unemployed, partnered, wave 1)

When we first met Andrew, we became aware that he had learning difficulties. He was attending a college course for Maths and English GCSEs, and later tried courses in plastering and preparation for the armed forces. He did not manage to complete these courses. Over the next few years Andrew's socio-economic circumstances deteriorated significantly. At the same time, relationships with the grandparents and his partner were highly volatile (see Chapters 5 and 6). It was not until his last interview with FYF that Andrew disclosed that he was unable to read, and had difficulties with writing, problems that had shaped and constrained his life since his primary school days. At wave 5, he had been unemployed and in receipt of Jobseekers Allowance for some years. Finding work was a remote dream, although he searched for work every day. He had received some support-in-kind from his mother and her partner (he was able to lodge with them for a while). Yet his mother was not able to assist him financially. His Jobseekers Allowance had recently been sanctioned; he had not read a letter informing him of an appointment that he needed to attend. He was demoralised and depressed by his precarious situation:

> 'If I got a job, it would change my life. … I wouldn't mind being a builder or something. But, like I say, I can't read any communications. So, it is hard. Like, I see a job going, and I put in for it and ten others who have, like, A for communications obviously will end up with it. … I've handed [my CV] in at Poundland … the Market, fish shops, pizza shops – as daft as it seems, everywhere. … If I got an interview, I think I'd be happy … I am going backwards on myself … I just look and look and look and never get anywhere. … I mean, people look at us, "oh look at him, on JSA [Jobseekers Allowance]. We're paying his benefits", but "hang on there, you are, but no one won't hand us any jobs". … It's the worst, most frustrating thing probably ever. … I've had a few problems and me money's been … stopped … for about three weeks now. It's a big thing … when you don't have any money. … I can't travel to get anywhere and have a look [for work]. … I've asked me mum, but she said "no" she hasn't got it. …

If I don't get any money or anything from anywhere, I'm going to be probably homeless. Sometimes I even think about crying ... It's really, really hard.' (Andrew, aged ʃ19, low-skilled, long-term unemployed, partnered, wave 5)

As other researchers report (Donald et al, 2022; Ladlow et al, 2023) a lack of employment can produce significant emotional turmoil and mental health challenges for young men who are unable to support their children. Andrew attached enormous importance to his relationship with his daughter (see his earlier account), which provided the motivation to keep searching for work. But, arguably, his fatherhood status, and the need to provide for his daughter placed extra pressure upon him, reinforcing the sense of futility and failure that pervaded his account.

Several other young men in similar circumstances had gone further along these downward paths. Adam had become homeless when he could no longer pay his board and lodging at home. Living in poverty on the minimum levels of benefits, he drifted from sofa-surfing with friends and family into emergency hostel accommodation, where there was no provision for bringing his child (see Chapter 8). As a final example, Callum (quoted earlier) had been on an upward trajectory between waves 1 and 2 of our study, moving from a college course to an apprenticeship. By wave 3, he was struggling financially, with cuts to his Educational Maintenance Allowance, and the loss of his free travel pass and free meal vouchers. By wave 4, his trajectory was downward. He had lost his apprenticeship and had not received payment for his casual employment. With barely enough funds to live on, he resorted once more to selling and using drugs, and his relationship with his children and with his mother became more strained.

As these cases show, the increased conditionality of benefits, and the threat or application of sanctions could further destabilise the fragile lives of these low-skilled, disadvantaged young men, leading to precarious housing and the risk of criminal practices. As Callum's and Andrew's accounts show, it was not uncommon for mental health issues to emerge, which added a further layer of complexity and challenge to the parenting efforts of these young men. Indeed, the growing discrepancy between their ideals of fatherhood and what they could actually achieve was, in itself, detrimental to their well-being and their identities as fathers. Such circumstances could derail their efforts to see and to support their children and their children's mothers, in some cases resulting in a loss of contact over time.

Concluding discussion

Our evidence shows a strongly held ideology among young fathers of the value of 'stepping up' to a breadwinner role and identity. As other researchers have found, breadwinning remains a powerful ideological component of young fatherhood (Shirani, 2015). At the same time, our evidence suggests that this economic model of young fatherhood does not eclipse notions of engaged fatherhood; the two have become closely intertwined to produce a more nuanced understanding of the roles and responsibilities of young fathers (Dermott, 2008). Both components, then, are integral to 'being there'. This was the case regardless of the young men's EET trajectories and skills levels, their relationships with the mothers, or their co-resident status with their children. The earning power of the young men is an important factor in securing their credentials as good fathers, and (as shown for Dominic and Jason in Chapter 5) could be used as a bargaining chip when access to their children was curtailed.

The findings presented here attest to the sheer hard work and determination of young fathers to pursue a breadwinning role, whether studying for a degree, juggling several jobs at a time or the relentless search for casual work. Many young men faced a triple burden of earning, learning and caring that required great commitment and fortitude. Such evidence should dispel any last vestige of the idea that young fathers are shirkers, who simply run away from their responsibilities.

At this point it is worth revisiting the well-established correlation between young fatherhood and indices of social deprivation, with a view to discerning more clearly how this correlation should be understood, and how young fathers themselves are implicated in these processes. As we have seen, this correlation was evident for a substantial number of the lower-income, low-skilled young fathers in this study. However, for the better resourced young men, no such correlation was evident. As we have seen, those with a steady accumulation of educational skills, and, crucially, with solid family resources and stable homes, were engaged in longer term planning, working with an imperative not so much to earn but to build a livelihood, a trade or a career. These were upward, future-oriented and, in some cases, strategically managed trajectories. The young men had a sustained sense of their own identities and confidence in pursuing their goals, borne of a more secure socio-economic foundation for their future lives. In these cases, the disruptions caused by early fatherhood were more likely to create a temporary fissure in an existing trajectory that had already been forged during their earlier years. These young men were continuing to thrive despite their early entry into parenthood.

An early and unexpected entry into fatherhood can be the catalyst to grow up a little faster, to 'make good', to try out new forms of adult identity, to find work or other sources of income in the shorter-term, or to redouble efforts to secure longer-term pathways into trades or careers. Yet, the accounts presented here show that while there was some movement over time in the skills categories inhabited by these young men, their EET trajectories had already begun to form during their childhoods, shaped by a constellation of socio-economic, educational, relational and familial factors. The disruptions or enhancements caused by early fatherhood, then, do not amount to permanent shifts in the direction of a life. They are more likely to create a temporary fissure or reappraisal of an existing trajectory that has already been forged prior to the arrival of a child.

As Furstenberg suggests, 'one cannot glibly conclude that parenthood in adolescence inevitably or irreversibly disrupts the life course' (Furstenberg, 2003: 28). Political rhetoric concerning a parenting 'deficit', i.e. that early parenthood is an individual failing that brings with it a range of social ills and leads to poor outcomes for parents and their children is not borne out by the evidence presented here. In line with wider evidence (Kiernan, 2002; Duncan, 2007), our findings show that it is not early parenthood that adversely affects the life chances of young people; rather it is pre-existing poverty that leads to social marginalisation and reduced opportunities in life. Longitudinal evidence on the lives of young mothers presents a similar picture: their medium to longer-term economic and social fortunes are comparable to their peers who started their families later in life (SmithBattle, 2013; Bekaert and Bradly, 2019).

These findings on the significance of poverty in shaping people's life chances are hardly surprising. There is, 'a growing polarisation between the advantaged and the disadvantaged ... a social fracturing which would have been unrecognisable in the society of 20 years ago' (Bynner, 2007: 377– 8). This picture has hardly abated since 2007; rather, it has been accentuated as welfare retrenchment policies have been introduced and youth services dismantled. The accounts of the young men presented here accord with this wider picture.

All of this suggests a pressing need for investment in a range of socio-economic measures to support the efforts of semi- and low-skilled young fathers to provide for their children. These include tailored training and employment pathways, careers advice and support, of the sort formerly provided through the Connexions service, and the provision of benefits packages to support training and apprenticeship schemes. The provision of an adequate minimum wage and improved work conditions for young people would be highly beneficial. This would require policies that refocus on the 'demand' side issues surrounding training and employment opportunities, as a counter to 'supply' side issues that focus on the willingness or otherwise of young people to take up paid work (Hutchinson et al, 2016).

Tailored EET support for young fathers that is provided earlier in the life course and sustained through the critical years of education and into training for work would seem to be essential. There is a pressing need, also, to tackle the generational inequalities that arise in a benefits system that favours older people, and that serves, perversely, to punish vulnerable young men through a harsh sanctions regime, rather than provide a safety net of social security. This would bring direct benefits to young fathers and mothers, their children and wider families, and it would have wider social value. Not least, it would help to prevent the cascade of further problems that can arise through precarity, including the loss of a home. It is to this issue of housing, and associated problems of locality and declining neighbourhoods, that we now turn.

8

Finding a place to parent: young fathers' housing needs and pathways

With Linzi Ladlow[1]

Introduction

In this chapter we broaden our perspective further to trace the varied housing pathways of young fathers, drawing on our earlier contributions (Neale and Ladlow, 2015b), a secondary analysis of Following Young Fathers (FYF) housing data, and conceptual ideas developed in Ladlow (2021) and other scholarly literature. Housing is a crucial resource and topic of concern for young parents. An adequate home environment is vital for a sense of security as a parent and a necessary foundation for the care of children. As a major domain within the political and socio-economic exosystem, it is a key factor that shapes the journeys of young fathers (Deslauriers and Kiselica, 2022). Yet housing is seldom explored in research on young people's transitions to parenthood, while research on the housing trajectories of young fathers is sparse.

In our discussion we map out the housing circumstances of the young fathers across the sample, explore their values and aspirations for finding a place to parent, and trace their housing journeys over time. Their accounts reveal significant diversity and fluidity in their housing journeys over time, including 'yo-yo' trajectories involving fluctuating states of independence from/dependence on their families, and on statutory and other forms of professional housing support. These possibilities are constrained and influenced by an increasingly precarious housing system, in which opportunities for young parents to set up an independent home have been progressively eroded. We situate our discussion in a political context in which policy makers tend to prioritise the issue of welfare and housing dependency, rather than the actual needs of young parents (Giullari and Shaw, 2005).

Young people, destandardised transitions and evolving housing welfare in the UK

Rising house prices, falling incomes and instability in the youth labour market and housing systems mean that finding a place to parent often involves 'walking a tightrope' (Ladlow, 2021) for many young people. This is especially true for those who lack existing financial, familial or housing resources. While rich, qualitative research about the housing trajectories and experiences of young fathers is relatively rare, the housing experiences and living arrangements of young people have become internationally recognised areas of academic and policy concern (Mackie, 2016). According to Mackie (2016), debates in policy coalesce around two concurrent challenges. The first is to ensure that all young people can leave home and live independently, an issue that may be more challenging when becoming a parent at a young age. The second is to improve both the suitability and availability of housing.

Despite these intentions, research consistently shows that young people aspire to secure sustainable housing that is independent of their parents, in a context where such provision is increasingly elusive. Trends in the UK and across Europe indicate that young people now rely on their families to house them for much longer periods of time (Holdsworth and Morgan, 2005; Stone et al, 2014). This has the effect for many young people of delaying their entry into independent adulthood (ONS, 2019). ONS (2019) figures confirm that more than 50 per cent of young people in the UK had left home for the first time at age 23; a trend also observed across Europe, where over half of young people continue to live with their parents until their mid-20s. The majority of these are young men (Eurostat, 2021).

A number of parallel trends explain the delay of housing independence to later in the life course. A combination of increasing youth unemployment and the rising costs of housing and education have contributed to the creation of constrained and prolonged transitions to employment, increasing the financial dependency of young people on their parents (Biggart and Walther, 2005; McKee, 2012; Banting and Myles, 2013; Mackie, 2016; Maroto and Severson, 2020, see also Chapter 7). Severe housing crises across Europe have also meant that access to and affordability of housing as a basic social good and foundational welfare resource have come under threat for more people (Garcia and Vicari Haddock, 2016). It is also worth noting that young people from families with limited material and socio-economic resources and/or where there has been a parental break-up, for example, are more likely to leave home at a younger age than those where parent relationships remain intact (van den Berg et al, 2018). Earlier transitions out of the family home may therefore also be indicative of multigenerational inequities across households (SmithBattle et al, 2019b).

As we saw in the Introduction to this book, the linear pattern and normative, progress biography of leaving education, securing employment, entering a stable relationship, starting a new family and securing a home has been eroded over the years, although it remains an ideal for many people, including young fathers (see, for example, Ben in Chapter 4). The destandardised youth transitions that have emerged include 'yo-yo' housing trajectories (Biggart and Walther, 2005) that are fluid, complex and sometimes reversible. For many young people, this has created a constellation of semi-dependency (Biggart and Walther, 2005) comprising varying states of dependence, semi-dependence and independence in relation to their families of origin and statutory housing provision.

The destandardisation of youth transitions has also been influenced by changes in the British housing welfare system and the austerity policies that have defined the second decade of the 21st century (see Chapter 2). An encroaching crisis in housing provision has impacted on young people's housing options and their ability to secure housing across all sectors (for example, Somerville, 2016; Lund, 2018). The radical reorientation of housing policy set in motion by the Coalition government (2010–15), and later accelerated by the Conservative government from 2015, has favoured support for models of homeownership, while simultaneously worsening financial and regulative conditions for those yet to secure a mortgage (Stephens and Stephenson, 2016). Owner-occupation and social renting have become increasingly tenuous options for young people, compounded by rising house prices and steadily falling incomes. Reduced mortgage lending, coupled with reduced loan-to-value ratios have also made it difficult for young people to buy their own homes without significant additional financial support (National Housing Federation, 2010 cited by Clapham et al, 2014; Coulter, 2018). In a context where British housing policy has redistributed rights from low-income groups to others (Stephens and Stephenson, 2016), existing familial support and the resources that may be passed on from the older generation have become crucial safety nets that shape young people's housing options and their timing.

When young people leave the family home, they tend to rely on the social and private renting sectors (Heath, 2008). The private rented sector (PRS) is one of the most accessible housing options for young people, but it is costly and not always adequate for families. Many young families consider PRS tenures to be unsuitable for their needs due to uncertainty about their short-term length and security (Clapham et al, 2014). Rents are unregulated and comparatively high (DCLG, 2012), placing constraints on longer-term housing goals. The standards of PRS homes are also reportedly poor and sometimes non-compliant with the Decent Homes Standard (DCLG, 2009).

The challenges of navigating the PRS system are compounded by reduced entitlements to, and availability of, social housing and state support for rented housing through the social security system. Since 2010, the stock of social housing has continually decreased. With increasingly large waiting lists for new social housing applicants, priority is given to those deemed most in need. For people under the age of 18, support is restricted to those who are homeless, threatened with homelessness, or who are primary caregivers. In this context, young fathers applying for social housing as individuals are likely to have low priority status unless they are registered as their child's primary carer, which is uncommon (see Chapter 5). More generally, the parental status of young fathers is rarely considered in the housing support system. This may result in their assignment to accommodation that is unsuitable as a place to parent, for example, in shared accommodation, singles hostels or bedsits. Housing options like these are rarely suitable for children and, as we have seen in earlier chapters, may present safeguarding risks. Council accommodation procedures and housing shortages also frequently lead to allocations at a distance from family and friends (Berrington et al, 2005; Alexander et al, 2010; Lau Clayton, 2016), sometimes resulting in isolation (Speak et al, 1997). This is part and parcel of the gendered neglect of young fathers in policy and professional practice circles that we highlighted in Chapter 2.

Moreover, changes to Universal Credit since 2017 mean that young people under the age of 21 are no longer eligible for housing benefit (GOV.UK, 2022). Under the new system, parents under the age of 25 receive a lower personal allowance than is paid to benefit claimants over the age of 25. These cuts to welfare entitlements for young people, coupled with substantial funding cuts to housing support services, leave vulnerable young people at heightened risk of homelessness (Homeless Link, 2013).

It is worth noting here that historically there have been some encouraging commitments among policy makers to improving the housing situations of young parents. As shown in Chapter 2, towards the end of the Teenage Pregnancy Strategy, the Teenage Parent Supported Housing Programme was piloted in seven local authorities (see Hadley and Ingham, 2018, for a full review). The aim was to provide enhanced support packages for young parents aged 16 and 17 who were not living with their own parents. An evaluation of the pilot (Quilgars, et al, 2011) found that 72 per cent of supported parents benefited from the support of understanding staff, practical help with housing issues, and increased confidence. Nearly 60 per cent observed benefits for their children too. Some 67 per cent also moved on to live independently following support from the programme. Similarly positive results were reported in an evaluation of a commissioned 'Action for Children' supported housing, tenancy and floating support service in Rochdale (Livesley et al, 2011). The young mothers described the scheme as lifesaving. They were supported to escape circumstances of extreme vulnerability and felt secure and safe. They were able to fulfil their aspirations for having a family life and their new housing security was a catalyst for positive life changes.

However, without a national framework for the provision of housing support, availability is patchy and uncoordinated across localities. Moreover, where the needs of young mothers are prioritised, as primary caring parents, young fathers are especially vulnerable and subject to an increasingly conditional framework of housing welfare. It is against this backdrop that we examine the fluid and patchwork housing trajectories of the young fathers in this study.

(In)stability and mobility in the housing trajectories of young fathers

The living situations of young fathers provide the foundation upon which important domains of their lives are built, including their parenting and family relationships, and their education and employment aspirations and achievements. Housing and 'home' provide people with ontological security – subjective and deeply rooted understandings of the quality, safety and security of one's living environment, which impacts on one's sense of self and capacity to flourish (Giddens, 1990; Padgett, 2007; Ladlow, 2021). The young men in this study described a diverse range of living arrangements and housing trajectories that were dynamic, variable in their quality and often unstable over time (Goldberg et al, 2013; Neale and Ladlow, 2015b; Deslauriers and Kiselica, 2022). These living environments were shaped by their family backgrounds and resources, and their gender and relationship status, as well as the housing options available to them.

Figure 8.1 maps the housing options and possible housing trajectories described by the young fathers in this study, revealing relative degrees of stability and (im)permanence in their places of residence. Notwithstanding some variation across cases, both 'horizontal' (between parental households) and 'vertical' (into private and/or social rented accommodation or homelessness) transitions were described.

There was also considerable yo-yoing between households and living arrangements, within and across the cases. Options for homeownership were unrealised by any of the fathers in this sample; none had access to the capital required to achieve this, although the skilled young men in the study had the potential to accrue such capital over time (see Chapter 7).

Of the sample of 31 young fathers, approximately two thirds lived with their parents for all or part of the early years of their parenting, with 15 young men sustaining this arrangement throughout the study period. Of these, 11 young men were in semi-skilled occupations, or still in education. This gave them some basic ontological security and a sense of having and being 'at home' (Padgett, 2007) and a place to parent, at least on a part-time basis. By the close of the study, a further three young men were residing in the maternal household and the remaining 13 were living independently, primarily in social housing. These participants described more fluid housing trajectories. 'Being there' for a child and the mother was a particular challenge for young fathers who were parenting at a distance, that is, who

Figure 8.1: Typology of living arrangements/ontological security for young fathers

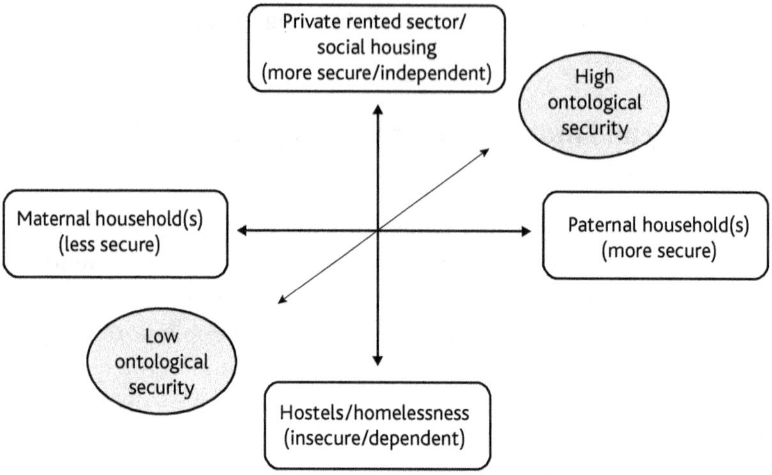

```
                    Private rented sector/
                       social housing
                  (more secure/independent)         High
                              ▲                  ontological
                              |                    security
                              |        ↗
  Maternal household(s) ◄─────┼─────► Paternal household(s)
      (less secure)           |          (more secure)
                         ↙    |
       Low                    |
   ontological                ▼
     security          Hostels/homelessness
                      (insecure/dependent)
```

were single and attempting to co-parent across households. Several of these young men were also living in overcrowded conditions and experiencing intergenerational conflicts with their parents (see Chapter 6).

Some described 'horizontal' and temporary moves into the homes of the maternal grandmother around the time of the birth. This arrangement enabled the young men to co-parent at close hand with the mothers of their children but, for reasons discussed in Chapter 6, this was often a short-lived option. Despite the ostensible stability and financial and material security provided by continued residence with parents, living with them long term became increasingly difficult and was rarely possible for extended periods of time. This resulted in higher residential mobility and fluidity in living arrangements as the young men sought or were sometimes forced into establishing independence in the PRS.

Pathways to housing independence and autonomy were therefore fluid and variable. Those with greater resources were more likely to secure some semblance of housing independence and stability, moving up the vertical plane across the study with less frequent house moves and longer-term tenancies. A larger proportion of the young fathers (16) described unstable housing trajectories characterised by dependence on the state (in hostel or social housing provision), or on informal networks (including sofa-surfing at friends' houses). In these more extreme cases, the young fathers were experiencing a hidden form of homelessness (Quail, 2007). Across the study, these young men experienced frequent moves, with high residential mobility that created greater challenges in sustaining relationships with their children. Those yo-yoing between states of independence, semi-dependence and dependence were also more likely to be low-skilled (12 out of 17) and their limited education and employment opportunities further compounded their precarious housing situations. Seven young fathers from the sample received specialist support from housing charities, enabling them to settle into independent stable households.

In what follows, young fathers' housing pathways are explored in relation to stable or chaotic experiences, and familial or state support. We consider how the participants narrated their aspirations for security, stability and independence by establishing secure housing and a 'home' as a central component of fulfilling their responsibilities as fathers. Presenting analyses of cases that are representative of each segment of the housing trajectories typology, we illustrate the yo-yo nature of continuity and change in the young fathers' housing arrangements over time, and what this residential mobility meant for their parenting efforts. We also draw out the different experiences of young men who were partnered, and developing their parenting at close hand, and those who were single, and parenting at a distance.

Housing journeys: aspirations, stability and change

Despite facing more complex transitions to adulthood, young fathers held conventional aspirations for their housing. They aspired to live in their own home and establish a suitable and stable location to bring up their children:

> 'I'd like to have my own house when I'm at least seventeen or something.' (Jackson, aged 15, lower income, partnered, lives with his mother and siblings, wave 1)

> 'Bringing them up in the right environment, in the right place. I mean right now I'm living in a flat and we've got noisy neighbours. And, you know, there's a lot going on. I'm still not finished decorating. And it's not suitable to bring a child into I don't think. I think, in reality, you need to have, you know, show 'em what environment you should be in. So then when they grow up they, they're gonna be in that environment. They won't wanna bring their kid up in, you know, in a different type of environment like what I'm living in now, so ...' (Callum, aged 19, lower income, single, social housing, wave 2)

> 'I'd ... stay away from a council estate ... and not go to a typical council estate school, where it's full of idiots. ... I'm unemployed ... and living in a council flat in a block of smackhead flats in [deprived areas of the city] wasn't ideal ... I can't give [my son] the best possible life. ... I've always wanted kids ... in a stable life, work, having a nice home, doing healthy things. ... didn't even have a garden for him to

play in. ... I would never consider putting [my son] in an ounce of life I've had – that's not a normal upbringing.' (Jason, aged 22 lower income, single, social housing, wave 1)

The disadvantaged young men typically framed their future housing aspirations around a narrative of intergenerational change and repair. They hoped to provide a better home and life for their children than they had experienced themselves. Trevor, for example, was living in a deprived neighbourhood and frequently experienced problems relating to crime in the local area. Like Callum and Jason, his aspirations for his daughter were linked to housing and neighbourhood:

'My views on bringing her up are completely different to how I got brought up. Like I'd like to bring her up in a nice area where there's no crime or anything like that. So I'd keep her away from all that sort of stuff. And I'm guessing [daughter's mother] will be the same to be quite honest. Different to how we've had it.' (Trevor, aged 16, lower income, single, living with parents, wave 2)

Jock, a skilled and well-resourced young man who was living with his parents did not experience these problems of degraded housing and neighbourhoods. However, his desire to set up his own home was no less evident. Like all the young men, this depended on his ability to secure employment, suitable housing and financial independence from his own parents:

'Finish university first, get my degree, get a decent job, get our own place, get settled down. And then take it from there. It's like I'm doing it all back to front! ... Financially, no, I haven't got a chance of finding anywhere of my own.

That's why I'm working so hard ... to get to that stage in my life where I can have my own place and, you know, hopefully make another go of it, trying to be a family.' (Jock, aged 20/21, higher income, co-parenting at a distance/partnered, living with family, waves 1 and 2)

In doing everything "back to front", Jock illustrates the potential mismatch between the individual biographies of young people and institutionally normative transitions to adulthood. Nevertheless, future orientations like these underscored the young fathers' decision making and choices around their living arrangements and were often thoughtfully balanced alongside considerations of existing family support, the affordability and accessibility of various housing options, and a determination to support their families.

Co-residence with the paternal family

While several of the young fathers expressed a desire to secure their own home, many continued to live with their own parents as they transitioned to parenthood. As shown in Chapter 6, this was perhaps the most tangible form of support offered to young fathers by the older generation. Where households are adequately resourced and relationships relatively amicable, young fathers value the opportunity to remain at home with their parents and consider this a safe, secure and supportive environment for their children. Family living also facilitated the young fathers' efforts to manage the triple shift of earning, learning and caring (see Chapter 7) and was a protective factor in a context when traditional linear transitions from adolescence to adulthood are no longer standardised. This living arrangement was often predicated on the secure financial position of the grandparents, the provision of informal kin care, finding a workable and amicable balance of responsibilities across the generations, and opportunities for the young fathers to maintain a social life and pursue education and/or employment opportunities.

School-age fathers who were in relatively amicable relationships were most likely to maintain a home base with their parents. In some cases, they moved in with the maternal grandparents, or made frequent moves between the two households. Across the sample, a young father's co-residence with parents was a natural continuation of previous patterns of living and the most common form of non-tenure arrangement. It represents a secure base from which to parent, a stepping-stone to eventual housing independence and was often the best housing option and comparably better than alternatives like the PRS or hostels:

> 'I'm only going to choose a right house 'cos I don't want to be in a hostel or anything like that because it's not a good environment for my little one. I want a decent environment for him. I'd sooner stay at my mum's where it's a nice environment. I'd prefer an environment like that so he can grow up without getting hurt.' (Jed, aged 16, partnered, lower income, living with mother, stepfather and siblings, wave 1)

> 'Yeah, I mean at the minute it's difficult for me to get my own place. To pay rent. ...When my partner at the time, she had [son], she was ... staying at her mum's and I was at my mum's. And it was, it was difficult again. And her mum actually invited me to stay. And we ended up, well I ended up staying for just over a year. She didn't have to do that. ... But she wanted to do that. ... And ... my mum's been great. ... And at the weekends ... my mum drives, so she'll take us out. ... to the seaside. It was just the help and support from family members. Yeah, don't know what we would have done without

them. ... But yeah, the main goal for me is to get maybe my own place. And obviously so the kids can have their own space at mine. Like I said, at the minute it's just, it's not possible at the moment.' (Kevin, aged 24, lower income, separated, formerly partnered and living with his mother, wave 1)

For young single men, co-residence with their own parents gave them space to establish a relationship with their child in a home environment that was not under the control of the mother or her family. Dominic considered this especially important in circumstances of strained relationships with his ex-partner and the maternal family:

'Like, everything's set in place for me to have him whenever. Like ... he's got his own bedroom at my house. He's got his own set of clothes. ... When I go and pick him up from, from her house, it's just him I pick up. I don't pick up anything else.' (Dominic, aged 21, higher income, single, living with parents, wave 4)

Living with parents, then, was commonly seen as an expedient solution in a context where the young men lacked employment and sufficient finances to fund an independent household. However, it was rarely considered as a sustainable or long-term solution. As shown in Chapter 6, tensions could arise over intergenerational family relationships and responsibilities, and there were fears of becoming too financially dependent on the older generation.

Overcrowding was identified as a significant issue for the young men that eroded their ontological security and sharpened their desire for a place of their own. Dominic, for example, reported sharing a bedroom with his siblings when his son came to stay, in order to give his son his own space:

'Cos I gave [son] my room and I just sleep on, when he's not there I sleep in his bed 'cos he's got a full-sized bed. When he's there my younger brother's got a bunk bed so I'll sleep there. But I've got no dedicated space to myself. I ain't got a room. All my stuff which were, which is kind of, which I could really show off and have in my bedroom is just packed away now. So I don't have anywhere to really relax. Just really sort of, just *be*, do you know what I mean? So that sometimes plays a bit havoc 'cos if you had nowhere to go and you're just like in the living room wi' your parents and, well you can go outside. You've got no, you've got no dedicated space. ... You're constantly in the same environment as your parents. ... It's a constant conflict. ... Yeah, if I had the financial muscle I would definitely just live on my own ... it's just, it's not ideal, but it's probably a lot better position than a lot of other people so I can't complain that much.' (Dominic, aged 21, higher income, single, living with parents, wave 4)

Other young men were living in smaller housing units in which they shared a bedroom with their child and co-parent. This was the case for Jayden, whose partner and daughter came to stay three nights per week. The small family home also housed his mother, stepfather and two brothers:

'[We] only live in a two-bedroom flat so it's not really that big. So I've got to share a room with my brothers. And like [daughter], she's got her own bed and like stuff like that. But we've all got to share a room. So I'm trying to blag [my mum] to get a bigger house but she's not having none of it! ... I moved out because of our daughter but mainly because of arguing and stuff like that as well. And because we were cooped up in one room because [my partner] stays like say four or five nights of week if you know what I mean? And the room, obviously one bedroom weren't big enough for three of us.' (Jayden, aged 21, lower income, single, living with parents, wave 1)

'Yeah ... there is a point where we want to, you know, move out and do things ourselves and stuff. ... if we had like an unlimited pot of money, like anyone probably would, but I mean it is quite practical living there right now because you can always ask for that like help and it's there, I guess, to an extent. So yeah, I mean maybe like later on, definitely.' (Zane, aged 18, higher income, partnered, living in maternal household, wave 1)

Five of the young men remained living with their fathers following the divorce or separation of their parents, or moved back and forth between the homes of their mothers and fathers as a variation on a horizontal yo-yo trajectory. This was the case for Richard. His parents' divorce was acrimonious, leading to fears that his mother would take over the family home and leave him with nowhere to live. Richard was not able to stay at his partner's parent's council house because of residence rules that would affect the benefit entitlements of the maternal household:

'Can't [stay over] 'cos that, she don't pay t' rent. Council does. ... I stay till, like one o'clock in t' morning and go home. [Then] I go back down to [partner's] before my daughter wakes up at like, I set off from my house at about half six. Get down to my partner's for about seven.' (Richard, aged 16, partnered, lower income, lives with father, wave 2)

As this case shows, a variety of relational and financial circumstances and regulations may arise in families to shape or unsettle the housing options of these young men.

Moves between paternal and maternal grandparent households

A second trajectory that involved continued reliance on family support networks for partnered young men involved 'horizontal' moves between paternal and maternal grandparent households. This trajectory provided continued financial, material security and semi-dependence for the young fathers and their families, albeit based on split residence or frequent moves between different households.

These split arrangements were especially helpful where the two households were located miles apart and the young fathers could not afford daily bus fares to visit their children. Some young families split their time evenly between their parents' homes. This facilitated frequent contact between grandparents and grandchild but gave them regular breaks from the intensity of supporting their children (see Chapter 6). The young couple, in turn, were able to spend every day together. They could develop a routine as co-parents of their child and established some autonomy and a sense of semi-independence as a young family, without the financial pressures or responsibilities of independent living. This was the case for both Jed and Jimmy in the early days of parenthood (although, as shown in Chapter 4, Jimmy's volatile relationships led to the eventual cessation of his contact with his child):

> 'It's got easier now, now we've got into like a routine. ... And like I've bought stuff ... she's bought stuff ... so we don't have to carry it all. ... I've got clothes at hers, she's got clothes at mine, [son's] got bottles at hers and that.' (Jed, aged 16, lower income, partnered, living across two households, wave 1)

> 'One night she just stayed 'cos she couldn't be bothered going home. Then since then she's been coming to stay all t' time. So, she just brings what she needs. Like she stays like three times a week. And I go to hers on t' weekend. So she just brings what she needs ... [It's] better than before. 'Cos I don't have to spend all my money going up to her house. And she's staying at mine. I get to see my son more, so yeah. And ma mum gets to see him so yeah ... If we do, we don't watch him, Mum'll watch him so we can go out and have a break. ... I hope it stays how it is for like maybe another year, year or two. Till I've finished all my courses at college. And then I can get a job and get my own house.' (Jimmy, aged 16, lower income, partnered and living across two households, wave 2)

Despite its advantages, however, this pattern of horizontal yo-yoing between grandparent households was not without its challenges, not least adjusting to different relationship dynamics across households and the inevitable tensions that could arise across the generations (see Chapter 6). Where tensions arose in these households, the arrangements were short-lived. Unusually, Jock's partner had moved into the well-resourced home of Jock's parents at the outset, but tensions ran high, the mother returned to the maternal household and the couple separated. Jock then aimed to develop a friendship with the mother as the basis for parenting at a distance (see Chapter 5) and by wave 2 the relationship with the mother had been rekindled. What was missing was an opportunity to find their own home as a solid base for a new family life together:

> 'This isn't how it's supposed to be. ... If I had one wish that'd be ... for all three of us to be together 'cos ... we've ended up in separate places and, you know, this bickering going on between, you know, our family members ... it's not great. ... And I just want him to be with me all the time, I'd like to have all three of us to have our own place but it's just frustrating having to go somewhere to see my son. ... I shouldn't, you know, have to go and pick him up and take him back to mine, just to spend a day with him.' (Jock, aged 21, higher income, rekindled relationship, living with family, wave 2)

Overall, regardless of whether young fathers were residing in the paternal or maternal household, or across both households, these arrangements were generally considered to be necessary but temporary solutions. While these arrangements supported young men in 'being there' for their children, they did not always guarantee stability and security. They were seen as stepping stones to a more independent future. Most young men wanted to live independently and aspired to homes of their own, free from the constraints of living with their families, but also with continued support where possible. However, opportunities to make 'vertical' moves to tenured housing arrangements were very limited for young fathers. Whatever their ideals for parenting in independent households, this goal was unrealisable for most young fathers, at least in the short to medium term. Even where it was achievable, moving on and up to independent living brought a new range of challenges for these young men.

Moving on and transitioning to 'tenured' independence

Across cases, there were two identifiable trajectories for the young men who had already transitioned out of the family home or who did so during the study period. These represented the 'vertical' moves involving some independence from family. The first were characterised by relatively stable, secure and prescribed transitions, where the young men were able to establish some independence in the PRS. This route was only open to a few of the well-resourced young men in this study. It was too expensive, the housing was inappropriate for raising a child, or tenures were too short-term. Darren moved into the PRS briefly only to find he couldn't afford the rent:

> 'I went into a private house. It wor nice as well, big conservatory and everything. £630 or £640 a month it wor. Turned out I couldn't afford it. So I ended up moving back into old 'ouse. But it wor more homesick than nowt else. It just didn't, you know, it didn't feel the same.' (Darren, aged 22, lower income, living with partner, wave 3)

For higher-income young men at the upper end of our age range, university placements provided what might be characterised as a more standardised and prescribed route into rented student accommodation, a transition experienced by many young people who enter higher education. Of the three young men who moved into the PRS under these circumstances, one was living in a shared student house that was unsuitable for children, while two others had married and moved into their own flats prior to the arrival of their children. For Martin, renting provided a sense of independence and stability: "I feel like we have our own lives" (Martin, aged 23, higher income, partnered, private rented accommodation, wave 1).

In other cases, young, partnered couples were able to move on via local authority housing that was offered to the mothers. This was the case for Kevin who, after a year of living in overcrowded conditions in the maternal household, moved with his then-partner and their child into their own flat: "[My partner] ended up getting her own place. And … we moved in together. I think that's, as a family, that's what you want. You want your own space, your own house. Yeah, it was our castle … It was, it was brilliant" (Kevin, aged 24, lower income, formerly partnered, local authority housing, wave 1).

However, access to safe, affordable housing is not always possible for young people, especially where they have limited financial security and/or do not have intact family support systems (McDowell and Bonner-Thompson, 2020). The single young men in this study, and those who were intermittently attached to their partners, had to find less-secure routes into independent living when staying with their parents became untenable. Local authority housing and housing benefits were important safety nets, but the provision was for single homeless men. The accommodation was often too far away from mother and child, and of poor quality or in degraded neighbourhoods that were seen as unsuitable for a child.

Instability and high residential mobility

The more disadvantaged young fathers experienced nomadic and precarious trajectories characterised by periods of homelessness or residence in hostels. Some 16 of the young men led what might be called a nomadic existence, characterised by high rates of residential mobility during their parenting journeys. This included living in precarious temporary abodes and sofa-surfing at the homes of friends, interspersed with frequent moves in and out of the homes of their mothers and/or fathers. In these cases, their state of semi-dependence included financial reliance on the state, reliance on friends and/or the need for professional intervention. These options offered partial, short-term resolutions to housing woes, but they were only temporary solutions that increased their precarity and dependence on others and constrained their ability to sustain a relationship with their child and co-parent. A typical housing trajectory identified among the more disadvantaged young fathers involved frequent moves. Jimmy, for example, moved seven times during the course of the study:

'It's harder for me, 'cos then I've got nowhere to go, nowhere to live. And I'm like sponging off people's mums and that. And then obviously I can't go and see [my child's mum], she can't bring [my son] down to see me. So ... it's just harder on me.' (Jimmy, aged 16, lower income, partnered, nomadic, wave 3)

Andrew moved four times over the course of the study. From his father's house he moved to a local authority singles hostel, then had a short spell in a social housing flat with his partner. This tenure ended when the partnership came to an end amid domestic violence and damage to the property. Residence in a hostel led to curtailed contact with his daughter. Visitation restrictions were in place because of the presence of drug users and alcoholics in the building: "I can't blame 'em basically. But I am a bit ... gutted like, but ... end of day all they're doing is a ... job really" (Andrew, aged 17, lower income, partnered, living in a hostel, wave 3). Andrew hoped to secure a home in the PRS, which he expected would enable him to spend more time with his daughter and partner. As a temporary measure he moved to his mother's house but he had no income, and when his mother's housing benefit was withdrawn, she could not afford to continue to house him (see his account in Chapter 7). Feeling like a temporary resident at his mother's house, Andrew's feared becoming homeless: "It's more I sleep at me mum's house. But like I say, if I don't get any money or anything from anywhere, I'm going to be probably homeless. So it is hard" (Andrew, aged 19, lower income, partnered, multiple residences, wave 5). The unstable and chaotic housing pathway Andrew describes is shaped in part by housing welfare reforms that disadvantage young people and their families. However, by the end of the study, Andrew had once more moved into a social housing unit with his partner and their daughter: "I think it's … it's amazing! But basically, I couldn't ask for owt else basically really. … For one, I have a home. I have my daughter and I have, I have my partner" (Andrew, aged 19, lower income, partnered, multiple residences, wave 5).

Adam provides a further example of the slippery slope towards homeless status. His housing journey as a parent had started at his father's flat and then moved on to the maternal household. But, as shown in Chapter 6, a violent argument with the maternal grandfather led to the young family moving in with Adam's mother. However, when Adam dropped out of college, his mother could no longer claim benefits for him as a dependent child. The young couple also [found] it hard to live together: "So I got kicked out of my mum's for not being able to pay to live there. So then I was homeless for about two or three months. I was living at my mates, at my dad's, just in and out of houses" (Adam, aged 17, lower income, partnered, nomadic, wave 2). After this intensely nomadic period of his life, Adam went to live in a hostel for single homeless men, arranged for him by a local housing charity. This gave Adam a roof over his head, but one that took no account of his status as a parent. As was the case for Andrew, Adam's son was not allowed to visit, and the location of the hostel, some miles from his partner and child, meant that he was unable to pay for transport to visit them. This left him missing his son and living in relative isolation:

> 'No, [son] can't come to visit … and I've got to be there at least four nights a week. So I just sit there, basically, doing nothing for hours on end. I can go out but if I haven't got money to get to my places, I've gotta walk it. … I've got loads of pictures and videos of [my son] so I just slideshow them and just watch him before I go to bed. … It makes me a bit upset now and then, but at least I get to see him on a picture.' (Adam, aged 18, lower income, partnered, singles hostel, wave 4)

These 'hidden' forms of homelessness (Quail, 2007) and the accompanying loss of ontological security provided a very difficult backdrop to the lives of these poorly resourced young men.

Five young men in the sample spoke explicitly about being homeless at some point in their lives. For Cade, the lack of a home address additionally meant he could not register with the Job Centre, potentially his only route into paid work and out of poverty:

> 'It's hard. It's harder than having a kid, trying to find a place and a job. I could go over to my friends still and stuff like that. But recently we

was homeless. Just finding me a room was hard. And I only got a room 'cos of the cold weather. ... I asked the [housing advisor], "what if it was summertime?" And they said that nothing would be done for me. I'd have to spend it on the street. ... It's hard to get a job because when you go to the Job Centre ... you tell them, 'I haven't got a place to stay'. ... Then they go, "well you've got to go [back] to housing". ... It's really hard ... it's awful. You don't feel like a man or a human being anymore. You know, you just don't feel like you're worth anything.' (Cade, aged 21, lower income, partnered, homeless, wave 1)

The nomadic lives of these young men were a constant disruption at a time when they were attempting to focus on their new identities as parents; without a stable home they had no foundation for the care a child. Their limited periods of semi-dependence from their birth families could be seen as akin to jumping out of the frying pan into the fire. This kind of housing trajectory, then, confounds the basic requirements needed for ontological security, and a sense of stability, control and constancy (Dupuis and Thorns, 1998). It was a trajectory that many of the young men hoped actively to avoid.

Professional housing support

Cade's account also points to the minimal advice and support that he received from housing agencies, and the very limited options that professionals have in offering advice. Accessing this provision is difficult: there is no cohesive national policy or approach, resulting in patchy provision across localities (Johnsen and Quilgars, 2010). Among the young men who sought professional help with their housing were seven who received support from housing charities. The nature and quality of this provision varied enormously. Marcel, for example, sought help because the local authority house he was living in with his partner and child was damp, in poor condition and causing health problems. The housing charity found him more suitable accommodation and helped the family settle in:

'They've just been coming to see me and seeing if things are going alright and things are getting taken care of. And I go up there if I ... need maybe some help or some, some questions that need answering ... I can go talk to them and ... they help me a lot ... So I appreciate that. ... So, it's like, it's nice to know that there's, there's people out there that do care about young fathers and young people. And even if they're a bit stuck that they can help them out. So, I'm really happy about that, yeah.' (Marcel, aged 24, lower income, cohabiting with partner, wave 1)

Alongside support to secure a tenancy, professionals can also provide floating support to help young fathers with the tasks of independent living (managing finances, paying household bills and so on). This was especially welcomed by young fathers who lacked support from their own families.

For single young men the support on offer was more limited. But it could provide an essential safety net and lifeline to young men in difficult circumstances, if only through the provision of substandard, temporary accommodation. Before getting a council house with his partner, Darren found temporary accommodation through a local charity that helped young homeless people. He was placed in a shared house. The charity only offered single-sex occupancy, but Darren struck up a good relationship with the manager, who used his discretion and worked around the system to arrange a one-bedroom house for Darren, his partner and child: "They don't work with partners, you know, like me and our lass, right. But like he said, what's not on the books is not on the books if you know what I mean!" (Darren, aged 23, lower income, cohabiting with partner, supported housing, wave 4). The manager was also helpful in finding accommodation that was local to the maternal household and provided floating support of the kind outlined earlier. This support for Darren bridged the gap between dependence and independence in the early days of his parenthood and specifically supported his housing needs as a father. Darren saw this opportunity for co-residence as better for the young couple, making their relationship 'stronger' (although see the account of their subsequent family dynamics and housing issues in Chapter 5).

Darren's account also points to the systemic difficulties housing agencies may face in supporting young fathers as service users and meeting their needs as parents. As we have seen, in the climate shaped under the Coalition and Conservative governments since 2010 (see Chapter 2), young fathers are adversely affected by housing policy rules and changes, especially if they do not live with the mother of their child. The housing system is predicated on the assumption that young mothers are parenting alone and that the young fathers are only peripherally attached to the family unit. The policies themselves tend to reinforce this state of affairs, thereby compounding the neglect that young fathers commonly face.

Concluding discussion

Affordable, accessible housing has become an increasingly limited resource in Britain. For young fathers, having a base from which to parent, whether at close hand or at a distance, is essential if they are to fulfil their intentions to be there for their children. Yet housing options for young fathers have become more constrained within a housing system that is in crisis, creating complex constellations of semi-dependency for young fathers. Far from incentivising them to improve their life chances, they have to navigate complex housing systems, welfare policy conditions and gendered processes that create precarity and uncertainty. Young fathers aspire to independence and a home of their own. Yet with increasingly limited housing options they face difficult choices about their future living conditions. Combined with increasing employment precarity, housing instability creates a *double precarity* (Desmond and Gershenson, 2016) in which a secure home, an essential prerequisite for developing skills and commitments as parents, is increasingly out of reach.

The longitudinal evidence presented here also illuminates the yo-yo dynamics of young fathers' housing trajectories, which flow back and forth between dependency, semi-dependency and independence. These fluid and volatile housing pathways reflect the increasingly destabilised trajectories of young people more generally. For young fathers, these trajectories are diverse, variable and non-linear, especially in the early years of their parenting journeys when, as we have seen in Chapter 4, their commitments to their children are built on particularly shaky ground.

For young parents who are dependent on older generations, it is evident that the ostensible stability of the grandparental home as a place to parent can be a lifeline. However, this is often only a short-term solution to young men's investments and engagements in their relationship with their partners and their children. Becoming a parent at a young age places inevitable and often unanticipated pressures on the financial and material resources of the grandparent generation. In reality, the stability of such provision is highly variable and rarely sustainable beyond the short term (see Chapter 6; Neale and Ladlow, 2015b).

For those young parents seeking to establish housing independence, the challenges are compounded by the increasingly limited options for accessing independent housing. The swell of temporary accommodation and shorthold tenancies in the PRS combined with high rents, means that these options are only viable for those with financial resources. Accessing statutory housing support is also challenging in times of welfare retrenchment. For young fathers the issues are compounded by the lack of recognition for their commitments to their children, and the responsibilities that they need to fulfil. They are simply not eligible for statutory support unless they are designated as a primary carer.

Yet where specialist housing support services are available, they are greatly valued and can make a huge difference to the quality and stability of these young lives. Quilgars et al (2011) argue that there is a need for more supported housing units that accommodate couples, although they caution that there should also be consideration of the age gap between young mothers and their partners, as well as the appropriateness of placing males in units that may accommodate victims of domestic violence. The development of such provision, however, would perpetuate a gap in thinking about the needs of single young fathers, whose commitment to their children and the development of a joint parenting project across households may be equally strong. In circumstances where young fathers find themselves leading nomadic lives, without a stable base to care for their children, social housing or homelessness may be the only pathways available to them. For these young men, the process of seeking a suitable place to parent has been likened to walking a tightrope, yet without an adequate safety net of statutory support (Ladlow, 2021).

Finally, it is worth broadening our focus to consider the emerging findings from Part II of this book. Taken together, these empirical chapters reveal that the constellation of factors that make a difference to the unfolding lives of young fathers are many, varied and interlocking. Housing concerns are intricately bound up with issues of a relational and socio-economic nature, as we have seen across these chapters. The quality of housing and local neighbourhoods is one of the most tangible and emotionally charged manifestations of people's socio-economic and relational fortunes or misfortunes. Housing is a vital structural and neighbourhood issue that is sorely in need of public investment. Yet the findings reported here show that the provision of a place to parent is also a deeply personal, interpersonal and intergenerational family issue that impacts on young people's ontological security, their perceptions and experience of 'home', their capacity to flourish in their daily lives and their ability to support and care for others, including their children. Seen in this light, the need for public investment to overcome the current housing crisis for disadvantaged young parents – fathers as well as mothers – becomes all the more vital.

PART III

Supporting young fathers: lived experiences and policy challenges

In the final part of this book, we explore young fathers' perspectives on their support needs and their experiences of engaging with practitioners across a range of services. A key objective is to shed light on how far policy responses are in tune with the lived experiences of young fathers (explored in earlier chapters). We also consider how a greater congruence between the two can be achieved through collaborative modes of professional practice and client engagement. In our conclusion to the book (Chapter 11), we draw together our empirical evidence, revisit the robustness of our methodology, and consider the implications of our findings for the development of compassionate social policy in the UK.

In Chapter 9 we set out a framework for understanding the responses of service providers to young fathers, focusing on how they balance and combine support for young fathers with surveillance (the safeguarding agenda), but also with sidelining and exclusion, based on unclear remits, limited resources and a view that young fathers are 'hard to reach', that is, that they are not interested in or necessarily deserving of professional support as parents. As a counter to this picture, we also highlight the work of specialist services that offer new ways to approach young fathers, based on a different orientation to their identities, needs and commitments.

Extending our earlier discussions, particularly in Chapter 2, what emerges here is a conventional landscape of statutory support for young parents that has been shaped in relation to two underlying and interrelated forces. The first is a traditional, gendered ideology of parenthood that frames the issue of young parenthood in terms of teenage pregnancy, thereby bringing young women centrally into the picture and often eclipsing young men, who are relegated to fleeting 'bit' players. The second is the institutional embedding of a *social problems* framework in professional practice, in which young fathers are rendered not simply as 'secondary' parents but potentially as 'deficient' parents whose very presence is treated with uncertainty and suspicion. In these circumstances, the stigma experienced by young fathers (see Chapters 2 and 4) is not simply an additional challenge. It emerges as a foundational problem that shapes their identities and practices, impacts on their confidence, and affects their capacity for social engagement with their children, the mothers and their wider support networks, both familial and professional.

This is a sorry state of affairs. The picture becomes most starkly evident at the coalface of professional practice, where lived experiences and policy responses intersect and collide. However, at this same coalface, innovative specialist services are inculcating a *social engagement* framework for working with young fathers that provides a model for future development. This brings us to Chapter 10 and the Responding to Young Dads impact initiative, where new modes of working based on collaborations between researchers, young fathers and the professionals who serve them are being imagined, crafted and developed. This initiative sought to shift the balance of professional responses away from a deficit view of young fathers. It did so by enabling selected young men to take on ambassadorial and training roles, to engage with practitioners in new ways, to actively demonstrate their capacity for social engagement, and to grow in confidence as experts by experience. In short, these chapters reinforce the insight that effective policy responses rest, fundamentally, on our capacity to 'see' young fathers in a different way.

9

Professional support for young fathers: support, surveillance, sidelining?

Introduction

Having built a detailed and dynamic picture of the parenting journeys of young fathers, this chapter considers how they experience formal support services. The discussion draws on a range of earlier contributions from the Following Young Fathers (FYF) team, notably, Neale and Davies (2015b); a secondary analysis of data from the FYF study, and wider scholarly debates about professional support for young fathers. The accounts of practitioners, generated through the FYF study, are also touched upon here but given greater attention in related publications (Davies and Neale, 2015; Davies, 2016).

Young fathers engage with a variety of services as they transition to fatherhood and through their parenting journeys. These socio-cultural institutions are a key part of the exosystem (Deslaurier and Kiselica, 2022) through which young fathers navigate when they become parents. We focus specifically on their engagements with formalised universal services (antenatal, maternity and family nurse support), and more specialised provision that supports young fathers with their education, housing, and employment, and when leaving custody. We consider the extent to which young men feel welcomed and supported within these services, particularly where they have a central remit to support mothers. Attention to young fathers' narratives about when, how and why they interact with services and institutions across their parenting journeys are revealing of their complex needs and the contexts and circumstances in which they actively seek help.

We illustrate the varied challenges faced by young fathers and those who support them, exploring how practitioners balance support with surveillance (the safeguarding agenda) and detailing practices of sidelining. Both strategies are based on unclear remits, limited resources and a view that young fathers are 'hard to reach'. We conclude by demonstrating the value of specialist provision for young fathers, which, when combined with peer models of support, act as a stabilising force with very real benefits for these young men.

'Hard-to-reach' young fathers?

The earliest research about young fathers, from the 1980s, demonstrates that young fathers have long been considered 'hard-to-reach' in professional support and policy contexts. Perpetuated by simplistic, stereotypical views that these young men are irresponsible, absent and uncaring, practitioners, policy makers and researchers during this era have contributed to their exclusion and biased treatment (Kiselica and Kiselica, 2014). Other factors include delivery of ill-conceived services premised on models created for teenage mothers, and overly rigid time schedules that lack sensitivity to the needs of young fathers who are most likely to seek help in times of crisis. The lack of research and understanding of young fathers' perspectives has also hampered their access to support (Kiselica and Kiselica, 2014).

The deficit view that sees young fathers as irresponsible and a potential risk to themselves or to their children remains widespread in professional practice in the UK (Maxwell et al, 2012). Little seems to have changed, at least at an institutional level, since the days when Nicoll et al (1999: 4) reported a pervasive view, held by professionals, that young fathers: 'do not push themselves to the front of the queue to be engaged by professionals. They will often do the opposite and make themselves scarce'.

Such a framing problematically underscores acceptance of low rates of service engagement with young fathers, while simultaneously placing responsibility for such engagement with the young men themselves (Neale and Davies, 2015b; Neale, 2016). It is a position that fails to consider the dynamics of relationships between service providers and users, and places expectations on young men to seek support and to engage with systems that do not cater to their needs. As shown in Chapter 2, where young fathers feel unacknowledged and excluded, they are more likely to avoid professional support (Reeves, 2006; Ross et al, 2010; Ferguson, 2016). These contrasting perceptions suggest that practitioners and young fathers operate in parallel universes, with limited understanding on either side (Neale and Davies, 2015b). Perversely, in a context where young fathers value their children, wish to 'be there' for them, and can make a positive contribution, this response from professionals creates the very conditions that constrain their involvement.

Perhaps a more productive question to ask is whether services are 'hard-to-access' for this client group (Hadley, 2014; Neale, 2016). Evidence about the broader exclusion of fathers from services have been linked to the complex mix of structural, organisational and cultural influences that characterise the existing landscape of support. Key factors that shape professional practice (Philip et al, 2019; Pfitzner et al, 2020) include the dominance of 'mother-centric' services, and corresponding cultural perceptions that assume that women are primarily responsible for children, and men are optional, absent and risky (Reeves, 2006; Maxwell et al, 2012). Increasingly punitive and conditional UK welfare and labour systems (see Chapter 2) have also eroded service provision for young people (the closure of Sure Start Centres and community centres being most notable), placing increased time and resource pressures on already stretched professionals. These processes also limit outreach opportunities and reduce time for gender-inclusive and cultural diversity training for professionals.

These barriers notwithstanding, the significant role of parenting interventions and formal support in improving engagement with fathers, including young fathers, is growing (see, for example, Bronte-Tinkew and Horowitz, 2010; and Buston, 2018 on the value of prison-based parenting interventions). Yet it is difficult to develop practice responses aligned directly with the needs of young fathers without a clear picture of the challenges they face or of how they navigate their encounters with services. To understand what works, we need to know what matters to young fathers, and how they perceive the landscape of service provision.

Across the FYF study, young fathers had significant support needs. These ranged from antenatal support during pregnancy, parenting skills, interpersonal (relational) skills, sexual health guidance, mental and emotional support/counselling and practical help with education, training, employment, housing and finances. However, universal or statutory support pathways for young fathers are lacking (Mensah, 2017), although the antenatal stage and birth are times when they are perhaps most visible. From a practice perspective, engagement with services around the time of pregnancy and birth is almost universal (especially by young mothers) so this is an ideal time for practitioners to foster engagement with young fathers and begin to build relationships of trust with them. The need for professional support for this client group is also beyond doubt. As Ferguson and Gates (2013) note, the vulnerability of these young men is striking.

Encounters with professionals in early pregnancy and birth

As shown in Chapter 4 and supported by wider evidence (Ross et al, 2010), young men can play an important role in the care and support of their partner during pregnancy and early parenthood. Moreover, early support provided by maternity and health services may be crucial in fostering young paternal identities and encouraging young fathers to manage and maintain their involvement over time (Maxwell et al, 2012; Ferguson and Gates, 2013; Mensah, 2017). But currently, the extent of such engagement is unclear, for it remains a matter for professional discretion.

Counter to the pervasive negative assumptions that young fathers are uninterested in pregnancy and birth and unlikely to engage, most of the young men attended scans and were invested in asking questions and learning about the process. This included the young fathers who were no longer in a relationship with the mother of their child:

'I'll go to midwife meetings with her, and mentors, I've been there sometimes when her mentor's talking to her. And I've just asked the mentor certain information. And I've asked the midwife a lot of information about the kids and things that I want. Such as like, you know, just bits of information to do with circumcision and, you know, when the kids [are] coming, if they're born at a certain age, what happens, how long do they have to stay in the hospital for. And just to make sure, you know, because it's a big transitional step for [mum of twins] but also me. So, I feel like I'm having to be more hands on. But, yeah we do, I do go to a lot of the things.' (Iman, aged 16, higher income, single, wave 1)

'With [ex-partner and the twins] I went to all the scans. I don't think I went to see midwives and stuff like that. I went to home visits and all that kind of stuff. ... I didn't go to any maternity classes or anything like that with her. But yeah I went to all the scans and that. And then with [third child and new partner], I went to everything. It were just different with [the fourth child] 'cos we weren't together at the time ... I went to one of the scans and I think that's all.' (Callum, aged 21, lower income, separated from the mothers, wave 4)

The young men had encounters with universal health services both during and after pregnancy and described a mix of experiences during the birth. Zane valued the inclusive and supportive approach of the midwife involved in the birthing process, while Trevor felt excluded from the birth, which was attended instead by his partner's foster mother:

'They were absolutely great. And you kind of knew the step-by-step things that were gonna happen. You knew what happened when she became this far dilated or anything like that. So you had a pretty good view and as you were going along anyway they were like, "okay this is what we're gonna do. This is what's happening now" and things like that. So you were always informed. You always knew what was gonna happen ... I mean not really. I think, again you can't really tell if I would have been older if they would have treated me differently. But it seemed like it was kind of like a routine thing, they did this to everyone irrespective of what age, gender is etc ... so they did seem kind of like very good professionals.' (Zane, aged 18, middle income, partnered, wave 1)

'I'm not going to say they was hypocrites and that they just went for her. But they was more mum-sided. ... Well, I turned up and then I was ready to go see my daughter. And then the professionals asked my baby mother whether I could come in. And she said, "no not yet". And I was like, "my daughter's in there though". But I didn't,

I couldn't kick off 'cos it was a happy day for me but she did get me mad that day. I was treated more like a grandparent than a parent. Like I had to wait to see my own daughter.' (Trevor, aged 15, lower income, single, wave 1)

As shown in Chapter 4, it was common for young mothers, especially those from lower-income families, to invite their mother or another female relative to be present at the birth. However, the exclusion of the young men from the birthing experience could undermine their investment in their fathering identities.

Multi-agency service engagements

Young fathers may be navigating numerous adversities, around poverty, employment, housing, mental health, insecure family lives and poor relationships, that could impact on their engagement with their children. In these circumstances they both need and may value professional support. This is likely to be especially pertinent for young fathers in their earlier teenage years, where entry into parenthood is unplanned, and/or where relationships with the mother are difficult or contact with a child is tenuous. Moreover, where young fathers are experiencing material disadvantages and/or a general lack of family support, their needs for professional help are likely to be extensive (Neale and Davies, 2015a).

Many of the young men in this study faced such difficulties. Some came into the orbit of surveillance services, such as social workers, especially where the young men had a history of poor family support, including issues of abuse or neglect in their childhoods, or where they had experienced spells in the care system, or had offended and spent time in custody. Across this cohort of young men, needs varied greatly, as did the nature and extent of their engagement with professionals over time. Some had more specific needs relating to their parenting circumstances, for example, those who had sought legal advice over contact issues. Those with more extensive needs often came into contact with multiple agencies, whose involvement needed to be managed and coordinated over time.

Adam and his partner were involved with 11 separate agencies over the course of the study, reflecting multi-agency working in the context of complex needs. The support was initially appreciated, especially that provided by the Family Nurse Partnership team and by Tim, the specialist learning mentor that Adam had been referred to via his school:

'I don't know where they came from actually. I don't know where Tim came from [interviewer laughs]. I think school got in touch with Tim. I don't know who got in touch with the Family Nurse Partnership nurse for [partner] ... but yeah, she helps support and does little lessons on how to do bathing and stuff like that. She talks to us about help and support we can get from, well me stopping smoking and stuff like that, NHS, child, whatever it is. For schools and stuff. She got us in touch with someone called [Family Nurse Partnership staff member] ... she does stuff like, she stays with us two years after he's born to help us get dental care, healthcare, stuff like that if we don't know what we're doing. So, the family nurse is kind of better than the midwife if you ask me.' (Adam, aged 16, lower income, partnered, wave 1)

The young fathers who received support from the Family Nurse Partnership placed high value on this service. As an intensive and effective home visitation service, the Family Nurse Partnership in England offers one-to-one support and utilises a skilled, therapeutically oriented and holistic approach directed primarily at young mothers. In some areas, it also engages the fathers as co-parents and promotes their capacity for caregiving (Ferguson and Gates, 2013; Ferguson, 2016).

However, over time it became clear that the intensity of involvement across agencies was not well coordinated in Adam's case, and he quickly reached saturation point: "sometimes it gets a bit too much with all the appointments and stuff. So like, I mean we didn't have any this week so I was really happy ... 'cos it's a break" (Adam, aged 16, lower income, partnered, wave 1). For young fathers who are seeking to secure employment or attend college, regular appointments became burdensome and impacted on their abilities to navigate the delicate balance required of engaged fathers, namely earning and caring.

Those engaged primarily with statutory agencies such as social services, the Child and Family Court Advisory and Support Service (CAFCASS), or the criminal justice system, were more likely to report feeling unsupported, overwhelmed and/or isolated as they grappled with adjustments to parenthood:

'I haven't got no one really to speak to in terms of, like, talking about what's happening with [my] son and all. So ... I'm on my own now pretty much. So I don't like speaking to people I know ... like ... my family. If you say something to them, they'd come back and say, "oh blah blah blah". ... They don't really listen to what you say. I'd like someone to speak to. ... Someone to listen and give me advice, but ... I wouldn't know where to start.' (Jimmy, aged 18, lower income, separated, former recipient of local authority mentoring scheme, engaged with CAFCASS and the criminal justice system, wave 4)

Four of the young men had been referred to community-based parenting programmes by social services protection teams or magistrates and were receiving specialist parenthood and relationship guidance. A further two had benefited from such provision while in custody. Seventeen of the young fathers had received specialist mentoring, including parenting classes for young fathers, as part of an expansion of provision for young parents under New Labour's ten-year Teenage Pregnancy Strategy. In general, though, the young men identified a lack of community-based and peer support and felt that the service environment was too regulatory. Signposting to social forms of support was seen as a good alternative:

> 'It depends on what sort of help as well. 'Cos it's like support is nice yeah. But if it were like through social services and social care and intensive family support and that lot, I don't think people'd really wanna know. It's just actual support basically, like "oh yeah you can call round here and, you know, socialise with these other parents" and stuff like that. That wouldn't be that bad. You know like a, a day care, no, I would say like a drop-in centre or summat. You know where you can take you and your kids and you can go chat with people on area and stuff. And they've brought their kids and that lot and your kids can play wi' their kids and all. Stuff like that'd be alright if you know what I mean.' (Darren, aged, 22, lower income, partnered, wave 2)

While specialist support groups for fathers exist and are beneficial (Robertson et al, 2018; Hanna, 2018), funding is highly fragmented across localities, making access for young fathers a postcode lottery. This suggests the need for a sustained, national programme of funding for services that support and facilitate contact between fathers and their children.

The accessibility of services (or lack thereof) is not simply about the presence of a service or its geographical location. The nature and quality of the engagements with professionals is a key factor that determines whether young fathers perceive services to be accessible and supportive. This was evident from the young men's accounts, as we will show.

Surveillance, sidelining and support

Practitioners used a variety of strategies to engage with young fathers, which we have conceptualised as surveillance, sidelining and support (Neale and Davies, 2015b). They may combine these strategies in creative ways, for example where surveillance is tempered by a supportive, redemptionist ethos. The complex and overlapping character of these practices reflects the considerable degree of discretion used by practitioners in their engagements with young fathers. In exploring these different approaches, we aim to move beyond blanket categorisations of fathers, or the practitioners who work with them, as 'good' or 'bad', and to recognise the complex constellation or dynamic factors – institutional, organisational and interpersonal – that create distinctive interactions between young fathers and practitioners over time (Deslauriers et al, 2012; Maxwell et al, 2012; Neale and Davies, 2015b; Ferguson, 2016).

Surveillance: 'they just linger'

Several of the young men felt subjected to practices of surveillance. These are foundational to a risk-based approach to support (Neale and Ladlow, 2015a; Ladlow and Neale, 2016) and essential where there are safeguarding concerns. However, the nature of these encounters was difficult for the young men. They had significant underlying fears that their parenting credentials could be discredited or unrecognised, or that contact would be denied and their children taken away. They felt overly visible and stigmatised by what they perceived as a lack of respect from professionals. As we saw in Chapter 4, supervised contact made young fathers feel uncomfortable, eroded their confidence and inhibited their spontaneity as parents:

'If I say summat, they don't really know what I'm on about. … They're using all these big fancy words. … "This is a recorded PPI"[1] … Just speak more English! … They do a lot of that when they want to confuse you. … I feel like I've got to act perfect. … do what they say and if I don't then summat bad is gonna happen. … So, I've got to just listen and keep it in. … We had a meeting with the social workers to discuss if [son] should go on the child protection plan. And the teachers that's supposed to be there to support me, said, "physical abuse, emotional abuse and neglect". And at that I nearly started crying because she said "physical abuse". And I thought "you think I'd harm my kid physically?!"' And I just like, I was just proper upset from it.' (Adam, aged 16, lower income, partnered, Social Services Case Review, wave 2)

'When someone's watching you … you feel stupid, 'cos … you've got people looking down on you. You can't play with your kids properly. … You just, you want to feel more confident. You … don't want to feel like a bloody criminal.' (Callum, aged 21, lower income, single, supervised contact, CAFCASS, wave 4)

'[They] should try to speak on [our] level. Give everyone a chance. Don't judge people. … But most (practitioners) did just look down at you a little bit.' (Cade, aged 18, lower income, partnered, antenatal services, wave 1)

More generally, interactions with 'surveillance' agencies like social services and the criminal justice system were considered unsupportive, and the young men felt stigmatised by what they perceived as a lack of respect. Some described having to "jump through hoops" to try to get these professionals "off our case". The young men talked of their encounters with these agencies as a kind of subterranean battle of wills, which required them to outwit their interrogators. They felt judged and spoken down to. Whatever the need for surveillance, the interactions reported by the young men were counterproductive and there was a greater likelihood that the interventions would be ineffective (Neale and Davies, 2015b). They could also perpetuate a vicious circle of disengagement and mistrust (Neale and Davies, 2015b).

Sidelining: "she weren't really interested in talking to me"

While surveillance involves an overt professional focus on young fathers, sidelining involves passively ignoring or neglecting them, or actively excluding them. Sidelining is a more subtle, but pervasive and arguably pernicious way in which professionals convey their negative perceptions of young fathers. Failure to accord recognition and respect to young men as parents may undermine their parenting efforts and impact on their self-confidence and their identities as parents:

> 'I went to all the scans. ... I was there all the way ... . I loved going to the scans. But the midwife ... she seemed not to really, well there was just something about her which made me feel like she didn't really like me or something ... it was just like she weren't really interested in talking to me or anything, which sort of gave me the impression.'
> (Jakie, aged 23, lower income, partnered, midwifery, wave 1)

> '[It was like I wasn't there. They didn't speak to me. They didn't involve me.] ... I said [to the midwife], "how come you never ever address me? When you've got anything to say about my son you never tell me, it's always my girlfriend. And I'm left in't dark, you're just talking in riddles"... . She just said it's easier and she's mum after all and all this.'
> (Jason, aged 25, lower income, single, midwifery, wave 4)

Sidelining can also occur at an organisational level, where services fail to publicise services to young men, sustaining their ignorance about what support is available, whether they are eligible and how to access it. Existing research also suggests that more active and targeted exclusion may be evident. In settings such as Children's Centres, young men may be politely shown the door, effectively barred from establishing their credentials as a parent, let alone being invited to express or discuss their needs (Davies and Neale, 2015; Osborn, 2015).

There are several underlying explanations for sidelining that, taken together, reinforce and entrench this practice. It is most often explained as gender bias – a perceived need to focus resources and services on mothers as the primary carers. As shown in Chapter 5, while the stigma of early parenthood touches both mothers and fathers, young mothers alone are seen to have a legitimate claim to their children, and the right to determine the nature and extent of the father's involvement (Gilligan et al, 2012). This creates ambivalence about the credentials of young fathers to be recognised as recipients of parenting services (Neale and Davies, 2015b). This gender bias may be reinforced by deficit views of young fathers that engender suspicion and distrust, creating ambivalence about young men's motives and credentials as parents, particularly where they are single, and/or from low-income families. They may quickly be rendered invisible in this context or at least, unseen in practice circles (Neale and Davies, 2015b; Osborn, 2015). These negative perceptions of young fathers represent a major barrier to their positive engagement.

As shown in Chapter 2, the young men themselves also engage in sidelining, either by avoiding services or by disengaging when they keenly feel the stigma of their early entry into parenthood, and when they are aware of the general ambivalence of professionals towards them (Shields and Pierce, 2006; Speak, 2006; Deslauriers et al, 2012). An experience of being sidelined in one setting can colour their perceptions, fuelling distrust in other settings (Neale and Davies, 2015b; Ferguson, 2016). Their reluctance to engage may also be reinforced by traditional masculine norms around help-seeking, which make them wary of appearing ignorant or in need of help (Osborn, 2015; Seidler et al, 2016):

> '[It was like] I weren't there. They didn't speak to me. They didn't involve me. ... Instead of just leaving me sat there, like, they could have engaged in conversation with me. And ... instead of just talking directly at [mother of the child] and [maternal grandmother] telling them what's going to happen, [they could] tell me, like explain it to me in a way I understand. ... But they didn't. ... Looking back, I'd tell [other young fathers] to ... stick their noses in. Like make sure they get involved and ask, definitely. Like, don't just get left sat there.' (Jimmy, aged 18, lower income, separated, Midwives/Health Visiting, wave 4)

As reported elsewhere (Tarrant and Hughes, 2019), for Karl, aged 16, and other young fathers seeking contact with their children via the courts, the problem of sidelining was especially critical, for it could result in the potential loss of contact with their child. Karl was not in a relationship with the mother of his two-week-old baby (unplanned) and explained that his baby had been taken into care after the mother had failed a care assessment. Karl was given only one hour after the baby was taken into care to source a solicitor to support a claim to paternity. Describing the contact arrangements at this time, Karl explained that he only saw his son twice a week for one hour during contact sessions. The involvement of social workers was stressful, and he wanted to go to court to try to arrange regular child-contact time. Here he notes how he and the paternal family were sidelined by the arrangements, which prioritised the mother and the maternal grandmother:

> '[Ex-partner] gets an hour and a half and I only get an hour. But then [maternal grandmother] gets half an hour. But I don't understand that 'cos it's like, again it's like her side t' family, it's like all her family's seeing him. And like nobody in my family's seen him at all. It's like my sister, she wants to go see him and so does my brother and so does my dad. But it's like they can't.' (Karl, aged 16, lower income, single, wave 1)

At this time, Karl was given limited opportunities to prove himself as an engaged father (Tarrant and Hughes, 2019). His continued investment in his son's life was thwarted by the unrealistic and inflexible requirements of social services to attend contact sessions over nine miles away, when at the same time he was required to attend his college course for three days per week:

> 'They tell you like to be, like really stupid places … . It's like tomorrow I'm over in, I'm at [area of city] about nine miles away and they expect me yeah … at nine o'clock in morning. So it's like I get up for bus, I have to get up about half past five in morning. And I get ready and it's off at six o'clock, six o'clock bus but sometimes I'm late. … and … if I'm later they start questioning but I can't do anything 'cos they've got cars. I'm on the bus … that's why I ain't doing my college course or nowt 'cos I won't be able to work round that. 'Cos if they are saying to me "you need to be here, like on Tuesday at half past nine" … that means my college course is gonna have to work round that.' (Karl, aged 16, lower income single, wave 1)

More generally, across the range of professional agencies, there were few opportunities for these young men to be listened to, to talk through problems, acquire skills, gain confidence or work out alternative strategies for managing their parental roles and relationships. While sidelining is a subtle process, it can be highly damaging, creating and reinforcing the absence of young men, edging them out of their social engagement as parents and increasing their vulnerability to losing their children (Tarrant and Hughes, 2019).

This occurred for Karl. His first child was adopted because he was deemed to have failed an assessment. But events leading up to this event and how it was organised reflected a lack of communication with this young man that may have made this outcome more likely:

> 'When [son's carers] took him on holiday and they didn't tell me where he were when he got back or owt. ... Then all of a sudden, I didn't, didn't know where they were 'cos nobody had phoned me, you know ... and [ex-partner] didn't tell me nowt. ... and I lost contact. ... I didn't see him for like a few week. ... And then when I rung [social worker] ... about eight times and I said to ring me back, 'cos she weren't answering. And then I rung office and I went up to t' office. And she didn't ring me back. She rung me back about five days ago and said "oh well if I need to go to contact it'll have to wait till I go back to court again" ... But basically, it's their fault 'cos ... they didn't tell me when court was or anything. But [ex-partner] never tells me owt either.'
>
> *How did that make you feel then that, you know, you were kept out of the loop?*
>
> 'I weren't happy. It were confusing as well. It's like when I was ringing her I thought "oh why ain't she rung back?" So then I went up to t' office and she was in a meeting. And then she said she'll ring me first thing in t' morning, she didn't ring. Took her ages to ring, well it took about three week to ring me. And she said that I failed my assessment.'
> (Karl, aged 16, lower income, single, wave 1)

In Karl's case, creative and compassionate thinking and responses on the part of practitioners could have made a difference. Recognition, good communication and more timely support for Karl, including help to navigate the structural challenges he faced around transport access and the clash of institutional expectations and timings, would have been invaluable in making contact more workable for him and his child (Tarrant and Hughes, 2019). Breaking the cycle by changing a sidelining culture, however, will take time and it is as much an organisational issue as the responsibility of individual professionals. It requires mainstream services to acknowledge and address their sidelining practices, and to adopt some of the creative and flexible strategies used in specialist services to temper surveillance with trust and support.

Support and effective engagement: 'rescue and repair'

Perhaps inevitably, a supportive ethos finds its clearest expression in specialist, targeted services that are tailored explicitly to the needs of young fathers.

These offer models for alternative ways to engage with these young men. 'Local champions' of young fathers, whether they are individuals working for existing services or targeted specialist services, can generate virtuous circles of engagement and support but they can also lead the way in brokering this ethos in mainstream settings (Neale and Davies, 2015b).

The development of such specialist support is part of a wider policy priority to support fathers in family services (Buston, 2018). Pockets of specialist support services for young fathers, typically funded through the voluntary sector, are growing, although they are currently limited to specific localities. The supportive ethos that drives these services is based on a social engagement framework for understanding these young men. Effective support and professional engagement involves strategies of 'rescue and repair' (Hughes and Tarrant, 2023). Young fathers may be 'rescued' through holistic support around the challenging circumstances they navigate, and then 'repaired' through specialist support designed to develop their skills, confidence, identities and citizenship. These services take as a starting point the potential contribution that young men can make to their children's lives, and the value that parenthood can have for the young men themselves.

The FYF team worked with a specialist mentoring service for young fathers, which was attended by 17 of the young men in the study and funded through the local education authority (Davies and Neale, 2015; Neale and Davies, 2015b). The high value placed on this service by the young men in the study was striking:

> '[It was] the best support you can have really. ... I didn't have a clue what I was doing, like, I was skiving school ... but he got me referred onto college, and that got me back into education, right. ... And like he'd take us out places ... So we'd get to bond with us kids instead of the mother being there ... And socialising with other young fathers, you know, in the same shoes as us. ... Well, I'd have been lost [without him].' (Darren, aged 23, lower income, partnered, local authority learning mentor scheme, wave 5)

> 'The support I got from college was to help me financially ... But he's helped me a lot emotionally. ... 'cos I didn't sort of have emotional boundaries, that – I couldn't care less about anything. So, to get things off my chest with him ... like someone I could talk to as a friend but wasn't a friend 'cos he was a professional. ... It helped me sort of stabilise myself.' (Adam, aged 18, lower income, partnered, local authority learning mentor scheme, wave 4)

> 'He's got his, like, professional voice and that. But when he's talking to you, he's, he's just like a mate. You can just tell him owt and talk

to him properly. And he's just totally down to earth. ... I did a fathers group that he ran ... like how to bath a baby. And one time [laughs] they brought in these pretend pregnancy things – in the belly it had loads of weights – so you'd know how it felt to be pregnant. ... [then] I was doing peer mentoring ... like you'd help other teenage fathers and stuff. ... It felt like I'm needed to do summat, like I'm wanted, if you know what I mean. ... I don't know where I'd be now if it weren't for him. ... He does teach you. And he makes you think about things ... in the right way. And makes you see sense. And that's helped me a lot in life 'cos I've been in a lot of dark places. ... If you can see yourself going downhill, you want to stop it. And he makes you see that.' (Callum, aged 19, lower income, separated, local authority learning mentor scheme, wave 3)

Wider evidence supports the findings here: young men value personalised support that is built on respect, trust, consistency, reliability and a sense of care and commitment (Ward et al, 2017).

The learning mentor service created a unique blend of holistic provision that included emotional support and counselling, practical help, coordinated referrals to other agencies, and an educational, peer mentoring and social programme exclusively for young fathers. Crucially, engagement with the service was triggered early in the young men's transitions into parenthood and sustained over time. Arguably, however, the flexible, impartial, genial and approachable style of the learning mentor was key to its success. He was able to engender trust and mutual respect in the young men, replacing the vicious circle with a virtuous one comprising engagement and support. He also advocated on behalf of his clients, attended referrals with them, and promoted an ethos of social engagement and support across mainstream provision (Neale and Davies, 2015b). As Pfitzner et al (2015: 537) note, 'whether clients are "hard to reach" or services are "too hard to access", the starting point for any intervention is engagement'.

It is difficult to gauge how far a supportive, social engagement framework of understanding has been adopted across health, social care and other mainstream agencies. Certainly, the young men in this study reported supportive encounters with a range of mainstream services, including health visiting, probation, the CAFCASS family law service and the Connexions employment service. However, sidelining practices and experiences in relation to young fathers have also been widely reported (Osborn, 2015), raising the possibility that, 'the vicious circle of disengagement has become embedded in institutional cultures, fuelled by broader cultural perceptions of "feckless" young fathers' (Neale, 2016: 75). Professional perspectives on this issue, generated through the FYF study, tend to support this view, indicating that the new ethos remains fragmented and subject to the discretion of individual practitioners:

'You see some individual hospitals or individual midwifery teams who've really taken the needs of young fathers on board, but, you know, if we're to look nationally, then they're few and far between.' (Young parent specialist, Connexions service)

'[There is] benign neglect. But it also tips into exclusion and rudeness.' (Head of Commissioning, Local Authority Children's Services)

Currently, the new approach seems to be driven by 'local champions' for young fathers, residing on the margins of statutory provision or in the voluntary sector, who are pioneering new ways to develop their services for young fathers. These practitioners are often prepared to 'go the extra mile' to understand their lived experiences and devise creative and tailored solutions to meet their needs (Deslauriers et al, 2012; Hogg, 2014; Neale, 2016).

Creating a more virtuous circle of engagement and support may mean more than bringing young fathers into the fold. It involves seeing young fathers in a different way; by replacing negative assumptions about their risky and 'feckless' behaviour with more positive images of their commitment to their children and their capacity to care (Neale, 2016). Where young fathers themselves have the capacity and confidence to engage, this can help to change the culture of professional practice. Here, Iman recounts his strategy for encouraging professional staff to engage with him:

'I'll observe, listen and then, you know, the midwife, I'll ask a question and then the midwife will answer. And then she'll be like, "oh yeah, yeah. Just to remind you, I'm not just here for the mother to be. Any questions you want to ask, I'll answer".' (Iman, aged 16, higher income, separated, antenatal services, wave 1)

Not all young men have the vocabulary, etiquette or confidence to engage with professionals in these ways. Trust and reciprocity must be nurtured over time. Self-help and peer-support schemes can be valuable in this regard, helping young fathers to find a collective voice in which they find solidarity through their common ground as young fathers (a theme developed further in Chapter 10). Johnson, for example, describes his experiences of developing a role as a spokesperson for young fathers through the Young Dads Council (Colfer et al, 2015):

'It's great that I get to represent the view of young dads. ... The first time I spoke in public about being a dad, I was nervous, but ... now I'm happy to do it. ... I want to help break [down] stereotypes ... I know now that it's OK for men to have a little gossip about things they're going through, you don't have to be afraid of what people think.' (Johnson, in Colfer et al 2015: 342–4)

Implications for professional practice

In this chapter we have seen that a vicious circle of disengagement, distrust and lack of respect can occur through sidelining and surveillance, particularly where these approaches damage young fathers' confidence and self-esteem. Young men are more likely to disengage from professional support when they feel keenly the stigma of their early entry into parenthood and are aware of the ambivalence of professionals towards them (Deslauriers et al, 2012). Such disengagement is particularly evident among highly marginalised young men, whose biographies are marked by persistent levels of poverty and emotional hardships (Ferguson, 2016).

It is worth clarifying here that practices of surveillance, sidelining and support may be used interchangeably by the same professionals at different times or in different contexts. They are not mutually exclusive strategies or confined to specific agencies. They are part of a repertoire of responses used by professionals in different settings and circumstances. However, a supportive ethos can foster a more virtuous circle of engagement, trust and mutual respect that serves to encourage young men's identities as parents. In criminal justice settings this approach forms part of an ethos of transformation or redemption, of moving on to better things (Meek, 2007; Neale and Ladlow, 2015a; Ladlow and Neale, 2016; Neale, 2016). It is also worth noting that sidelining young men who may be deemed 'risky' does nothing to address the issues they are facing and may do little to address safeguarding issues for their children and the mothers (Kate Bulman, pers. comm.; Ferguson, 2016; Neale, 2016).

As shown in Chapter 2, young fathers aspire not only to engage with their children but to be treated as clients of services. They place a high value on professional support where it is built on an ethos of recognition, respect and social engagement, and where they are treated as a potential asset rather than a risk to their children (Neale and Davies, 2015b; Davies, 2016). Moreover, such engagement can help to foster their identities as fathers and increase their self-confidence as parents (Robertson et al, 2018). It may also give them the resources to tackle some of the relational challenges that they might face, not least the skills to develop as co-parents (see Chapter 5).

A key theme of this study, representing a departure from much existing research, concerns the importance of thinking dynamically in understanding the lives of young fathers and building a life course perspective into policy and practice responses. Tailored support needs to be *timely*, provided at an *early* stage in the journey into parenthood and *sustained* over time (Neale, 2016). Early support is vital. Interventions at key moments, including the period immediately following a conception and through the pregnancy are likely to make a significant difference (Cundy, 2016). As we saw in Chapter 4, these are times when young fathers' fledgling identities are on particularly shaky ground and their status as prospective parents can seem unreal. It is at this time too when they are likely to be most willing to acquire new skills without the stigma of seeming vulnerable or 'in need'.

However, the needs of young fathers are continually evolving, and new challenges of a relational and socio-economic nature are likely to become more critical over time. The focus on early engagement should not detract from the value of sustained support that can be mobilised flexibly as and when needed to provide a safety net of longer-term support. This is particularly important for vulnerable and highly marginalised young men, whose deep experiences of social suffering may require sustained therapeutic interventions from specialist practitioners (Ferguson, 2016; Neale, 2016). Support for young fathers then is a process that needs to be tailored to the lived realities and dynamics of young men's parenthood journeys.

Organisational issues are also critical factors. While effective engagement relies on transformative and caring client–practitioner relationships (Davies, 2016), the responses of individual service providers represent only one dimension of the process. It is also vital to address the infrastructure and service ethos within which practitioners operate, the policy directives that guide their engagement, and the funding and resources that facilitate their work (Davies, 2016; Neale, 2016). These are the vital prerequisites for changing the culture of professional practice so that young fathers are no longer discounted as hard to reach, uninterested or risky, but sought out and welcomed as parents with a valuable contribution to make (Neale and Davies, 2015a: 311).

As we have seen, an ethos of support and engagement is a vital part of the repertoire of practitioner responses in a variety of health, social care and other professional settings. Presently, it is more likely to be tacked on in mainstream settings, or to be the product of practitioner discretion, than to be robustly embedded in the culture, organisation and governance of mainstream provision (Osborn, 2015). As Osborn (2015) cautions, there is a danger that the 'hard to reach' label may justify hiving off provision to specialist services alone (Osborn, 2015). This is problematic in a context where specialist service provision is fragmented across the statutory and voluntary sectors, and something of a postcode lottery in terms of its accessibility (Davies and Neale, 2016; Tarrant and Neale, 2017a). As Osborn (2015) argues, there is a pressing need to include the needs of young fathers in mainstream strategic planning and service delivery plans, rather than seeing them as the sole purview of specialist teams.

In accounting for the different ways in which practitioners engage (or fail to engage) with young fathers, it is important to move beyond a culture of blame and avoid blanket categorisations of fathers and the practitioners who work with them, as 'good' or 'bad'. As Ferguson (2016) notes, it is more productive to recognise the complex constellation of dynamic factors – institutional, organisational and interpersonal – that create distinctive interactions between young fathers and practitioners over time (Deslauriers et al, 2012; Maxwell et al, 2012; Neale and Davies, 2015b; Neale, 2016). It is also worth exploring the factors that enable or constrain a new ethos of professional support and social engagement in relation to young fathers, and what might be done to overcome the constraints.

Concluding discussion

In this chapter we have explored how professionals working in generic and specialist services, both statutory and voluntary, respond to young fathers, and how they temper a culture of support and social engagement with the exclusionary practices of surveillance and sidelining. The need to create a better balance between these responses and give young fathers due recognition and respect has been highlighted here. Perhaps the first step in making young fathers 'count' in mainstream settings is the simple expedient of counting them. As shown in Chapter 1, effective provision is currently hampered by a lack of routinely collected information about young fathers. Without data, professionals operate with little knowledge of these young men's lives and lack strategies and the confidence to engage with them (Deslauriers et al, 2012; Neale and Davies, 2015b). Effective engagement also requires investment in professional training and the provision of coordinated support between agencies, and across the mix of generic and specialist services (Reeves et al, 2009; Neale and Davies, 2015b; Osborn, 2015; Davies, 2016). The recent development of digital (internet and mobile-based) support services have enormous potential as coordinating and training platforms across agencies and may also help to push these agendas forward (Tarrant et al, 2021; see, for example, Mniszak et al, 2020 and DigiDAD, an e-learning programme that has been co-created by the North East Young Dads and Lads, professionals and researchers to support young fathers: https://www.digidad.uk/).

This chapter has reinforced the insight that effective policy responses rest, fundamentally, on our capacity to 'see' young fathers in a different way (Neale, 2016). In this regard, there is scope for young fathers, as experts by experience, to take on ambassadorial roles and engage directly with practitioners in training and conference settings. Through such strategies, the capacity of young fathers for social engagement is not simply promoted by researchers, but actively demonstrated by the young men themselves. This development is documented in our final empirical chapter, to which we now turn.

10

Enhancing the social engagement of young fathers through qualitative longitudinal impact research

Introduction

This chapter reports on a novel impact initiative outlined briefly in Chapter 3, called Responding to Young Dads in a Different Way (hereafter, RYD, Tarrant and Neale, 2016–17; Tarrant and Neale, 2017b; Tarrant, 2023). Building cumulatively on the knowledge generated and relationships fostered with young fathers and professionals in the Following Young Fathers (FYF) study, we worked with national partners for an additional year to develop new father-inclusive, evidence-based pathways of support. As an extended process of stakeholder engagement, the RYD initiative illustrated the value of collaborative, partnership-based working with multi-agency professionals, as a means to create impact in real time, facilitated through the longitudinal design of the research process (Neale and Morton, 2012; Neale, 2021a; Neale, 2022). The RYD initiative facilitated opportunities for modest social transformation within existing support systems, in particular, through the promotion of father-inclusive practice, driven by and for young fathers and the professionals who champion them.

The two collaborative case studies, comprising strands one and two of the initiative, included:

- a post-custody settlement project that sought to identify and capture the value of alternative support pathways for young fathers leaving the criminal justice system (reported on in Bulman and Neale, 2017); and
- an adaptation of a pre-existing, London-based social intervention called the Young Dads Collective, which was rolled out to the North of England (reported on in May et al, 2017).

The learning from both strands was foundational to a third strand of work, in which a group of young fathers developed ambassadorial and advocacy roles in professional settings. These young men were supported to craft their narratives about their lived experiences of young fatherhood and to share them with an audience of multi-agency professionals. Instigating early research and practice innovations, the study sought to raise the visibility of young fatherhood through advocacy, and through the refinement of bespoke training and support pathways. These were designed to challenge deficit views of young fathers and to encourage and enhance young fathers' opportunities for positive engagement with their children and co-parents (Tarrant and Neale, 2017b).

The Responding to Young Dads (RYD) study: sustaining stakeholder engagement

In extending already productive relationships with partners established in the FYF study, the RYD initiative developed a sustained programme of multi-stakeholder engagement. Stakeholder engagement facilitates an active relationship among all those involved in a service as well as collaborative input into service delivery and development. A fundamental aim of the FYF study and its follow-on initiatives has been to drive and effect meaningful social change. Overseen by Anna, the study had three core objectives:

- to maintain the momentum established during the FYF study by acting on the practice-informed knowledge produced;
- to respond to practice gaps that were identified by the young fathers and professionals who engaged with the study, through the implementation of bespoke solutions; and
- to support a group of young fathers and practitioners to collaborate and establish new evidence-based models of practice and training.

In extending the participatory ethos of FYF, RYD facilitated innovative ways to co-produce knowledge across the research/policy/practice interface (Neale and Morton, 2012; Tarrant and Neale, 2017a). From the outset, FYF sought to make a difference in the real world (Holstein and Minkler, 2007, cited in Neale, 2021a) through empirical engagement with professionals and consideration of strategies to ensure the dissemination and uptake of the developing findings. As we argue in Chapter 3, qualitative longitudinal (QL) studies, especially those with an applied policy and/or practice orientation, have great capacity to operate as navigational devices and facilitators of change (Neale, 2021a). These are described in detail elsewhere but, to briefly recap, they involve real-time, flexible and iterative modes of knowledge production, which shed light on 'what works' and 'how things work' through the simultaneous generation of practice-informed research and research-based practice (Neale, 2021a, 2022).

The credentials of such an approach have been established through action research and participatory methodologies, whereby research processes are designed to facilitate change, rather than simply capturing change in the making. RYD ensured that the research evidence generated with young fathers and professionals was more effectively taken up, translated, and applied with and for a wider community of young fathers and multi-agency professional groups in real time. As an action research study, not only did we walk alongside partners instigating change, but we also documented the methods of implementation, and captured the evolving impacts this had on the key stakeholders. Uniquely, we were positioned to intervene with evidence where necessary to steer the process in an evidence-informed way. Our approach was therefore iterative, flexible and cumulative, and supported tentative transformations within what is a complex and dynamic landscape of support with distinctive challenges in seeing young fathers and supporting their engagement (see also Chapter 9).

Shifting from a 'social problems' to a 'social engagement' ethos in practice

A core aim of RYD was to consider how the dominant social problems and associated deficit models of young fatherhood might be shifted towards a recognition of the value of their family engagement. The social problems framework, introduced in Chapter 1, is underscored by evidence that young fathers face a range of disadvantages, have various health and social care needs and are often dependent themselves at the time they enter parenthood. They therefore present numerous challenges for health and social care policy and professional practice.

While pockets of good practice clearly exist within organisations (see Chapter 9), responsibilities for enacting change are often individualised; they are more often taken on by young father champions or 'change-makers' rather than embedded in organisational cultures and policies. As we saw in Chapter 2, the social problems framework tends to dominate as the starting point for professional practice, while a social engagement framework remains substantially underdeveloped. More generally, the evidence from FYF demonstrates that young fathers are 'doubly excluded'; by virtue of their age and gender, they are more likely to be written off as troublesome and troubling (Ferguson, 2016). In addition, as Chapter 9 illustrates, pervasive stereotypes and assumptions about young fathers often translate into practices of surveillance or sidelining by practitioners, practices that can exacerbate their marginalisation and exclusion from vital support. The idea that young fathers are necessarily 'hard to reach' or, even worse, that they are not interested in their children or that they may pose a risk to them, is pervasive and difficult to challenge (Hadley, 2014; see also Chapters 2 and 9). The visibility of young fathers is also hampered by the simple problem of identifying and recognising them, let alone meeting their needs, in a context where they are not counted. It is only by addressing and questioning stigmatising representations of young fathers that more effective support can be developed.

A foundational starting point for the RYD initiative, based on the knowledge produced through FYF, is that the invisibility and exclusion of young fathers can only be effectively challenged if their ambitions to be there for their children are acknowledged as important, and are encouraged by professionals and support organisations. Good practice for individual fathers requires a joined-up and integrated approach including consistent ways of working by professionals and services. Such issues should not be seen simply as interpersonal issues that are negotiated and contested between young fathers and professionals alone. They are structural and institutional. It is essential that positive change should not be considered the sole responsibility of particular providers (Deslauriers et al, 2012; Neale and Davies, 2015a; Osborn, 2015; Ferguson, 2016). Change is required at multiple levels, including a shift in culture in professional settings and policy discourse (Tarrant, 2023).

Existing research indicates that parenthood services should endeavour to adhere to a universal commitment to *father-inclusive practice*; an approach that promotes fathers' well-being, builds their capacity to support mothers, promotes maternal health behaviours, and supports children with their mental health and well-being (Bateson et al, 2017). Embedding a commitment to father-inclusion has potential to engender systems change that recognises, values and encourages more positive forms of engagement, not only by young fathers, but by all fathers in the lives of their children.

Drawing on these staunch findings and bringing them into practice settings and policy discourse, the RYD initiative was designed to address some overarching methodological questions:

- How do we effectively mobilise the knowledge generated in the FYF study to instigate the vital changes needed to address these pressing practice and policy challenges?
- How do we bring key stakeholders on this journey with us and in a way that has multifaceted and directional benefits for those implicated in these processes?

We consider these questions through our two pilot case studies. As shown, these sought to address two pressing problems for policy and professional practice that were observed by our partners: first, how to improve post-settlement processes for young offender fathers, and second, how to create spaces for young fathers to communicate directly with practitioners and thereby contribute to a sea change in professional perceptions.

RYD was co-designed with three practice partners to pilot new ways of working *with* young fathers and to enable practitioners who support or engage with them to develop new ideas and hone their working practices. The key strands of the three-part initiative built cumulatively from the established stakeholder relationships within the FYF study and were led by

Strand one: post-incarceration and resettlement support for young fathers

This case study was led by Kate Bulman, a Health Education lead nurse at Oakhill Secure Training Centre based in the Midlands (UK). The broad aim was to explore how support for young fathers who were leaving prison could be more effectively delivered and sustained over the longer term (drawing on Neale and Ladlow, 2015a; Ladlow and Neale, 2016; also see Tarrant and Neale, 2017b). The strand supported Kate in exploring ways in which continuity of support might be developed for vulnerable young fathers when they are released from prison and return back to their communities. An observation from the FYF study was the high value young fathers place on receiving specialist support as fathers while they are in prison. However, they receive much less tailored or bespoke support when they return to their communities. FYF demonstrated that continuity of care upon release is sorely needed if men's fledgling identities as young fathers are to be consolidated.

Kate recruited five young fathers who had engaged well with professional support in custody and supported them over a year as they made the transition to resettlement following their release from the secure training centre. Methods for more effective and sustainable support delivery in the longer term were explored, alongside consideration of what issues might arise for practitioners in meeting this objective. This strand piloted and tested new ways of developing sustained support for these young men upon their release from custody, built upon a redemptive ethos focused on investments in their fathering identities, rather than their criminal trajectories (Ladlow and Neale, 2016). As such, it was an ideal test case for understanding the particular issues facing some of the most marginalised and vulnerable young men in the UK, and piloting new and more robust forms of support for them in a way that acknowledged the dynamic, open-ended nature of their parenting journeys.

Improving resettlement support for young offender fathers

For young fathers in prison or with a history of incarceration, the challenges of assuming and maintaining a parenting role and identity and proving their worth, are all the greater (Ladlow and Neale, 2016; also see Jason, Chapter 4). While there is no formal auditing of men's parental status in UK prisons, teenage fatherhood among incarcerated young men is reportedly high (Buston et al, 2012). Many of these young men have biographies like those evidenced through the social problems framework (see Chapter 1).

They reflect myriad 'risk' factors that accumulate over time and may become antecedents for the increased likelihood of engagement in criminal activity and possible incarceration. These young men, for example, are more likely to have been exposed to verbal, physical or sexual abuse, and to be living in households where there has been parental separation, domestic violence, mental illness, and drug and alcohol misuse. The complex array of challenges they face, associated with poverty, lack of social support, volatile relationships, mental health problems and low educational attainment, are only likely to be magnified by time spent in the criminal justice system (Ladlow and Neale, 2016). Trajectories through and beyond the criminal justice system are fraught with challenge. When young men are in prison, maintaining contact with children in custody settings is a primary difficulty. This may be restricted for several reasons, including troubles experienced in relationships with partners or co-parents; institutional constraints linked to inflexible or limited visitation policies; and/or inadequate contact environments (see also Chapter 4).

In terms of resettlement processes, having a criminal record can make it harder for young men to secure employment and child-appropriate housing, although being in a co-residential partnership with the mother can help (see Jax, Chapter 5, also, Chapters 7 and 8). Limited material or financial resources may also severely constrain their parenting efforts and relationships with partners and wider family members (Buston et al, 2012; Tarrant and Neale, 2017a). The complexity of these issues needs to be both addressed and overcome, if these young men are to establish and sustain trusting and supportive relationships in adulthood, maintain healthy relationships with their partners or co-parents, and fulfil their ambitions to be engaged fathers.

Evidence from the FYF study demonstrates that specialist services that operate with an ethos of compassion and support are even more vital for prison-experienced young fathers. While punitive, punishment-based regimes, grounded in a risk framework, serve to reinforce the offending identities of young fathers (Ladlow and Neale, 2016), professional interventions based on an ethos of redemption can foster renewed investments by young men in their fathering identities, with potential benefits beyond the criminal justice system. In this context, parenthood identities may offer a route to desistence and an anchor for pursuing alternative pathways (Neale and Ladlow, 2015a; Ladlow and Neale, 2016). There is burgeoning evidence to suggest that when family support programmes are delivered in prisons, they are essential mechanisms for the maintenance of family connections and for fostering relational identities (Buston et al, 2012, for instance). A recent evaluation of three family support services provided by the Prison Advice and Care Trust, demonstrates their essential work in facilitating contact between young fathers and their families, through the provision of advocacy and therapeutic support, and the brokering of relevant services (Ugwudike, 2018).

The award-winning Fatherhood Programme, developed by Kate Bulman at Oakhill Secure Training Centre, UK, is a prime example of how a professional intervention can successfully nurture parenting identities among young fathers. This programme aimed to reduce the risk of early parenthood for young offenders and enhance the parenting capacity of young men who had become fathers or were expecting a child. Designed and delivered by Kate, the programme was based on the premise that being a good parent relies on the capacity of young men to develop their own lives in positive ways. In direct engagement with young men, it promotes the understanding that young fathers need to care for themselves and commit to working with a spirit of trust, respect and commitment with their partners or co-parent, if they are to sustain a role in their children's lives (see Chapter 5, also Neale and Davies, 2015b; Neale and Patrick, 2016).

Feedback on the training programme has been uniformly positive. Young fathers reflect that the course offers them a renewed sense of purpose and identity, an understanding of the importance of having a non-abusive, supportive and respectful relationship with their child's mother, and the confidence to develop their skills as a parent (Neale and Ladlow, 2015a; Ladlow and Neale, 2016). The effects of such interventions may be short-lived, however, especially upon resettlement. Highly vulnerable young fathers often return to their communities to face the same considerable and insurmountable barriers in their family lives and communities that they did before they were incarcerated. A review of resettlement literature by Markson et al (2015) demonstrates that, upon release from prison, offenders have to secure key resources and may have a complex set of needs relating to housing, employment, health, addictions, finances, family relationships, and changing attitudes and behaviours. Being able to meet these needs is key to desistence from crime (Markson et al, 2015). Yet sustained support that would enable young men to achieve these aims following their release is in short supply.

The FYF findings indicated that professional support for incarcerated young fathers is likely to be most effective when it is tailored to the needs of the individual, offered and delivered as early as possible in their offending and parenthood journeys, and then sustained beyond their incarceration (Neale and Ladlow, 2015a). Further development of this work therefore aimed to explore how such follow-on support could be put into practice, and what the issues were in terms of supporting young men over the longer term to build pro-social lives for themselves and nurture positive relationships with their children and families.

The pilot initiative: young fathers, youth justice and resettlement support

Strand one sought to address these identified gaps in support for young fathers in such circumstances by engaging with five young men as they transitioned from custody to resettlement in their communities. These young men had engaged well with the Oakhill Fatherhood Programme and agreed to participate in the pilot. Adopting a part-time fatherhood support role after the young men left custody, Kate followed up these young men on a regular basis over a ten-month period and offered flexible and tailored support when needs arose. She was supported in this role by young fathers involved with the Young Dads Collective (YDC, see later) who provided one-to-one befriending support in accordance with the individual needs of these post-custodial young men. Through this initiative, Kate and the YDC fathers were simultaneously afforded detailed and privileged insights into the challenges these young fathers were required to navigate. She observed strengths and weaknesses in the current support landscape and put into practice a responsive and personalised support offer (reported in Bulman and Neale, 2017).

The young fathers who volunteered for this pilot initiative varied greatly in their circumstances, although each had extensive needs associated with their disadvantaged backgrounds and custody experience. Prior to going into custody none had been living with biological parents. Three had been in care placements or were living with extended family. Most, at some point in their childhoods, had had no fixed abode and were homeless for periods of time. Care leavers are especially likely to need more focused and targeted support than other young people as they make their transition to adulthood. Lack of support from their families, or from the state as corporate parents, can mean that they struggle to meet their own basic physical, psychological and social needs. The young men, who ranged in age from 15 to 17, had all experienced chaotic and disconnected childhoods of this nature. The lack of familial and state support that characterised their lives prior to entering custody not only continued but was amplified in the aftermath.

All five young men reported a range of severe problems throughout the settlement process. Key issues included navigating problematic family relationships, disjointed services that created gaps in support, and relocation to areas distant from their children. Following release, only one of the five young men returned to live with a biological parent. This relationship fell apart soon afterwards. Another, who was a care leaver, went to live with his biological father whom he had not lived with since he was a baby (see Chapter 6 on the importance of relationships with the grandparent generation). This initially provided an opportunity to repair his connections with his family and offered some short-term stability. Over time however, it became increasingly difficult for his father to cope with his mental health and behavioural issues. Later, he was asked to leave.

Complex safeguarding issues also arose in each of the cases, bound up with the potential risk of these young men to others, but also with risks to the young men themselves. Their own life chances were highly constrained and, confirming the findings of FYF, most lacked any dedicated or tailored formal support to help them to address their personal health and development needs. Four of the young men had maintained a relationship with the mothers of their children while in custody, which gave them a vital springboard upon which to build a fatherhood identity (see Chapter 5). However, one young man had an acrimonious relationship with the mother of his child, increasing the precarity of his position as a parent.

For those without family support to rely on, varied and inconsistent housing provision was especially problematic and exacerbated their ability to secure independence (see also Chapter 8). One of the fathers was initially provided with accommodation in a different local authority from that where his child lived. He was also evicted on two different occasions without sufficient grounds. These evictions were overturned through Kate's intervention, who worked closely with an advocate and solicitors. It was clear, however, that the local authority did not understand the need for this young man to live near his child. Their priority had been to provide cheaper housing in their own local area.

Wider evidence shows that while a menu of services may be signposted before and immediately after a release from prison, practitioners reportedly struggle to connect fathers to post-release services in the longer term (McKay et al, 2018). Post-custodial support is currently patchy and variable in terms of the emphasis on an ethos of redemption (Ladlow and Neale, 2016). Where redemptive provisions do exist, it is usually at the discretion of committed individuals, rather than built into the remit of a support worker's role. The disjointed nature of provision, both statutory and specialised, also reinforces this fragmentation. The time and care provided by Young Offender Teams who support the resettlement process for a short while, is vital and a period when young people's needs are most likely to be met. Social services support often steps back at this time but, when the Young Offender Teams withdraw, the support that is reinstated by social services can be inadequate. Statutory provision provided through Children's Centres is also patchy (and has been increasingly defunded during a period of political austerity that began in the early 2010s). It is not typically designed for fathers and commonly reinforces the gendered nature of young parenthood. More specialist support, such as that offered through parenting groups specifically for fathers, is also fragmented. The availability of support is therefore a postcode lottery for many young fathers.

The findings of this strand of the RYD initiative suggest that the high levels of complexity and vulnerability found among this small sample of young fathers were deeply compounded by the structural inequalities that they faced, and a lack of support linked to the disjointed nature of post-resettlement support. The extent of support required for each of these young men was significant and varied over time, both in terms of accessibility and degree of need. This placed a great burden on Kate in her support role. It required a great deal of flexibility, time and resource that were constrained by the conditions of her existing employment. The findings here suggest that a dedicated support worker is vital but also requires the backing and resourcing of a more robust organisational infrastructure.

A key tenet of the role was to implement an open, exploratory and responsive approach, which frequently involved the provision of counselling and emotional support. Time was dedicated to getting to know and understand the young fathers' perspectives but also those of their family members, including the mothers of their children and the parents of the young men. The role also involved working alongside other professionals and, in some cases, advocating on the young men's behalf in their negotiations with local authorities.

In one case, Kate was asked to support a young father who needed to open a bank account, a process that proved to be drawn out and complicated. In this example, a range of interlocking factors made it difficult for this young man to establish and sustain his own life. With no access to his birth certificate and a lack of knowledge, confidence and literacy skills to fill in the key forms or negotiate support, either in person or on the phone, this proved an extremely difficult processes to navigate. The basic underpinning requirements of adulthood that are often taken for granted, like having ID and a bank account (needed for receiving payment for work or benefits), are therefore often difficult for young people to acquire or preserve without parental support, yet they must be prioritised. What was worryingly clear was just how difficult it was for these young men to invest in their roles and identities as fathers when their own basic needs as young citizens were not being met.

Practice recommendations

This strand produced several recommendations for practice development. One-to-one specialist provision led by a specialist practitioner is essential to help bring about systemic change to the practice landscape; to meet the extensive needs of these highly vulnerable young fathers; and to help them in the process of navigating a complex bureaucracy of state agencies. Key elements of support provision for young fathers engaging in resettlement and desistence processes, which distinctly overlap with what we already know about the provision of effective, father-inclusive practice, might include:

- emotional support and counselling for the management of negative feelings and problems (using monitoring tools to gauge these states where possible);
- relationship support, including referral to perpetrator programmes for young men who show signs of controlling or abusive behaviour in relationships;

- mediating relationships of trust and respect between the young men, the mothers and wider family members;
- practical support with childcare skills;
- bringing young fathers together for peer support and the building of new social networks;
- advocacy on behalf of young fathers;
- brokering generic services, including accompanying young fathers to appointments with housing, educational, employment and benefits workers; and
- coordinating referrals to other agencies and arranging extra support where needed, for example, the mentoring and befriending service that Kate organised for these young men through the Young Dads Collective (Bulman and Neale, 2017).

These findings and recommendations, which confirmed and extended insights generated in the FYF study, were reported at a dedicated policy event, as well as the final project dissemination event marking the end of the RYD initiative, and in the final project report (Bulman and Neale, 2017). Of most significance here, these findings were based on a new pilot initiative which was designed and implemented by a practitioner on the basis of evidence from the FYF study, and with support from the FYF team.

Strand two: establishing the Young Dads Collective North

The second case study, which ran in parallel with the first, was more explicitly practitioner-led. It involved a national collaboration between the YDC in London (established by Family and Childcare Trust, now rebranded as the Coram Family and Childcare), and the Teenage Pregnancy and Parenthood Team located within the Health and Well-being Service at a West Yorkshire city council. The YDC evolved from an advocacy project called Young Dads TV, which was designed to promote the voices and engagement of young fathers via a collaborative digital project (Colfer et al, 2015). Via this model, young fathers participate as experts by experience who share their accounts of the realities of young fatherhood and their engagements with professionals. A key aim of the YDC is to influence how services engage with young men and break down barriers that might exclude them from key avenues of support and learning.

This strand established a new iteration of the Young Dads Collective in the North of England (YDC North). The expertise of the London group was drawn upon to facilitate this process, and to explore and assess the extent to which this model might map on to, and operate in, a statutory local authority setting offering generic family support. The opportunity to roll out and develop the work of the YDC in a new region of the UK was seen as a crucial strand of this practitioner initiative and a way of addressing the FYF-identified postcode lottery of support for young fathers.

The initiative was founded on the perceived capacity of young fathers to be recognised as experts by experience, that is, to speak for themselves, to provide peer support, to be involved in the delivery of professional training and to take on ambassadorial roles for young fathers everywhere. This was seen as a vital means to instigate a change in culture and challenge the pervasive social deficit view of young fathers. The process not only empowered and gave voice to a marginalised group, but also created a space and an audience primed to effect a change in professional cultures. The work of this strand involved sustained professional support and training for the young fathers who had signed up to take part. YDC in London fed directly into the design of the implementation process, supported by insights provided by the researchers whose involvement ensured an evidence-based approach (Colfer et al, 2015; Neale and Davies, 2015a; Neale et al, 2015).

Development of the pilot initiative

A partnership approach across organisations (including a national children's charity and a West Yorkshire city council) was essential to the success of this initiative. Both organisations were known to the FYF research team and had national reputations for championing young fathers in their localities. We were able to facilitate the roll-out of the very successful work of the YDC to the North of England. The process also enabled the sharing of good practice and strategies for development across organisations, importing creative ideas generated in the voluntary sector into the provisions of a statutory service.

The YDC model was selected as an exemplar of co-producing best practice and promoting effective ways to challenge the exclusion of young fathers and pervasive negative views of them. Uniquely, the YDC model empowers selected young fathers as experts by experience, providing opportunities among an otherwise isolated population for young men to come together to develop a shared identity and an 'authentic' voice (Colfer et al, 2015; see also Tarrant, 2023). The development of the young men's personal accounts of their experiences as fathers, and as seekers of professional support, creates opportunities for them to gain the confidence and skills needed to articulate their experiences of disadvantage in the context of broader socio-economic and political structures (Levac, 2013). Supported by professionals who champion young fathers and promote father-inclusive practice, the young men were trained to educate mutli-agency professionals by influencing their views around effective practice.

In the delivery of their narratives, the young fathers actively encourage reflexivity among professionals in their localities. The input of the young men helped to reach a shared understanding of the barriers to supporting young fathers and inspired new considerations of the strategies needed to dismantle them. In this way, the young fathers engaged directly in practitioner consultation and training, fostering new dialogues and relationships and opportunities for change. Creating spaces for dialogue and the development of shared understandings between a marginalised group and the practitioners who serve them is a vital part of the process of breaking down prejudices and enabling young men to be seen in a different way (we develop this theme further in Chapter 11).

In creating a new version of the YDC model in a new locality, the work of this strand of the RYD initiative represented a new way of changing the culture of professional support, one based on giving young fathers a unique voice and input into policy processes, and a captive audience, who were receptive to their lived experiences. By giving young fathers a voice, the YDC strand of this initiative was designed to build on and further develop the engagement work with young fathers that was initiated under the FYF study (detailed in Chapter 3). It afforded 'shared authority' for the participants, a participatory principle that aligns with and underscores the ethos of the FYF study (Neale, 2013; Neale et al, 2015).

In rolling out the YDC model to the North of England, a key aim was to extend and enhance the support being offered to young fathers through the provisions of the local city council. Four capable young fathers drawn from the local area were recruited and trained as experts by experience. Three of them had taken part in the original FYF study. The young men were provided with sustained support over a year to develop advocacy, mentoring and training roles, which they were also able to test out at a national practitioner training event at the end of the study (see later).

At the outset of the process, the young fathers attended a 'train the trainer' session run by members of the YDC team in London, and with support from Anna, who shared evidence from the FYF study. This led to the co-production of an 'Ask a Dad' workshop, a bespoke training package designed to be co-delivered by young fathers and professionals across health and social care settings, initially in West Yorkshire. As a new initiative, the co-deliverers of YDC North committed to offering training to over 300 professionals in the city. The local lead of the model calculates that this was achieved through a range of workshops, presentations and engagements with influential local organisations, and meetings with senior service providers and policy makers, including a local MP (Tarrant and Neale, 2017b). These organisations straddled health and social care agencies across the statutory and voluntary sectors.

The young men were able to develop their skills and confidence, with predominantly positive outcomes. One young father reflected that he was: "Buzzing, love being listened to. It's not just the work with the professionals it's about meeting up with other dads when we do the planning.

We all want other dads to have a better experience" (YDC North member). Practitioner responses were equally positive: "It has been really useful to hear the other side. I will try to make time to ask the right questions in future" (Health Professional).

"So powerful: until you hear it said, you don't realise how hard it is" (Teenage Pregnancy Worker).

Over the course of the study, a novel and innovative programme of work comprising components of activism and advocacy was also implemented. One young man directly informed a new draft action policy plan for the support of young fathers in the local city and was invited to join the board as a user representative. The young dads also worked together to create a media campaign, designed to promote positive messages about young fatherhood and raise awareness locally.

There were also benefits for the YDC members based in London who, as part of the RYD initiative, were able to influence policy and practice via their attendance at a meeting at the House of Lords. Selected young fathers also presented at the All-Party Parliamentary Group on Fatherhood, where they campaigned for urgent parental policy reform (Tarrant and Neale, 2017b). In finding common ground as young fathers, these young men were able to collectively address the stigma faced by young fathers. They were at the vanguard of a new resistance movement that promotes alternative narratives for understanding their lived experiences and the challenges that they face (see Bekaert and Bradly, 2019 on young mothers).

Key learning and insights

The implementation of a YDC North produced impacts for young fathers and professionals in the West Yorkshire city, and a strengthened evidence base for the YDC in London (Tarrant and Neale, 2017b). The relative success of the model was premised on several key factors. The young dads who were recruited were already well known to the Teenage Pregnancy and Parenthood Team, with whom trusting and positive relationships had already been built. Those relationships are ongoing and have facilitated re-access to these young men for new research, which is generating retrospective accounts of the YDC North implementation, its impacts and challenges (Tarrant, 2023).

The two RYD initiatives illustrate the value of investing in participatory and partnership-based approaches to the creation and delivery of training and consultation for professionals, that is premised on the authentic voices of young fathers. Key to the transformative power of the model is the development of a new, evidence-informed theoretically rich model of father-inclusive practice, that challenges established ways of working in practice and professional settings (Tarrant and Neale, 2017b). Indeed, it is only by promoting engaged fathering premised on a strengths-based approach and challenging stigmatising narratives about young fathers, that more effective support can be developed. The YDC model does just this, offering an innovative solution by training young fathers to articulate their own capabilities and needs in a collaborative environment including a broad, interdisciplinary audience of practitioners and professionals.

It also offers routes for young men's wider social and economic participation by upskilling and investing in young men and by tackling social isolation through peer support. By the end of the study, for example, three of the young fathers who were not in permanent employment prior to their involvement in the YDC North training had been significantly upskilled and had secured paid work and training opportunities. Their contributions were also greatly valued by delegates and a matter of pride for the young men themselves. Their capacity and commitment for effective social engagement with practitioners was a key finding from the FYF study and their own voices had been used to demonstrate this to a practice audience (see Chapter 3). But the RYD initiative represented a leap forward in this collaborative work, for it enabled participatory principles to be embedded within the work of a local authority, thereby demonstrating the potential to change the shape of organisational cultures and mindsets from within. In these ways, we might see the YDC model as an exemplar of an emerging 'paternal commons' of young fathers, in which their voices become a powerful form of public persuasion against their neglect and marginalisation in policy and professional practice (see also Morriss, 2018).

Strand three: co-disseminating education and training about father-inclusive practice

This strand of work involved a collaborative effort across the group, and the culmination of the professional development work conducted over the course of the year. The core aims were to promote the new learning from strands one and two, to test new ways to deliver practitioner training, based on the direct involvement of young fathers themselves, and to consider the feasibility of rolling this training out to multi-agency professionals operating across other regions of the UK.

The power of the collaborative, partnership working that evolved across the year was forcefully highlighted during a final practitioner conference, called Young Dads Talk, held at the end of the study. In consultation with numerous academic and non-academic partners nationally, Young Dads Talk was a research- and practice-informed national training event for practitioners, held in April 2017. Modelled on the Ask a Dad workshops (strand two) this event created a space for genuine multi-direction engagement between national researchers, professionals and young fathers. More than 80 national delegates, including social workers, health visitors, service managers, maternity service workers, youth offending teams, youth workers and family outreach workers, were in attendance.

As well as managing some of the logistics of the event, selected young fathers from YDC London and YDC North co-disseminated knowledge, shedding their anonymity to convey their experiences to the delegates. With the support of their key workers, they co-designed the conference and supported its organisation and running. Knowledge exchange was facilitated by young fathers who presented about their experiences and in workshops that encouraged practitioners to share their experiences of best practice and how they might employ father-inclusive practice in future to promote a more gender-equal professional culture. Following the event, delegates made pledges to change their practice and/or to promote good practice in their organisations. The aim of challenging misrepresentations and stigma and the provocation for professionals to see young fathers differently was the key message of the event, conveyed not only by the narratives presented by young men but also embodied by their contributions and visibility on the day.

Establishing the Grimsby Dads Collective (2020–24)

Building on the knowledge and expertise acquired from the FYF study and extending the collaborative relationships established during the RYD initiative (Tarrant and Neale, 2017a, 2017b), the Following Young Fathers Further (FYFF) team, under the leadership of Anna, has been exploring how the effective practices of support offered by the YDC model might be adapted to a new UK location and policy and practice context. This work assumes the benefits of a similarly dynamic view of policy making and support practices for young fathers, exploring how research and practice innovation based on the principles of co-production and participation can be sustained through the longitudinal frame of a research programme. This work introduces the language of co-creation to interrogate the value of driving collaboratively created evidence-based interventions with young fathers and professionals, while simultaneously employing transformative approaches to evaluation (for example, Tarrant et al, 2022; Tarrant, 2023).

From the outset of this new phase of the programme, new practice partners from the voluntary sector in Grimsby, a relatively deprived coastal town on the east coast of England, have been able to explore whether the model would work effectively to establish a more cohesive father-inclusive policy and practice environment locally. Coram Family and Child Care, YMCA Humber (a youth, community and housing support service) and NSPCC Together for Childhood have collaborated as a new consortium to implement this new YDC hub. Like the YDCs in London and the North, the Grimsby Dads Collective[1] has been driven by a shared commitment to transforming deficit representations and images of young fathers and the national expansion of interventions that enable young fathers to establish and promote their own voices. Indeed, this new iteration of the model, with its own place-based identity as the Grimsby Dads Collective, complete with local input from young fathers, responds to a community-identified need for preventative work for boys and young men in the town. It also provides an opportunity to explore the replicability of the model to another area of the UK with a different practice and policy landscape.

This new iteration of the YDC model continues to be grounded in the principles of partnership working. The extended QL design of the initiative has enabled the documentation of the implementation process, evidence that it is actively shaping key decision making in real time, as well as adaptations to local conditions and responses. Interviews with young fathers and core project partners are being conducted to evaluate the relative success and sustainability of the process, and to examine how the key beneficiaries and stakeholders (commissioners of services and practitioners in Grimsby, a new cohort of local young fathers, and young fathers from the original YDC group) connect and collaborate during times of change. The research is also exploring the extent to which these new relationships, or relational ecologies (Tarrant, 2023), can promote more democratic, collaborative ways of working in Grimsby with the purpose of shaping a collective ability to respond and adapt in a national and regional practice landscape that remains largely 'mother-centric' and 'risk'/problem-oriented.

At the time of writing, the implementation and development of the Grimsby Dads Collective is ongoing. This has been impacted in distinctive and unanticipated ways by the COVID-19 pandemic, including the requirement to work remotely. Findings and learning from the first two years of the implementation process are discussed in an interim report (Way and Tarrant, 2022). As case studies, the expansion of the YDC from London to West Yorkshire and more recently to Grimsby, demonstrate the combined value of QL and participatory modes of impact research (Neale, 2021a) that can be mobilised to address the complex needs of marginalised communities and populations.

A key finding across these studies is that the effectiveness of the YDC model lies in its flexibility and ability to enable the voices of young fathers to be heard and incorporated at individual, operational and strategic levels. Individually, young men are upskilled, while operationally they can influence the design and delivery of services and education. Strategically, young fathers are at the heart of systems change, driving new forms of policy and professional practice through the telling of their experiences of young fatherhood and their engagement with services. Significantly, they are not made solely responsible for systems change. The training and education of professionals and policy makers ensures that everyone who operates within the system has the knowledge and the power required to collectively effect change on behalf of young fathers and their families.

Concluding discussion

This chapter has outlined innovative modes of collaborative impact research designed to support young fathers. We have illustrated the case for participatory and action research methods, facilitated through QL impact studies, that both capture and promote 'what works', 'what matters' and 'how things work' for young fathers in diverse welfare and support settings (Neale, 2021a, 2021b). We demonstrate how democratic, collaborative approaches to research and innovation that involve working in partnership with young fathers and professionals can prompt modest social transformations by fostering a climate of compassion and strengths-based practice among professionals.

Unlike evidence in previous reviews (for example, Trivedi et al, 2007) and other co-produced projects with young fathers (Lohan et al, 2017), we have not focused here on interventions in sexual reproduction or policies intended to reduce teenage pregnancies. Instead, our focus has been on refining and enhancing interventions and programmes that aim to support young men who are already fathers. Our early observations indicate that young fathers' engagement in their family lives improves when they benefit from tailored support and from investments in them as fathers and men of the future. They place a high worth on peer support and derive confidence from developing narratives about their shared identities as young fathers. These narratives not only influence professional practice; they are transformative for young fathers themselves in developing their skills and confidence in key domains of their lives, not least their education, health, employment and their family relationships.

Effective, sustained stakeholder engagement has been vital to the realisation of the RYD impact initiative. The two work packages were practitioner-led and collaborative across a range of stakeholders. From the basis of co-producing and promoting clear narratives about the importance of young fatherhood, the evidence base has been disseminated and translated more effectively and efficiently in real time with policy makers, think tanks, and generic and specialist providers in grassroots organisations (Neale et al, 2015). These methods have been especially fruitful in embodying and taking forward the evidence generated in the FYF study and in providing new forms of support and engagement for young fathers.

All three strands of the RYD study yielded additional, rich insights about the experiences and support needs of young fathers and professional responses, while also attending to key policy issues and gaps in knowledge exchange and translation. These included enhanced understanding of the complex nature of young fathers' lives, the values and aspirations that they hold, the challenges they face across a range of domains (relationships, employment, housing, finances and so on); and the support that they need in establishing and sustaining a relationship with their children.

Our findings suggest that these models of practice transformation have great potential for mobilising change at multiple institutional levels. Relatedly, in making tentative steps towards father-inclusion, these innovations have the potential to engender a radical theoretical shift in practice and social policy responses more generally, so that they reflect a commitment to an ethos of compassion and concern for others rather than those premised on punitive and deficit views and approaches. In our final chapter, we broaden our thinking to consider the radical potential for embedding compassion in the ethos and operation of UK social policy, for the benefit of vulnerable young fathers and others who are marginalised and poorly resourced.

11

Rethinking young fatherhood: citizenship and compassionate social policy

Introduction

In this final chapter we revisit our findings on the lived experiences and support needs of young fathers and draw together the rich constellation of factors that shape their lives over time. In considering how our findings fit with the existing body of research set out in Chapter 1, we return to the methodological groundings for this study, appraise the robustness of our sampling strategy and identify gaps in knowledge that are ripe for further investigation. Finally, we return to the policy context within which this study was conducted. We introduce the idea of compassionate social policy as a means of reframing the landscape of policy and professional practice and responding more effectively to vulnerable young fathers and their families, along with other stigmatised groups in society.

The lived experiences of young fatherhood

Through the Following Young Fathers (FYF) study we have traced the unfolding journeys of a longitudinal sample of 31 young men as they conceived a child, transitioned through the pregnancy, and attempted to establish a role and identity as a parent in the early years of their child's life. In ten cases, the Following Young Fathers Further (FYFF) study has followed their journeys over nearly a decade to gain insights into their longer-term parenting trajectories. We focused not simply on their capacity to contribute to their children's lives; we explored their own needs for care and support in a context where many were of a tender age and dependent, vulnerable and/or disadvantaged themselves.

We know from wider evidence that young fathers are heterogeneous, warning against the tendency to make blanket assumptions about their lives. These young men shared an urban environment in a Northern industrial city in the UK, and a local landscape of service provision. But beyond this, the sample reflected a diverse range of circumstances, including the age at which the young men conceived a child (ranging from 14 to 24); their relationship status (partnered, single, parenting at close hand or at a distance from their children); their family relationships (stable to unstable) and their socio-economic circumstances (ranging from well to poorly resourced). Ten of these young men, around a third of our sample were relatively well resourced, while a further ten were leading highly impoverished lives, including instances of offending behaviour. This socio-economic variation was a novel feature of this study, yielding important insights into the cumulative impact of poverty on these unfolding lives.

Our reporting has been shaped through two complementary frameworks for understanding the lives of young fathers. The first is a *social problems* framework, which has provided an underpinning for much of the earlier literature on young fathers (and young parents more generally) and has fed into policy and practice responses to these young men. The key finding in this literature is the strong correlation between young fatherhood and a range of social ills. As we have seen, this framework shades all to easily into a *social deficit* understanding of young fathers, a moral condemnation of them for running away from their responsibilities and 'causing' the ills that they suffer (we return to this theme later).

An alternative *social engagement* framework sees these young men in a different way – as young fathers who are committed to their children and doing their best to 'be there' despite the raft of challenges that they face. This alternative reading has emerged from a considerable body of qualitative research evidence based on the lived experiences of young fathers. Our own findings very much support this view. Twenty-one young men had sustained a solid and regular fatherhood role and identity over the course of the study, while a further six had some intermittent contact with their children. Moreover, the ten young men who took part in our longer-term follow-up study had all retained their commitment to their children. We have seen that what it means to 'be there' for a child, and how it is practised varied enormously across this sample. In some quarters it involved an intermittent or 'fun' engagement in a child's life rather than an enduring responsibility for the day-to-day care of a child. Nevertheless, the overriding message from a social engagement perspective is that young fathers matter. They care about and want to be there for their children. This major counterbalance to the rhetoric surrounding 'deadbeat dads' and 'problem youth' has been slow to gain ground, although there is evidence to suggest that it is beginning to find its way into public discourses and mainstream professional practice.

In summing up our evidence, we begin with some important commonalities in the journeys of these young men, which hold our sample together and, through the wider body of evidence, link these young men to young fathers everywhere. Our findings reveal that the tender age of young fathers is just one of many challenges that they face as they make the transition into parenthood. We have seen that they commonly conceive a child 'in the moment', often in fleeting or relatively casual relationships, and without forethought. Their use of contraception may be unskilled or sporadic but, in many cases, it is seen as the responsibility of the young women. Moreover, young men have little agency over the decision to keep a child. In these contexts, the news of a pregnancy creates a rupture in these young lives: it is likely to be an unwelcome shock that brings emotional turmoil, fear of the future and anxieties about their capacity to turn themselves at relatively short notice from carefree lads to responsible dads. These young men felt they had been catapulted into adult responsibilities at what they saw as too young an age, when they felt they were not ready, when they had too few resources to contribute, with little experience of looking after a child or negotiating adult relationships, and with no strong desire to do either. The young men's lack of reproductive agency is a significant finding of this study, with implications for Relationship and Sex Education provision, which currently remains limited in its impact and effectiveness.

The anxieties that young fathers face may continue throughout a pregnancy, sharpened in a context where fatherhood is an unreal, socially constructed state that becomes tangible only through the support and recognition of others (notably, the mothers, but also wider family and health and social care practitioners). Moreover, the stress is likely to continue over time, particularly in relation to the dynamics of their family relationships, and their employment and housing journeys, as they try to find ways to step up to their new responsibilities.

The pernicious social stigma that surrounds an early and unplanned entry into parenthood hovers in the background of these processes, shaping the young men's sense of self and impacting on their fragile paternal identities. Sometimes they encounter this stigma directly in the responses of the maternal grandparents and/or frontline professional staff. This can sharpen their efforts to distance themselves from the stereotypical absent young father, while simultaneously reinforcing their anxieties and sense of shame about the impending birth. It seems that a social deficit model of young fatherhood cannot easily be taken out of the picture; it creates a moral benchmark against which young men judge the responses and behaviour of themselves and others, and against which others judge them. Moreover, as we have seen, its impact is by no means short-lived; it may have pernicious effects on the mental health and well-being of young fathers for years to come.

Yet the rather woeful plight of these young men in the early stages of their journeys represents only half the picture. Alongside the stress, they commonly reported the joy of becoming a parent and finding a natural connection to a newborn child. The arrival of a child was seen as a major turning point and a source of pride and achievement. Their accounts reveal the rise of a new emotional literacy surrounding the power of emotionally engaged fatherhood. In many cases, entering fatherhood was transformative, providing a fundamental source of meaning and identity and opening new pathways and aspirations for the future. Wider evidence supports this picture: an unplanned child is by no means an unwanted child.

For those with fragile family ties, or fragile identities through offending, drinking or drug taking, entering parenthood offered a new purpose and direction in life, the chance to forge new and positive family lives that would enable them to move on from the deep suffering of their own childhoods. In short, regardless of their family background, socio-economic circumstances or their relationship with the child's mother and her family, the young men in this study embraced the ethos of engaged fatherhood and tried, with varying degrees of success, to put this ethos into practice.

We turn now to the factors that made a difference to the parenting journeys of these young men. Their transitions through the early years of parenthood did not occur in a linear direction, at a uniform pace, or follow a set path. They were fluid, contingent and unpredictable. Their trajectories converged and diverged through time, shaped by a complex constellation of individual, relational, socio-economic and environmental opportunities and constraints. The challenges ranged from managing fragile relationships with the mothers of their children, and by extension with the maternal grandparents; trying to fulfil a breadwinner role through education, employment or training; seeking a place to parent in a volatile housing market; and their mixed experiences of professional support. The complex intertwining of these challenges gave a unique edge to each life, while their cumulative impact created additional pressures for these young men. We have tried to convey this complexity through our ecological reporting, building layers of insight through accounts that range from micro to macro, from the interpersonal, to the familial, to wider institutional and structural opportunities and constraints.

The efforts of our participants to become good fathers and to overcome the challenges were laudable. We have also documented the anguish felt by poorly resourced young men whose family relationships were fragile and volatile over time; who had no stable homes; who dropped out of school or training or could not find paid work; who might (especially in these circumstances) descend into debt, domestic violence and/or criminal behaviour; who had further unplanned pregnancies; and who faced mental health problems and/or the loss of contact with their children. For some of these impoverished fathers this was a slippery slope, involving a relentless cumulation of many of these difficulties over time.

In distilling our evidence, we focus here on two key challenges, of a relational and socio-economic nature, that not only shaped the journeys of our participants, but created major divergencies in their trajectories across the sample.

Relational factors

The gendered and generational dimensions of young parenthood emerged as key factors that shaped the young men's parenting journeys. Young mothers, as the primary caring parents (often with the help of maternal grandmothers), hold the power to make decisions about keeping a child, and how a child will subsequently be cared for and by whom. In all but one case, the young men were told of the impending birth and given an option to be involved, even where they were not in a relationship with the mother. But one father was excluded from the pregnancy and birth in the context of a deep rift between him and the maternal family. He was unable to forge a meaningful connection with his child in the aftermath, and opted to drop out of his child's life.

Our evidence shows that whatever the strength of the ethos of engaged fatherhood, it sits alongside and remains in uneasy tension with the enduring ethos of the mother/child dyad. Whatever the strength of the young men's aspirations in relation to their children, their roles and identities as fathers were predicated on their ability to sustain a productive co-parenting relationship with the mothers, as primary carers of their children (and, by extension, the maternal grandparents, who to varying degrees help to deliver this primary care). While these gendered patterns are evident in some measure for all fathers, they are particularly pronounced for this age group, where an entry into parenthood is largely unplanned, and where co-parental relationships are fragile from the outset. Moreover, in these circumstances, power and responsibility could flow vertically down the generations in the maternal household, in the process, constraining the development of 'horizontal' co-parenting relationships between the young parents themselves.

We have seen that mothers could act as gate-openers, instilling confidence in the young men and encouraging and facilitating their relationships with their children. This was most likely to occur where the fathers were parenting at close hand, through a couple relationship or shared residence with the mother. But where fathers were attempting to parent at a distance, without a stable relationship with the mothers or a shared home as the basis for their parenting, young mothers were more likely to act as gatekeepers. In these circumstances, fathers often had to work harder to prove their parenting credentials. Many were developing distinctive moral scripts around good fatherhood. Alongside their commitment to 'stepping up', and 'being there' for their children, they were promoting ideals of friendship, respect and teamwork with the mother. In this way, they were asserting the viability of non-partnered co-parenting that could operate across separate households. And they were challenging the idea that 'being there' for a mother and child necessarily means being in an intimate and exclusive relationship with the mother. As their accounts show, they commonly denigrated what they saw as the dubious maternal practice of using a child as a weapon in disputes over money, lifestyles or a father's commitment to the mother. These moral scripts were not operating simply at an ideological level; they were feeding into and unsettling young parenting practices and negotiating processes.

In some cases, the mothers acted as gate-closers, barring the young men from seeing their children. The personal qualities of the young men were important factors here. Where they had engaged in domestic violence, coercive or unstable behaviour, drug taking or criminal activities they could be perceived as a risk to mother or child. In these circumstances, the barring of contact was seen by the young men as understandable. However, the practice of barring contact was condemned when it was triggered purely by the end of a relationship between the parents, or the re-partnering of either parent. In several of these cases, the fathers were successful in brokering contact arrangements through the family courts, or through family mediation. However, the recourse to family law was regarded as a last resort, and the costs were seen as prohibitive, especially after the withdrawal of legal aid. Whatever the outcome, these ruptures in relationships undermined the young men's efforts to establish a friendship with the mothers as the basis for their co-parenting, and in some cases, damaged the parenting efforts of the young men.

Overall, the nature and quality of the young men's relationships with the mothers (and, by extension, with the mother's family) emerged as critical factors in how or whether they could sustain a role as a parent. Their parenting became largely conditional on the goodwill of the mothers and maternal grandparents. There is an evident need for good relational skills as the basis for co-parenting: a need for cooperation, tact, trust, mutual respect, flexibility, the ability to negotiate and compromise, emotional maturity and a joint focus on the needs of the child. Being an engaged father requires a great deal more than simply 'being there'. These skills have to be learned, yet their inculcation may take time for younger men who lack confidence in their relational abilities.

Our discussion suggests a limited understanding of these delicate and fragile interpersonal and family dynamics in policy circles and in professional practice. This reinforces the need for Relationship and Sex Education and other forms of early intervention that would better prepare young people for the essential tasks of establishing and sustaining personal relationships of intimacy, care, trust and respect in their adult lives. Recognising the counselling support that young fathers might need to manage the effects of impoverished childhoods, and the relational work of engaged fatherhood, would be equally helpful, enabling young fathers to care for their own mental and physical well-being, alongside caring for others. Whatever the strength of the ethos of engaged fatherhood, it emerges in this study as a contingent state, dependent on a range of relational, reputational and intergenerational factors that determine whether or to what extent young men can be there for their children.

Socio-economic factors

Maintaining these crucial family relationships relies not only on the personal qualities of the fathers, but on their socio-economic credentials. As we have seen, a commitment to an ethos of engaged fatherhood does not replace a breadwinning ideology. Indeed, among this sample, economic and material provision for a child was seen as central to the ethos of engaged fatherhood. The young men's access to basic socio-economic resources (their capacity to take on a breadwinner role, and the income levels and resources of the paternal household) were also crucial in shaping their parenting journeys over time, with impact on their capacity to sustain contact with their children. A lack of personal resources was an issue for all of the young men in the study, given their relative youth. Falling back on the resources available in the grandparent households was a vital lifeline across the sample, although as we also show, these resources varied greatly in their quality, extent and sustainability over time.

The efforts of young fathers to step up to their breadwinner responsibilities were laudable. Some of the young men faced a triple burden of learning, earning and caring. This involved a great deal of juggling of their time and effort as they attempted to combine paid work and care of their child with further education or training. Others faced the challenges of holding down more than one job, striving to improve their employment and training circumstances, or relentless state-mandated searching for low-paid casual employment. These balancing acts were not short-term contingency measures; they could continue to shape the employment trajectories of young fathers over many years.

On the whole, the most well-resourced young men fared best in terms of fulfilling their role as engaged young fathers. The economic security of their childhoods and family lives gave these young men greater support, stability and confidence in managing their family relationships. They had the capacity, often supported through their parents, to make a material, financial and emotional contribution to their children's lives. This is not to downplay the emotional and relational difficulties that they faced, sometimes over many years. But their supportive home and family lives cushioned these problems. They had already begun to accrue educational skills and qualifications before entering parenthood and had good prospects for economic security in the future. Being able to draw upon these resources enabled them to incorporate a positive fatherhood role and identity into their lives with relative ease.

In contrast, the most disadvantaged young men had no such foundation in their early lives to draw upon, making it difficult to generate and sustain new family relationships or take on new parenting and employment responsibilities. Their EET strategies were short-term and expedient, based on the imperative to earn. Their aspirations to find work and provide economically remained largely unfulfilled, linked to ongoing insecurities in the labour market and the greater conditionality of welfare provision in the UK. Their credentials as potential providers and their employment prospects were hanging very much in the balance. As we have seen, in some circumstances, the offer of cash-in-hand support to a mother would be used as a bargaining chip to gain access to or reinstate contact with a child. Yet, since the earning power of these disadvantaged young men was highly constrained, they sometimes resorted to selling drugs, or other risky and illegal practices as the only way to contribute to the maternal household.

These young men lived with an accumulation of daily hardships in which time horizons shrink and resources become increasingly fragile. The ability to formulate plans and mobilise aspirations for the future is, arguably, integral to social citizenship, yet for those facing cumulative hardships, this capacity may be eclipsed in the overriding preoccupation with day-to-day survival. This can lead to downward paths, risky and sometimes criminal practices, and the erosion of health. We were struck by the mental health problems that beset many of these impoverished young men, and their need for professional support in coping with a range of adverse life events. It was among this poorly resourced group that contact between father and child was most fragile over time, and, in several cases, ceased over the course of the study.

In terms of housing, the better-resourced young men in this study retained their homes with their parents as a basis for their parenting or adopted a yo-yo pattern of moving between the maternal and paternal households. However, many of the disadvantaged young men had no secure place to parent; they were not deemed eligible for state housing, for their parental status was simply unrecognised. Some of the young men were leading nomadic lives, moving in quick succession from temporary and often overcrowded homes with grandparents or foster parents, to sofa-surfing with aunties or friends, to being on remand, and on to emergency hostel accommodation where children are not allowed.

The quality of housing and local neighbourhoods is one of the most tangible and emotionally charged manifestations of people's socio-economic and relational fortunes or misfortunes. For disadvantaged young men, the lack of a home represents the most visible aspect of parenting on shaky ground, the culmination of a cascade of problems that could wear these young men down over time. These unstable, patchwork lives offer little emotional or material security for vulnerable young fathers, let alone for their offspring. Housing is a vital structural and neighbourhood issue that is badly in need of public investment. Yet the findings reported here show that the lack of a place to parent is also a deeply personal, interpersonal and intergenerational family issue that impacts on young people's ontological security, their perceptions and experience of 'home', their capacity to flourish in their daily lives and their ability to support and care for others, including their children. These unmet needs for housing and home could, in turn, unsettle the fatherhood identities and family relationships of these young men, and undermine their basic capacity to be there for their children.

Across the lower-income young men in this study there were striking accounts of school-age fathers saving their pocket money to buy nappies; of school leavers tramping the streets every day to distribute their CVs to shops and factories; of young men struggling to complete training courses with low educational skills and problems of illiteracy. There were stark tales of living hand to mouth, when young men were sanctioned for missing appointments and had no state support, or were leading nomadic lives, moving frequently between a range of temporary accommodation, including homeless hostels in inaccessible locations and without provision for children. And there were young men who did not have the bus fare to search for work, attend appointments or visit their children. These accounts reflect more than the lived experiences of young fatherhood; they reflect the everyday realities of living in poverty as a young father with a child to support. Such experiences are: 'almost always overwhelmingly negative and can have psychological, physical, relational and practical effects on people's lives. Poverty is a highly stigmatised social position and the experience of poverty in an affluent society can be particularly isolating and socially damaging' (Ridge 2009: 3).

These precarious patterns of living show in stark relief how wider institutional and structural forces can filter back to impede and unsettle the delicate balance of young fathers' family relationships.

Methodological considerations

Before turning to the policy implications of our findings, we briefly revisit the methodological design of this study and consider what our findings have added to the wider body of evidence about the lives of young fathers. We also set out here some further gaps in our understanding that are ripe for further investigation. Our detailed review of research on young fatherhood in Chapter 1 revealed a rich body of international and historical evidence about their lives, which has informed the analysis of data in this study. This involved piecing together a scattered evidence base to create a coherent picture of the lives of young fathers and bringing together the *social problems* and *social engagement* literatures as complementary frames of reference for enhancing our insights.

The nature of young fathers' general experiences, particularly during their transition into parenthood, are remarkably similar across time and place, creating important synergies between the wider body of evidence and the findings reported here. However, in two important respects, this study represents a departure from existing studies. First, the utilisation of qualitative longitudinal (QL) methods has enabled detailed insights into the unfolding lives of these young men over the early years of their parenting, moving beyond 'snapshot' understandings to capture change in the making. This is a robust methodology (Neale, 2021a), not least because it is embedded in the ebbs and flows of lived experiences. The longitudinal reach achieved here is unique in qualitative studies of young fatherhood, enabling detailed insights into the causal processes that shape young men's journeys beyond the first year of a child's life. It is an approach that is rarely used in this field, and it is ripe for further development.

The second departure relates to the sampling strategy used in this research. Securing extra funding for this study in 2012 enabled us to adopt a targeted, purposively driven sampling strategy in preference to the small-scale opportunity samples that typically characterise this field of study. Opportunity sampling offers a quick and relatively easy way to access a sample and is justified in the context of small-scale exploratory studies in new fields of scholarship. But, as we have suggested, young fatherhood research is now coming of age and no longer fits into this category.

Purposive samples do not need to be large. But they need to encompass a strategically chosen range of experiences and circumstances across a study population. Our targeted approach enabled us to sample across well- and poorly resourced young men, to yield insights into how their socio-economic fortunes are implicated in their parenting journeys. Again, this represents a departure from most existing research. Above all, however, it was the heterogeneity of this sample, combined with the longitudinal reach of the design, that enabled us to explore the diverging journeys of those young men who sustained their engagement with their children over time, and those who were unable to do so. In the process we have shed light on the complex causal processes that led to these different outcomes across the sample.

One final sampling issue is worth revisiting here. It concerns the commitment to engaged fatherhood, which was strongly evident across this sample, and the vexed question of whether this pattern is the product of a skewed and unrepresentative sample. As we have seen, it is not clear how prevalent 'absent' young fathers are in the wider population of young fathers, particularly where they become disengaged at the outset. However, we have suggested that public perceptions of an overriding prevalence of these young men are vastly exaggerated, given the evidence from a range of studies that young men are strongly committed to being there for their children. Since absent young fathers do not have a paternal identity (or only a residual one) they tend to fall outside the orbit of studies such as FYF. We have pieced together some limited evidence on the circumstances that may lead young men to disengage at an early stage, including evidence from one young man in this study who was precluded from establishing a relationship with his son. But beyond this, our knowledge of these young men is woefully inadequate. This suggests the need for a targeted study that would focus on the lived experiences of absent young fathers.

There are other areas too, where we have identified gaps in knowledge that deserve more focused investigation. There is huge potential, of course, for qualitative longitudinal designs that can tap into the unfolding biographies of young fathers in a variety of circumstances and settings, and for the use of purposive sampling that can create more robust axes of comparison across different life experiences. There is also huge scope for international comparative studies, of the sort being undertaken in the FYFF study. Researchers are endlessly creative and will find many new avenues of enquiry for the future. But some possibilities are set out here:

- housing needs and experiences in different welfare regimes;
- comparative understandings of EET trajectories;
- intergenerational relationships in different cultural/familial settings;
- co-parenting (at close hand/at a distance) and the impact of domestic violence;
- commonalities and differences in the experiences of young mothers and young fathers;
- the experiences of primary caring young fathers;
- family law and mediation, in the context of family law reform in the UK
- experiences of state care/leaving care as a young father;
- the journeys of young offender fathers into custody and into resettlement;
- ethnicity and cultural constructions of parenthood;
- mental health experiences and needs; and
- qualitative longitudinal impact studies that facilitate change by supporting and charting the building of new services and interventions (see Neale, 2021a for a detailed description and discussion, and for an example, see Chapter 10 and Tarrant, 2023).

Seeing young fathers in a different way

In the remainder of this chapter, we examine the policy implications of our findings and return to an underlying theme that has shaped much of the discussion in this book. It concerns the social problems framework for understanding young fathers, which, in policy, practice and public responses, slides almost seamlessly into a social deficit model of these young men. Through a potent mixture of problem-focused neglect, sidelining and public denigration, these frameworks have become institutionally embedded in UK policy and professional practice since the 1990s. In the process, the social engagement framework for understanding young fathers (that is, that they aspire to be there for their children and engage with support agencies) has been almost entirely eclipsed from view.

There are a number of linked components to the deficit model of young fatherhood. As observed, gendered ideologies of parenthood provide a broad grounding: the focus on teenage pregnancy brings young women centrally into the picture and eclipses young men, who are relegated to 'bit' players who are not recognised or accorded legitimacy as parents. In this policy vacuum a social deficit understanding of young fathers has flourished. It is presumed (without foundation in empirical evidence) that these young men are overwhelmingly absent, irresponsible, and potentially risky for mothers and children. This colours professional perceptions, leading to practices of sidelining and/or extra surveillance. Here, young fathers are rendered not simply as 'secondary' parents, but as potentially 'deficient' parents, whose very presence is treated with suspicion and uncertainty. More benignly, perhaps, professionals may regard them as 'hard to reach'. But, either way, these are deficit views of young fathers, part of a culture of blame in a policy regime that tends to shun, sideline or neglect those who are in need.

Wider policy responses reinforce the picture: early parenthood is seen as the product of ignorance and low expectations, an individual failing that brings with it, indeed causes, a range of social ills that lead to poor outcomes for parents and their children (an assumption that is clearly refuted across a range of studies, including our own). Linked to this is the idea that a parenting deficit runs across the generations in impoverished families, creating an inevitable cycle of disadvantage (see, for example, SEU, 1999). Political rhetoric and media commentary complete the picture: young fathers are commonly portrayed as morally reprehensible and deviant for impregnating young women, running away from their responsibilities and 'causing' the social ills that they suffer.

As we have noted, the stigma that arises from these public and political discourses is palpable, with resulting impacts on young men's mental health (see Chapter 2). Young fathers who are unemployed, homeless or otherwise living in poverty may be doubly disadvantaged: the stigma of welfare dependency, and the charge of being 'shirkers' who are unworthy and/ or untrustworthy is also present, compounding their marginalised status (Ridge, 2002; Patrick, 2017). Overall, it is striking that, since the 1990s, UK policy and practice responses to young fathers have been shaped largely in relation to a range of stigatising discourses that are adrift from empirical reality. This creates a significant mismatch between policy processes and the lived experiences of young fathers. It also has deleterious impacts on young fathers themselves, colouring their perceptions of their own worth and legitimacy as parents. This is why there is an evident need to see young fathers in a different and more compassionate way in policy and practice settings (Neale and Davies, 2015a; 2015b).

Compassionate social policy

Before exploring how policy and professional practice might be reframed to give greater support to young fathers, it is necessary to take a step back, to consider, in broader context, the ethical principles that shape the operation of welfare states, and how these may feed into the lived experiences of those who seek state support. As Gregory (2015: 349) notes, countries with universal welfare provision, where all people are entitled to certain benefits or services as a right of citizenship, are likely to have stronger and more effective welfare states than countries where support is highly conditional and targeted only on those with the greatest need. Targeted regimes (such as the UK and US) invest less in welfare and the quality of its provision, have lower levels of public support for the welfare state and, consequently, do less well in tackling poverty and disadvantage. Regimes with more generous or universal coverage (typically, the Nordic countries) fare much better in eradicating or reducing these social ills (Gregory, 2015).

Comparative evidence (of the sort utilised by Ridge, 2002, and Gregory, 2015) is very useful here, for it enables us to see more clearly the link between the ethical principles and operation of different welfare regimes and the effects of their interventions on their clients. Nativel and Daguerre (2006: 228), for example, found that in Norway, Denmark and France, benefits and state support had been organised in ways that supported all lone parents, regardless of age, thereby avoiding the stigmatisation of young parents. Wider comparative evidence (Grundy and Foverskov, 2016) shows that public acceptance of young parents and staunch state support can make significant differences to their longer-term health outcomes, while similar findings are reported for young fathers in the context of British and Swedish welfare regimes (Andreasson et al, 2023).

One of the key features that makes a difference in these contrasting welfare states is the underlying sets of ethical principles that drive interventions and that pervade public perceptions. Highly targeted regimes tend to value the principles of self-reliance and self-sufficiency, along with an ethic of justice (Collins et al, 2012). And, as shown in Chapter 2, they are also characterised by high levels of stigma for vulnerable and dependent populations (Gregory, 2015). The whole system relies on, indeed inculcates, wider public perceptions that makes scapegoats of those deemed to be undeserving. In the UK, this neoliberal stance harks back to the 19th century Poor Law, which consciously divided the deserving from the undeserving poor.

In contrast, welfare systems that operate on universal principles of support are likely to be underpinned by an ethos of compassion rather than self-sufficiency. The place of compassion in social policy has received some welcome attention in recent years. There are some long-running debates about the precise meaning of the term in political, legal and moral philosophy and whether it should be viewed as a 'virtue' that requires action as part of a flourishing society, or as a more abstract 'value' that is open to interpretation and where follow-up action is discretionary. There are also questions about the extent to which this ethos can operate beyond individual responses and be built into institutional cultures as the basis for delivering health and social care (see Nussbaum, 1996; Collins et al, 2012, 2015; Gregory, 2015;

Finkel, 2019; Bierre and Howden-Chapman, 2022). Despite the debates, it is generally agreed that if societies are to be more caring, inclusive and equitable, then the ethos of compassion has a crucial role to play.

Compassion has no settled meaning but for our purposes here we take a lead from the moral philosophies of David Hume and Adam Smith (Gregory, 2015). It is a moral sensibility that produces sympathy for and solidarity with those who suffer misfortune. As a broad umbrella term, compassion is closely aligned with Richard Tawney's long-established ideals of fellowship (social relations founded on recognition and mutual respect; see Deacon, 2007). It is also closely aligned with the development of social models of citizenship for children and young people, based on an entitlement to recognition, respect and participation (Neale, 2004; Neale and Flowerdew, 2007). Taylor (1992: 26) reminds us that 'due recognition is not just a courtesy that we owe people. It is a fundamental human need'. These basic needs underpin young people's citizenship and are just as crucial for their well-being as their needs for care and protection. It is also worth noting that a culture of compassion can run alongside and complement the values of justice and self-sufficiency, for, by fostering self-worth, confidence and hope, it may empower people to develop more self-reliant lives in the future.

While compassion is bound up with the range of moral sensibilities we have outlined, it is important to note that in a policy context it is not a one-way or passive process. It is essentially empathetic, relational and collaborative. It requires the observer to engage positively with the person, put themselves into their shoes, be a good listener and, where possible, to reach a joint understanding of how they have arrived at their current circumstances and how they might move on. This is the case regardless of whether the observer condones a person's past actions and choices or judges them to be 'deserving'; compassion does not require a surrender of one's own moral position or interests (Collins et al, 2012; Gregory, 2015). But as an exercise in personal judgement, involving ongoing reflection and dialogue, it requires a capacity to understand the lives of others and to avoid prejudging likely outcomes.

As these observations imply, compassion feeds into and shapes human responses and practical action; here it becomes a civic virtue, a political and policy driving force, rather than an abstract value. It requires an active response that goes beyond sympathy to offer emotional and practical support, encouragement and advocacy. Compassionate responses are essentially collaborative; they seek to diminish power differentials and encourage the agency of those in need (Bierre and Howden-Chapman, 2022). Finally, as practical action, a compassionate ethos is essentially dynamic. It works through time to understand and move on from past circumstances. It is also future oriented, on the basis that change is always possible and that hope can be rekindled. The aim is to help identify and facilitate new pathways that may be transformative and, in some cases, redemptive for those in need:

> In providing and receiving care in conditions of mutual respect we learn and enact the practical ethics of being attentive to others: responsibility, trust, being adaptable and accommodating to others' differences, toleration for our own and others' human frailty, and how to sustain and repair relationships. These are not just personal qualities but contribute to social cohesion. They can be seen as civic virtues and therefore as part of what it means to be a citizen. (Williams, 2004: 76)

Steering a delicate path guided by a compassionate ethos is not an easy option. There may be pitfalls to guard against. Where compassion is the product of individual discretion, without embodiment in organisation cultures, it may be harder work for the individuals involved, and less effective or widespread or sustainable over time (Collins et al, 2012; Bierre and Howden-Chapman, 2022). Moreover, there is a tendency for compassion to shade into paternalism, pity or charity in ways that may be demeaning rather than empowering for the person in need (Collins et al, 2012). As Horsell (2017) notes, the language of compassion may be highjacked by neoliberal governments, who may espouse an ethos of compassion but do nothing to tackle the structural conditions that perpetuate social inequalities. That is why compassion needs to operate at both individual and wider institutional levels of policy making, and embody solidarity, collective decision making and an ethic of respect for those who are suffering.

Social policy interventions that enable a compassionate treatment of people in need are hardly new; they can be found in many welfare regimes through time and space (Finkel, 2019). In the UK, despite the dominance of a self-seeking neoliberal approach to welfare provision, we can see compassion in operation among dedicated professionals across a range of care settings, along with recent attempts to build it into institutional cultures. In 2008, New Labour introduced a compassion index into the metrics used for gauging the quality of nursing care in the NHS, on the basis that empathetic care is as important to recovery as the skills of doctors (Carvel, 2008). Under the Coalition government, a compassionate care policy, designed to ensure that people are treated with respect, dignity and compassion, was extended to all health and social care services in the UK (DoH, 2015). In the wake of these changes, compassion was declared as a core value, derived from the founding principles of the NHS, which could be remobilised to shape the operation of the whole organisation (West, 2016).

The drivers for these developments are significant here. They occurred in the wake of discoveries of widespread abuse of vulnerable patients by care staff in hospital and residential care settings (DoH, 2015) and a culture of bullying within the NHS workforce (West, 2016). The new measures were designed to counter further tendencies towards controlling, punitive, threatening or uncaring behaviour within the NHS, and to guard against the danger of institutionalised bullying, abuse and neglect (West, 2016). In a welfare regime that is driven by neoliberal values, such problems are deeply rooted, and they remain in evidence today, in the early 2020s. But a culture of compassion can help not only to expose them, but to offer an alternative, and a more humane and civilised way of shaping social relationships that would enable people to flourish.

More recently, there have been calls to build cultures of compassion across other domains of social policy, for example, in the operation of the private rental sector (Bierre and Howden-Chapman, 2022); in supporting homeless people (Horsell, 2017); in social work practice (Mickel, 2008; Frontline/CPI, 2019); and in the treatment of asylum seekers who arrive on our shores (Hudson-Wilkin, 2023). In the wake of 13 years (at the time of writing) of neoliberal welfare retrenchment and the application of punitive sanctions under the Coalition and Conservative governments, there has been a recent call for a new values-based approach to social policy in the UK, which would embed dignity, respect and recognition into the fabric of public services (Vizard and Hills, 2021).

How these changes might be achieved is an open question. Solutions would need to be tailored to particular settings of support and professional practice. It is generally recognised that building a culture of compassion into welfare institutions is no easy task, particularly where governments need to respond not only to individual suffering and tackle the stigma that people face, but also work at institutional levels to tackle structural inequalities in employment and housing and ensure an adequate safety net of welfare benefits. Despite the basic challenges, there are some components of an institutional culture of compassion that are worth considering here:

- Compassionate interventions that are person-centred, interactive and action-based require the inculcation of broad sets of principles that can be interpreted and applied with discretion and fine judgement by professional workers in specific contexts to tailor solutions to people's needs (Gregory, 2015).
- Professionals need enough autonomy, time, staffing and resources to work flexibly and use their judgement to respond creatively and appropriately to individual need; to devise thoughtful, collaborative plans of action, and to provide continuity of care over time. Large caseloads, fixed schedules and bureaucratic form-filling that serve the system rather than the clients can undermine compassionate care.
- This kind of provision rests, in turn, on high-quality training, trust in professionals, and local empowerment: the devolving of responsibility and decision making to local teams who operate at the frontline of service delivery and have a collective and intuitive grasp of local problems.

- Institutional leaders, as the carriers of culture in an organisation, need to work collectively and by example to embody and promote a culture of compassion both in the workplace and beyond it, and to counter the stigma that stalks their clients (West, 2016). At higher levels of government, too, policy makers have a crucial role to play in inculcating broader sets of compassionate values and principles in society. This may help to counter the public cultures of blame that arise when people are stigmatised, 'othered' and labelled in ways that discredit them.
- Policy makers need to build compassion directly into their provisions for welfare support, employment and housing, to tackle the wider structural inequalities that exist between those who are well and poorly resourced. Greater provision for universal benefits in welfare systems will ensure a greater buy-in to, and acceptance of, these systems by the public, and lead to more effective safety nets of support for vulnerable citizens.

Changing the hearts and minds of people at all levels of an organisation, let alone beyond it, may be an uphill struggle in a deeply entrenched neoliberal welfare regime. However, as our example in the NHS shows, this makes a compassionate response to the provision of care and welfare all the more vital.

Rethinking support and citizenship for young fathers

Compassionate social policy responses of the sort we have outlined would make a significant difference to the lives of young fathers. They would provide a mechanism for challenging deficit understandings of these young men, dissipating the stigma that they currently face, and enabling their aspirations as socially engaged and responsible fathers to be given due recognition and respect. The practices of sidelining and neglect seen in the operation of UK policy and professional practice fail to meet the most basic test of social citizenship for young fathers, for they fail to accord recognition to these young men as fathers, let alone enable and support their engagement with their children. Arguably, the capacity to see young fathers in a different way is a necessary precursor to providing appropriate support for them.

Some of the young men in this study benefited from the provision of specialist counselling, emotional and peer-support services, as the accounts in Chapter 9 reveal. This was vital support for school-aged and impoverished young men. Yet such provision has always been patchy and under-resourced in mainstream services, and it is under further strain in the current political climate. Moreover, for those who are offending or resorting to illegal activities, the need for compassionate professional interventions and a redemptive approach to their futures is all the greater, providing a much-needed complement to the 'risk' and 'surveillance' frameworks that shape mainstream social work and social justice provision.

As shown in Chapter 9, the specialist services that played a central role in this study were distinctive, effective and highly valued by the young men precisely because they bore all the hallmarks of a compassionate ethos of care and respect (Davies and Neale, 2015; Neale and Davies, 2015a; Neale and Ladlow, 2015a; Ladlow and Neale, 2016). Kate Bulman, the specialist nurse working in a secure unit with young offender fathers explained her approach when we first went to meet her: the core requirement in helping the young men was to be able to love them. In these cases, compassionate care was being pioneered by exceptional individuals, who were acting as local champions for young fathers. These pioneering local champions were given some limited backing from their institutions. However, they were often working on their own initiative, and without the resources and encouragement to develop their work further or to sustain it over time. This meant that they made personal sacrifices to respond to the needs of their clients, for example, working long hours and keeping young fathers on their caseload beyond the time when they should have been referred on to other agencies. This finding reinforces the need for institutional backing and the provision of sufficient resources to enable a culture of compassion to flourish.

For Gregory (2015), one of the most effective ways to mobilise compassion across settings, to change hearts and minds, is to bring disparate communities together, to break down the barriers of prejudice and lack of knowledge and enable a face-to-face understanding of the lives of others through the simple expedient of listening to them. As demonstrated in Chapter 10, we were able to mobilise this approach through our stakeholder and impact work with selected young fathers in this study. Working with the principle of shared authority, selected young men took on ambassadorial roles for young fathers. They were given both a voice and a captive audience of practitioners. Their very presence was critical in our ability to convey the central message of this study to a broad policy and practice audience: that young fathers wish to engage with their children, to be counted, to be seen as clients of services and to be supported in their parenting journeys. We did not need to speak for them; their own words were much more powerful.

Such initiatives have powerful effects, not only in changing perceptions of young fathers but empowering them to become part of the solution as advocates for young fathers and trainers of new generations of professionals. The mobilisation of qualitative longitudinal impact designs, rooted in new forms of collaborative enterprise that embrace the efforts of young men themselves, are emerging as important and innovative mechanisms for facilitating such work (Neale, 2021a, 2021b; Tarrant, 2023). Such initiatives illustrate new and compassionate ways of developing research/practice collaborations that can break down prejudices, promote the social citizenship of young fathers and enable them to be seen in a different way.

Concluding discussion

In this final chapter we have drawn together the findings from this study on young fathers, revisited our dynamic methodology, and placed our findings in the context of the existing body of research evidence. We have seen that young fathers wish to 'be there' for their children but face a raft of challenges in doing so, not least, those of a relational and socio-economic nature. The very different trajectories of young fathers who are well or poorly resourced is a key finding from this study, with implications for policy and professional practice in the UK.

We have also argued for a compassionate response to these young fathers in policy and professional practice, one that recognises and respects their social citizenship, that seeks to understand the challenges they face, and that offers sustained support of a socio-economic and relational nature that can facilitate their efforts to be good dads. Early intervention policies are vital for families. But sustained support over time is no less vital, particularly for vulnerable young men who have experiences of deep suffering in their earlier family lives. In these cases, offers of sustained support that embody the principles of compassion, redemption and hope for the future are likely to be needed. Disadvantaged young fathers are more likely to flourish in welfare and labour-market conditions that support their positive and progressive involvement in their families, and that facilitates their participation, rather than attributing blame and punishing their efforts (Tarrant, 2021).

However, in the political climate of the early 2020s, the prospect of rolling out specialist support for these young men, building a more compassionate ethos into mainstream service provision, or attending to the socio-economic and housing needs of young fathers who are living 'on the margins' seems remote. Government interest in tackling the challenges of young pregnancies and supporting young people into parenthood has waned over the years, along with initiatives to support young people into work, and early intervention services designed to tackle family hardship. In 2012, Maxwell and colleagues observed that the potential for young fathers to make a positive contribution to their children's lives and to improve their own life chances was still far from being realised (Maxwell et al, 2012). Despite the efforts of pioneering services that have made a real difference to the lives of some young fathers, relatively little has changed in the broader landscape of policy and professional support over the intervening decade. Moreover, the continuing shifts towards neoliberal policies threatens to eradicate what little progress has been made. Nevertheless, young fathers still matter, and they deserve better.

On a final note, we have observed that research that seeks to understand the changing lives of young fathers through time remains scarce. We have tried to convey the importance of such research in shedding light on young men's parenting journeys and the complex causes and consequences of family change. Through this study we have been able to recognise the value of young fathers, to appreciate their efforts to support their families, and to feel compassion for them when things go wrong. And we have piloted new collaborative modes of engagement for young fathers with service providers that recognise and enhance their social citizenship, and that nurture their potential to engage positively with their children and their families, for the benefit of all.

APPENDIX

Pen portraits of the participants

Adam

Eleven-year follow-up, five waves (FYF); three waves (FYFF)

Adam was 16 years old when he first became a parent. He was interviewed five times for FYF between 2011 and 2015. During this time, he was subject to involvement with 11 statutory agencies because of safeguarding concerns in his family of origin and concerns about his newborn child. He had benefited from specialist support through the learning mentor scheme, and the Family Nurse Partnership. From a lower income family, Adam left school early without any qualifications and was unable to find work or sustain a college course. He was in a partnership with the mother of his child, which he valued, although their relationship was highly volatile over the course of the study. Adam was one of the most nomadic young men in our study and spent some time without a home, and in a local authority hostel where he could not bring his child. His partner terminated a second pregnancy at Adam's request, because of social services intervention in their lives.

Subsequently Adam was interviewed for two follow-up studies when he was 18 and 19 years old. These showed that he suffered from serious mental health issues, especially while his son had a child protection plan. While his mother informally took on the care of his son and sought to become formally recognised as a kin carer, Adam and his partner resisted this by attending parenting, domestic violence/victim courses and supervised contacts. By the time he is 19, Adam is attending college and has moved into a temporary flat while bidding for social housing.

When re-accessed for the Following Young Fathers Further study, Adam is 28 years old and still has one son, who is 12. He is a 'stay-at-home' dad and is supporting his son but expresses guilt about not working and the financial struggles this creates. He does cash-in-hand work but is worried about how his mental health may impact on his employment prospects in future. Following early difficulties in his relationship with the mother of his son, the couple got married and were together for six years. However, our most recent, informal conversations with Adam reveal that he and his wife have since separated.

Andrew

Four-year follow-up, five waves (FYF)

Andrew was one of the younger parents in our study, having become a dad at the age of 15. His daughter was 18 months old when he first participated in the study. We traced his parenting journey from 2011 to 2014, between the ages of 16 and 19. This journey reflects long-term socio-economic disadvantage both prior to and through his entry into parenthood. While Andrew has completed secondary education and is enrolled on several training courses, he remains unemployed. This is, in part, associated with his ongoing learning needs. He is unable to read as a result of earlier disengagement from primary school education and limited support from his family. Andrew's parents are separated, and he has a complicated ongoing relationship with his father, who is drug involved.

When Andrew makes the transition into fatherhood, this complicates an already complex set of familial circumstances. The mother of Andrew's child is the teenage daughter of his father's new partner. The mother of his child is therefore his new de facto stepsister. Theirs is a volatile relationship involving instances of domestic violence. Andrew separates from her when his father returns to prison and she and her mother relocate, but they subsequently reunite. It is decided through a court hearing that they should share custody of their daughter. Despite the fragility of their relationship, he manages to sustain contact with his child. However, his involvement is complicated by an insecure housing trajectory when his disconnection from his birth family results in a period spent in a hostel. Given the complexity of Andrew's circumstances, he comes into the orbit of social services, who provide him with learning support and with the family courts and surveillance services given the concerns over domestic violence.

Bekele

Two-year follow-up, two waves (FYF)

Bekele was interviewed twice in 2013 and 2014. He had his first child at the age of 21. He is of African origin, but migrated to the UK as a refugee when he was age 20. Unusual for this sample of young fathers, he is a single father and the primary caregiver of his two children, aged two and four. His ex-partner does not see the children. Given his status as a single father and the challenges bound up with balancing childcare costs with care responsibilities, he is unemployed and experiencing financial difficulties. Bekele receives support with childcare from church friends, neighbours and family where he can, which helps him to manage. He is ambitious and keen to support his children, so he later secures a part-time security job and enrols on an English course at a local college. The college provides childcare, so he can attend three days a week.

Ben

Eight-year follow-up, two waves (FYF); two waves (FYFF)

With a stable and well-resourced family background, Ben first became a father when he was 18 years old. He was interviewed twice for our study a year apart, in 2013 and 2014. Ben discovered he was going to become a father just as he had embarked on his undergraduate degree and initially struggled to come to terms with the pregnancy. He separated from the mother during this time. Despite missing the birth, he expresses a clear commitment to being involved in the upbringing of his daughter. Despite some early challenges, he manages to establish a good relationship with the mother, which supports him in his efforts to sustain contact with his daughter. In his first interview, Ben regularly visits her at the maternal grandparents' home, and weathers a number of tensions in the maternal household. Later, he is able to collect his daughter and spends time with her at his own parent's house. His parents are particularly supportive of him at this time, facilitating contact and helping him with finances when he is struggling to get by on his student loan. Ben was heavily invested in his university degree and future career prospects. He continued on this track and undertook a placement abroad during the first year of his child's life.

His interviews for the FYFF study began when he was 28. He had just embarked on a master's course, having worked in IT since finishing his undergraduate degree. He is single, after coming out of a more recent relationship. He has given up his own flat and moved into a flat share with other young professionals, an option that enables him to maintain some independence from his parents but that makes it tricky to spend quality time with his daughter at home. He lives an hour's drive from his daughter (who is now ten) but continues to see her every other weekend at his parents' home. They have a good relationship, and he enjoys taking her to gigs to watch the band he performs in. He remains close friends with his daughter's mother and says that their relationship has greatly improved since she re-partnered. He likes his daughter's stepdad and is also friends with him. He reveals long-term issues with the stigma of his early entry into parenthood.

Cade

Participated in one wave (FYF)

Cade was interviewed when he was 21 in 2013. At that time he was living with his three-year-old son and the mother of his child, his partner. Their son was unplanned but welcomed. Before meeting and moving in with his partner, Cade was homeless and was known to a local housing organisation. While homeless, Cade was struggling to find work and was unable to receive welfare support because of a lack of postal address to add to job application forms. His unemployment status undermines his confidence and self-esteem and is a key source of mental ill health. Despite this, he finds parenting rewarding and has a close relationship with his son. He does not have the support of his family and feels unable to ask them for help. However, he values the supportive, stable relationship he has with his partner.

Callum
Three-year follow-up, four waves (FYF)

Callum was interviewed four times for the FYF study between 2011 and 2013. Aged 19 in his first interview, he explains that he became the father of twins at the age of 15. His experiences of fatherhood are highly complex, involving high rates of service interactions and legal intervention and difficulties sustaining contact with his children. His parenting journey also reflects one of long-term socio-economic disadvantage, both prior to and beyond his entry into parenthood.

Callum has four children by the age of 19: twin boys, who were unplanned and conceived while Callum and his partner were at school, and two daughters in quick succession with another mother. Despite a strong commitment to his children, his parenting efforts are spread very thin and the arrival of his fourth child plunges him into depression. His relationship with the mother of his twins is especially difficult and, with advice from his mother, he seeks to secure contact with the children through the family courts. This initiates a long process involving CAFCASS, which eventually results in him securing some contact at the weekend. Callum finds it challenging to maintain his relationships with his children. He is struggling financially as he moves between insecure, low-paid, commission-based and cash-in-hand work. He was unable to sustain a college course and reports severe mental health problems. He has also resorted to selling drugs to make money. Despite these challenges, his mother and stepfather are important influences and sources of support to Callum.

Darren
Five-year follow-up, five waves (FYF)

Darren first participated in the study when aged 21 and was interviewed between 2011 and 2014. He first became a father aged 15. Despite being unemployed and of a lower socio-economic status than some young fathers, Darren remains partnered with the mother of the child throughout the study. They have a six-year-old son and later, at age 24, they have another son unplanned, following several miscarriages and problems with contraception. His housing trajectory takes a linear route from supporting his family in his parents' home to finding accommodation through a local housing organisation. Despite the rules, a housing support officer finds accommodation for him and his partner and son. The family have sustained social services involvement from the outset of their parenting journey, which is re-established when concerns of abuse and neglect are raised by his son's school. Darren is long-term unemployed because of a shoulder injury for which he receives benefits. Despite his disability, he has ambitions to go back to college and wants to work in the future.

Dominic
Thirteen-year follow-up, five waves (FYF); three waves (FYFF)

Dominic participated in the FYF study five times between the ages of 18 and 23. He comes from a higher-income background and has a secure and supportive family and a stable home base with them. He has one son. The couple met when Dominic was aged 14 and had a child when Dominic was 16. He was barred from seeing his partner during the pregnancy but rekindled the relationship in time to be there for his son. He ended the relationship with the mother a year after the birth, having established frequent contact of four days per week with his son. The break-up led to a cessation of contact, but Dominic sought help through the family courts. He reached a mediated agreement with the mother in which he sees his son every other weekend. This enabled him to secure a sustained relationship with his son over the years but led to ongoing tensions in his relationship with the mother; he felt unable to develop a friendship with her. Financial challenges, including paying child maintenance and paying off a loan to cover childcare fees incurred by his ex-partner, contribute to longer-term problems in their relationship with each other. With a relatively stable family background and good qualifications, Dominic was on a semi-skilled employment trajectory at the start of the FYF study, having given up his studies. He later went part-time in order to do a part-time degree and felt his life was back on track.

Interviewed another three times for the FYFF study (2020–23), Dominic is aged between 28 and 31. His son is aged between 12 and 15. He continues to be a non-resident father and his son stays with him at his flat every Monday night. Contact arrangements for his son have changed over time, reflecting the evolution of his relationship with his son, who is more independent now that he is older, and the mother of his son over time. His relationship with his ex-partner remains steady overall, but he describes a fraught history of disputes over maintenance payments and further cessation of contact, resulting in further applications to court. His earning power has been a critical factor in his efforts to reinstate contact when these disputes have arisen. He works full-time in the financial sector and is enjoying career progression and financial security. Despite some fleeting relationships, he remains single. His financial security is reduced slightly by his relationship status, but he has a mortgage and lives in a safe area located 4.5 miles away from his son.

Iman
Two-year follow-up, two waves (FYF)

Iman was interviewed twice in 2013 and 2014 between the ages of 16 and 17. He is of mixed Asian/Caribbean heritage. At age 16 he is expecting twins with a friend from school. Iman and his friend do not form a romantic partnership, but Iman nevertheless demonstrates his commitment to his fathering role through visits to the midwife with her during the pre-birth period. Iman lives with his mother and is completing his GCSEs, with aspirations to go to college and later to university. He is very ambitious and is doing well in his education, which he believes will lead to a better future for himself and his children. When the twins are born, Iman sees them every other week initially, but later is estranged from the maternal household and contact reduces. His mother is a lifeline in facilitating his relationships with his children. With her advice, he puts his efforts into his education and future career as a way of providing material support for his children.

Jackson
Two-year follow-up, two waves (FYF)

Jackson was interviewed for the FYF study in 2013 and 2014. His early parenting journey was captured when he was aged 15–16 years old. He was 15 when he first discovered he was to become a father and still at secondary school when his girlfriend fell pregnant. Although the pregnancy is unplanned, he is excited about the birth of his child. He has a close relationship with both of his parents; he lives with his mum and siblings and his dad also lives nearby. When his son is born, he and the baby's mother receive professional support through the pre-birth assessment process. Having left school at age 16, he is not in college or work, constrained by his young age and lack of work experience. His relationship with his eight-month-old son is impacted by his arrest for assault. His partner's social worker informs him that he is not able to see his son until he completes his probation period and the terms associated with this. The couple are also involved in some form of monthly group family assessment meetings with other professionals, but he is unclear what this process is.

Jakie
Single interview in 2013 (FYF)

Jakie has a relatively stable parenting trajectory despite having relocated and living in an area with limited family support. He was 22 years old when he had his daughter; the child was nearly one when he was interviewed. The couple had been dating for four years prior to that. They live together and look after their daughter together. Jakie is unemployed but has instigated the process of enrolling on a plastering course through college, which is taking some time, so he has signed on for unemployment benefits. The family do not have any childcare support from Jakie's family because they do not live locally, but he has a close relationship with his mother. They also sometimes receive help with childcare from his partner's father (the maternal grandfather). A voluntary housing organisation has been very helpful to the couple in sourcing a larger house in order to support their family, and additionally has provided practical advice about budgeting and finances.

Jason
Four-year follow-up, four waves (FYF)

Jason was interviewed from 2011 to 2014, when he was between the ages of 22 and 25. He has an impoverished background, having been taken into care during his adolescence when his mother died of a drug overdose. He has anger management problems and has a prison sentence for violent assault after he has been drinking. At the time of our interviews, he is living in local authority housing in a degraded neighbourhood. He first became a father when he was 22. This was unplanned, but he describes being transformed by the birth of his son and seeing potential for new opportunities in his future. However, he returned to prison for a 15-month sentence at the age of 23, after a violent pub brawl. This meant that he lost precious time with his son, although the mother facilitated his contact. Upon his release, when he was trying to rekindle contact with his child, he had another unplanned child with the same mother. His relationship with the mother is volatile and on-off, and, although he tries, he finds it difficult to establish a friendship with her as the basis for co-parenting. He can see his child when he has some cash in hand to provide for the mother. When Jason explores new relationships, contact is curtailed and Jason's subsequent erratic behaviour and threats of violence lead to his arrest. Jason receives a restraining order, which is heartbreaking for him as he begins to lose contact with his children. Jason aspires to go back into education but struggles with this. He has remained unemployed and disengaged from EET opportunities throughout the study. He makes some money by working for a friend.

Jax
Two-year follow-up, two waves (FYF)

Jax was interviewed for the FYF study between 2013 and 2014, aged 18–19. He has a daughter and lives with his partner. He loves his family life but describes himself as lazy and lets his partner do most of the work of caring for the baby. He describes a troubled trajectory both prior to becoming a father and beyond. He discovered he was to be a parent on his 18th birthday, which he spent in custody. He spent five of the first eight months of his relationship in custody. He was 'bashed' as a child and has anger management problems. His time in custody is the result of involvement with burglary, theft and assault. He has a history of drug and drink problems. He is present for the birth of his daughter, and they are moved to local authority housing in a new area to keep him away from his old 'criminal' peer group. Given his custody experiences, Jax in unemployed and in receipt of Job Seekers Allowance, although his access worker supports him to enrol on college courses. He is disappointed following ten unsuccessful interviews for work because he wants to 'provide' for his family and does not like being reliant on social security support.

Jayden

Eight-year follow-up, one-off interview (FYF); three waves (FYFF)

Jayden, who has a three-year-old daughter, became a father at the age of 18. He was only interviewed once for the FYF study but has been followed up three times since. At the time of his first interview, he is separated from the mother of his child. He lives with his mother, her partner and his two younger brothers in a two-bedroom house where he shares the care of his daughter, who stays three nights per week. The house is overcrowded; his daughter has to share a room with Jayden and his two brothers. Despite some qualifications in bricklaying he is unemployed, following a period of navigating low-or poorly paid work placements. He has past experience as a sales assistant but makes ends meet through various cash-in-hand jobs and some factory work secured through an agency.

Jayden has experience of the criminal justice system, including being placed in custody for a day at a time, generally for fighting or drunk and disorderly behaviour. On one occasion he receives 200 hours of community service for an affray. During the COVID-19 pandemic, his employment trajectory is fraught. He is furloughed from his job as a forklift driver so does cash-in-hand jobs to make extra money. He later works with his friend doing joinery but eventually goes back to forklift driving. He has a positive relationship with the mother of his child and sofa-surfs at her house, where she lives with her new partner, the child, and her parents. This gives Jayden the opportunity to see his daughter every day. He has always had a mostly equal share of care for his daughter.

Jed

Two-year follow-up, two waves (FYF)

Jed is aged 16–17 when he participates in the FYF study, between 2013 and 2014. He is 16 when he conceives an unplanned son with a partner he had been seeing for three months. He lives with his mother, stepfather and siblings, and his girlfriend lives nearby. Jed is very close to his mother, who raised him as a single parent when his father left. He has a disrupted education history including reduced time at secondary school as a result of 'behavioural problems'. To support their son, the young couple divide their time on a weekly basis between the maternal and paternal parents' houses. Jed is in the process of trying to find a flat to live in with his son but, having left education, is struggling to find work. A Connexions (employment) worker supports him to job search and complete college applications. After enrolling at college, Jed finds he can't cope and quickly leaves. He also splits up from the mother of his child and his contact with his son ceases when she moves to another town. Jed considers going to court to gain access to his son but has limited resources available to him to go through the process.

Jimmy

Four-year follow-up, five waves (FYF)

Jimmy is first interviewed in 2011, when he is 16, just one month after his son is born. By his final interview in 2014, he has turned 19. His trajectory reflects one of socio-economic disadvantage that extends beyond the birth of his child. The pregnancy was unplanned, occurring one to two months into his relationship with the mother. Initially the couple split their time between their parents' houses, but Jimmy moves out and lives with a friend. His homelessness results in reduced time to see his son, whom he sees twice a week. By age 18, this has led to the breakdown of his relationship with the mother of his child, and a loss of contact with his son, so he is advised by wider family to see a solicitor. Jimmy was able to obtain legal aid while unemployed leading to an informal, mutual agreement between the couple around contact times. Despite the mutual agreement over contact, the couple still had to attend court because the process was already in motion. During the court session, the judge decided that Jimmy should spend less time with his son. Jimmy was unhappy with the decision and did not think that the reduced hours made sense. By the time his son is two years old, Jimmy is permitted only 11 hours per week to see his son. Jimmy remains unemployed after leaving school and at age 19, is struggling to find work because he is underqualified and lacks work experience. By the time of his last interview, Jimmy has not seen his son for some months, although the couple continue to attend court about contact times. Jimmy has been asked to attend a domestic violence course because of allegations from his ex-partner, and also because of a recent arrest.

Jock
Nine-year follow-up, two waves (FYF), three waves (FYFF)

Jock's early parenting experiences are captured in the Following Young Fathers study between 2013 and 2014 when he is studying on a foundation degree at university, aged 22. Jock has a well-resourced, higher-income background. Soon after the birth of his son, he and the mother move into his parents' house. When tensions in the household arise, the couple break up and mother and child move to the maternal grandparents' house. Despite the fleeting nature of their relationship, they sustain contact, with an arrangement that Jock sees his son one night per week at the maternal grandparents' home and has him to stay overnight once a week at the paternal grandparents' home. He is unsure if he will rekindle the relationship with the mother but aims for them to be friends.

Jock is followed up three times for the Following Young Fathers Further study, between the age of 29 and 31. During the COVID-19 pandemic, Jock sees less of his son because his contact is curtailed by the lockdowns, and fears of the maternal family about the risk of spreading the virus. Jock does not pursue the courts, despite being advised by his parents, because he wants to maintain an amicable relationship with his ex-partner. Post-pandemic he sees his son more regularly again. More recently he has him over to stay every other weekend, visits him a few times during the week and takes him to football matches. By this time, he has also secured a Master's degree and has a stable and secure job. This enables him to pay child maintenance and to live in a privately rented house. He maintains a friendship with the mother, and has re-partnered.

Joe
Two-year follow-up, two waves (FYF)

Joe is interviewed between the ages of 17 and 18 and comes from a lower-income background with a complex, disrupted family history. He has a history of care experience/kinship care and grew up living with his aunt when his mother was deemed 'unfit' to care for him, following her separation from Joe's father. His parenting trajectory is captured over the space of a year, starting when Joe is aged 17, and his daughter is one month old. Joe and the mother of his child met at secondary school and despite not being in a relationship when their daughter is born, they sustain a positive relationship. This enables them to develop an amicable shared parenting arrangement and later, to rekindle their romantic relationship. Joe remains unemployed but is investing in a 'progression' course that helps young people to find employment. While he aspires to join the armed forces, he fails the entrance exams. He later secures work washing dishes at a restaurant with hopes of advancing to be chef. Given his family history and socio-economic disadvantage, he is managing intensive professional intervention, including an assigned social worker, a support worker in relation to his new independent living arrangement and a Connexions worker. He felt that his support worker was the most helpful and supportive.

Karl

Four-year follow-up, four waves (FYF)

Karl's parenting trajectory is captured between 2011 and 2014 and is highly complex. He has a low-income family background and at age 16, while living with his father, he becomes a father. He is not in a relationship with the mother of his two-week-old baby (unplanned) and has limited control over care arrangements for him. His son is taken into care after the mother failed a care assessment associated with a turbulent upbring and mental health concerns. Karl has limited access to the midwives and social workers pre-birth, and once his son is born, he can only see his son twice a week for contact. He struggles to attend contact sessions because his college is reticent to give him the time and he has to travel on multiple buses very early in the morning just to reach the appointments. Later his father tries to advocate for him. He feels ignored by professionals. At the end of this process, he is devastated when a decision is made that his son is to be adopted.

Karl experiences similar challenges in sustaining contact with his second unplanned child, a daughter born to a new partner. He and her mother go through a three-month residential foster placement together after the birth and are continually assessed during this time. Karl also benefits from specialist support through voluntary sector organisations. The couple later split up, but he maintains an amicable relationship with this second mother. This enables him to see his daughter daily at the home of the mother, and on his own three days per week. Karl later contacts a solicitor to go to court to secure full custody of his daughter because of reports his daughter's mother is taking drugs. During this time, Karl leaves school and engages in training; a groundwork course to gain his gardening qualifications, which he hopes will enable him to work for his friend's gardening company. He is in receipt of benefits at this time while he is unemployed.

Kevin

Interviewed in 2013 (FYF)

Kevin is aged 24 when he is interviewed and about to turn 25. He became a young father at the age of 18. He has a son who is seven and a daughter aged three who he says are "his life". Both pregnancies were unplanned but occurred while in a relatively stable relationship with the mother. The couple eventually separate but maintain an amicable relationship. While the children live with their mother, the couple are co-parenting, which means that Kevin sees them when he takes them to school and at weekends at his house, where he lives with his mother. As an engaged father, he feels it is very important to see his children as much as possible. Both the maternal and paternal grandmothers are highly supportive of the couple in terms of helping out and providing childcare. He has been in employment for seven years doing stock control for an engineering firm and is just beginning an NVQ in warehousing. Kevin was advised by his college tutor to drop out of his college course and seek work to support his family. He hopes to return to college in the future.

Manuel
Seven-year follow-up, one wave (FYF), one wave (FYFF)

Manuel first became a father at the age of 17, and has two children, a daughter and a son. He is from a Mediterranean country and came to England aged 11, with his mother and younger siblings. Before his children are born he spends some time in a hostel having struggled to live with his mother and being asked to move out by his dad and stepmum. He describes difficult and distant relationships with both of his parents. The mother of Manuel's children first became pregnant a year after they had been together. The mother lives in the maternal grandmother's house. Manuel moves between his mother's house and his own accommodation. They later have a second child, a daughter, described as a "second chance", following an incident that resulted in his arrest and the arrest of his father. Manuel describes a court case to determine the care arrangements for his son, who sustained unexplained injuries at five weeks old. Neither are charged, but both his son and daughter live with the maternal grandparents who are seeking a Special Guardianship Order.

For his follow-up interview, some years later, Manuel continues to see the children regularly, but the COVID-19 pandemic impacted heavily on his continued contact with them. During the pandemic, some years later, Manuel loses his long term employment as a cleaner/bar tender in a pub (which closed down during the pandemic) and is about to start a zero-hours contract. He is now in a new relationship and is expecting a third child.

Marcel
One-year follow-up, two waves (FYF)

Marcel is 24 years old and has a one-year-old daughter. Born in Western Europe, he moved to England with his mother and siblings when he was

18 years old. Marcel starts a business course at college, where he meets his girlfriend. The pregnancy was unplanned, but a happy and exciting time for the couple. Marcel holds traditional ideas about being the provider for the family. After the news of the pregnancy, Marcel left college to find work and has been in between jobs since. He often works in temporary posts and will claim benefits when not in work to keep the family afloat.

Martin
Ten-year follow-up, two waves (FYF); two waves (FYFF)

Martin was married when he had his first child at the age of 23. He remains in a secure, stable relationship with his wife who he met at their local church. Martin is from a higher-income family, and is well-resourced and educated. He has positive relationships with his wider family.

For his follow-up with FYFF, Martin is 33 years old and a father of two children. Following the successful completion of his degree, he had embarked on a doctoral research study, but later withdrew when his second child was born. He subsequently enrolled in teacher training. He is now a full-time teacher at a secondary school, has a mortgage that he hopes to pay off in ten years and the couple are settled in an area that they like. Martin represents the most stable and settled of the young men in the FYF study and this continues over time.

Orlando
Two-year follow-up, two waves (FYF)

Orlando is originally from Africa but moved to the UK as a child with his mother and siblings because of civil unrest in his country. His parenting journey is captured between 2013 and 2014, when he is aged 24 and 25. His son was born when he was 24. Orlando was shocked about the pregnancy and the couple split up when they found out about it. However, he remains an engaged father after the birth, living with mother and child for a short time in temporary accommodation until they later move into a larger house. Despite not being in a relationship with his son's mother, this is an arrangement Orlando thought was best so that they were looked after. Orlando continues to share parenting for his son. He sees him every day because they live near to one another. There are also set days when he will look after his son on his own because his ex-partner has returned to work. Following a period of insecure agency work, Orlando later gains employment although he remains on a low income. He and his ex-partner pay the maternal grandmother to babysit when they are both working because she has reduced her hours at work to do this.

Peter

Two-year follow-up, two waves (FYF)

Peter's parenting journey is captured during 2013–14 when he is aged 16 to 18. At age 16, his daughter is five months old. He is separated from the mother of his child and despite having a fraught relationship after their initial break-up, they manage to negotiate a shared parenting arrangement for their daughter in the longer term. Throughout this period he remains living with his parents, who are very supportive and provide him with financial help. They encourage and support him to find employment, leading to a secure role with a parcel delivery company. While his shift pattern impacts on his time with his daughter, whom he sees three times a week, he is also able to provide financial support for her.

Raymond

Ten-year follow-up, one-off interview (FYF); 3 waves (FYFF)

Raymond was 15 years old when he first became a father and was 20 in 2014, when he was first interviewed for the FYF study. He was recruited because of his experiences as a young offender father, who had benefited from a specialist fatherhood programme when in a secure training centre for young offenders. He was concerned about how he would financially provide for his child, so he started to sell drugs to make money. He was subsequently arrested and received a custodial sentence but his child and relationship with the mother provided stability for him and a new direction in life during resettlement.

His follow-up interviews with the FYFF study begin in 2020, when he is 26. He is no longer with the mother and now seeking a divorce. He is engaged to a new partner who has children from a previous relationship, whom he considers to be his stepchildren. In 2023, his new partner has announced that she is pregnant again. He is only able to speak to his eldest son a couple of times of month because they have moved 70 miles away. In 2020, he is balancing two jobs; one as a manager in a restaurant and another as a care worker, but is able to do the school runs for his children. He leaves the restaurant on bad terms and seeks support from an employment tribunal. Following a short period working for a supermarket, he works in a café that enables him to manage employment around his childcare responsibilities.

Richard

Four-year follow-up, five waves (FYF)

Richard's fathering journey is followed between 2011 and 2014, when he is aged between 16 and 18. He lives with his father, who is in the process of divorcing Richard's mother. Richard found out that his partner was pregnant when he was 13. They had been in a relationship when the unplanned pregnancy occurred. Their relationship breaks down two years after the birth of their daughter, following a spate of arguments. Over time, their relationship deteriorates leading to a reduction in his contact with his daughter and then a loss of contact altogether. Despite efforts to sustain contact, the mother of his child does not respond to his requests, and while he would like, ideally, to contact solicitors and secure a court order, the costs are high and he lacks knowledge and support to navigate the legal system. During this time he "goes off the rails" and is arrested on several occasions, for reasons he won't disclose. He moves into his mother's home following her suggestion, which provides him with some stability. Richard describes an insecure employment trajectory after leaving education and when unemployed he relies on his dad for money. However, he later secures steady employment in a local garage, working for six days a week.

Senwe

Four-year follow-up, four waves (FYF)

Senwe participates in the FYF study between 2011 and 2014, when he is aged between 16 and 19. He is Black African-British and was born in Africa before migrating to the UK with his mother when he was eight years old. He met his girlfriend at school and the unplanned pregnancy occurred one year into their relationship when he was 15. His daughter lives round the corner with the mother of the child. The young couple later break up, but they manage to sustain a 'formal' but positive relationship meaning Senwe is able to negotiate contact. Having finished his first year of a decorating course at college, a Connexions worker supports him to secure an apprenticeship in bricklaying, for which he trains with a company four days a week. He also attends college for his diploma at the same time. He is enjoying the apprenticeship, and the salary he receives for it and hopes to secure a job at the end of the training. He continues to live with his mother during this time and she supports him financially, emotionally and with childcare for his daughter.

Simon

Three-year follow-up, four waves (FYF)

Simon participates in the FYF study between 2011 and 2013. He is 16 years old when he is first interviewed. He discovered the pregnancy when taking his GCSEs and just two weeks before the birth, when the maternal grandmother rang to inform him. Simon had been going out with the mother for a year but the couple split up due to arguments and an estrangement with the maternal family. Simon wanted to see his son two weeks after the birth, but this was not arranged by the maternal grandparents' family. Two months later, his involvement with his son continues to be hindered by disagreements with the maternal family. He was given very limited access to visit his son at the maternal household and had had no time to adjust to the idea of being a father. The disagreements lead to his withdrawal from seeing his son as this was the least stressful option for him and his mother. He is also investing in a new and more positive relationship and would like children one day in the future. Simon has received his GCSE results and started a vehicle maintenance course but did not like it. At 18 years old, Simon found a position in a metal supply company but continues to look for another job. In the future he would like to apply for the armed forces or become an HGV driver.

Steven

One-off interview in 2014 (FYF)

Steven, aged 26, had his first child at the age of 20. He was recruited to explore his experiences as a young offender father. He has two daughters, aged two and three, by different mothers and another is on the way with a third partner with whom he lives. The mother of his eldest daughter is restricting contact so he is in touch with the courts to see if he can contest it. Stephen has a history as a persistent offender and reports past problems with school, his family and housing. He received his first custodial sentence aged 14 and has served five prison sentences, spending a total of seven years in prison. At the time of his interview, Steven had been out of prison for a few months and had been working as a tradesman, having gained qualifications inside. He has ambitions to run his own business, so signed up to benefits to fund him to do a course needed to become self-employed. Steven is living with the partner of his third child and has moved to a new area so he could make a "fresh start" away from his network of peers who might lead him back to a life of crime.

Tarrell

Eleven-year follow-up, three waves (FYF); two waves (FYFF)

Tarrell is 20 years old when first interviewed for the FYF study, having become a parent in his mid-teens. He participates three times with a gap in between because he is in prison. He has a complex parenting journey, characterised by multiple partnerships and pregnancies. He has a lower-income, poorly resourced family background, is Black British, unemployed, and when we first met him, he was living with his mother. By the mid-point in the study, he had three children, twins (aged five) with the first mother, and a younger son (19 months) from a second relationship. He pays child support for each of his children. Tarrell sees his youngest boy more regularly than the twins as he is on better terms with their mother, although he has contacted solicitors to establish contact with his twins. He is unemployed having "dropped out" of school and completed NVQs at college when younger. He later moves in with the mother of his youngest son and they have another unplanned child. Tarrell also impregnates another girl when he was on a relationship break from her. This son (his fifth child) is nine weeks old. Aged 25, he spends some time in prison linked to a drug charge. On his release he sees his children at weekends and returns to live with his mother. He secures a part-time cleaning job with help from a friend who supported him to ensure his conviction does not restrict him, but later loses his job following a disagreement with a co-worker.

Subsequently, he participates twice in the FYFF study between the ages of 31 and 32. He still lives on and off with his mum, whom he remains close to. He now has six children and also lives for part of the time with the mother of his sixth child. His first children (twins) are aged 16 now, but he has not seen them since they were two. He sees his third and fourth children (aged 11 and 13) regularly but does not see his fifth child because of a difficult break-up. This is despite going to court to try to secure contact with her. He is unemployed, having lost his job during the COVID-19 pandemic.

Tommy

Two-year follow-up, two waves (FYF)

Tommy was interviewed between 2012 and 2014 for the FYF study. When first interviewed, he is a 24-year-old undergraduate student studying a mixed humanities and languages course. He has academic skills and a potentially solid role as a provider. He is White British, married and has a son who is two and half years old. The pregnancy was planned; Tommy says he had always wanted children. The couple were married for three years before their relationship broke down. His partner was unfaithful to him and asked him to leave. This left Tommy homeless and with no money. He lived with the maternal grandmother for a short period of time, who was very supportive of him and facilitated his relationship with his son. Without familial support and while waiting for his student loan over the summer, he struggled financially. He tried to request housing and maintenance money early from the university, but they were not very helpful or understanding. At wave 2, Tommy continues to see his son each weekend at the maternal grandmother's house and stays over there for affordability reasons. Tommy later finds student accommodation to live in but does not take his son there because it is not considered child friendly (that is, he lives with other students who are partying and taking drugs). Tommy later starts a new, serious relationship and would like more children in future, but he keeps his new relationships and his relationship with his son as separate parts of his life.

Trevor
Ten-year follow-up, two waves (FYF); three waves (FYFF)

Trevor is interviewed twice for the FYF study between 2013 and 2014. He is White British and lives in a lower income family with his parents, with whom he has a positive relationship. Trevor conceived a child when he was 14. He is 15 years old when he is first interviewed so is still in education and has a six-week-old daughter. Trevor is not in a relationship with his daughter's mother and had only seen his daughter on five occasions. Social services support Trevor to come to a childcare arrangement to see his daughter every other weekend when contact stops completely, but they advise that the mother of the child wants to proceed through solicitors to arrange formal contact times. He therefore finds a solicitor and they later come to an informal arrangement including child maintenance payments.

Trevor has participated in three interviews for the FYFF study. During the COVID-19 pandemic he sees his daughter more often having established a better relationship with her mother. Trevor goes on to have a second daughter following a brief relationship with another mother, but he loses contact with her and the child. He tries to secure contact via mediation and applies for legal aid but discovers he is not entitled to it. Throughout this period, he sustains employment in a call centre but experiences a period of furlough. He then becomes temporarily homeless when his mother stops paying rent and they lose their home. He is supported back into temporary housing by a housing charity, which he resides in with a new partner.

Zane
Two-year follow-up, two waves (FYF)

Zane's fathering journey is captured from 2012 to 2014, when he is between the ages of 18 and 20. He is White British and lives with his partner and son at the maternal grandmother's house. Both he and his partner remain in a secure relationship, and both are students, with skills and potential careers ahead of them. Zane is a first-year law student at university and works part-time in retail. He aspires to be either a barrister or to remain in higher education. He is working part-time for the Citizens Advice Bureau to gain work experience that will support his career intentions. He has a close relationship with his son and shares the childcare duties with his partner so that they can support one another through their studies.

Notes

Chapter 4
[1] We have recorded the pseudonyms of the young men, their age, income level, and relationship status at the time of interview. These characteristics change over the course of the study. Other characteristics have been added as appropriate across the chapters.

Chapter 5
[1] Following Young Fathers data on family law matters are relatively sparse and were not generated in a systematic way, although they impinged on a relatively large number of these young men. While we touch upon this important theme, we have been unable to give it detailed consideration here.

Chapter 8
[1] To cite this chapter: Ladlow, L., Neale, B. and Tarrant, A. (2024) Finding a place to parent: young fathers' housing needs and pathways, in B. Neale and A. Tarrant, *The Dynamics of Young Fatherhood: Understanding the Parenting Journeys and Support Needs of Young Fathers*, Bristol: Policy Press, pp 159–178.

Chapter 9
[1] PPI refers to Patient Public Involvement, the process of involving patients in the planning, commissioning, delivery and evaluation of health and social care services.

Chapter 10
[1] https://fyff.co.uk/projects/grimsby-dads-collective

References

Achatz, M. and MacAllum, C.A. (1994) *Young Unwed Fathers: Report from the Field*, Philadelphia, PA: Private/Public Ventures. Available from: https://www.issuelab.org/resources/12136/12136.pdf [Accessed 29 August 2023].

Alexander, C., Duncan, S. and Edwards, R. (2010) 'Just a mum or dad': experiencing teenage parenting and work-life balances, in S. Duncan, R. Edwards and C. Alexander (eds) *Teenage Parenthood: What's the Problem?*, London: Tufnell Press, pp 135–56.

Alldred, P., Fox, N. and Kulpa, R. (2016) Engaging parents with sex and relationship education: a UK primary school case study, *Health Education Journal*, 75(7): 855–68.

Allen, G. (2011) *Early Intervention: The Next Steps – An Independent Report to Her Majesty's Government*, London: Cabinet Office. Available from: https://www.gov.uk/government/publications/early-intervention-the-next-steps--2 [Accessed 29 August 2023].

Allen, G. and Crow, G. (2001) *Families, Households and Society*, Basingstoke: Palgrave.

Allen, L. (2007) 'Sensitive and real macho all at the same time': young heterosexual men and romance, *Men and Masculinities*, 10(2): 137–52.

Allen, L. (2008) 'They think you shouldn't be having sex anyway': young people's suggestions for improving sexuality education content, *Sexualities*, 11(5): 573–94.

Andreasson, J., Tarrant, A., Johansson, T. and Ladlow, L. (2023) Perceptions of gender equality and engaged fatherhood among young fathers: parenthood and the welfare state in Sweden and the UK, *Families, Relationships and Societies*, 12(3): 323–40.

APPGPF/APPGSM (All-Party Parliamentary Group on Parents and Families/All-Party Parliamentary Group on Social Mobility) (2015) *The Parliamentary Inquiry into Parenting and Social Mobility: Enhancing Parenting Support Across the UK*, London: Family and Childcare Trust. Available from: https://www.familyandchildcaretrust.org/parliamentary-inquiry-parenting-and-social-mobility [Accessed 29 August 2023].

APPGYE (All-Party Parliamentary Group on Youth Employment) (nd) *Inquiry into Pathways from Education to Employment: A Report of the All-Party Parliamentary Group on Youth Employment*, Kettering: Youth Employment UK. Available from: https://www.youthemployment.org.uk/dev/wp-content/uploads/2017/04/Youth-Employment-Pathways-from-Education-to-Employment-Report-Youth-Employment-APPG.pdf [Accessed 29 August 2023].

Arai, L. (2009) *Teenage Pregnancy: The Making and Unmaking of a Problem*, Bristol: Policy Press.

Arber, S. and Timonen, V. (2012) *Contemporary Grandparenting: Changing Family Relationships in Global Contexts*, Bristol: Policy Press.

Arney, W.R. and Bergen, B.J. (1984) Power and visibility: the invention of teenage pregnancy, *Social Science & Medicine*, 18(1): 11–19.

Astuti, A.W., Hurst, J. and Kaur Bharj, K. (2021) Adolescent fathers' experiences in Indonesia: a qualitative study, *International Journal of Adolescence and Youth*, 26(1): 201–10.

Ayoola, L., Gates, P. and Taylor, M. (2010) *Exploring the Needs and Experiences of Teenage Fathers in the City of Nottingham: Creating Families, Building Futures*, Nottingham: Leslie Ayoola Consultants and the City of Nottingham.

Ayton, R. and Hansen, E. (2016) Complex young lives: a collective qualitative case study analysis of young fatherhood and breastfeeding, *International Breastfeeding Journal*, 11: art 6. Available from: https://doi.org/10.1186/s13006-016-0066-9 [Accessed 29 August 2023].

Banting, K. and Myles, P. (eds) (2013) *Inequality and the Fading of Redistributive Politics*, Vancouver: UBC Press.

Barnardo's (2012) *'Are We Nearly There Yet, Dad?' Supporting Young Dads' Journeys Through Fatherhood*. Available from: https://www.barnardos.org.uk/sites/default/files/2020-11/are_we_nearly_there_yet_dad.pdf [Accessed 29 August 2023].

Barret, R.L. and Robinson, B.E. (1982) A descriptive study of teenage expectant fathers, *Family Relations*, 31(3): 349–52.

Bate, A. and Foster, D. (2017) *Sure Start (England)*, Briefing Paper, no. 7257, London: House of Commons Library.

Bateson, K., Darwin, Z., Galdas, P and Rosan, C. (2017) Engaging fathers: acknowledging the barriers, *Journal of Health Visiting*, 5(3): 126–32.

Baxter, A., Dundas, R., Popham, F. and Craig, P. (2021) How effective was England's teenage pregnancy strategy? a comparative analysis of high-income countries. *Social Science & Medicine*, 270: art 113685. Available from: https://doi.org/10.1016/j.socscimed.2021.113685 [Accessed 29 August 2023].

Bekaert, S. and Bradly, J. (2019) The increasingly leaky stigma of the 'pregnant teen': when does 'young motherhood' cease to be problematic?, *Studies in the Maternal*, 11(1): art 8. Available from: https://doi.org/10.16995/sim.267 [Accessed 29 August 2023].

Ben-Galim, D. and Silim, A. (2013) *The Sandwich Generation: Older Women Balancing Work and Care*, IPPR, https://www.ippr.org/files/images/media/files/publication/2013/08/sandwich-generation-August2013_11168_11168.pdf [Accessed 27 September 2023].

Berger, L.M. and Langton, C.E. (2011) Young disadvantaged men as fathers, *Annals of the American Academy of Political and Social Science*, 635(1): 56–75.

References

Berrington, A.M., Cobos Hernandez, M.I., Ingham, R. and Stevenson, J. (2005) *Antecedents and Outcomes of Young Fatherhood: Longitudinal Evidence from the 1970 British Birth Cohort Study*, Working Paper No. A 05/09, Southampton: Southampton Statistical Sciences Research Institute.

Best, A. and Holmes, B. (2010) Systems thinking, knowledge and action: towards better models and methods, *Evidence and Policy*, 16(2): 145–59.

Bierre, S. and Howden-Chapman, P. (2022) The theory and practice of a politics of compassion in the private rental sector: a study of Aotearoa, NZ and 'kindness' during the COVID-19 pandemic, *International Journal of Housing Policy*, Online First. Available from: https://doi.org/10.1080/19491247.2022.2133341 [Accessed 29 August 2023].

Biggart, A. and Walther, A. (2005) Coping with yo-yo transitions: young adults' struggle for support, between family and state in comparative perspective, in C. Leccardi and E. Ruspini (eds) *A New Youth? Young People, Generations and Family Life*, Farnham: Ashgate, pp 41–62.

Birbeck, S. (2004) *Lads to Dads*, unpublished report on Young Fathers Research Project, commissioned for Worcester Sure Start.

Black, A. (2009) *Lads to Dads*, BBC Northern Ireland, 16 November, Documentary produced and directed by Aaron Black.

Bochel, H. and Daly, G. (2021) Research, evidence and social policy, in H. Bochel, and G. Daly (eds) *Social Policy*, 4th edn, Abingdon: Routledge, pp 111–29.

Bochel, H. and Powell, M. (eds) (2016) *The Coalition Government and Social Policy: Restructuring the Welfare State*, Bristol: Policy Press.

Bradshaw, J., Stimson, C., Skinner, C. and Williams, J. (1999) *Absent Fathers?*, Abingdon: Routledge.

Brandon, M., Philip, G. and Clifton, J. (2017) *'Counting Fathers In': Men's Experiences of the Child Protection System*, Norwich: Centre for Research on Children and Families, University of East Anglia.

Brannen, J. and Nilsen, A. (2006) From fatherhood to fathering: transmission and change among British fathers in four-generation families, *Sociology*, 40(2): 335–52.

Braye, S. and McDonnell, L. (2013) Balancing powers: university researchers thinking critically about participatory research with young fathers, *Qualitative Research*, 13(3): 265–84.

Bronte-Tinkew, J. and Horowitz, A. (2010) Factors associated with unmarried, non-resident fathers' perceptions of their coparenting, *Journal of Family Issues*, 31(1): 31–65.

Brook (2011) *Sex and Relationships Education for the 21st Century: We Need it Now*, London: Brook. Available from: https://legacy.brook.org.uk/images/brook/professionals/documents/press_releases/sreforthe21stcentury reportfinal.pdf [Accessed 24 November 2022].

Brown, S. (1990) *If the Shoes Fit: Final Report and Program Implementation Guide of the Maine Young Fathers Project*, Portland, ME: Human Services Development Institute. Available from: https://www.fatherhood.gov/sites/default/files/resource_files/e000000029_0.pdf [Accessed 29 August 2023].

Brown, S. (2016) *Teenage Pregnancy, Parenting and Intergenerational Relations*, London: Palgrave Macmillan.

Brown, S. and McQueen, F. (2020) Engaging young working-class men in the delivery of sex and relationships education, *Sex Education: Sexuality, Society and Learning*, 20(2): 186–201.

Buchanan, A. and Rotkirch, A. (2016) *Grandfathers: Global Perspectives*, London: Palgrave Macmillan.

Bulman, K. and Neale, B. (2017) Developing sustained support for vulnerable young fathers: journeys with young offenders, in A. Tarrant and B. Neale (eds) *Learning to Support Young Dads: Responding to Young Fathers in a Different Way*, Leeds: School of Sociology and Social Policy, University of Leeds, pp 5–13. Available from: https://followingfathers.leeds.ac.uk/wp-content/uploads/sites/79/2017/04/SYD-final-report.pdf [Accessed 29 August 2023].

Bunting, L. and McAuley, C. (2004) Teenage pregnancy and parenthood: the role of fathers, *Child & Family Social Work*, 9(3): 295–303.

Burghes, L., Clarke, L. and Cronin, N. (1997) *Fathers and Fatherhood in Britain*, London: Family Policy Studies Centre.

Buston, K. (2018) Recruiting, retaining and engaging men in social interventions: lessons for implementation focusing on a prison-based parenting intervention for young incarcerated fathers, *Child Care Practice*, 24(2): 164–80.

Buston, K., Parkes, A., Thomson, H., Wight, D. and Fenton, C. (2012) Parenting interventions for male young offenders: a review of the evidence on what works, *Journal of Adolescence*, 35(3): 731–42.

Bynner, J. (2007) Re-thinking the youth phase of the life-course: the case for emerging adulthood?, *Journal of Youth Studies*, 8(4): 367–84.

Caldwell, C.H. and Antonucci, T.C. (1997) Childbearing during adolescence: mental health risks and opportunities, in J. Schulenburg, J.L. Maggs and K. Hurrelmann (eds) *Health Risks and Developmental Transitions During Adolescence*, New York: Cambridge University Press, pp 220–46.

Carabine, J. (2007) New Labour's teenage pregnancy strategy: constituting knowing, responsible citizens, *Cultural Studies*, 21(6): 952–73.

Carlson, M.J. and McLanahan, S.S. (2010) Fathers in fragile families, in M.E. Lamb (ed) *The Role of the Father in Child Development*, 5th edn, Hoboken, NJ: Wiley, pp 241–69.

Carvel, J. (2008) Nurses to be rated on how compassionate and smiley they are, *The Guardian*, 18 June. Available from: https://www.theguardian.com/society/2008/jun/18/nhs60.nhs1 [Accessed 29 August 2023].

Chili, S. and Maharaj, P. (2015) 'Becoming a father': perspectives and experiences of young men in Durban, South Africa, *South African Review of Sociology*, 46(3): 28–44.

Chirawatkul, S., Rungreangkulkij, S., Jong-Udomkarn, D., Sawangchareon, K., Anusornteerakul, S., Wattananukulkiat, S. and Charoenwong, S. (2011) *Prevention of and dealing with teenage pregnancy*. Bangkok: Bureau of Gender Equity Promotion, Office of Women's Affairs and Family Development.

Churchill, H. (2016) One step forward, two steps back: children, young people and the Conservative–Liberal Democrat coalition, in H. Bochel and M. Powell (eds) *The Coalition Government and Social Policy: Restructuring the Welfare State*, Bristol: Policy Press, pp 265–84.

Clapham, D., Mackie, P., Orford, S., Thomas, I. and Buckley, K. (2014) The housing pathways of young people in the UK, *Environment and Planning A: Economy and Space*, 46(8): 2016–31.

Clark, D. (ed) (1991) *Marriage, Domestic Life and Social Change: Writings for Jacqueline Burgoyne (1944–88)*, London: Routledge.

Clark, E. (2002) *Baby Fathers: New Images of Teenage Fatherhood*, London: Teenage Pregnancy Unit.

Clayton, C. and Fletcher, K. (2023) *A Qualitative Evaluation of the 'Dads at Their Best' Service*, Leeds: Leeds Trinity University.

Clayton, C., Lee, H.S. and May, J. (2021) *New Pathways for Young Fathers*, Policy Briefing Paper, March, Leeds: Leeds Trinity University. Available from: https://www.daddilife.com/wp-content/uploads/2021/04/03-New-Pathways-Young-Fathers-Policy-Briefing-2.pdf [Accessed 30 August 2023].

Clayton, C., Fletcher, K., Lee, H.S., Rallings, J., Cookson, D. and May, J. (2022) *Connected Young Fatherhood: Rural and Urban Experiences During the Pandemic*, Leeds: Leeds Trinity University. Available from: https://www.daddilife.com/wp-content/uploads/2022/09/FINAL-Connected-Young-Fatherhood-3.pdf [Accessed 30 August 2023].

Coleman, J. and Dennison, C. (1998) Teenage parenthood, *Children and Society*, 12(4): 306–14.

Coles, B. (2000) *Joined-Up Youth Research, Policy and Practice*, Leicester: Youth Work Press.

Colfer, S., Turner-Uaandja, H. and Johnson, L. (2015) Young Dads TV: digital voices of young fathers, *Families, Relationships and Societies*, 4(2): 339–45.

Collins, M.E. and Mead, M. (2021) Social constructions of children and youth: beyond dependents and deviants, *Journal of Social Policy*, 50(3): 493–510.

Collins, M.E., Cooney, K. and Garlington, S. (2012) Compassion in contemporary social policy: applications of virtue theory. *Journal of Social Policy*, 41(2): 251–69.

Collins, M.E., Garlington, S. and Cooney, K. (2015) Relieving human suffering: compassion in social policy, *Journal of Sociology and Social Welfare*, 42(1): 95–120.

Conn, B.M., de Figueiredo, S., Sherer, S., Mankerian, M. and Iverson, E. (2018) 'Our lives aren't over': a strengths-based perspectives on stigma, discrimination and coping among young parents, *Journal of Adolescence*, 66(1): 91–100.

Cook, M.C. and. and Cameron, S.T. (2017) Social issues of teenage pregnancy, *Obstetrics, Gynaecology & Reproductive Medicine*, 25(9): 243–248.

Corlyon, J. and McGuire, C. (1999) *Pregnancy and Parenthood: The Views and Experiences of Young People in Public Care*, London: National Children's Bureau.

Cornock, D. (2013) MP tells ministers: 'put feckless fathers in chains', *BBC News*, 12 November. Available from: www.bbc.co.uk/news/uk-wales-politics-24916242 [Accessed 30 August 2023].

Coulter, R. (2018) Parental background and housing outcomes in young adulthood, *Housing Studies*, 33(2): 201–23.

Cundy, J. (2016) Supporting young dads' journeys through fatherhood, *Social Policy and Society*, 15(1): 141–53.

Daguerre, A. (2006) Teenage pregnancy and parenthood in England, in A. Daguerre and C. Nativel (eds) *When Children Become Parents: Welfare State Responses to Teenage Pregnancy*, Bristol: Policy Press, pp 67–88.

Davies, B. (2019) *Austerity, Youth Policy and the Deconstruction of the Youth Service in England*, Cham: Palgrave Macmillan.

Davies, L. (2016) Are young fathers 'hard to reach'? Understanding the importance of relationship building and service sustainability, *Journal of Children's Services*, 11(4): 317–29.

Davies, L. and Neale, B. (2015) Supporting young fathers: the promise, potential and perils of statutory service provision, *Families, Relationships and Societies*, 4(2): 331–8.

DCLG (Department for Communities and Local Government) (2009) *The Private Rented Sector: Professionalism and Quality*, London: DCLG.

DCLG (Department for Communities and Local Government) (2012) *English Housing Survey: Households – Annual Report on England's Households, 2010–11*, London: DCLG.

DCSF and DoH (Department for Children, Schools and Families and Department of Health) (2007) *Teenage Parents: Next Steps – Guidance for Local Authorities and Primary Care Trusts*, London: DCSF.

DCSF and DoH (Department for Children, Schools and Families and Department of Health) (2010) *Teenage Pregnancy Strategy: Beyond 2010*, London: DCSF.

Deacon, A. (2002) *Perspectives on Welfare*, Buckingham: Open University Press.

Deacon, A. (2007) Fellowship, in A.H. Halsey (ed) *Democracy in Crisis? Ethical Socialism for a Prosperous Country*, London: Politico's, pp 135–46.

Dermott, E. (2008) *Intimate Fatherhood: A Sociological Analysis*, Abingdon: Routledge.

Dermott, E. (2016) Non-resident fathers in the UK: living standards and social support, *Journal of Poverty and Social Justice*, 24(2): 113–25.

Dermott, E. and Miller, T. (2015) More than the sum of its parts? contemporary fatherhood policy, practice and discourse. *Families, Relationships and Societies*, 4(2): 183–95.

Deslauriers, J.M. (2011) Becoming a young father: a decision or an 'accident'?, *International Journal of Adolescence and Youth*, 16(3): 289–308.

Deslauriers, J.M. and Kiselica, M.S. (2022) An ecological approach to understanding the paternal commitments of young fathers: from the pregnancy test to the child's first birthday, *Child & Adolescent Social Work Journal*, online. Available from: https://doi.org/10.1007/s10560-022-00845-5 [Accessed 30 August 2023].

Deslauriers, J.M., DeVault, A., Groulx, A.P. and Sévigny, R. (2012) Rethinking services for young fathers, *Fathering*, 10(1): 66–90.

Desmond, M. and Gershenson, C. (2016) Housing and employment insecurity among the working poor, *Social Problems*, 63(1): 46–67.

DfE (Department for Education) (2013) *Funding for Sure Start Children's Centres*. Available from: https://www.gov.uk/government/publications/funding-for-sure-start-childrens-centres [Accessed 30 August 2023].

DfE (Department for Education) (2020) *Relationships Education, Relationships and Sex Education (RSE) and Health Education Statutory Guidance for Governing Bodies, Proprietors, Head Teachers, Principals, Senior Leadership Teams, Teachers*, London: DfE. Available from: https://assets.publishing.service.gov.uk/government/uploads/system/uploads/attachment_data/file/1090195/Relationships_Education_RSE_and_Health_Education.pdf [Accessed 30 August 2023].

DfES (Department for Education and Skills) (2006a) *Teenage Pregnancy: Accelerating the Strategy to 2010*, London: DfES.

DfES (Department for Education and Skills) (2006b) *Teenage Pregnancy Next Steps: Guidance for Local Authorities and Primary Care Trusts of Effective Delivery of Local Strategies*, London: DfES.

DHSC and DfE (Department for Health and Social Care and Department for Education) (2022) *Family Hubs and Start for Life Programme Guide*. Available from: https://www.gov.uk/government/publications/family-hubs-and-start-for-life-programme-local-authority-guide [Accessed 2 January 2023].

Diverse Dads Collective (2021) *Researching Inclusive Support for (Young) Fathers: A Community-Led Study*, Lincoln: University of Lincoln/North East Young Dads and Lads Project. Available from: https://fyff.co.uk/files/a1cc7f6026608e57385f20c4cf159e74c4f5a840.pdf [Accessed 2 January 2023].

DoH (Department of Health) (2012) *Public Health Outcomes Framework*, London: DoH.

DoH (Department of Health) (2013) *Sexual Health Improvement Framework for England*, London: DoH.

DoH (Department of Health) (2015) *2010 to 2015 Government Policy: Compassionate Care in the NHS*. Available from: https://www.gov.uk/government/publications/2010-to-2015-government-policy-compassionate-care-in-the-nhs/ [Accessed 30 August 2023].

Donald, L., Davidson, R., Murphy, S., Hadley, A., Puthussery, S. and Randhawa, G. (2022) How young, disadvantaged fathers are affected by socioeconomic and relational barriers: a UK-based qualitative study, *Families, Relationships and Societies*, 11(3): 447–64.

Doughty, S. (2009) Teachers should tell boys the joys of teen fatherhood, government advice reveals, *Mail Online*, 17 February. Available from: https://www.dailymail.co.uk/news/article-1147201/Teachers-tell-boys-joys-teen-fatherhood--government-advice-reveals.html [Accessed 30 August 2023].

Dukes, A. and Palm, G. (2019) Reproductive justice and support for young fathers, *Infant Mental Health Journal*, 40(5): 710–24.

Duncan, S. (2007) What's the problem with teenage parents? and what's the problem with policy?, *Critical Social Policy*, 27(3): 307–34.

Duncan, S., Edwards, R. and Alexander, C. (eds) (2010) *Teenage Parenthood: What's the Problem?*, London: Tufnell Press.

Dupuis, A. and Thorns, D.C. (1998) Home, home ownership and the search for ontological security, *Sociological Review*, 46(1): 24–47.

DWP (2010) *Equality Impact Assessment: Strengthening Families, Promoting Parental Responsiblity: The Future of Child Maintenance*, London: Department for Work and Pensions. Available from: https://assets.publishing.service.gov.uk/media/5a7c5d2140f0b626628ab895/eia-strengthening-families.pdf [Accessed 28 November 2023].

Dwyer, P., Scullion, L., Jones, K., McNeil, J. and Stewart, A.B.R. (2023) *The Impacts of Welfare Conditionality: Sanctions, Support and Behaviour Change*, Bristol: Policy Press.

Early, V., Fairbrother, H. and Curtis, P. (2019) Displaying good fathering through the construction of physical activity as intimate practice, *Families, Relationships and Societies*, 8(2): 213–29.

Edin, K. and Nelson, T.J. (2013) *Doing the Best I Can: Fatherhood in the Inner City*, Berkeley: University of California Press.

Edwards, R. and Gillies, V. (2016) Family policy: the Mods and Rockers, in H. Bochel and M. Powell (eds) *The Coalition Government and Social Policy: Restructuring the Welfare State*, Bristol: Policy Press, pp 243–64.

Eisenstadt, N. (2011) *Providing a Sure Start: How the Government Discovered Early Childhood*, Bristol: Policy Press.

Elke Graf, T. and Wojnicka, K. (2023) Post-separation fatherhood narratives in Germany and Sweden: between caring and protective masculinities, *Journal of Family Studies*, 29(3): 1022–42.

Elkington, A. (2017) The everyday lives of young Māori fathers: an explorative study, *Journal of Indigenous Wellbeing*, 2(3): 3–17.

Elley, S. (2013) *Understanding Sex and Relationship Education, Youth and Class: A Youth Work-Led Approach*, Basingstoke: Palgrave Macmillan.

Ellis-Sloan, K. (2013) Teenage mothers, stigma and their 'presentations of self', *Sociological Research Online*, 19(1): art 9. Available from: http://www.socresonline.org.uk/19/1/9.html [Accessed 30 August 2023].

Ellis-Sloan, K. (2021) Former young mothers' pathways through higher education: a chance to rethink the narrative, *Educational Review*, Online First.

Emmel, N. and Hughes, K. (2014) Vulnerability, intergenerational exchange and the conscience of generations, in J. Holland and R. Edwards (eds) *Understanding Families Over Time: Research and Policy*, Basingstoke: Palgrave Macmillan, pp 161–75.

Emmel, N., Hughes, K., Greenhalgh, J. and Sales, A. (2007) Accessing socially excluded people: trust and the gatekeeper in the researcher–participant relationship, *Sociological Research Online*, 12(2): 43–55. Available from: https://doi.org/10.5153/sro.1512 [Accessed 30 August 2023].

Enderstein, A.M. and Boonzaier, F. (2015) Narratives of young South African fathers: redefining masculinity through fatherhood, *Journal of Gender Studies*, 24(5): 512–27.

Epstein, D., O'Flynn, S. and Telford, D. (2003) *Silenced Sexualities in Schools and Universities*, Stoke-on-Trent: Trentham Books.

Eurostat (2021) *Age of young people leaving their parental household, 2020*. Available from: https://ec.europa.eu/eurostat/statistics-explained/index.php?title=Age_of_young_people_leaving_their_parental_household&oldid=539345 [Accessed 25 November 2022].

Fatherhood Institute (2011) *Different Sorts of Dads: The Research on Fathers' Impact on Their Children*, Marlborough: Fatherhood Institute.

Fatherhood Institute (2013a) *Research Summary: Young Fathers*, London: Fatherhood Institute. Available from: http://www.fatherhoodinstitute.org/2013/fatherhood-institute-research-summary-young-fathers/ [Accessed 30 August 2023].

Fatherhood Institute (2013b) *Invisible Fathers: Working with Young Dads Resource Pack*. Available from: http://www.fatherhoodinstitute.org/2013/invisible-fathers-working-with-young-dads-resource-pack/ [Accessed 30 August 2023].

Featherstone, B. (2009) *Contemporary Fathering: Theory, Policy and Practice*, Bristol: Policy Press.

Ferguson, H. (2016) Patterns of engagement and non-engagement of young fathers in early intervention and safeguarding work, *Social Policy and Society*, 15(1): 99–111.

Ferguson, H. and Gates, P. (2013) Early intervention and holistic, relationship-based practice with fathers: evidence from the work of the Family Nurse Partnership, *Child and Family Social Work*, 20(1): 96–105.

Finkel, A. (2019) *Compassion: A Global History of Social Policy*, London: Red Globe Press.

Florsheim, P. and Moore, D. (2020) *Lost and Found: Young Fathers in the Age of Unwed Parenthood*, Oxford: Oxford University Press.

Florsheim, P., Moore, D. and Edgington, C. (2003) Romantic relations among adolescent parents, in P. Florsheim (ed) *Adolescent Romantic Relations and Sexual Behavior: Theory, Research, and Practical Implications*, Mahwah, NJ: Lawrence Erlbaum, pp 297–322.

Flouri, E. (2005) *Fathering and Child Outcomes*, Chichester: Wiley.

Formby, E., Hirst, J. and Owen, J. (2010) Pathways to adulthood: reflections from three generations of young mothers and fathers, in S. Duncan, R. Edwards and C. Alexander (eds) *Teenage Parenthood: What's the Problem?*, London: Tufnell Press, pp 85–110.

Forrest, S. (2007) *Boys, Young Men and Sexual Health Services: A Summary of a Review of the Academic Literature*, London: Brook/Working with Men.

France, A. (2008) From being to becoming: the importance of tackling youth poverty in transitions to adulthood, *Social Policy and Society*, 7(4): 495–505.

Frontline/Centre for Public Impact/Buurtzorg (2019) *A Blueprint for Children's Social Care: Unlocking the Potential of Social Work*. London: Frontline/CPI/Buurtzorg. htpps://www.centreforpublicimpact.org/assets/documents/Blueprint-for-childrens-social-care.pdf.

Fry, P. and Trifiletti, R. (1983) Teenage fathers: an exploration of their developmental needs and anxieties and the implications for clinical–social intervention and services, *Journal of Psychiatric Treatment and Evaluation*, 5(2/3): 219–27.

Furlong, A. and Cartmel, F. (2007) *Young People and Social Change: New Perspectives*, 2nd edn, Maidenhead: McGraw-Hill/Open University Press.

Furstenberg, F. (1976) Premarital pregnancy and marital instability, *Journal of Social Issues*, 31(1): 67–86.

Furstenberg, F. (2003) Teenage childbearing as a public issue and private concern, *Annual Review of Sociology*, 29: 23–39.

Furstenberg, F. and Cherlin, A.J. (1991) *Divided families: What Happens to Children When Parents Part*, Cambridge, MA: Harvard University Press.

Furstenberg, F., Brooks-Gunn, J. and Morgan, S.P. (1987) *Adolescent Mothers in Later Life*, Cambridge: Cambridge University Press.

Garcia, M. and Vicari Haddock, S. (2016) Special issue: housing and community needs and social innovation responses in times of crisis, *Journal of Housing and the Built Environment*, 31(3): 393–407.

Garthwaite, K., Patrick, R., Power, M., Tarrant, A. and Warnock, R. (eds) (2022) *COVID-19 Collaborations: Researching Poverty and Low-Income Family Life During the Pandemic*, Bristol: Policy Press.

Gibbin, D. (2003) *The P Files: Hartlepool Teenage Pregnancy Research Report*, Hartlepool: North Tees and Hartlepool NHS Trust.

Giddens, A. (1990) *Consequences of Modernity*, Oxford: Polity Press.

Gilligan, P., Manby, M. and Pickburn, C. (2012) Fathers' involvement in children's services: exploring local and national issues in 'Moorlandstown', *British Journal of Social Work*, 42(3): 500–18.

Giullari, S. and Shaw, M. (2005) Supporting or controlling? New Labour's housing strategy for teenage parents, *Critical Social Policy*, 25(3): 402–17.

Glikman, H. (2004) Low-income young fathers: contexts, connections, and self, *Social Work*, 49(2): 195–206.

Goldberg, W.A., Tan, E.T., Davis, C.R. and Easterbrooks, M.A. (2013) What predicts parental involvement by young fathers at psychosocial risk?, *Fathering*, 11(3): 280–91.

Goldman, R. and Burgess, A. (2017) *Where's the Daddy? Fathers and Father-Figures in UK Datasets*, Marlborough: Fatherhood Institute.

GOV.UK (2022) *Housing Costs and Universal Credit*. Available from: https://www.gov.uk/housing-and-universal-credit [Accessed 18 July 2023].

Graham, H. and McDermott, E. (2005) Qualitative research and the evidence base of policy: insights from studies of teenage mothers in the UK, *Journal of Social Policy*, 35(1): 21–37.

Graham, M. (2013) *'It's About Family, Innit?': Towards an Understanding of the Lives of Teenage Mothers and Fathers as They Make the Transition to Parenthood*, doctoral thesis, London: City University. Available from: https://openaccess.city.ac.uk/id/eprint/3018/ [Accessed 31 August 2023].

Grau Grau, M., las Heras Maestro, M. and Bowles, H.R. (2022) *Engaged Fatherhood for Men, Families and Gender Equality: Healthcare, Social Policy, and Work Perspectives*, Cham (Switzerland): Springer.

Gregory, J. (2015) Engineering compassion: the institutional structure of virtue, *Journal of Social Policy*, 44(2): 339–56.

Griffiths, S.M., Jewell, T., Rae, M. and de Gruchy, J. (2021) Editorial: the future of public health in England. *British Medical Journal*, 372(662). Available from: https://doi.org/10.1136/bmj.n662 [Accessed 29 August 2023].

Griggs, J. (2010) *Protect, Support, Provide: Examining the Role of Grandparents in Families at Risk of Poverty*, London: Grandparents Plus.

Grundy, E. and Foverskov, E. (2016) Age at first birth and later life health in Western and Eastern Europe, *Population and Development Review*, 42(2): 245–69.

Hadley, A. (2014) Teenage pregnancy: huge progress … but more to do, *Community Practitioner*, 87(6): 44–7.

Hadley, A. (2023) *Rise in Teen Conception Rates Signals a Warning Against Complacency*, Brook, 3 May. Available from: https://www.brook.org.uk/blog/rise-in-teen-conception-rates/ [Accessed 31 August 2023].

Hadley, A. and Evans, D.T. (2013) Teenage pregnancy and sexual health, *Nursing Times*, 109(46): 22–7.

Hadley, A. and Ingham, R. (2018) *Teenage Pregnancy and Young Parenthood: Effective Policy and Practice*, Abingdon: Routledge.

Hanna, E. (2018) *Supporting Young Men as Fathers: Gendered Understandings of Group-Based Community Provisions*, Cham: Palgrave Macmillan.

Hanna, E. and Lau-Clayton, L. (2012) *Capturing Past and Future Time in Qualitative Longitudinal Field Enquiry: Timelines and Relational Maps*, Timescapes Methods Guide No. 5, Leeds: Timescapes, University of Leeds. Available from: https://followingfathers.leeds.ac.uk/wp-content/uploads/sites/79/2015/10/esmee_online.pdf [Accessed 20 December 2022].

Heath, S. (2008) *Housing Choices and Issues for Young People in the UK, Findings*, November, York: Joseph Rowntree Foundation.

Hendricks, L. and Montgomery, T. (1983) A limited population of unmarried adolescent fathers: a preliminary report on their views of fatherhood and the relationship with the mothers of their children, *Adolescence*, 18: 201–10.

Hennessy, P. (2011) Runaway fathers are like drink drivers, blasts David Cameron, *The Telegraph*, 18 June. Available from: https://www.telegraph.co.uk/news/politics/david-cameron/8583752/Runaway-fathers-are-like-drink-drivers-blasts-David-Cameron.html [Accessed 31 August 2023].

Higginbottom, G.M.A., Mathers, N., Marsh, P., Kirkham, M., Owen, J.M. and Serrant-Green, L. (2006) Young people of minority ethnic origin in England and early parenthood: views from young parents and service providers, *Social Science & Medicine*, 63(4): 858–70.

Hilpern, K. (2009) Young fathers: 'I love my child as much as any older dad', *Mail Online*, 26 June. Available from: https://www.dailymail.co.uk/home/you/article-1194221/Teenage-fathers-I-love-child-older-dad.html [Accessed 31 August 2023].

Hogg, S. (2014) *The Dad Project: A Knee-High Design Challenge Project*, London: Design Council and NSPCC.

Holdsworth, C. and Morgan, D. (2005) *Transitions in Context: Leaving Home, Independence and Adulthood*, Maidenhead: Open University Press.

Holmberg, L.I. and Wahlberg, V. (2000) The process of decision-making on abortion: a grounded theory study of young men in Sweden, *Journal of Adolescent Health*, 26(3): 230–4.

Holstein, M.B. and Minkler, M. (2007) Critical gerontology: reflections for the 21st century, in M. Bernard and T. Scharf (eds) *Critical Perspectives on Ageing Societies*, Bristol: Policy Press, pp 13–26.

Homeless Link (2013) *Young People's Experiences of Homelessness are Distinct From Adults*. Available from: https://homeless.org.uk/areas-of-expertise/meeting-diverse-needs/young-people/ [Accessed 31 August 2023].

Horsell, C. (2017) A politics of compassion: informing a new social policy for homelessness?, *International Social Work*, 60(4): 966–75.

House of Commons Education Committee (2015) *Life Lessons: PSHE and SRE in Schools*. Fifth report of session 2014–15. HC 145. London: House of Commons.

Hudson, F. and Ineichen, B. (1991) *Taking It Lying Down: Sexuality and Teenage Motherhood*, Basingstoke: Macmillan Education.

Hudson-Wilkin, R. (2023) *Seeking Sanctuary: The Rights of People to Cross Borders*, presentation for the Project Bonhoeffer Online Conference, February. Available from: https://www.youtube.com/watch?v=OYPk01_geSU&ab_channel=ProjectBonhoeffer [Accessed 31 August 2023].

Hughes, K. and Emmel, N. (2011) *Intergenerational Exchange: Grandparents, Their Grandchildren, and the Texture of Poverty*, Timescapes Policy Briefing Paper No. 6, Leeds: Timescapes, University of Leeds. Available from: http://www.timescapes.leeds.ac.uk/assets/files/Policy-Conference-2011/paper-6.pdf [Accessed 11 July 2023].

Hughes, K. and Tarrant, A. (2020) *Qualitative Secondary Analysis*, London: Sage.

Hughes, K. and Tarrant, A. (2023) *Men, Families, and Poverty: Tracing the Intergenerational Trajectories of Place-Based Hardship*, Cham: Palgrave Macmillan.

Hughes, K., Hughes, J. and Tarrant, A. (2021) Working at a remove: continuous, collective, and configurative approaches to qualitative secondary analysis, *Quality & Quantity*, 56(3): 375–94.

Hunt, J. (2018) Grandparents as substitute parents in the UK, *Contemporary Social Science*, 13(2): 175–86.

Hutchinson, J., Beck, V. and Hooley, T. (2016) Delivering NEET policy packages? A decade of NEET policy in England, *Journal of Education and Work*, 29(6): 707–27.

Ingham, R. (2005) Teenage pregnancy policy in England, *Sexuality Research and Social Policy*, 2(3): 56–67.

Jaffee, S.R., Caspi, A., Moffitt, T.E., Taylor, A. and Dickson, N. (2001) Predicting early fatherhood and whether young fathers live with their children: prospective findings and policy reconsiderations, *Journal of Child Psychology and Psychiatry*, 42(6): 803–15.

Jamie, K. and Brown, S. (forthcoming) Introduction: exploring the lives and lived experiences of young parents, *Frontiers in Sociology*. Available from: www.frontiers.org

Johanssen, T. and Hammarén, N. (2014) 'Imagine, just 16 years old and already a dad!': the construction of young fatherhood on the Internet, *International Journal of Adolescence and Youth*, 19(3): 366–81.

Johnsen, S. and Quilgars, D. (2010) *Teenage Parent Supported Housing Pilot Evaluation*, York: Centre for Housing Policy, University of York.

Johnson, D. (2015) Not your stereotypical young father, not your typical teenage life, *Families, Relationships and Societies*, 4(2): 319–22.

Johnson, W.E. Jr (2001) Parental involvement among unwed fathers, *Children and Youth Services Review*, 23(6/7): 513–36.

Jones, G. (2002) *Leaving Home*, Buckingham: Open University Press.

Jupp, E. (2013) Enacting parenting policy? the hybrid spaces of Sure Start Children's Centres. *Children's Geographies*, 11(2): 173–87.

Khatun, M., Al Mamun, A., Scott, J., William, G.M., Clavarino, A. and Najman, J.M. (2017) Do children born to teenage parents have lower adult intelligence? A prospective birth cohort study, *PLoS ONE*, 12(3): art e0167395. Available from: https://doi.org/10.1371/journal.pone.0167395 [Accessed 31 August 2023].

Kidger, J. (2004) Including young mothers: limitations to New Labour's strategy for supporting teenage parents. *Critical Social Policy*, 24(3): 291–311.

Kiernan, K. (1995) *Transitions to Parenthood: Young Mothers, Young Fathers: Associated Factors and Later Life Experiences*, Welfare State Programme Discussion Paper WSP 113, London: LSE STICERD.

Kiernan, K. (2002) Disadvantage and demography: chicken and egg?, in J. Hills, J. Le Grand and D. Piachaud (eds) *Understanding Social Exclusion*, Oxford: Oxford University Press, pp 84–96.

Kiernan, K. (2005) *Non-Residential Fatherhood and Child Involvement: Evidence from the Millennium Cohort Study*, CASE paper No. 100. London: Centre for Analysis of Social Exclusion, London School of Economics.

Kirkman, M., Harrison, L., Hillier, L. and Pyett, P. (2001) 'I know I'm doing a good job': canonical autobiographical narratives of teenage mothers, *Culture, Health & Sexuality*, 3(3): 279–94.

Kiselica, M. (2011) *When Boys Become Parents: Adolescent Fatherhood in America*, New Brunswick, NJ: Rutgers.

Kiselica, M. (forthcoming) Moving beyond stigma: re-examining the lives of teenage fathers, in M. Lafrance, J. Deslauriers and G. Trembly (eds) *The Forgotten Realities of Men*, Vancouver: UBC Press.

Kiselica, M.S. and Kiselica, A.M. (2014) The complicated worlds of adolescent fathers: implications for clinical practice, public policy, and research, *Psychology of Men & Masculinity*, 15(3): 260–74.

References

Klinman, D.G., Sander, J.H., Rosen, J.L., Longo, K.R. and Martinez, L.P. (1985) *The Teen Parent Collaboration: Reaching and Serving the Teenage Father*, New York: Bank Street College of Education. Available from: https://files.eric.ed.gov/fulltext/ED270714.pdf [Accessed 31 August 2023].

Kost, K.A. (1997) The effects of support on the economic well-being of young fathers, *Families in Society*, 78(4): 370–82.

Ladlow, L. (2021) *Housing Young Parents: A Micro-Dynamic Study of the Housing Experiences and Support Needs of Young Mothers and Fathers*, PhD thesis, Leeds: University of Leeds.

Ladlow, L. and Neale, B. (2016) Risk, resource, redemption? the parenting and custodial experiences of young offender fathers, *Social Policy and Society*, 15(1): 113–27.

Ladlow, L., Tarrant, A. and Way, L. (2023) *A Dynamic Perspective of Young Fathers' Well-Being: Predictive and Protective Factors Across Their Mental Health Pathways*, Following Young Fathers Further Briefing Paper No. 4. Available from: https://fyff.co.uk/files/9924206dac296bcb0927f7623168dd34a1ecc1e2.pdf [Accessed 31 August 2023].

Lammy, D. (2015) Bringing young fathers into the fold: policy challenges and developments, *Families, Relationships and Societies*, 4(2): 315–17.

Landers, M.D., Mitchell, O. and Coates, E.E. (2015) Teenage fatherhood as a potential turning point in the lives of delinquent youth, *Journal of Child and Family Studies*, 24(6): 1685–96.

Lane, T.S. and Clay, C.M. (2000) Meeting the service needs of young fathers, *Child and Adolescent Social Work Journal*, 17(1): 35–54.

Larson, N.C., Hussey, J.M., Gilmore, M.R. and Gilchrist, L.D. (1996) What about dad? Fathers of children born to school-age mothers, *Families in Society: Journal of Contemporary Human Services*, 279–89.

Lau Clayton, C. (2015) *Young Fatherhood: Sharing Care with the Mother of the Child*, Briefing Paper no. 2, Leeds: University of Leeds. Available from: https://followingfathers.leeds.ac.uk/wp-content/uploads/sites/79/2015/10/Brieifing-Paper-2-V8.pdf [Accessed 21 December 2022].

Lau Clayton, C. (2016) The lives of young fathers: a review of selected evidence, *Social Policy and Society*, 15(1): 129–40.

Lau Clayton, C. (2017) Young fathers and their perspective of health and well-being: examples from the ERSC 'Following Young Fathers Study', in F. Portier-Le Cocq (ed) *Fertility, Health and Lone Parenting: European Contexts*, Abingdon: Routledge, pp 162–79.

Lau Clayton, C. and May, J. (2011) *Following Fathers: The Experiences and Support Needs of Young Dads*, Timescapes Policy Conference, Queen Elizabeth II Conference Centre, Westminster, London, 14 June.

Laub, J.H. and Sampson, R.J. (2003) *Shared Beginnings, Divergent Lives: Delinquent Boys to Age 70*, Cambridge, MA: Harvard University Press.

Law, J. (2004) *After Method: Mess in Social Science Research*, Abingdon: Routledge.

Lawton, K. (2013) *The Condition of Britain Briefing 2: Growing Up and Becoming an Adult*, London: Institute of Public Policy Research.

Leite, R. (2007) An exploration of aspects of boundary ambiguity among young, unmarried fathers during the prenatal period, *Family Relations*, 56(2): 162–74.

Lemay, C.A., Cashman, S.B., Elfenbein, D.S. and Felice, M.E. (2010) A qualitative study of the meaning of fatherhood among young urban fathers, *Public Health Nursing*, 27(3): 221–31.

Levac, L. (2013) 'Is this for real?' Participatory research, intersectionality, and the development of leader and collective efficacy with young mothers. *Action Research*, 11(4): 423–41.

Lewin, A., Mitchell, S.J., Waters, D., Hodgkinson, S., Southammakosane, C. and Gilmore, J. (2015) The protective effects of father involvement for infants of teen mothers with depressive symptoms, *Maternal and Child Health Journal*, 19(5): 1016–23.

Limmer, M. (2010) Young men, masculinities and sex education, *Sex Education*, 10(4): 349–58.

Lindberg, L.D. and Maddow-Zimmet, I. (2012) Consequences of sex education on teen and young adult sexual behaviors and outcomes, *Journal of Adolescent Health*, 51(4): 332–8.

Livesley, J., Long, L., Fallon, D., Myers, S., de Lopez, J., Chadwick, R. and Cappleman, J. (2011) *Evaluation of the Action for Children: Supported Housing, Supported Tenancy and Teenage Pregnancy Floating Support Services*, Salford: University of Salford. Available from: https://www.basw.co.uk/system/files/resources/basw_101213-8_0.pdf [Accessed 18 July 2023].

Lloyd, T. (2010) *Young Fathers and Midwives: An Opportunity Missed?* London: Brook.

Lohan, M., Cruise, S., O'Halloran, P., Alderdice, F. and Hyde, A. (2010) Adolescent men's attitudes in relation to pregnancy and pregnancy outcomes: a systematic review of the literature from 1980–2009, *Journal of Adolescent Health*, 47(4): 327–45.

Lohan, M., Aventin, A., Maguire, L., Curran, R., McDowell, C., et al (2017) Increasing boys' and girls' intentions to avoid teenage pregnancy: a cluster randomised controlled feasibility trial of an interactive video drama-based intervention in post-primary schools in Northern Ireland, *Public Health Research*, 5(1). Available from: https://doi.org/10.3310/phr05010 [Accessed 31 August 2023].

Lowenthal, B. and Lowenthal, R. (1997) Teenage parenting: challenges, interventions and programs, *Childhood Education*, 74(1): 29–32.

Luker, K. (1996) *Dubious Conceptions: The Politics of Teenage Pregnancy*, Cambridge, MA: Harvard University Press.

Lund, B. (2018) *The Housing Crisis as the Long-term Casualty of Austerity Politics, 1918–2018*, History & Policy Policy Paper. 6 December. Available from: https://www.historyandpolicy.org/policy-papers/papers/the-housing-crisis-as-the-long-term-casualty-of-austerity-politics-1918-201 [Accessed 18 July 2023].

MacDonald, R. (2011) Youth transitions, unemployment and underemployment: plus ça change, plus c'est la même chose?, *Journal of Sociology*, 47(4): 427–44.

MacDonald, R. (2013) Underemployment and precarité: the new condition of youth?, *Lifelong Learning in Europe (lLinE) Newsletter*, 2013(1): 1–7.

MacDonald, R. and Marsh, J. (2005) *Disconnected Youth: Growing up in Britain's Poor Neighbourhoods*, Basingstoke: Palgrave Macmillan.

MacDonald, R., Shildrick, T. and Furlong, A. (2020) 'Cycles of disadvantage' revisited: young people, families and poverty across generations, *Journal of Youth Studies*, 23(1): 12–27.

Mackie, P.K. (2016) Young people and housing: identifying the key issues, *International Journal of Housing Policy*, 16(2): 137–43.

MacLeod, J. (2009) *Ain't No Makin' It: Aspirations and Attainment in a Low-Income Neighbourhood*, 3rd edn, Boulder, CO: Westview Press.

Madiba, S. and Nsiki, C. (2017) Teen fathers' perceptions and experiences of fatherhood: a qualitative exploration with in-school teen fathers in a rural district in South Africa, *Current Pediatric Research*, 21(1): 501–6.

Mann, E., Cardona, V. and Gómez, C. (2015) Beyond the discourse of reproductive choice: narratives of pregnancy resolution among Latina/o teenage parents, *Culture, Health & Sexuality*, 17(9): 1090–104.

Mann, R. Khan, H. and Leeson, G. (2009) *Age and Gender Differences in Grandchildren's Relations with their Maternal Grandfathers and Grandmothers*, Working Paper 209, Oxford Institute of Ageing Working Papers.

Mann, R., Tarrant, A. and Leeson, G. (2016) Grandfatherhood: shifting masculinities in later life. *Sociology*, 50(3): 594–610.

Markson, L., Lösel, F., Souza, K. and Lanskey, C. (2015) Male prisoners' family relationships and resilience in resettlement, *Criminology & Criminal Justice*, 15(4): 423–41.

Maroto, M. and Severson, M. (2020) Owning, renting, or living with parents? changing housing situations among Canadian young adults, 2001 to 2011, *Housing Studies*, 35(4): 679–702.

Mason, J., May, V. and Clarke, L. (2007) Ambivalence and the paradoxes of grandparenting, *Sociological Review*, 55(4): 687–706.

Matlakala, F.K., Makhubele, J.C. and Mashilo, M.W. (2018) Challenges of teenage fathers towards fatherhood in Vaalbank, Mpumalanga province, *Gender & Behaviours*, 16(3): https://hdl.handle.net/10520/EJC-1366854ede.

Mawn, L., Oliver, E., Akhter, N., Bambra, C., Torgerson, C., Bridle, C. and Stain, H. (2018) Are we failing young people not in employment, education or training (NEETs)? a systematic review and meta-analysis of re-engagement interventions, *Systematic Reviews*, 6: art 16. Available from: https://doi.org/10.1186/s13643-016-0394-2 [Accessed 31 August 2023].

Maxwell, N., Scourfield, J., Featherstone, B., Holland, S. and Tolman, R. (2012) Engaging fathers in child welfare services: a narrative review of recent research evidence, *Child & Family Social Work*, 17(2): 160–9.

May, J., Turner-Uaandja, J., Dawson, H. and Vemba, R. (2017) Developing the Young Dads Collective North, in A. Tarrant, and B. Neale (eds) *Learning to Support Young Dads: Responding to Young Fathers in a Different Way*, Leeds: School of Sociology and Social Policy, University of Leeds, pp 14–22. Available from: https://followingfathers.leeds.ac.uk/wp-content/uploads/sites/79/2017/04/SYD-final-report.pdf [Accessed 20 December 2020].

Mazza, C. (2002) Young dads: the effects of a parenting program on urban African-American adolescent fathers, *Adolescence*, 37(148): 681–93.

McAllister, F., Burgess, A., Kato, J. and Barker, G. (2012) *Fatherhood: Parenting Programmes and Policy – A Critical Review of Best Practice*, London: Fatherhood Institute.

McDowell, L. (2014) The sexual contract, youth, masculinity and the uncertain promise of waged work in austerity Britain, *Australian Feminist Studies*, 29(79): 31–49.

McDowell, L. and Bonner-Thompson, C. (2020) The other side of coastal towns: young men's precarious lives on the margins of England, *Environment and Planning A: Economy and Space*, 52(5): 916–32.

McKay, S. and Rowlingson, K. (2016) Social Security under the coalition and Conservatives: shredding the system for people of working age; privileging pensioners, in H. Bochel and M. Powell (eds) *The Coalition Government and Social Policy: Restructuring the Welfare State*, Bristol: Policy Press, pp 179–200.

McKay, T., Lindquist, C., Feinberg, R., Steffey, D., Landwehr, J. and Bir, A. (2018) Family life before and during incarceration, *Journal of Offender Rehabilitation*, 57(2): 96–114.

McKee, K. (2012) Young people, homeownership and future welfare, *Housing Studies*, 27(6): 853–62.

McNulty, A. (2010) Great expectations: teenage pregnancy and intergenerational transmission, in S. Duncan, R. Edwards and C. Alexander (eds) *Teenage Parenthood: What's the Problem?*, London: Tufnell Press, pp 111–34.

Meek, R. (2007) Parenting education for young fathers in prison, *Child & Family Social Work*, 12(3): 239–47.

Mensah, K. (2017) *Young Fathers: Where We Are Now?*, London: Working With Men. Available from: https://futuremen.org/wp-content/uploads/2020/03/Future-Men-Young-Fathers-Report-2017-1.pdf [Accessed 31 August 2023].

Menzel, A. (2022) The coronavirus pandemic: exploring expectant fathers' experiences, *Journal for Cultural Research*, 26(1): 83–101.

Mickel, A. (2008) The role of compassion in social work, *Community Care*, 29 July. Available from: https://www.communitycare.co.uk/2008/07/29/the-role-of-compassion-in-social-work/ [Accessed 2 September 2023].

Miller, D.B. (1997) Adolescent fathers: what we know and what we need to know, *Child and Adolescent Social Work Journal*, 14(1): 55–69.

Miller, T. (2011) *Making Sense of Fatherhood: Gender, Caring and Work*, Cambridge: Cambridge University Press.

Miller-Johnson S., Winn D.C., Coie J.D., Malone P.S. and Lochman J. (2004) Risk factors for adolescent pregnancy reports among African-American males, *Journal of Research on Adolescence*, 14(4): 471–95.

Mirza-Davies, J. and Brown, J. (2016) *NEET: Young People Not in Education, Employment or Training*, Briefing Paper No. SN 06705, London: House of Commons Library.

Mniszak, C., O'Brien, H.L., Greyson, D., Chabot, C. and Shoveller, J. (2020) 'Nothing's available': young fathers' experiences with unmet information needs and barriers to resolving them, *Information Processing & Management*, 57(2): art 102081. Available from: https://doi.org/10.1016/j.ipm.2019.102081 [Accessed 2 September 2023].

MoJ (Ministry of Justice) (2020) *Assessing Risk of Harm to Children and Parents in Private Law Children's Cases: Final Report*, June, London: Ministry of Justice.

Mollborn, S. (2017) Teenage mothers: What we know and how it matters, *Child Development Perspectives*, 11(1): 63–9.

Mollborn, S. and Jacobs, J. (2015) 'I'll be there for you': teen parents' coparenting relationships, *Journal of Marriage and Family*, 77(2): 373–87.

Morris, K. and Featherstone, B. (2010) Investing in children, regulating parents, thinking family: a decade of tensions and contradictions, *Social Policy and Society*, 9(4): 557–66.

Morriss, L. (2018) Haunted futures: the stigma of being a mother living apart from her child(ren) as a result of state-ordered court removal, *Sociological Review*, 66(4): 816–31.

Mortune, C. (2021) *Care-Experienced Young People: What Supportive Relationships Facilitate Transition to and Participation in Post-16 Education, Employment or Training (EET)?* Doctoral thesis (DEdPsy), London: UCL (University College London). Available from: https://discovery.ucl.ac.uk/id/eprint/10130138/ [Accessed 2 September 2023].

Mukuna, R.K. (2020) Exploring Basotho teenage fathers' experiences of early fatherhood at South African rural high schools, *Journal of Psychology in Africa*, 30(4): 348–53.

National Housing Federation (2010) *Cuts to Area-Based Grants Could Have Dire Effect on Vulnerable People*, National Housing Federation media release, 11 June.

Nativel, C. with Daguerre, A. (2006) Conclusion: welfare states and the politics of teenage pregnancy: lessons from cross-national comparisons, in A. Daguerre and C. Nativel (eds) *When Children Become Parents: Welfare State Responses to Teenage Pregnancy*, Bristol: Policy Press, pp 225–40.

Nayak, A. (2006) Displaced masculinities: chavs, youth and class in the post-industrial city, *Sociology*, 40(5): 813–31.

Nayak, A. and Kehily, M.J. (2013) 'Chavs, chavettes and pramface girls': teenage mothers, marginalised young men and the management of stigma. *Journal of Youth Studies*, 17(10): 1330–45.

Ncayiyane, Z. and Nel, L. (2023) Young Black fathers' perceptions of fatherhood: a family systems account, *Journal of Family Issues*, Online First. Available from: https://doi.org/10.1177/0192513X231172955 [Accessed 2 September 2023].

Neale, B. (2004) Introduction: young children's citizenship, in B. Neale (ed) *Young Children's Citizenship: Ideas into Practice*, York: Joseph Rowntree Foundation, pp 6–18.

Neale, B. (2013) Adding time into the mix: stakeholder ethics in qualitative longitudinal research, *Methodological Innovations Online*, 8(2): 6–20.

Neale, B. (2016) Introduction: young fatherhood – lived experiences and policy challenges, *Social Policy and Society*, 15(1): 75–83.

Neale, B. (2021a) *The Craft of Qualitative Longitudinal Research*, London: Sage.

Neale, B. (2021b) Fluid enquiry, complex causality, policy processes: making a difference with qualitative longitudinal research, *Social Policy and Society*, 20(4): 653–69.

Neale, B. (2021c) *Lived Experiences, Policy Responses: The Role of Qualitative Longitudinal Research in Evaluating Schemes to Alleviate Poverty*, thematic discussion paper for the fifth meeting of the EU Minimum Income Network, April. Brussels: EU Commission. Available from: https://timescapes-archive.leeds.ac.uk/wp-content/uploads/sites/47/2021/06/EU-MINET-final-circulated-paper-Bren-Neale.pdf [Accessed 21 December 2022].

Neale, B. (2022) *Analytical Principles in Qualitative Longitudinal Research*, presentation to the Time in QCA International Workshop, Rotterdam, 5 October.

Neale, B. and Davies, L. (2015a) Seeing young fathers in a different way: editorial introduction. *Families, Relationships and Societies*, 4(2) 309–13.

Neale, B. and Davies, L. (2015b) *Hard to Reach? Re-thinking Support for Young Fathers*, Briefing Paper no. 6, Leeds: University of Leeds. Available from: https://followingfathers.leeds.ac.uk/wp-content/uploads/sites/79/2015/10/Brieifing-Paper-6-V7.pdf [Accessed 2 September 2023].

Neale, B. and Davies, L. (2016) Becoming a young breadwinner? The education, employment and training trajectories of young fathers, *Social Policy and Society*, 15(1): 85–98.

Neale, B. and Flowerdew, J. (2007) New structures, new agency: the dynamics of child–parent relationships after divorce, *International Journal of Children's Rights*, 15(1): 25–42.

Neale, B. and Ladlow, L. (2015a) *Young Offender Fathers: Risk, Resource, Redemption?*, Following Young Fathers Briefing Paper no. 5, Leeds: University of Leeds. Available from: https://followingfathers.leeds.ac.uk/wp-content/uploads/sites/79/2015/10/Brieifing-Paper-5-V5.pdf [Accessed 2 September 2023].

Neale, B. and Ladlow, L. (2015b) *Finding a Place to Parent? Housing Young Fathers*, Following Young Fathers Briefing Paper No. 7, Leeds: University of Leeds. Available from: https://followingfathers.leeds.ac.uk/wp-content/uploads/sites/79/2015/10/Briefing-Paper-7-V3.pdf [Accessed 2 September 2023].

Neale, B. and Lau Clayton, C. (2011) *Following Young Fathers: The Lived Experience of Teenage Parenting Over Time*, Timescapes Policy Briefing Paper no. 1, Leeds: Timescapes, University of Leeds. Available from: https://timescapes-archive.leeds.ac.uk/wp-content/uploads/sites/47/2020/07/paper-2.pdf [Accessed 2 September 2023].

Neale, B. and Lau Clayton, C. (2014) Young parenthood and cross-generational relationships: the perspectives of young fathers, in J. Holland and R. Edwards (eds) *Understanding Families Over Time: Research and Policy*, London: Palgrave Macmillan, pp 69–87.

Neale, B. and Lau Clayton, C. (2015) *Grandparent Support? The Views of Young Fathers*, Following Young Fathers Briefing Paper no. 3, Leeds: University of Leeds. Available from: https://followingfathers.leeds.ac.uk/wp-content/uploads/sites/79/2015/10/Brieifing-Paper-3-V7.pdf [Accessed 2 September 2023].

Neale, B. and Morton, S. (2012) *Creating Impact Through Qualitative Longitudinal Research*, Timescapes Methods Guide No. 20, Leeds: Timescapes, University of Leeds. Available from: https://timescapes-archive.leeds.ac.uk/wp-content/uploads/sites/47/2020/07/timescapes-neale-creating-impact.pdf [Accessed 2 September 2023].

Neale, B. and Patrick, R. (2016) *Engaged Young Fathers? Gender, Parenthood and the Dynamics of Relationships*, Following Young Fathers Working Paper No. 1. Available from: https://followingfathers.leeds.ac.uk/wp-content/uploads/sites/79/2015/10/FYF-Working-Paper-Engaged-young-fathers.pdf [Accessed 21 December 2022].

Neale, B. and Smart, C. (2002) Caring, earning and changing: parenthood and employment after divorce, in A. Carling, S. Duncan and R. Edwards (eds) *Analysing Families: Morality and Rationality in Policy and Practice*, London: Routledge, pp 183–98.

Neale, B., Lau Clayton, C., Davies, L. and Ladlow, L. (2015) *Researching the Lives of Young Fathers: The Following Young Fathers Study and Dataset*, Following Young Fathers Briefing Paper no. 8, Leeds: University of Leeds. Available from: https://followingfathers.leeds.ac.uk/wp-content/uploads/sites/79/2015/10/Researching-the-Lives-of-Young-Fathers-updated-Oct-22.pdf [Accessed 2 September 2023].

Negura, L. and Deslauriers, J. (2010) Work and lifestyle: social representations among young fathers, *British Journal of Social Work*, 40(8): 2652–68.

Newton, B. (2014) Evaluation of the Youth Contract for 16–17 year-olds, *Employment Studies*, 20: 1–2.

Nicoll, A., Catchpole, M., Cliffe, S., Hughes, G., Simms, I. and Thomas, D. (1999) Sexual health of teenagers in England and Wales: Analysis of national data, *British Medical Journal*, 318: 1321–22.

Norman, H. and Davies, J. (2023) *What a Difference a Dad Makes: Paternal Involvement and its Effects on Children's Education*. PIECE study Leeds: University of Leeds.

NPI (New Policy Institute) (2015) *Poverty Among Young People in the UK*, London: New Policy Institute. Available from: https://www.npi.org.uk/files/7114/2892/2456/Poverty_among_young_people_in_the_UK_FINAL.pdf [Accessed 2 September 2023].

Nussbaum, M. (1996) Compassion: the basic social emotion, *Social Philosophy and Policy*, 13(1): 27–58.

Ofsted (Office for Standards in Education, Children's Services and Skills) (2013) *Not Yet Good Enough: Personal, Social, Health and Economic Education in Schools*. Available from: https://assets.publishing.service.gov.uk/government/uploads/system/uploads/attachment_data/file/413178/Not_yet_good_enough_personal__social__health_and_economic_education_in_schools.pdf [Accessed 2 January 2023].

ONS (Office of National Statistics) (2013) *An Overview of Forty Years of Data (General Lifestyle survey overview - a report of the General Lifestyle Survey 2011)*. London: Office of National Statistics.

ONS (Office for National Statistics) (2019) *Milestones: Journeying into Adulthood*, ONS, 18 February. Available from: https://www.ons.gov.uk/peoplepopulationandcommunity/populationandmigration/populationestimates/articles/milestonesjourneyingintoadulthood/2019-02-18 [Accessed 2 September 2023].

ONS (Office for National Statistics) (2020) *Young People Not in Education, Employment or Training (NEET), UK*: November 2020, ONS, 19 November. Available from: https://www.ons.gov.uk/employmentandlabourmarket/peoplenotinwork/unemployment/bulletins/youngpeoplenotineducationemploymentortrainingneet/november2020 [Accessed 2 January 2023].

ONS (Office for National Statistics) (2021) *Parenting in Lockdown: Coronavirus and The Effects on Work-life Balance*. Census data, 2021.

ONS (Office for National Statistics) (2022) *Birth Characteristics in England and Wales: 2017*, ONS. Available from: https://www.ons.gov.uk/peoplepopulationandcommunity/birthsdeathsandmarriages/livebirths/bulletins/birthcharacteristicsinenglandandwales/2017 [Accessed 2 September 2023].

ONS (Office for National Statistics) (2023) *Conceptions in England and Wales 2021*, ONS. Available from: https://www.ons.gov.uk/peoplepopulationandcommunity/birthsdeathsandmarriages/conceptionandfertilityrates/bulletins/conceptionstatistics/2021 [Accessed 2 September 2023].

Osborn, M. (2007) *'Being There': Young Men's Experience and Perception of Fatherhood*, doctoral thesis, Chelmsford: Anglia Ruskin University.

Osborn, M. (2015) Young fathers: unseen but not invisible, *Families, Relationships and Societies*, 4(2): 323–29.

Owens, R. (2022) 'It's the way they look at you': why discrimination towards young parents is a policy and practice issue, *Children & Society*, 36(6): 1280–95.

Padgett, D.K. (2007) There's no place like (a) home: ontological security among persons with serious mental illness in the United States, *Social Science & Medicine*, 64(9): 1925–36.

Paranjothy, S., Broughton, H., Adappa, R. and Fone, D. (2009) Teenage pregnancy: who suffers? *Archive of Disease in Childhood*, 94(3): 239–45.

Parikh, S.S. (2005) The other parent: a historical policy analysis of teen fathers, *Praxis*, 5: 13–21.

Parikh, S.S. (2009) Validating reciprocity: supporting young fathers' continued involvement with their children, *Families in Society: The Journal of Contemporary Social Services*, 90(3): 261–70.

Paschal, A. (2006) 'I'm doing what I have to do': African American teens and their experiences of fatherhood, *Dissertations Abstracts International, A: Humanities and Social Sciences*, 64: 2663-A.

Paschal, A., Lewis-Moss, R.K. and Hsiao, T. (2011) Perceived fatherhood roles, and parenting behaviours among African-American teen fathers, *Journal of Adolescent Research*, 26(1): 61–83.

Patrick, R. (2017) *For Whose Benefit? The Everyday Realities of Welfare Reform*, Bristol: Policy Press.

Pfitzner, N., Humphreys, C. and Hegarty, K. (2015) Engaging men: a multi-level model to support father engagement, *Child & Family Social Work*, 22(1): 537–47.

Pfitzner, N., Humphreys, C. and Hegarty, K. (2020) Bringing men in from the margins: Father-inclusive practices for the delivery of parenting interventions, *Child & Family Social Work*, 25(1): 198–206.

PHE and LGA (Public Health England and Local Government Association) (2018) *Teenage Pregnancy Prevention Framework*, London: PHE. Available from: https://assets.publishing.service.gov.uk/government/uploads/system/uploads/attachment_data/file/836597/Teenage_Pregnancy_Prevention_Framework.pdf [Accessed 20 December 2022].

PHE and LGA (Public Health England and Local Government Association) (2019 [2016]) *A Framework for Supporting Teenage Mothers and Young Fathers*, 2nd edn, London: PHE. Available from: https://assets.publishing.service.gov.uk/government/uploads/system/uploads/attachment_data/file/796582/PHE_Young_Parents_Support_Framework_April2019.pdf [Accessed 2 September 2023].

Philip, G., Clifton, J. and Brandon, M. (2019) The trouble with fathers: the impact of time and gendered-thinking on working relationships between fathers and social workers in child protection practice in England, *Journal of Family Issues*, 40(16): 2288–309.

Piachaud, D. and Sutherland, H. (2001) Child poverty in Britain and the New Labour government, *Journal of Social Policy*, 30(1): 95–118.

Pirog, M.A., Jung, H. and Lee, D. (2018) The changing face of teenage parenthood in the United States: evidence from NLSY79 and NLSY97, *Child & Youth Care Forum*, 47(3): 317–42.

Pirog-Good, M.A. (1995) The family background and attitudes of teen fathers, *Youth and Society*, 26(3): 351–76.

Pirog-Good, M.A. (1996) The education and labor market outcomes of adolescent fathers, *Youth and Society*, 28(2): 236–62.

Pollock, S., Trew, R. and Jones, K. (2005) *Young Black Fathers and Maternity Services*, London: Fathers Direct.

Poole, E., Speight, S., O'Brien, M., Connolly, S. and Aldrich, M. (2014) *Father Involvement with Children and Couple Relationships*, Modern Fatherhood Briefing Paper. Available from: http://www.modernfatherhood.org/wp-content/uploads/2014/10/Fathers-relationships-briefing-paper.pdf [Accessed 2 September 2023].

Poole, E., Speight, S., O'Brien, M., Connolly, S. and Aldrich, M. (2016) Who are non-resident fathers? A British socio-demographic profile, *Journal of Social Policy*, 45(2): 223–50.

Quail, K. (2007) Housing difficulties for teenage parents and their children: an East Midlands study, in P. Baker, K. Guthrie, C. Hutchinson, R. Kane and K. Wellings (eds) *Teenage Pregnancy and Reproductive Health*, London: Royal College of Obstetricians and Gynaecologists. Chapter 18.

Quilgars, D., Fitzpatrick, S. and Pleace, N. (2011) *Ending Youth Homelessness: Possibilities, Challenges and Practical Solutions*, July. Available from: https://www.york.ac.uk/media/chp/documents/2011/EndingYouthHomelessness.pdf [Accessed 2 September 2023].

Quinton, D., Pollock, S. and Golding, J. (2002) *The Transition to Fatherhood in Young Men: Influences on Commitment*, Report to the ESRC, Bristol: University of Bristol. Available from: https://research-information.bris.ac.uk/files/189625291/Final_report.doc [Accessed 2 September 2023].

Rantho, K. and Matlakala, F. (2021) Psychological and socio-economic challenges faced by teen fathers: a narrative review, *Humanities & Social Sciences Reviews*, 9(5): 62–7.

Rao, A.H. (2021) Gendered interpretations of job loss and subsequent professional pathways, *Gender and Society*, 35(6): 884–909.

RCPCH (Royal College of Paediatrics and Child Health) (2021) *Conceptions in Young People*, RCPCH, May. Available from: https://stateofchildhealth.rcpch.ac.uk/evidence/health-behaviours/conceptions-in-young-people/ [Accessed 2 September 2023].

Reeves, J. (2006) Recklessness, rescue and responsibility: young men tell their stories of the transition to fatherhood, *Practice*, 18(2): 79–90.

Reeves, J., Gale, L., Webb, J., Delaney, R. and Cocklin, N. (2009) Focusing on young men: developing integrated services for young fathers, *Community Practitioner*, 82(9): 18–21.

Rhein, L.M., Ginsburg, K.R., Schwarz, D.F., Pinto-Martin, J.A., Zhao, H., Morgan, A.P. and Slap, G.B. (1997) Teen father participation in child rearing: family perspectives, *Journal of Adolescent Health*, 21(4): 244–52.

Ridge, T. (2002) *Childhood Poverty and Social Exclusion: From a Child's Perspective*, Bristol: Policy Press.

Ridge, T. (2009) *Living with Poverty: A Review of the Literature on Children's and Families' Experience of Poverty*, Department for Work and Pensions, Research Report No. 594, Norwich: HMSO.

Ridge, T. (2015) *Understanding the Family-Work Project: Researching Low-Income Families Over Time*, conference presentation: Researching Relationships Across Generations and Through Time, FLAG Research Centre, University of Leeds, 9 June.

Roberts, S. (2013) 'Boys will be boys ... won't they?' Change and continuities in contemporary young working-class masculinities, *Sociology*, 47(4): 671–86.

Roberts, Y. (2013) Too young to be a dad?, *The Observer*, 11 August. Available from: https://www.theguardian.com/lifeandstyle/2013/aug/11/young-dad-teenage-fathers [Accessed 2 September 2023].

Robinson, B.E. (1988) *Teenage Fathers*, Lexington, MA: D.C. Heath.

Robinson, M., Templeton, M., Kelly, C., Grant, D., Buston, K., Hunt, K. and Lohan, M. (2023) Addressing sexual and reproductive health and rights with men in prisons: co-production and feasibility testing of a relationship, sexuality and future fatherhood education programme, *International Journal of Prisoner Health*, 19(3): 322–39.

Rolph, J. (1999) *Young, Unemployed, Unmarried … Fathers Talking*, London: Working with Men.

Romo, C., Bellamy, J. and Coleman, M.T. (2004) *TFF Final Evaluation Report*, Austin, TX: Texas Fragile Families Initiative.

Ross, N.J., Church, S., Hill, M., Seaman, P. and Roberts, T. (2010) The perspectives of young men and their teenage partners on maternity and health services during pregnancy and early parenthood, *Children & Society*, 24(6): 304–15.

Rouch G. (2005) *Boys Raising Babies: Adolescent Fatherhood in New Zealand*, New Zealand: Barnardos.

Rouch, G. (2009) *Low-Skilled, Low Socio-economic, Young, Co-resident, Working Fathers: Their Experience of Fatherhood*, PhD dissertation, Palmerston North, New Zealand: Massey University. Available from: https://mro.massey.ac.nz/bitstream/handle/10179/1283/01front.pdf [Accessed 2 September 2023].

Roy, K. (2004) 'You can't eat love': negotiating provider role expectations from low income fathers and families, *Fathering*, 2(3): 253–76.

Rua, M. (2015) *Māori Men's Positive and Interconnected Sense of Self, Being and Place*, PhD thesis, Hamilton, New Zealand: University of Waikato. Available from: http://hdl.handle.net/10289/9440 [Accessed 2 September 2023].

Sadler, L.S. and Clemmens, D.A. (2004) Ambivalent grandmothers raising teen daughters and their babies, *Journal of Family Nursing*, 10(2): 211–31.

SEF (Sex Education Forum) (2015) *Sex and Relationship Education: The Evidence*, Sex Education Forum Evidence Briefing, London: SEF. Available from: https://www.sexeducationforum.org.uk/sites/default/files/field/attachment/SRE - the evidence - March 2015.pdf [Accessed 2 September 2023].

SEF (Sex Education Forum) (2016) *Heads or Tails? What Young People Tell Us About SRE*, London: SEF. Available from: https://www.sexeducationforum.org.uk/resources/evidence/heads-or-tails-what-young-people-are-telling-us-about-sre [Accessed 2 September 2023].

SEF (Sex Education Forum) (2018) *Statutory RSE: Are Teachers in England Prepared?*, London: SEF. Available from: https://www.sexeducationforum.org.uk/resources/evidence/statutory-rse-are-teachers-england-prepared [Accessed 2 September 2023].

SEF (Sex Education Forum) (2022) *New Polling Shows Young People are being Failed by Poor Relationships and Sex Education in Schools and at Home*, Sex Education Forum Press Release, 1 February. Available from: https://www.sexeducationforum.org.uk/news/news/new-polling-shows-young-people-are-being-failed-poor-relationships-and-sex-education [Accessed 2 September 2023].

Seidler, Z., Dawes, A., Rice, S., Oliffe, J. and Dhillon, H. (2016) The role of masculinity in men's help-seeking for depression: a systematic review, *Clinical Psychology Review*, 49: 106–18.

SEU (Social Exclusion Unit) (1999) *Teenage Pregnancy: Report by the Social Exclusion Unit*, Cm. 4342, London: HMSO. Available from: https://dera.ioe.ac.uk/id/eprint/15086/1/teenage-pregnancy.pdf [Accessed 2 September 2023].

Shannon, S.K.S. and Abrams, L.S. (2007) Juvenile offenders as fathers: perceptions of fatherhood, crime and becoming an adult, *Families in Society*, 88(2): 183–91.

Sheeran, N., Jones, L., Bernardin, S., Wood, M., Doherty, L. et al (2021) Immoral, incompetent, and lacking warmth: how stereotypes of teenage fathers compare to those of other parents, *Sex Roles*, 84: 360–75.

Shepherd, J., Ludvigsen, A. and Hamilton, W. (2011) *Parents of Teenage Parents: Research, Issues and Practice, Summary Report*, Brighton: Young People in Focus.

Sherriff, T. (2007) *Supporting Young Fathers: Examples of Promising Practice*, Brighton: Trust for the Study of Adolescence.

Shields, N. and Pierce, L. (2006) Controversial issues surrounding teen pregnancy, in H.S. Holgate, R. Evans and F.K.O. Yuen (eds) *Teenage Pregnancy and Parenthood: Global Perspectives, Issues and Interventions*, Abingdon: Routledge, pp 122–39.

Shildrick, T., MacDonald, R., Webster, C. and Garthwaite, K. (2012) *Poverty and Insecurity: Life in Low-Pay, No-Pay Britain*, Bristol: Policy Press.

Shirani, F. (2015) 'I'm bringing back a dead art': continuity and change in the lives of young fathers, *Families, Relationships and Societies*, 4(2): 253–66.

Simmons, R., Russell, L. and Thompson, R. (2014) Young people and labour market marginality: findings from a longitudinal ethnographic study, *Journal of Youth Studies*, 17(5): 577–91.

Simpson, B., McCarthy, P. and Walker, J. (1995) *Being There: Fathers After Divorce*, Newcastle upon Tyne: Relate Centre for Family Studies.

Smart, C. and Neale, B. (1999) *Family Fragments?*, Cambridge: Polity Press.

SmithBattle, L. (1996) Intergenerational ethics of care for teenage mothers and their children, *Family Relations*, 45(1): 56–64.

SmithBattle, L. (2013) Reducing the stigmatization of teen mothers, *MCN: The American Journal of Maternal/Child Nursing*, 38(4): 235–41.

SmithBattle, L., Phengnum, W., Shagavah, A.W. and Okawa, S. (2019a) Fathering on tenuous ground: a qualitative meta-synthesis on teen fathering. *MCN: The American Journal of Maternal/Child Nursing*, 44(4): 186–94.

SmithBattle, L., Punsuwun, S. and Phengnum, W. (2019b) An umbrella review of qualitative research on teen mothering, *Western Journal of Nursing Research*, 43(5): 488478–488.

Somerville, P. (2016) Coalition housing policy in England, in H. Bochel and M. Powell (eds) *The Coalition Government and Social Policy: Restructuring the Welfare State*, Bristol: Policy Press, pp 153–78.

Speak, S. (2006) Being there: roles and aspirations of young single non-residential fathers, in H.S. Holgate, R. Evans and F.K.O. Yuen (eds) *Teenage Pregnancy and Parenthood: Global Perspectives Issues and Interventions*, Abingdon: Routledge, pp 140–9.

Speak, S., Cameron, S. and Gilroy, R. (1997) *Young Single Fathers: Participation in Fatherhood, Bridges and Barriers*, Oxford: Family Policy Studies Centre/York: Joseph Rowntree Foundation.

Srion, N. (2014) *Fathering Experience of Male Teenagers*, Master's thesis of nursing science, Bangkok: Chulalongkorn University. Available from: http://cuir.car.chula.ac.th/handle/123456789/44506 [Accessed 4 July 2016].

Sriyasak, A., Almqvist, A., Sridawruang, C., Neamsakul, W. and Häggström-Nordin, E. (2016) Struggling with motherhood and coping with fatherhood: a grounded theory study among Thai teenagers, *Midwifery*, 42: 1–9.

Statista (2023) *Number of Live Births in the United Kingdom from 1887 to 2021*, https://www.statista.com/statistics/281981/live-births-in-the-united-kingdom-uk/ [Accessed 26 September 2023].

Stephens, M. and Stephenson, A. (2016) Housing policy in the austerity age and beyond, in M. Fenger, J. Hudson and C. Needham (eds) *Social Policy Review 28: Analysis and Debate in Social Policy*, Bristol: Policy Press, pp 63–85.

Stone, J., Berrington, A. and Falkingham, J. (2014) Gender, turning points, and Boomerangs: returning home in young adulthood in Great Britain, *Demography*, 51: 257–76.

Swann, C., Bowe, K., McCormick, G. and Kosmin, M. (2003) *Teenage Pregnancy and Parenthood: A Review of Reviews, Evidence Briefing*, London: Health Development Agency.

Swartz, S. and Bhana, A. (2009) *Teenage Tata: Voices of Young Fathers in South Africa*, Cape Town: HSRC Press.

Tabberer, S., Hall, C., Prendergast, S. and Webster, A. (2000) *Teenage Pregnancy and Choice: Abortion or Motherhood – Influences on the Decision*, York: Joseph Rowntree Foundation.

Tach, L., Mincy, R. and Edin, K. (2010) Parenting as a 'package deal': relationships, fertility and nonresident father involvement among unmarried parents, *Demography*, 47(1): 181–204.

Tan, J.P., Buchanan, A., Flouri, E., Attar-Schwartz, S. and Griggs, J. (2010) Filling the parenting gap? Grandparent involvement with UK adolescents. *Journal of Family Issues*, 31(7): 992–1015.

Tarrant, A. (2012) 'Grandfathering: the construction of new identities and masculinities', in S. Arber and V. Timonen (eds) *Contemporary Grandparenting: Changing Family Relationships in Global Contexts*, Bristol: Policy Press, pp 181–202.

Tarrant, A. (2014) Grandfathering as spatio-temporal practice: conceptualizing performances of ageing masculinities in contemporary familial carescapes, *Social & Cultural Geography*, 14(2): 192–210.

Tarrant, A. (2017) Getting out of the swamp? Methodological reflections on using qualitative secondary analysis to develop research design, *International Journal of Social Research Methodology*, 20(6): 599–611.

Tarrant, A. (2018) Care in an age of austerity: men's care responsibilities in low-income families, *Ethics and Social Welfare*, 12(1): 38–48.

Tarrant, A. (2021) *Fathering and Poverty: Uncovering Men's Participation in Low-Income Family Life*, Bristol: Policy Press.

Tarrant, A. (2023) Instigating father-inclusive practice interventions with young fathers and multi-agency professionals: the transformative potential of qualitative longitudinal and co-creative methodologies, *Families, Relationships and Societies*, Early View. Available from: https://doi.org/10.1332/204674321X16913136250482 [Accessed 3 September 2023].

Tarrant, A. and Hughes, K. (2019) Qualitative secondary analysis: building longitudinal samples to understand men's generational identities in low income contexts, *Sociology*, 53(3): 538–53.

Tarrant, A. and Neale, B. (eds) (2017a) *Learning to Support Young Dads: Responding to Young Fathers in a Different Way*, Leeds: School of Sociology and Social Policy, University of Leeds. Available from: https://followingfathers.leeds.ac.uk/wp-content/uploads/sites/79/2017/04/SYD-final-report.pdf [Accessed 20 December 2020].

Tarrant, A. and Neale, B. (2017b) *Supporting Young Fathers in Welfare Settings: An Evidence Review of What Matters and What Helps*, Leeds: Social Sciences Institute, University of Leeds. Available from: https://followingfathers.leeds.ac.uk/wp-content/uploads/sites/79/2016/06/Evidence-Report.pdf [Accessed 20 December 2020].

Tarrant, A., Featherstone, B., O'Dell, L. and Fraser, C. (2017) 'You try to keep a brave face on but inside you are in bits': grandparent experiences of engaging with professionals in Children's Services, *Qualitative Social Work*, 16(3): 351–66.

Tarrant, A., Ladlow, L., Johansson, T., Andreasson, J. and Way, L. (2022) The impacts of the COVID-19 pandemic and lockdown policies on young fathers: comparative insights from the UK and Sweden, *Social Policy and Society*, Online First. Available from: https://doi.org/10.1017/S1474746422000586 [Accessed 3 September 2023].

Tarrant, A., Ladlow, L. and Way, L. (2020a) *From Social Isolation to Local Support: Relational Change and Continuities of Young Fathers in the Context of the COVID 19 Crisis*, Following Young Fathers Further Briefing Paper Two, December, Lincoln: University of Lincoln. Available from: https://fyff.co.uk/files/a755c5d5a520438e2deb94c843d53de523d04b23.pdf [Accessed 2 January 2023].

Tarrant, A., Way, L. and Ladlow, L. (2020b) *Negotiating 'Earning' and 'Caring' through the COVID-19 Crisis: Change and Continuities in the Parenting and Employment Trajectories of Young Fathers*, Following Young Fathers Further Briefing Paper One, December, Lincoln: University of Lincoln. Available from: https://fyff.co.uk/files/a3f0c3fb94e33eddceca475dbfdf051382eb3212.pdf [Accessed 2 January 2023].

Tarrant, A., Way, L. and Ladlow, L. (2021) *Supporting at a Distance: The Challenges and Opportunities of Supporting Young Fathers Through the COVID-19 Pandemic*, Following Young Fathers Further Briefing Paper Three, June, Lincoln: University of Lincoln. Available from: https://fyff.co.uk/files/96385a305eda72b7f8396b1075c81472d8b27c8d.pdf [Accessed 2 January 2023].

Taylor, C. (1992) The politics of recognition, in A. Gutmann (ed) *Multiculturalism and 'The Politics of Recognition'*, Princeton, NJ: Princeton University Press, pp 25–73.

Telegraph (2009) Teenage fatherhood and underage sex glamorised in Government guidance, *The Telegraph*, 17 February. Available from: https://www.telegraph.co.uk/women/mother-tongue/4644539/Teenage-fatherhood-and-underage-sex-glamorised-in-Government-guidance.html [Accessed 3 September 2023].

Tillman, K.H., Brewster, K.L. and Holway, G.V. (2019) Sexual and romantic relationships in young adulthood, *Annual Review of Sociology*, 45: 133–53.

Toledo-Dreves, V., Zabin, L.S. and Emerson, M.R. (1995) Durations of adolescent sexual relationships before and after conception, *Journal of Adolescent Health*, 17(3): 163–72.

Torres de Lacerda, A., Lucena de Vasconcelos, M., Nascimento de Alencar, E., Osório, M.M. and Pontes, C.M. (2014) Adolescent fathers: knowledge of and involvement in the breast feeding process in Brazil, *Midwifery*, 30(3): 338–44.

Townsend, N.W. (2002) *The Package Deal: Marriage, Work and Fatherhood in Men's Lives*, Philadelphia, PA: Temple University Press.

TPIAG (Teenage Pregnancy Independent Advisory Group) (2002) *First Annual Report*, London: TPIAG.

TPIAG (Teenage Pregnancy Independent Advisory Group) (2010) *Teenage Pregnancy: Past Successes, Future Challenges, Final Report*, London: TPIAG.

TPU (Teenage Pregnancy Unit) (2000) *Guidance for Developing Contraception and Sexual Health Advice Services to Reach Boys and Young Men*, London: TPU.

Trinder, L. (2008) Maternal gate closing and gate opening in postdivorce families, *Journal of Family Issues*, 29(10): 1298–324.

Trivedi, B., Bunn, F., Graham, M. and Wentz, R. (2007) *Update on Review of Reviews on Teenage Pregnancy and Parenthood*, Report for the National Institute for Health and Clinical Excellence (NICE). Hatfield: Centre for Research in Primary Community Care, University of Hertfordshire.

Trivedi, D., Brooks, F., Bunn, F. and Graham, M. (2009) Early fatherhood: a mapping of the evidence base relating to pregnancy prevention and parenting support, *Health Education Research*, 24(6): 999–1028.

Tuffin, K., Rouch, G. and Frewin, K. (2010) Constructing adolescent fatherhood: responsibilities and intergenerational repair, *Culture, Health & Sexuality*, 12(5): 485–98.

Tuffin, K., Rouch, G. and Frewin, K. (2018) The 'missing' parent: teenage fathers talk about the meaning of early parenthood, in A. Kamp, and M. McSharry (eds) *Re/assembling the Pregnant and Parenting Teenager: Narratives from the Field(s)*, Oxford: Peter Lang, pp 269–90.

Tyrer, P., Chase, E., Warwick, I. and Aggleton, P. (2005) 'Dealing with it': experience of young fathers in and leaving care, *British Journal of Social Work*, 35(7): 1107–121.

Uengwongsapat, C., Kantaruksa, K., Klunklin, A. and Sansiriphun, N. (2017) Growing into teen fatherhood: a grounded theory study, *International Nursing Review*, 65(2): 244–53.

Ugwudike, P. (2018) *Supporting Young Fathers in Prison: An Evaluation of PACTS Family Support Service*, Southampton: University of Southampton. Available from: https://eprints.soton.ac.uk/429629/1/Policy_Brief.pdf [Accessed 3 September 2023].

UNICEF (2021) *Early Childbearing*, UNICEF, December. Available from: https://data.unicef.org/topic/child-health/adolescent-health/ [Accessed 3 September 2023].

van den Berg, L., Kalmijn, M. and Leopold, T. (2018) Leaving and returning home: a new approach to off-time transitions, *Journal of Marriage and Family*, 81(3): 679–95.

Vizard, P. and Hills, J. (eds) (2021) *The Conservative Government's Record on Social Policy from May 2015 to pre-COVID 2020: Policies, Spending and Outcomes*, Summary Reports, London: London School of Economics. Available from: https://sticerd.lse.ac.uk/dps/case/spdo/SPDO_overview_paper_summary.pdf [Accessed 3 September 2023].

Walker, C. and Roberts, S. (eds) (2018) *Masculinity, Labour, and Neoliberalism: Working-Class Men in International Perspective*, Cham: Palgrave Macmillan.

Walker, R. (ed) (1999) *Ending Child Poverty: Popular Welfare for the 21st Century?*, Bristol: Policy Press.

Ward, M.R.M. (2015) *From Labouring to Learning: Working-Class Masculinities, Education and De-Industrialization*, Basingstoke: Palgrave Macmillan.

Ward, M.R.M., Tarrant, A., Terry, G., Featherstone, B., Robb, M. and Ruxton, S. (2017) Doing gender locally: the importance of 'place' in understanding marginalised masculinities and young men's transitions to 'safe' and successful futures, *Sociological Review*, 65(4): 797–815.

Way, L. and Tarrant, A. (2022) *Establishing the Young Dads Collective in Grimsby: Support for Young Fathers 'By Grimsby, For Grimsby'*, October, Lincoln: University of Lincoln. Available from: https://fyff.blogs.lincoln.ac.uk/files/2021/02/YDC-Grimsby-Webinar-Report.pdf&hl=en [Accessed 3 September 2023].

Way, L., Tarrant, A., Ladlow, L., York, J., Gorzelanczyk, A., Brown, D. and Patterson, W. (2022) Co-creating with young men: producing community informed training videos to foster more inclusive support environments for young fathers, *Sociological Research Online*, 27(3): 675–83.

Weber, J.B. (2012) Becoming teen fathers: stories of teen pregnancy, responsibility, and masculinity, *Gender & Society*, 26(6): 900–21.

Weber, J.B. (2018) 'It changed my life': rethinking the consequences of teenage fatherhood, in A. Kamp and M. McSharry (eds) *Re/assembling the Pregnant and Parenting Teenager: Narratives from the Field(s)*, Oxford: Peter Lang, pp 105–26.

Weber, J.B. (2020) Being there (or not): teen dads, gendered age, and negotiating the absent-father discourse, *Men and Masculinities*, 23(1): 42–64.

Weed, K., Nicholson, J.S. and Farris, J.R. (2015) *Teen Pregnancy and Parenting: Rethinking the Myths and Misperceptions*, Abingdon: Routledge.

Wei, E., Loeber, R. and Stouthamer-Loeber, M. (2002) How many of the offspring born to teenage fathers are produced by repeat serious delinquents? *Criminal Behaviour and Mental Health*, 12(1): 83–98.

Wellard, S., Meakings, S., Farmer, E. and Hunt, J. (2017) *Growing Up in Kinship Care: Experiences as Adolescents and Outcomes in Young Adulthood*, London: Grandparents Plus.

Weller, S., Davidson, E., Edwards, R. and Jamieson, L. (forthcoming) *Big Qual: A Guide to Breadth and Depth Analysis*, London: Palgrave Macmillan.

Wellings, K. and Kane, R. (1999) Trends in teenage pregnancy in England and Wales: how can we explain them?, *Journal of the Royal Society of Medicine*, 92(6): 277–82.

Wellings, K., Jones, K.G., Mercer, C.H., Tanton, C., Clifton, S., Datta, A., et al (2013) The prevalence of unplanned pregnancy and associated factors in Britain: findings from the 3rd National Survey of Sexual Attitudes and Lifestyles, *Lancet*, 382(9907): 1807–16.

Wellings, K., Palmer, M., Geary, R., Gibson, L., Copas, A., Datta, A., et al (2016) Changes in conception in women younger than 18 years and the circumstances of young mothers in England in 2000–2012: an observational study, *Lancet*, 6(388): 586–95.

Welshman, J. (2008) The cycle of deprivation: myths and misconceptions, *Children & Society*, 22(2): 75–85.

Wenham, A. (2013) Teenage pregnancy and parenthood: implications for policy and practice, in S. Curran, R. Harrison and D. Mackinnon (eds) *Working with Young People*, 2nd edn, London: Sage, pp 37–47.

West, M. (2016) *Compassion is the Core NHS Value – Not Bullying*. Formerly available from: https://leadershipacademy.nhs.uk/.

Wiggins, M., Oakley, A., Sawtell, M., Austerberry, H., Clemens, F. and Elbourne, D. (2005) *Teenage Parenthood and Social Exclusion: A Multi-Method Study, Summary Report of Findings*, London: University of London Institute of Education. Available from: https://discovery.ucl.ac.uk/10003007/1/Wiggins2005TeenageParenthood.pdf [Accessed 3 September 2023].

Wilkes, L., Mannix, J. and Jackson, D. (2012) 'I am going to be a dad': experiences and expectations of adolescent and young adult expectant fathers, *Journal of Clinical Nursing*, 21(1/2): 180–8.

Williams, F. (2004) *Rethinking Families*, London: Calouste Gulbenkian Foundation.

Williamson, H. (2021) *The Milltown Boys at Sixty: The Origins and Destinations of Young Men from a Poor Neighbourhood*, Abingdon: Routledge.

Wilson, K.R. and Prior, M.R. (2011) Father involvement and child well-being, *Journal of Paediatrics and Child Health*, 47(7): 405–7.

Wyn, J. (2014) Conceptualising transitions to adulthood, *New Directions in Adult and Continuing Education*, 143: 5–16.

Youth Parliament (2007) *SRE: Are You Getting It?*, London: UK Youth Parliament. Available from: https://web.archive.org/web/20081107152553/http://www.ukyouthparliament.org.uk/campaigns/sre/AreYouGettingIt.pdf [Accessed 3 September 2023].

Youth Employment UK (nd) *Youth Unemployment*. Available from: https://www.youthemployment.org.uk/youth-unemployment/ [Accessed 2 January 2023].

Index

References to figures appear in *italic* type.

A

abortion 35, 78, 79, 92, 122, 218
absent fathers
  'breadwinner' ideologies 138
  difficulties in researching 22, 59, 225
  Following Young Fathers (FYF) study 60
  social engagement framework 22–3
  social problems framework 2
  young fathers' own 17, 120
abstinence, promotion of 75
abuse 107, 112, 115, 130
Action for Children 160
action research 67
Adam
  adjusting to the pregnancy 80–1
  constrained contact 89, 92–3
  contraception 76
  employment 137
  engagement with support services 183–4, 186, 191
  fragile father-child relationships 87
  homelessness 92, 153
  housing 125, 172
  learning childcare skills 103–4
  multi-agency professional support 183–4
  multiple children 92–3
  paternal grandparents 125
  pen portrait 236
  reactions to pregnancy 77
  Relationship and Sex Education (RSE) 74
  relationship with child's mother 103, 104–5, 108, 129, 172
  relationship with grandparents 132, 172
adulthood transitions
  compassionate social policy 217–18
  delayed 158
  destandardisation of 159
  education, employment and training (EET) 138, 141, 143, 154–5
  emerging adult responsibility narratives 80
  fast-tracking to adulthood 80–3, 104, 121
  housing 163
  intergenerational care and support 121
  new parenthood as 2–4
  see also transition to young fatherhood
Alexander, C. 15
Allen, G. 4

ALSPAC (Avon Longitudinal Study of Parents and Children) 16
ambassadorial roles 178, 196, 197, 208, 233
Andreasson, J. 69, 228
Andrew
  constrained contact 89
  education 152
  employment 152–3
  housing 171–2
  pen portrait 236–7
  providing for children 143
  reactions to pregnancy 78
  relationship with child's mother 103, 108, 152, 171
  relationship with own father 130–1
anger management 89, 105, 108, 115
antenatal classes 81
antenatal support for young fathers 181–3
Anthony (Young Dad's Council) 66
anxiety 87
APPGF (All-Party Parliamentary Group on Fatherhood) 65, 210
APPGPF/APPGSM (All-Party Parliamentary Group on Parents and Families/All-Party Parliamentary Group on Social Mobility) 50, 65
APPGYE (All-Party Parliamentary Group on Youth Employment) 140, 141
apprenticeships 149, 151, 153, 155
Arai, L. 32, 33, 42
'Ask a Dad' workshop 209, 211
attendance at birth 83–4
attrition rates 60
austerity 4, 40, 135, 140, 159
Australia 15
average age of fatherhood 15
Ayton, R. 15

B

Barnardo's 64
Bateson, K. 200
'being there'
  'breadwinner' ideologies 138
  co-parenting relationships 103, 104, 105, 109, 114, 115, 220
  financial support 143, 154
  grandparents 122, 127
  housing 161, 169
  providing for children 104, 143

Index

social engagement framework 2, 20, 217
sustained father-child relationships 85–7
transition to young fatherhood 81, 82
Bekele, pen portrait 237
Ben
  birth as a turning point 84, 124
  challenges of being a dad 82–3
  decision to keep child 79
  education 145
  housing 158
  parenting at a distance 86–7
  pen portrait 237–8
  reactions to pregnancy 77, 78, 82
  relationship with child's mother 102–3, 109
  relationship with grandparents 128
  work aspirations 145, 146
benefit sanctions 141, 152, 156, 224
Berger, L.M. 18
Berrington, A.M. 16, 160
Biggart, A. 159
birth as a turning point 83–4, 85, 124
Birth Cohort Study (BCS70) 16
birth registration 23
birth statistics 14
birthing partners 124
Blair, Tony 33, 39
blame 43, 44, 122, 196
breadwinning 24, 126, 137–56, 222
British Household Panel Study 15, 17
Bulman, K. 64–5, 67, 194, 197, 201, 203, 204, 205, 206, 233
Bunting, L. 27
bus fares 168
buying a home 159, 161
Bynner, J. 4, 155

C

Cade
  birth as a turning point 124
  engagement with support services 186
  housing 172–3
  pen portrait 238–9
CAFCASS (Child and Family Court Advisory and Support Service) 184, 186, 192
Callum
  birth as a turning point 83
  constrained contact 89
  contraception 76
  decision to keep child 123
  drugs and alcohol 144
  education, employment and training (EET) 153
  engagement with support services 186, 191–2
  financial struggles 144, 153
  financial support 126
  grandparent support 127

housing 163
mental health issues 144
multiple children 93–4
parenting at a distance 111–12, 132–3, 153
pen portrait 239
recruitment to study 95
relationship with child's mother 103, 182
relationship with grandparents 132–3, 153
relationship with stepfather 122
support during pregnancy 182
Cameron, David 44
Canada 55
care, children being taken into 89, 189
care, young fathers' history of being in 89, 120, 139, 204
'Care to Learn' grants 139
career motivations, children as 145
'caring' as core attribute of fatherhood 143
caring roles 138
'cash and care' model of parenting 138
casual relationships 27
casualised workforces 140, 150, 153, 154
causal factors 6, 16, 54, 60, 142, 225
census data 14
change for the better, children bring about 85–7, 105–6
child benefits 130, 131
child poverty 38–9, 40
child protection 89, 92, 108, 131
Child Support Agency 47
child support payments 147
childcare
  funding for 139
  grandparents 118, 125
  inexperience in baby care 103
  lack of affordable 141
  sustaining relationships at close hand 103–4
childhoods, young fathers' own 17, 95, 105, 108, 130, 139, 183, 202
Children Act 1989 21
Children and Families Act 2014 21
Children's Centres 34, 35, 40, 47, 65, 187, 205
citizenship 229, 232–4
Clay, C.M. 11, 12
Clayton, C. 52
'clean break' divorce/split 26
close hand, parenting at 103–8
close layering of generations 118, 120, 131
Coalition government 31, 35–8, 40, 44–5, 47, 50, 139, 141, 159, 174, 231
co-dissemination of education and training 211–13
co-habitation 27–8, 99, 100, 174
cohort studies 13, 16, 55
Coles, B. 3
Colfer, S. 66, 193–4, 207, 208

collaborative research design 62–6, 68
collaborative writing project 66
community-based parenting programmes 184–5
comparative studies 12, 69, 226
compassionate social policy 7, 19, 216, 227–33
conception patterns 1, 4, 14, 15, 19, 34, 38, 42, 57, 75, 95
conference for practitioners 66
Connexions 35, 36, 149, 155, 192, 193
Conservative governments 31, 32–3, 35–8, 39, 44, 47, 119, 141, 159, 174, 231
contact with children
  constrained contact 89–92, 103
  court proceedings 90, 92, 93, 110, 111, 188–9, 190, 221
  curtailing of contact 89–92, 93, 98, 103, 110–14, 146–7, 154, 168, 183, 188, 221
  dual residency for children 86
  'every other weekend' 110, 146
  legal advice for contact issues 183
  overnights 86, 109
  parenting at a distance 26, 27, 86, 103, 108–14, 161, 220
  sidelining by professional support agencies 189
  supervised visits 88, 90, 91, 92, 93–4, 108, 186
  typology of child contact 99, *101*
  whilst in prison 202
  see also co-parenting relationships
continuity questions 61
contraception
  to avoid second pregnancy 92
  Conservative governments 33
  free NHS 32
  knowledge about contraception 75–7
  left to female partners 75–7
  preference to delay parenthood 35
  priority given to 76
  young men learning about 74–5
controlling behaviours 107
co-parenting relationships
  engaged fatherhood 25–9, 84
  gendered dynamics of young relationships 97–116
  housing *162*
  intergenerational care and support 124, 126–7, 129, 168
  living with grandparents 168
  professional support 194
  relational skills 220–1
  work aspirations 146
co-production of knowledge 63, 198
co-research methods 66
co-residence 99, 165–8
Corlyon, J. 26

costs of supporting young parents 32, 33
counselling 181, 192, 206, 221, 232
court proceedings 90, 92, 93, 110, 111, 188–9, 190, 221
COVID-19 38, 140, 213
criminal activity 144, 223
criminal justice system 88–9, 186–7, 194, 201–7
cross-sectional research approaches 65–6
Crow, G. 4
curtailing of contact 89, 93, 98, 103, 110–14, 146–7, 154, 168, 183, 188, 221
cycles of deprivation/disadvantage 36, 119

D

Daguerre. A. 44
dangerous pastimes, stopping 81
Daniel (contributions to research dissemination) 66
Darren
  adjusting to the pregnancy 80
  birth as a turning point 124
  contraception 76
  decision to keep child 79
  engagement with support services 185, 191
  grandparent reactions to pregnancy 121
  housing 170, 174
  multiple children 92
  pen portrait 239–40
  reactions to pregnancy 77, 82
  Relationship and Sex Education (RSE) 75
  relationship with child's mother 107, 174
  relationship with grandparents 132
  relationship with own father 130
data analysis 61, 62, 68
Davies, David 45
Davies, Laura 31, 48, 56, 65, 66, 111, 137, 179, 180, 183, 185, 186, 187, 188, 191, 192, 194, 195, 196, 200, 203, 208, 227, 233
'deadbeat' dads 46, 217
Decent Homes Standard 159
defeatist staff mindsets 34
deficit model of young parenthood
  conceptions of early parenthood 2, 18–19, 22
  education, employment and training (EET) 138, 155
  gendered dynamics of young relationships 112, 115
  'hard to reach' label 180
  implications for policy 226–7
  intergenerational care and support 119
  policy context 43–4
  unemployment 140
  see also social deficit framework
definition of 'young father' 14

Index

delinquency 18–19
demographic data 14
denial of paternity 22
depression 87
see also mental health issues
depth versus breadth of investigation 70
Deslauriers, J.M. 23, 62, 157, 179, 193, 194, 196, 200
deviance 43
different mothers, children with 93–4
DigiDAD 196
digital support services 196, 207
dignity, respect and recognition 41
disadvantaged young fathers
  employment 141
  grandparents 118, 227
  housing 163–4, 223
  less likely to be involved fathers 18
  likelihood of relationship breakdown 27
  losing contact with children 26
  low-skilled work 150–3
  need for professional support 183–5
  NEET (not in education, employment or training) 139
  policy context 40
  poverty as main factor in poor life chances 155
  stereotypes 18
  see also childhoods, young fathers' own
disengagement from services 194–6
dissemination of research 65–7
distance, parenting at a 26, 27, 86, 103, 108–14, 161, 220
Diverse Dads Collective 21
diversity of sample 59
doctors' appointments, attending 81
doing better than own father, as goal 20
domestic violence 108, 112, 115, 130, 131, 132, 171, 175–6, 206, 221
domestic/housework 103
Dominic
  birth as a turning point 84
  contraception 76
  decision to keep child 79, 123
  grandparent reactions to pregnancy 121
  housing 166–7
  parenting at a distance 86, 103, 110–11, 129, 146, 154, 166
  pen portrait 240
  Relationship and Sex Education (RSE) 75
  relationship with grandparents 129, 130
  skilled work 146–7
  sustained father-child relationships 85, 86, 147
Donald, L. 18, 27, 29, 94, 119, 153
double precarity 175, 227
drugs and alcohol 81, 107, 112, 130, 131, 153, 223

dual residency for children 86
Duncan, S. 2, 42
DWP (Department for Work and Pensions) 65
dynamic nature of young fatherhood 4–5, 55, 102–14, 194–5, 196, 201

E

Early Intervention Foundation 65
early intervention services 36, 116, 194
early onset of sexual activity 19
early parenthood patterns 1–2
earning, learning and caring burden 145–7, 154, 165, 184, 222
ecological approach to social inquiry 62
Economic and Social Research Council 1, 52, 53
economic views of fatherhood 138, 154
ecosystemic frameworks 23
Edin, K. 11, 25, 26, 76, 82, 86, 114, 143
education
  earning, learning and caring burden 145–7, 154, 165, 184, 222
  education, employment and training (EET) 33–4, 41, 137–56, 161, 163, 222
  education funding 139
  educational achievement and likelihood of early fatherhood 17
  extension beyond traditional school-leaving age 3
  higher education 142, 145, 146, 148, 170
Educational Maintenance Allowance 141
e-learning programmes 196
emerging adult responsibility narratives 80
Emmel, N. 4, 118, 119, 135
emotional connectedness 86
emotional disengagement 91
emotional engagement 85, 86, 95, 104, 218
emotional literacy 84
employment 137–56
  casualised workforces 140, 150, 153, 154
  earning, learning and caring burden 145–7, 154, 165, 184, 222
  grandparent care 118
  insecure work 3, 149, 150
  low-paid work 149, 222
  low-skilled work 140, 142, 144, 149, 150–3, 163
  part-time work 145, 147
  preoccupation with work forced by pregnancy 81
  semi-skilled work 142, 146, 147–50, 161
  separation from children for 24
  skilled work 145–7
  temporary work 140, 148
  training opportunities 139, 141, 149, 151–2, 155, 198

underemployment 140
in-work poverty 41, 140
work-based aspirations 143–53
Young Dads Collective 211
young people generally 41
zero-hours jobs 140
see also precarity; unemployment
engaged fatherhood
  benefits of engaged fatherhood 20–1
  co-parenting relationships 25–9, 84
  cultural shift towards 116
  disengagement from services 188
  economic views of fatherhood 154
  limited opportunities to demonstrate 189
  providing for children 222
  social engagement framework 20–1
  see also 'being there'; social engagement framework
engagement with support services 180
engaging young fathers in research 66–7
ethics of longitudinal studies 53
ethnic minorities 16, 59
Eurostat 158
'every other weekend' 110, 146
evidence-based policy 51
evidence-informed practice 210
existing evidence, nature of 11–12
exosystem 157, 179
  see also policy context
experts by experience 6, 66, 178, 196, 207–9

F

family courts 110, 221
family hubs 47
family law 116, 192, 221, 226, 254
Family Nurse Partnership scheme 35, 36, 48, 104, 183–4
family support services 65
Fatherhood Programme, Oakhill Secure Training Centre 203
father-inclusive practices 200
Featherstone, B. 50
'feckless' label 2, 43, 46, 50, 73, 74, 129, 192, 193
Ferguson, H. 181, 184, 186, 194, 195, 196, 199, 200
financial support
  'breadwinner' ideologies 138–9
  child support payments 147
  earning, learning and caring burden 145–7, 154, 165, 184, 222
  education, employment and training (EET) 137–56
  grandparents 125–6, 130
  saving up 81
  work-based aspirations 143–53
floating support for tenants 160, 174
Flowerdew, J. 66, 107, 229

focus groups 60–1, 65
Following Young Fathers (FYF) study
  design 4–5, 55–62
  inclusion in DCSF/DoH guidance 37
  methodology 52–70
  policy context 40
  qualitative longitudinal methodology 5
Formby, E. 82, 83
'Fragile Families' study 27
fragile father-child relationships 87–92, 102
fragile relationships with child's mother 100, 102
friendship with child's mother 87, 108, 111, 113, 115, 126, 128, 220
Fry, P. 24
'fun' dad 86–7
Furstenberg, F. 4, 28, 155
Future Jobs Fund 141
FYFF (Following Young Fathers Further) 52, 53, 57, 64, 67–9, 117, 212, 216, 226

G

gatekeeping strategies 98, 113, 126–9, 138, 220–1
  see also curtailing of contact
Gates, P. 181, 184
gender bias in service provision 188, 226
gendered dynamics of young relationships 97–116, 160, 219–21
gendered ideologies of 'breadwinning' 138–9
gendered patterns of grandparenting 118, 134
geopolitical factors 23–4
Gilligan, P. 27
global trends in early parenthood 14
'good' versus 'bad' fathers 43–4
grandparents
  grandfathers 118, 125, 134
  interference from grandparents 127–30
  intergenerational care and support 117–36
  involvement in birth itself 182–3
  living with grandparents 99, 120, 125, 129, 135, 161, 162, 165–9, 171, 175
  maternal grandparents 118, 120, 122–3, 124, 126, 127, 130, 134, 162, 165, 168–9, 220
  mediating role of grandparents 126
  oppressive grandparent relationships 130–1
  paternal grandparents 118, 120, 124, 125, 165–9
  relationships with 220
  as resource 222
Grandparents Plus 135
Gregory, J. 228, 229, 231, 233
'grey' literature 13

Index

Grimsby Dads Collective (2020–24) 212–13
guilt 24

H

Hadley, A. 1, 15, 33, 34, 35, 36, 37, 38, 45, 46, 50, 160, 180, 199
Hamlyn, C. 45–6
Hanna, E. 61
Hansen, E. 15
'hard to reach' label 2, 49, 63, 179–81, 192, 195, 227
'hard-to-access' services 180, 192
Health of the Nation initiative 33
Health Security Agency 38
health visitors, contact with 49
'helping out' 103
higher education 142, 145, 146, 148, 170
Hills, J. 40, 41
historical reach 68–9
historicising young fatherhood research 11–12
holistic/'whole system' approaches 36, 41, 191, 192
Holmberg, L.I. 79
'home,' concepts of 161, 162, 163, 176, 223
homelessness 61, 92–3, 153, 160, 162, 171–3
Horsell, C. 230
hostels 92, 131, 133, 153, 160, 171, 172, 223, 224
household chores 103
housing 157–76, 223
 buying a home 159, 161
 co-habitation 27–8, 99, 100, 174
 dual residency for children 86
 housing costs 3
 instability of 18, 99, 120, 161, 162, 171–3
 living with grandparents 99, 120, 125, 129, 135, 161, 162, 165–9, 171, 175
 local authority housing 170, 174
 private rented sector (PRS) 159, 162, 170, 171, 175
 resettlement support 201–7
 shared accommodation unsuitable for parenting 160, 170, 171, 172
 social housing 159, 161, 170, 171, 173–4
 student accommodation 170
 supported housing 160, 175
 Teenage Pregnancy Strategy (UK) 33–4
 temporary accommodation 3, 224
 'yo-yo' housing trajectories 158–9, 161–3, 168–9, 175, 223
housing benefits 141, 159, 160, 170
housing charities 64, 163, 172, 173
Housing Young Parents 52
Hudson, F. 19
Hughes, K. 4, 68, 118, 119, 120, 135, 189, 190, 191
Hume, D. 229
Hutchinson, J. 155

I

identity as father 73, 80, 194–5, 201, 205, 206, 208, 220
illiteracy 152, 224
Iman
 engagement with support services 193
 pen portrait 241
 relationship with child's mother 103, 126, 128, 148, 181–2
 semi-skilled work 148
 support during pregnancy 181–2
 supporting pregnancy 81
'in the moment,' living 75, 77, 93, 95, 217
income see employment; low-incomes; precarity; welfare state
independence
 aspiring to 169
 elusiveness of 158, 159
 housing 160, 162, 174, 175
 semi-independence 168
 'tenured' independence 169–70
Ineichen, B. 19
inequality 39, 119, 141, 155, 158
Ingham, R. 1, 15, 33, 34, 35, 36, 45, 46, 50, 160
insecure work 3, 149, 150
intergenerational care and support 117–36, 165–9
Intergenerational Exchange dataset 68
intergenerational transfer of poor outcomes 227
international research 12, 13, 17–18
internet-based support 196
interpretivist research tradition 53
interview methods 61, 62, 65
invisibility of young fathers 12, 13, 48–9, 188, 200
in-work poverty 41, 140
isolation 17, 160, 172, 184, 211, 224

J

Jackson
 housing 163
 pen portrait 241
 providing for children 143
Jakie
 engagement with support services 187
 pen portrait 241–2
 work-based aspirations 151
Jason
 birth as a turning point 83
 contraception 76
 decision to keep child 79
 engagement with support services 187

greater availability for children than own father 85
housing 163–4
on interview methods 62
multiple children 93
parenting at a distance 112, 154
pen portrait 242
reactions to pregnancy 78
relationship with child's mother 103, 112–14
relationship with grandparents 128
young offending history 88–9, 112, 201
Jax
  avoidance of second pregnancy 92
  pen portrait 242–3
  providing for children 143
  reactions to pregnancy 77
  relationship with child's mother 105–7, 202
Jayden
  housing 167
  pen portrait 243
Jed
  engagement with education 150–1
  housing 165, 168
  pen portrait 243–4
Jimmy
  contraception 76
  decision to keep child 78–9, 123
  engagement with support services 188
  housing 168, 171
  lack of contact with children 90, 112, 168
  pen portrait 244
  relationship with grandparents 130
  statutory agency contacts 184
Jobseeker's Allowance 141, 152
Jock
  education 145, 146
  housing 164, 169
  pen portrait 245
  relationship with child's mother 109
Joe
  pen portrait 245–6
  sustained father-child relationships 85
Johnson (Young Dads Council) 193–4
joint birth registration 23
Joseph, K. 119

K

Karl
  child taken into care 93, 189, 190
  engagement with support services 188–9, 190
  pen portrait 246
  Relationship and Sex Education (RSE) 75
keeping a child, decision-making 78–80
Kevin
  birth as a turning point 83–4
  housing 165, 170
  pen portrait 246–7

semi-skilled work 148–9
supporting pregnancy 81
sustained father-child relationships 85–6, 148
work-based aspirations 143
Khatun, M. 19
Kickstart scheme 141
Kiernan, K. 27
kinship care 118, 119, 132, 134, 135
Kiselica, M. 11, 12, 15, 17, 23, 62, 157, 179, 180
Klinman, D.G. 11, 12
knowledge co-production 63, 198

L

Ladlow, L. 52, 56, 57, 62, 65, 88, 89, 92, 120, 125, 144, 153, 157, 158, 175, 176, 186, 194, 201, 202, 203, 205, 233
Lammy, D. 65
Lane, T.S. 11, 12
Langton, C.E. 18
Larson, N.C. 28
Lau Clayton, C. 11, 16, 21, 52, 56, 60, 61, 66, 97, 99, 117, 118, 119, 123, 126, 127, 130, 132, 134, 160
Law, J. 54–5
learning difficulties 152
learning mentors 183–4, 192
leaving home, age of 158
legal advice for contact issues 183
legal guardianships 118
legislation reflecting engaged fatherhood 21
Leverhulme Trust 68
life chances, early parenthood does not necessarily disrupt 155
life course trajectories, changing 2–4, 194–5
life maps 61, *87*, *88*
Lilley, Peter 44
literacy problems 152, 224
literature review 11–30
Livesley, J. 160
living wage 141
local authority housing 170, 174
local champions 191, 193, 233
local government 35, 38
Lohan, M. 214
longitudinal cohort surveys 16
longitudinal impact research 6, 52, 53, 62–3, 67, 226
longitudinal studies into relationship with mother 28
long-term support, need for 194–5, 201
loose partnerships 99
love 21, 81, 233
low-incomes
  close layering of generations in low-income communities 4

and early fatherhood 17–18
EET trajectories 142
intergenerational care and support 120
young fathers burdened by 24, 144, 150, 224
low-paid work 149, 222
low-skilled work 140, 142, 144, 149, 150–3, 163

M

MacDonald, R. 3, 119, 140
Mackie, P.K. 158
mainstream support, need for 195–6
maintenance payments 147
'manning up' 81
Manuel
  grandparent reactions to pregnancy 121
  pen portrait 247
Marcel
  housing 173
  pen portrait 247–8
  work-based aspirations 151
Markson, L. 203
marriage 25–6, 77, 99
Martin
  housing 170
  pen portrait 248
  reactions to pregnancy 77
  relationship with grandparents 128
  supporting pregnancy 82
  sustained father-child relationships 85
masculine ideologies 76, 138, 188
maternal grandparents 118, 120, 122–3, 124, 126, 127, 130, 134, 162, 165, 168–9, 220
maternity services 181–3
Matlakala, F.K. 12, 29
Maxwell, N. 234
May, J. 63–4, 66, 197
McAuley, C. 27
McGuire, C. 26
McNulty, A. 119
media portrayals 51
mediating role of grandparents 126
mediation 110, 111, 221
mental health issues 87, 89, 92, 94, 144, 153, 218, 227
mentoring 185, 191, 209
  see also learning mentors
meta-synthesis of research 13–14
methodological challenges in young fatherhood research 12–14, 58–60, 224–6
midwives, contact with 49
Miller, D.B. 11, 24
Miller, T. 20, 55, 84, 103, 115, 116, 138
moral panic 2, 32, 44
moral prescriptions against early sexual practices 74

moral scripts 115, 220
moral sensibilities 79–80, 81, 229
Morris, K. 50
Morton, S. 63, 197
mother (of child)
  decision to keep child 78–9
  gatekeeping strategies 98, 113
  gendered patterns of parenthood 98–9
  mother/child dyad 25, 98, 100, 114, 115, 123, 129, 134, 220
  primary carer role 25, 97, 160, 175, 188, 220
  relationships with 25–9, 93–4, 97–116
  as typical focus of research 13
  wish to support 103–4
mother-centric professional support services 180, 188
moving away 111
MPLC (Men, Poverty and Lifetimes of Care) 52, 53, 68
multi-agency joined-up working 33, 41, 183–5, 198–9
multigenerational inequities 158
multiple children 74, 92–5, 131

N

National Child Development Study 17
National Longitudinal Survey of Labor Market Experiences (US) 19
Ncayiyane, Z. 24–5
Neale, B. 2, 3, 20, 21, 26, 31, 35, 48, 49, 52, 53, 54, 56, 57, 58, 59, 60, 61, 62, 63, 64, 65, 66, 67, 70, 84, 86, 88, 89, 92, 95, 97, *101*, 107, 111, 117, 118, 119, 120, 123, 125, 126, 127, 130, 132, 134, 137, 144, 157, 175, 179, 180, 183, 185, 186, 187, 188, 191, 192, 193, 194, 195, 196, 197, 198, 200, 201, 202, 203, 204, 205, 206, 208, 210, 212, 214, 224, 226, 227, 229, 233
NEET (not in education, employment or training) 139, 142–3
neglectful relationships 132–3
Nel, L. 24–5
Nelson, T.J. 11, 25, 26, 76, 82, 86, 114, 143
neoliberalism 39, 40, 46, 140, 228, 230, 231
'new' fathers 3, 20
New Labour 31, 33, 35, 39, 40, 42, 44, 47, 185
New Pathways for Young Fathers 52
Nicoll, A. 180
nomadic lives 171–3, 175, 223
non-linearity in life courses 54, 84, 158, 164, 175, 219
North East Young Dads and Lads 196
NVQs (national vocational qualifications) 148, 149

O

Oakhill Secure Training Centre 203
offending 105
  see also young offender fathers
ONS 1, 15, 23, 25, 26, 158
ontological security 161–2, 166, 172–3, 176, 223
opportunity sampling 57
opportunity versus catastrophe 21
Orlando
  pen portrait 248
  reactions to pregnancy 77
  relationship with child's mother 109
  supporting pregnancy 81
  sustained father-child relationships 85
  work-based aspirations 150
Osborn, M. 49, 192, 195, 196, 200
'othering' 43, 73
outreach services 181
overcrowding 166–7, 170
overnights 86, 109

P

package deal 25
Padgett, D.K. 161
parental rights 132–3
parenting at a distance 26, 27, 86, 103, 108–14, 161, 220
parenting at close hand 26, 98, 102, 103, 107, 108, 163, 220
parenting classes 107, 116, 185
parenting skills support 181, 183–4, 185, 209
parenting support programmes 116
Parikh, S.S. 12, 13
participatory research tools 61, 62–6, 67, 69, 198, 209, 210
partnership models of service provision 135–6
part-time work 145, 147
Paschal, A.M. 19, 22, 46, 81
'paternal commons' 211
paternal grandparents 118, 120, 124, 125, 165–9
Patrick, R. 84, 86, *101*, 134, 203, 227
peer interviewers 66
peer support 179, 185, 192, 193, 208, 232–3
Peter
  pen portrait 249
  reactions to pregnancy 77
Pfitzner, N. 192
PHE/LGA 1, 34, 36–7
Piachaud, D. 39
Pirog, M.A. 15, 17, 18, 119
Pirog-Good, M.A. 19, 138
planned early parenthood 4, 75–7
plans to have children 78

policy context
  collaborative research design 62–6, 70
  compassionate social policy 227–32
  education, employment and training (EET) 139–42
  grandparents 135
  housing 158, 159–60
  public discourses neglect young fathers 31–51
  rethinking young fatherhood 216–35
  specialist support 190–4
Pollock, S. 80
Poole, E. 26, 27
'positive ambivalence' 77
positive reactions to pregnancy 77
post-custody settlement project 197, 201–7
poverty 38–41, 119, 130, 131, 139, 140, 155, 224
practice-informed knowledge 198
practitioners as research participants 65
precarity
  double precarity 175
  education, employment and training (EET) 139, 141, 142, 150, 151, 156
  financial insecurity 18
  housing 157, 171, 175
pregnancy
  multiple 92–5
  responses, young fathers 77–80, 81–4, 218
  responses, grandparents 120–3, 124
  responses, policy/professional practice 32–3, 36, 38, 42, 44, 50, 119, 181–2, 192, 210
  support during 22, 38, 181–3
  teenage 11, 14, 15, 16, 24, 27, 32–5
preventative parenting programmes 116
pride in fatherhood 21
primary carer role
  usually mother 25, 97, 160, 175, 188, 220
  young fathers in 86, 160
Prison Advice and Care Trust 202
prison-based parenting interventions 181
private rented sector (PRS) 159, 162, 170, 171, 175
professional mentors 66
professional support 173–4, 179–96, 232–4
psychology 18–19
public health concerns 32, 35
Public Health England (PHE) 36–8, 48
purpose, fatherhood offers 24, 203, 219
purposive sampling 225
'pushed out' versus 'dropped out' 26

Q

qualitative longitudinal methodology 52–66, 197–215, 224–6
quantitative research 13, 50

Index

Quilgars, D. 160, 175
Quinton, D. 28, 47, 58, 80, 120

R

Rantho, K. 12, 29
Raymond, pen portrait 249
RCPCH (Royal College of Paediatrics and Child Health) 15, 38, 48
reactions to pregnancy 77–8, 120–3, 217–18
recruiting research participants 5, 13, 57–60, 66–7
'redemption' scripts 62
relational factors 29, 71, 96, 114, 219
relational skills 221
Relationship and Sex Education (RSE)
  implications of study for 96, 116, 218
  knowledge about contraception 75–7
  knowledge/practice gap 75
  policy context 31, 33
  previous research 64
  relational skills 221
  unsuitability for young men 74–5
relationship breakdown 27, 99
  see also separation (adult relationships)
religion 122–3
rented housing 159, 170
re-partnering 26, 110, 221
reproductive agency 25, 73, 75, 77, 80, 93, 94, 218, 220
reproductive decision-making 78–80
'rescue and repair' 118, 190–4
research questions 56
research-based practice 198
resettlement support 201–3
respect 41, 109, 110, 111, 112, 115, 187, 192, 194, 229
Responding to Young Dads in a Different Way (RYD) Impact Initiative 52, 53, 67, 197–215
restraining orders 113
Reuben (Young Dad's Council) 66
Richard
  grandparent reactions to pregnancy 121–2
  housing 167
  parenting at a distance 111
  pen portrait 249–50
  work-based aspirations 150
Ridge, T. 224, 227, 228
right to see child 111, 132–3
risk, assumed potential 2, 49, 65, 88, 89, 180, 194, 199, 202, 213
risk factors associated with young parenthood 18
risk profile for heightened chance of early fatherhood 17
risk-based approaches to support 186–7
role models 17, 122, 134
Ross, N.J. 124

S

safeguarding 179, 194, 204–5
sampling 5, 57–60, 225
Scandinavia 69, 228
scans, attending 81, 182
school, engagement with 150, 165
'scumbags' 82, 95
secondary data analysis 68, 157, 179
secrecy about pregnancy 79
Seeing Young Fathers in a Different Way 66
self-help schemes 193
semi-dependency 159, 168
semi-independence 173, 174, 175
semi-skilled work 142, 146, 147–50, 161
Senwe
  adjusting to the pregnancy 80
  financial support 126
  grandparent support 127
  pen portrait 250
  relationship with child's mother 108
  work-based aspirations 149–50
separation (adult relationships) 27, 99, 108–14, 120, 167, 221
separation (from children) 112
  see also contact with children
serial partnerships 94, 99
SEU 32, 33, 34, 39, 47
Sex education 35
  see also Relationship and Sex Education (RSE)
sexual agency 73, 74–5
sexually transmitted infections 74
shared accommodation, unsuitability for parenting 160, 170, 171, 172
'shared authority' 66, 209
shared bedrooms 167
shared care 86, 109
Shirani, F. 145, 149, 154
'shirkers' and 'strivers' 140, 154, 227
siblings 166
sidelining 179, 185, 187–90, 192, 194, 199, 226, 232
signposting to support 185, 206
Simon
  contraception 76
  decision to keep child 78–9, 80
  lack of contact with children 90–1, 112
  pen portrait 250–1
  relationship with child's mother 128
  work-based aspirations 150
skilled work 145–7
Smart, C. 3, 20, 26, 107
Smith, A. 229
Smith, I.D. 44
SmithBattle, L. 12, 13, 20, 23, 43, 44, 46, 58, 77, 80, 87, 130, 155, 158
snapshot studies 14, 30, 53, 57, 224
social capital 119

social citizenship 66
social complexity theory 54
social construction of young
  fatherhood 80
social deficit framework 11, 18–19, 43–4,
  119, 138, 217, 218, 226–7
  see also deficit model of
  young parenthood
social deprivation
  correlation with early parenthood 2, 16,
    32, 50, 154
  cycles of deprivation 119
  EET trajectories 142–3
  housing 164
  see also disadvantaged young fathers; poverty
social engagement framework
  'being there' 2, 20, 86, 217
  definition 2, 11, 19–23
  policy context 42, 48, 217, 226–32
  as research focus 56
  versus 'social problems'
    framework 199–201
  see also engaged fatherhood
social housing 159, 161, 170, 171, 173–4
social networks 80
social problems framework 2, 11, 16–18,
  42, 199, 217
social services 108, 131, 132, 183, 184,
  186–7, 189
socio-demographic profiling 14–16
socio-economic contexts of
  young fatherhood
  breadwinning 137–56
  compassionate social policy 221–4
  EET trajectories 142–53
  intergenerational care and support 119
  oppressive grandparent relationships 130
  policy context 40, 50
  previous research 23–5
  see also disadvantaged young
    fathers; poverty
sofa-surfing 99, 153, 162, 171, 223
solidarity between young fathers 193
South Africa 20, 24
Speak, S. 22, 28, 58, 81, 138, 160
specialist support 48, 163, 185, 190–4,
  195, 201–7, 232–3
stakeholder engagement 65, 197, 198–9,
  200, 214
statistics on early parenthood 1, 14–15, 32,
  34–5, 38
stepfathers 121, 122, 134
'stepping up' 81, 82, 115, 220
stepsiblings 130
stereotypes
  'breadwinner' ideologies 138
  'deadbeat' dads 46, 217
  'feckless' label 2, 43, 46, 50, 73, 74, 129,
    192, 193

'hard to reach' label 2, 49, 63, 179–81,
  192, 195, 199, 227
previous research 12, 18
risk 2, 49, 65, 88, 89, 180, 194, 199,
  202, 213
'scumbags' 82, 95
'shirkers' and 'strivers' 140, 154, 227
social deficit framework 43
Steven, pen portrait 251
stigma
  absent fathers 59
  of early parenthood 218
  grandparent reactions to pregnancy 120–1,
    122, 129
  'hard to reach' label 2, 49, 63, 179–81,
    192, 195, 199, 227
  lasting effects of 82
  mental health issues 227
  policy context 31, 43, 49, 50, 227
  poverty 224
  previous research 19, 22
  risk-based approaches to support 186
  'stepping up' and 'being there' 82
  vulnerability 195
  and young fathers' entitlement to
    services 188
  young offender fathers 88
Strategic Family Partnership Initiative on
  young fatherhood 64
street culture 18
strengths-based approaches 210–11
structural inequalities 40–1, 45, 119
student accommodation 170
study design 56–62
supervised visits 88, 90, 91, 92, 93–4, 108, 186
support packages 160, 163, 173–4, 175–6,
  232–4
supported housing 160, 175
Sure Start 21, 58, 180
  see also Children's Centres
Sure Start Plus 34
surveillance 48–9, 88, 126–8, 179, 183,
  185, 186–7, 194, 199
survival crime 144
sustained father-child relationships 85–7
sustained relationships with child's
  mother 100–2
sustained support, need for 194–5, 201
Sutherland, H. 39

T

Tach, L. 26
targeted welfare systems 44, 48, 228
Tarrant, A. 21, 31, 48, 52, 53, 67, 68, 69,
  118, 120, 135, 140, 188, 189, 190, 191,
  195, 196, 197, 198, 200, 202, 208, 209,
  210, 212, 213, 226, 233, 234
Tarrell
  multiple children 94

pen portrait 251–2
sustained father-child relationships 85
Tawney, Richard 229
Teenage Pregnancy and Parenthood Team 65
Teenage Pregnancy Independent Advisory Group (TPIAG) 33, 34, 47
Teenage Pregnancy Knowledge Exchange 36
Teenage Pregnancy Strategy (UK)
  'Care to Learn' grants 139
  education, employment and training (EET) 33–4
  parenting classes 185
  policy context 15, 31, 33–5, 36, 42, 45, 47, 50
  Relationship and Sex Education (RSE) 74
  Teenage Parent Supported Housing Programme 160
temporary accommodation 3, 224
temporary work 140, 148
'tenured' independence 169–70
terminations 35, 78, 79, 92, 122, 218
Thatcher, M. 44
thematic framework grids 62
therapeutic interventions 195, 202, 206
think tanks 65
Timescapes Initiative 53, 63, 66, 68
Toledo-Dreves, V. 27
Tommy
  on becoming a young father 73
  pen portrait 252–3
  reactions to pregnancy 77, 82
  relationship with child's mother 103, 126
training opportunities 139, 141, 149, 151–2, 155, 198
transformative effects of fatherhood 85–7, 105–6
transition to young fatherhood 73–96, 105, 121–2, 141, 194–5, 217–18
see also adulthood transitions
trauma 17, 95
Trevor
  adjusting to the pregnancy 80
  experiences during birth 182–3
  housing 164
  paternal grandparents 125
  pen portrait 253
Trifiletti, R. 24
Trinder, L. 98
Trivedi, D. 12, 13, 14, 17, 47, 214
'troubled' families 36, 44
trust 109, 110, 111, 112, 115, 128, 188, 192, 193, 194, 202
turning point, birth as 83–4, 85, 124, 143, 155, 218
twins 93, 94, 126, 148

U

UKRI Future Leaders Fellowship 52, 69
underclasses 119
underemployment 140
Understanding Society Study 27
unemployment 3, 17, 120, 139–40, 152, 153, 158
UNICEF 14
Universal Credit 160
universal support pathways (lack of) 181
University of Leeds 52, 67
unknown fatherhood 15
unplanned, most early parenthood is 15, 75–6, 218–19
US 15, 19, 20, 22, 24, 25, 26, 27, 42, 55

V

values-based approach to social policy 41
vertical decision-making patterns 123, 124, 134
violence 108, 113, 129, 130
see also domestic violence
virtuous circles of engagement 193, 194
visual mapping methods 61
Vizard, P. 40, 41
voluntary sector support 48, 50, 191, 193, 195, 208–9

W

Wahlberg, V. 79
Walther, A. 159
Ward, M.R.M. 192
Way, L. 69, 213
Weber, J.B. 2, 18, 58, 81, 82, 103, 138, 145, 150
Weed, K. 42, 43
'weekend dads' 138
Wei, E. 18
welfare benefits
  child benefits 130, 131
  conditionality 141, 153, 161, 180
  housing 157, 159–60, 171–2
  Jobseeker's Allowance 141, 152
  sanctions 141, 152, 156, 224
  Universal Credit 160
welfare state
  austerity 4, 40, 135, 140, 159
  compassionate social policy 230
  education, employment and training (EET) 139, 140, 141, 155
  intergenerational care and support 135
  policy context 39, 40, 45
  retrenchment 38, 40, 135, 155, 175, 231
  typology of welfare states 228
'whole system'/holistic approaches 36, 41, 191, 192

Wiggins, M. 28
Williams, F. 230
Worcester Sure Start 58
work *see* employment; unemployment
writing project 66
Wyn, J. 4

Y

Young Dads Collective North 207–11
Young Dads Collective (YDC) 197, 204, 206, 207, 210
Young Dad's Council 66, 193–4
Young Dads Talk 211–13
Young Lives and Times study 56

young offender fathers 64–5, 67, 88–9, 105, 112, 185, 201–7, 233
Young Offender Teams 205
Youth Contract 141
'yo-yo' housing trajectories 158–9, 161–3, 168–9, 175, 223

Z

Zane
 housing 167
 pen portrait 253
 relationship with child's mother 104
 support during pregnancy 182
zero-hours jobs 140

www.ingramcontent.com/pod-product-compliance
Lightning Source LLC
Chambersburg PA
CBHW070910030426
42336CB00014BA/2362